Recent Advances in Face Recognition

Edited by

Kresimir Delac,
Mislav Grgic
and
Marian Stewart Bartlett

Recent Advances in Face Recognition

Edited by Kresimir Delac, Mislav Grgic and Marian Stewart Bartlett

Republished by InTech

Janeza Trdine 9, 51000 Rijeka, Croatia

Technical Editor Teodora Smiljanic

Cover Designer Dino Smrekar

Additional hard copies can be obtained from orders@intechopen.com

Recent Advances in Face Recognition, Edited by Kresimir Delac, Mislav Grgic and Marian Stewart Bartlett
p. cm.
ISBN 978-953-7619-34-3

For EU product safety concerns:
IN TECH d.o.o., Prolaz Marije Krucifikse Kozulić 3, 51000 Rijeka, Croatia,
info@intechopen.com or visit our website at intechopen.com.

Meet the editors

K. Delac received his B.Sc.E.E. degree in 2003 and is currentlypursuing a Ph.D. degree at the University of Zagreb, Faculty of Electrical Engineering andComputing. His current research interests are digital image analysis, pattern recognition andbiometrics.

Mislav Grgic received the B.Sc., M.Sc. and Ph.D. degrees in electrical engineering from the University of Zagreb, Faculty of Electrical Engineering and Computing, Croatia, in 1997, 1998 and 2000, respectively. From July 1997 he has worked at the Department of Wireless Communications, Faculty of Electrical Engineering and Computing, University of Zagreb, Croatia. He was on a research study at the Department of Electronic Systems Engineering, University of Essex, Colchester, United Kingdom (1999/2000). In April 2007 he was promoted to Associate Professor. He participated in 4 scientific projects financed by the Ministry of Science, Education and Sports of the Republic of Croatia and 4 international COST projects of the European Commission in the field of Information and Communication Technologies (ICT). Currently he is a project leader of the research project: Intelligent Image Features Extraction in Knowledge Discovery Systems (036-0982560-1643), supported by the Ministry of Science, Education and Sports of the Republic of Croatia (2007-2009). He published more than 90 papers in journals and conference proceedings in the areas of image and video compression, image retrieval (MPEG-7), and face recognition. Dr. Grgic is a senior member of IEEE and a member of IEEE Region 8 GOLD Team, IEEE Computer Society, IEEE Communications Society, IEEE Signal Processing Society, EURASIP, ELMAR, and AMAC-FER. He was a chair of the IEEE Croatia Section GOLD Affinity Group (2005-2006). Currently he is a secretary of the IEEE Croatia Section where he serving as a chapter coordinator and conference coordinator. He is a collaborating member of the Croatian Academy of Engineering (HATZ). Dr. Grgic participates in more than 30 international programs, review and conference organizing committees and he serves as a technical reviewer for various scientific journals. He is a member of the Editorial Board of the Int. Journal of Signal and Imaging Systems Engineering. Dr. Grgic received bronze medal Josip Loncar from the Faculty of Electrical Engineering and Computing, University of Zagreb for an outstanding B.Sc. thesis work, silver medal Josip Loncar for an outstanding M.Sc. thesis work, and Vera Johanides award from the Croatian Academy of Engineering for scientific achievements in the area of multimedia communications, in 1997, 1999 and 2005, respectively.

Sonja Grgic received the B.Sc., M.Sc., and Ph.D. degrees in electrical engineering from the Faculty of Electrical Engineering and Computing, University of Zagreb, Zagreb, Croatia, in 1989, 1992, and 1996, respectively. She is currently an Assistant Professor in the Department of Radiocommunications and Microwave Engineering, Faculty of Electrical Engineering and Computing, University of Zagreb. Her research interests include television signal transmission and distribution, picture quality assessment, wavelet image compression, and broadband network architecture for digital television. She is a member of the international program and organizing committees of several international workshops and conferences. She was a Visiting Researcher in the Department of Telecommunications, University of Mining and Metallurgy, Krakow, Poland. Prof. Grgic was the recipient of the Silver Medal "Josip Loncar" from the Faculty of Electrical Engineering and Computing, University of Zagreb, for outstanding Ph.D. dissertation work.

Preface

Face recognition is still a vividly researched area in computer science. First attempts were made in early 1970-ies, but a real boom happened around 1988, parallel with a large increase in computational power. The first widely accepted algorithm of that time was the PCA or eigenfaces method, which even today is used not only as a benchmark method to compare new methods to, but as a base for many methods derived from the original idea.

Today, more than 20 years after, many scientists agree that the simple two frontal images in controlled conditions comparison is practically a solved problem. With minimal variation in such images apart from facial expression, the problem becomes trivial by today's standards with the recognition accuracy above 90% reported across many papers. This is arguably even better than human performance in the same conditions (especially if the humans are tested on the images of the unknown persons). However, when variations in images caused by pose, aging or extreme illumination conditions are introduced, humans' ability to recognize faces is still remarkable compared to computers', and we can safely say that the computers are currently not even close.

The main idea and the driver of further research in this area are security applications and human-computer interaction. Face recognition represents an intuitive and non-intrusive method of recognizing people and this is why it became one of three identification methods used in e-passports and a biometric of choice for many other security applications. However, until the above mentioned problems (illumination, pose, aging) are solved, it is unrealistic to expect that the full deployment potential of face recognition systems will be realized. There are many technological issues to be solved as well, some of which have been addressed in recent ANSI and ISO standards.

This goal of this book is to provide the reader with the most up to date research performed in automatic face recognition. The chapters presented here use innovative approaches to deal with a wide variety of unsolved issues.

Chapter 1 is a literature survey of the usage of compression in face recognition. This area of research is still quite new and there are only a handful of papers that deal with it, but since the adoption of face recognition as part of the e-passports more attention should be given to this problem. In chapter 2 the authors propose a new parallel model utilizing information from frequency and spatial domain, and using it as an input to different variants of LDA. The overall performance of the proposed system outperforms most of the conventional methods. In chapter 3 the authors give an idea on how to implement a simple yet efficient facial image acquisition for acquiring multi-views face database. The authors have further incorporated the acquired images into a novel majority-voting based recognition system using five views of each face. Chapter 4 gives an insightful mathematical introduction to tensor analysis and then uses the discriminative rank-one tensor projections with global-local tensor representation for face recognition. At the end of the chapter authors perform extensive experiments which demonstrate that their method outperforms previous discriminative embedding methods. Chapter 5 presents a review of related works in what the authors refer to as intelligent face recognition, emphasizing the connection to artificial intelligence. The artificial intelligent system described is implemented using supervised neural networks whose task were to simulate the function and the structure of human brain that receives visual information.

Chapter 6 proposes a new method to improve the recognition rate by selecting and generating optimal face image from a series of face images. The experiments at the end of the chapter show that the new method is on par with existing methods dealing with pose, with an additional benefit of having the potential to extend to other factors such as illumination and low resolution images. Chapter 7 gives and overview of multiresolution methods in face recognition. The authors start by outlining the limitations of the most popular multiresolution method - wavelet analysis - and continue by showing how some new techniques (like curvelets) can overcome them. The chapter also shows how these new tools fit into the larger picture of signal processing, namely, the Comprehensive Sampling of Compressed Sensing (CS). Chapter 8 addresses one of the most difficult problems in face recognition - the varying illumination. The approach described synthesizes an illumination normalized image using Quotient Image-based techniques which extract illumination invariant representation of a face from a facial image taken in uncontrolled illumination conditions. In chapter 9 the authors present their approach to anti-spoofing based on a liveness detection. The algorithm, based on eye blink detection, proved its efficiency in an experiment performed under uncontrolled indoor lighting conditions.

Chapter 10 gives an overview of the state-of-the-art in 2D and 3D face recognition and presents a novel 2D-3D mixed face recognition scheme. Chapter 11 explained an important aspect of any face recognition application in security - disguise - and investigates how it could affect face recognition accuracy in a series of experiments. Experimental results suggest that the problem of disguise, although rarely addressed in literature, is potentially more challenging than illumination, pose or aging. In chapter 12 the authors attempt to analyze the uncertainty (overlapping) problem under expression changes by using kernel-based subspace analysis and ANN-based classifiers. Chapter 13 gives a comprehensive study on the blood perfusion models based on infrared thermograms. The authors argue that the blood perfusion models are a better feature to represent human faces than traditional thermal data, and they support their argument by reporting the results of extensive experiments. The last two chapters of the book address the use of color information in face recognition. Chapter 14 integrates color image representation and recognition into one discriminant analysis model and chapter 15 presents a novel approach to using color information based on multi layer neural networks.

October 2008

Editors

Kresimir Delac,
Mislav Grgic
University of Zagreb
Faculty of Electrical Engineering and Computing
Department of Wireless Communications
Unska 3/XII, HR-10000 Zagreb
Croatia

Marian Stewart Bartlett
Institute for Neural Computation
University of California, San Diego, 0523
9500 Gilman Drive
La Jolla, CA 92093-0523
United States of America

Contents

Preface VII

1. Image Compression in Face Recognition - a Literature Survey 001
Kresimir Delac, Sonja Grgic and Mislav Grgic

2. New Parallel Models for Face Recognition 015
Heng Fui Liau, Kah Phooi Seng, Li-Minn Ang and Siew Wen Chin

3. Robust Face Recognition System Based on a Multi-Views Face Database 027
Dominique Ginhac, Fan Yang, Xiaojuan Liu, Jianwu Dang and Michel Paindavoine

4. Face Recognition by Discriminative Orthogonal Rank-one Tensor Decomposition 039
Gang Hua

5. Intelligent Local Face Recognition 055
Adnan Khashman

6. Generating Optimal Face Image in Face Recognition System 071
Yingchun Li, Guangda Su and Yan Shang

7. Multiresolution Methods in Face Recognition 79
Angshul Majumdar and Rabab K. Ward

8. Illumination Normalization using Quotient Image-based Techniques 97
Masashi Nishiyama, Tatsuo Kozakaya and Osamu Yamaguchi

9. Liveness Detection for Face Recognition 109
Gang Pan, Zhaohui Wu and Lin Sun

10. 2D-3D Mixed Face Recognition Schemes 125
Antonio Rama Calvo, Francesc Tarrés Ruiz, Jürgen Rurainsky and Peter Eisert

11. Recognizing Face Images with Disguise Variations 149
Richa Singh, Mayank Vatsa and Afzel Noore

12. Discriminant Subspace Analysis for Uncertain Situation in Facial Recognition 161
Pohsiang Tsai, Tich Phuoc Tran, Tom Hintz and Tony Jan

13. Blood Perfusion Models for Infrared Face Recognition 183
Shiqian Wu, Zhi-Jun Fang, Zhi-Hua Xie and Wei Liang

14. Discriminating Color Faces For Recognition 207
Jian Yang, Chengjun Liu and Jingyu Yang

15. A Novel Approach to Using Color Information in Improving Face Recognition Systems Based on Multi-Layer Neural Networks 223
Khalid Youssef and Peng-Yung Woo

1

Image Compression in Face Recognition - a Literature Survey

Kresimir Delac, Sonja Grgic and Mislav Grgic
University of Zagreb, Faculty of Electrical Engineering and Computing
Croatia

1. Introduction

Face recognition has repeatedly shown its importance over the last ten years or so. Not only is it a vividly researched area of image analysis, pattern recognition and more precisely biometrics (Zhao et al., 2003; Delac et al., 2004; Li & Jain, 2005; Delac & Grgic, 2007), but also it has become an important part of our everyday lives since it was introduced as one of the identification methods to be used in e-passports (ISO, 2004; ANSI, 2004).
From a practical implementation point of view, an important, yet often neglected part of any face recognition system is the image compression. In almost every imaginable scenario, image compression seems unavoidable. Just to name a few:

i. image is taken by some imaging device on site and needs to be transmitted to a distant server for verification/identification;
ii. image is to be stored on a low-capacity chip to be used for verification/identification (we really need an image and not just some extracted features for different algorithms to be able to perform recognition);
iii. thousands (or more) images are to be stored on a server as a set of images of known persons to be used in comparisons when verifying/identifying someone.

All of the described scenarios would benefit by using compressed images. Having compressed images would reduce the storage space requirements and transmission requirements. Compression was recognized as an important issue and is an actively researched area in other biometric approaches as well. Most recent efforts have been made in iris recognition (Rakshit & Monro, 2007; Matschitsch et al., 2007) and fingerprint recognition (Funk et al., 2005; Mascher-Kampfer et al., 2007). Apart from trying to deploy standard compression methods in recognition, researchers even develop special purpose compression algorithms, e.g. a recent low bit-rate compression of face images (Elad et al., 2007).
However, to use a compressed image in classical face recognition setups, the image has to be fully decompressed. This task is very computationally extensive and face recognition systems would benefit if full decompression could somehow be avoided. Working with partly decompressed images is commonly referred to as working in the compressed domain. This would additionally increase computation speed and overall performance of a face recognition system.
The aim of this chapter is to give a comprehensive overview of the research performed lately in the area of image compression and face recognition, with special attention brought to

performing face recognition directly in the compressed domain. We shall try to link the surveyed research hypotheses and conclusions to some real world scenarios as frequently as possible. We shall mostly concentrate on JPEG (Wallace, 1991) and JPEG2000 (Skodras et al., 2001) compression schemes and their related transformations (namely, Discrete Cosine Transform and Discrete Wavelet Transform). We feel that common image compression standards such as JPEG and JPEG2000 have the highest potential for actual usage in real life, since the image will always have to decompressed and presented to a human at some point. From that perspective it seems reasonable to use a well-known and commonly implemented compression format that any device can decompress.
The rest of this chapter comprises of four sections. In section 2 we shall give an overview of research in spatial (pixel) domain, mainly focusing on the influence that degraded image quality (due to compression) has on recognition accuracy. In section 3 we shall follow the same lines of thought for the transform (compressed) domain research, also covering some research that is well connected to the topic even though the actual experiments in the surveyed papers were not performed with face recognition scenarios. We feel that the presented results from other research areas will give potential future research directions. In section 4 we review the presented material and try to pinpoint some future research directions.

2. Spatial (pixel) domain

In this section, we shall give an overview of research in spatial (pixel) domain, mainly focusing on the influence that degraded image quality (due to compression) has on recognition accuracy. As depicted in Fig. 1, the compressed data is usually stored in a database or is at the output of some imaging equipment. The data must go through entropy decoding, inverse quantization and inverse transformation (IDCT in JPEG or IDWT in JPEG2000) before it can be regarded as an image. Such a resulting decompressed image is inevitably degraded, due to information discarding during compression. Point A thus represents image pixels and we say that any recognition algorithm using this information works in spatial or pixel domain. Any recognition algorithm using information at points B, C or D is said to be working in compressed domain and is using transform coefficients rather than pixels at its input. The topic of papers surveyed in this section is the influence that this degradation of image quality has on face recognition accuracy (point A in Fig. 1). The section is divided into two subsections, one describing JPEG-related work and one describing JPEG2000-related work. At the end of the section we give a joint analysis.

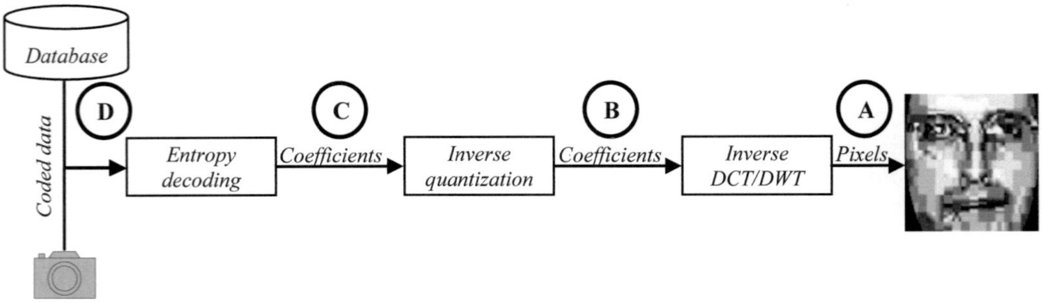

Fig. 1. Block diagram of decompression procedure in transform coding scenario

2.1 JPEG

In their FRVT 2000 Evaluation Report, Blackburn et al. tried to evaluate the effects of JPEG compression on face recognition (Blackburn et al., 2001). They simulated a hypothetical real-life scenario: images of persons known to the system (the gallery) were taken in near-ideal conditions and were uncompressed; unknown images (the probe set) were taken in uncontrolled conditions and were compressed at a certain compression level. Prior to experimenting, the compressed images were uncompressed (thus, returning to pixel domain), introducing compression artifacts that degrade image quality. They used standard galley set (*fa*) and probe set (*dup1*) of the FERET database for their experiments. The images were compressed to 0.8, 0.4, 0.25 and 0.2 bpp. The authors conclude that compression does not affect face recognition accuracy significantly. More significant performance drops were noted only under 0.2 bpp. The authors claim that there is a slight increase of accuracy at some compression ratios and that they recommend further exploration of the effects that compression has on face recognition.

Moon and Phillips evaluate the effects of JPEG and wavelet-based compression on face recognition (Moon & Phillips, 2001). The wavelet-based compression used is only marginally related to JPEG2000. Images used as probes and as gallery in the experiment were compressed to 0.5 bpp, decompressed and then geometrically normalized. System was trained on uncompressed (original) images. Recognition method used was PCA with L1 as a nearest neighbor metric. Since they use FERET database, again standard gallery set (*fa*) was used against two also standard probe sets (*fb* and *dup1*). They noticed no performance drop for JPEG compression, and a slight improvement of results for wavelet-based compression.

Wat and Srinivasan (Wat & Srinivasan, 2004) explored the effects of JPEG compression on PCA and LDA with the same setup as in (Blackburn et al., 2001) (FERET database, compressed probes, uncompressed gallery). Results were presented as a function of JPEG quality factor and are therefore very hard to interpret (the same quality factor will result in a different compression ratios for different images, dependent on the given image's statistical properties). By using two different histogram equalization techniques as a preprocessing, they claim that there is a slight increase in performance with the increase in compression ratio for LDA in the illumination task (*fc* probe set). For all other combinations, the results remain the same or decrease with higher compressions. This is in slight contradiction with results obtained in (Blackburn et al., 2001).

2.2 JPEG2000

JPEG2000 compression effects were tested by McGarry et al. (McGarry et al., 2004) as part of the development of the ANSI INCITS 385-2004 standard: "Face Recognition Format for Data Interchange" (ANSI, 2004), later to become the ISO/IEC IS 19794-5 standard: "Biometric Data Interchange Formats - Part 5: Face Image Data" (ISO, 2004). The experiment included compression at a compression rate of 10:1, later to become an actual recommendation in (ANSI, 2004) and (ISO, 2004). A commercial face recognition system was used for testing a vendor database. There are no details on the exact face recognition method used in the tested system and no details on a database used in experiments. In a similar setup as in previously described papers, it was determined that there is no significant performance drop when using compressed probe images. Based on their findings, the authors conjecture that compression rates higher than 10:1 could also be used, but they recommend a 10:1 compression as something that will certainly not deteriorate recognition results.

Wijaya and Savvides (Wijaya & Savvides, 2005) performed face verification on images compressed to 0.5 bpp by standard JPEG2000 and showed that high recognition rates can be achieved using correlation filters. They used CMU PIE database and performed two experiments to test illumination tolerance of the MACE filters-based classifier when JPEG2000 decompressed images are used as input. Their conclusion was also that compression does not adversely affect performance.
Delac et al. (Delac et al., 2005) performed the first detailed comparative analysis of the effects of standard JPEG and JPEG2000 image compression on face recognition. The authors tested compression effects on a wide range of subspace algorithm - metric combinations (PCA, LDA and ICA with L1, L2 and COS metrics). Similar to other studies, it was also concluded that compression does not affect performance significantly. The conclusions were supported by McNemar's hypothesis test as a means for measuring statistical significance of the observed results. As in almost all the other papers mentioned so far some performance improvements were noted, but none of them were statistically significant.
The next study by the same authors (Delac et al., 2007a) analyzed the effects that standard image compression methods (JPEG and JPEG2000) have on three well-known subspace appearance-based face recognition algorithms: PCA, LDA and ICA. McNemar's hypothesis test was used when comparing recognition accuracy in order to determine if the observed outcomes of the experiments are statistically important or a matter of chance. Image database chosen for the experiments was the grayscale portion of the FERET database along with accompanying protocol for face identification, including standard image gallery and probe sets. Image compression was performed using standard JPEG and JPEG2000 coder implementations and all experiments were done in pixel domain (i.e. the images are compressed to a certain number of bits per pixel and then uncompressed prior to use in recognition experiments). The recognition system's overall setup that was used in experiments was twofold. In the first part, only probe images were compressed and training and gallery images were uncompressed. This setup mimics the expected first step in implementing compression in real-life face recognition applications: an image captured by a surveillance camera is probed to an existing high-quality gallery image.
In the second part, a leap towards justifying fully compressed domain face recognition is taken by using compressed images in both training and testing stage. In conclusion, it was shown, contrary to common opinion, not only that compression does not deteriorate performance but also that it even improves it slightly in some cases (Fig. 2).

2.3 Analysis

The first thing that can be concluded from the papers reviewed in the above text is that all the authors agree that compression does not deteriorate recognition accuracy, even up to about 0.2 bpp. Some papers even report a slight increase in performance at some compression ratios, indicating that compression could help to discriminate persons in spite of the inevitable image quality degradation.
There are three main experimental setups used in surveyed papers:

1. training set is uncompressed; gallery and probe sets are compressed;
2. training and gallery sets are uncompressed; probe sets are compressed;
3. all images used in experiment are compressed;

Each of these setups mimics some expected real life scenarios, but most of the experiments done in research so far are performed using setup 2. Rarely are different setups compared in

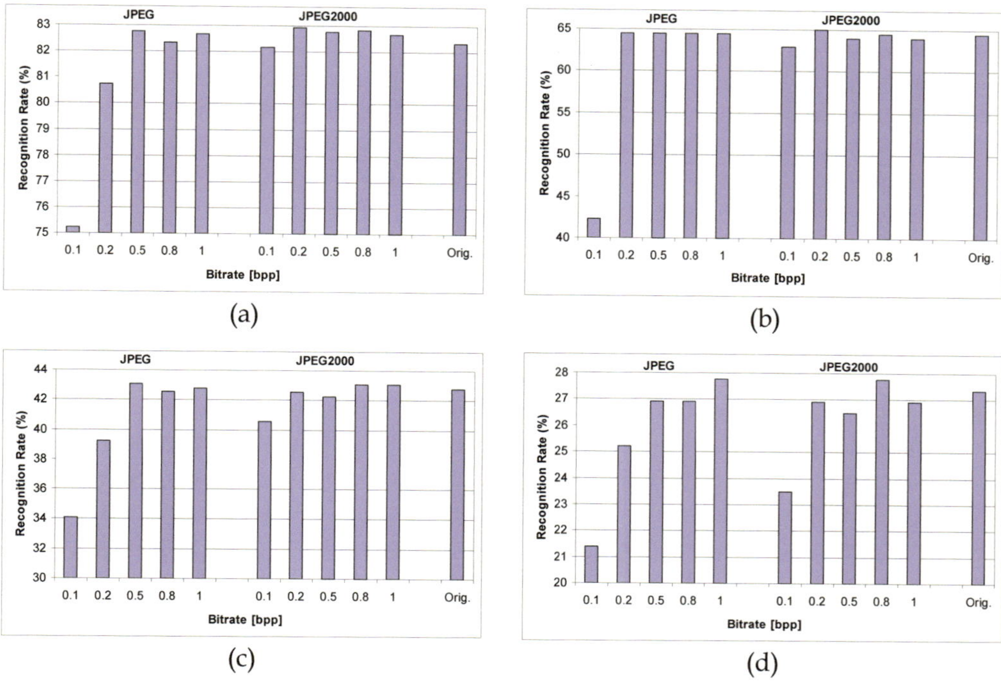

Fig. 2. ICA+COS performance as a function of bpp: (a) *fb* probe set, (b) *fc* probe set, (c) *dup1* probe set, (d) *dup2* probe set from (Delac et al., 2005)

a single paper. All the papers give the results in a form of a table or some sort of a curve that is a function of compression ratio, using an identification scenario. Verification tests with ROC graphs are yet to be done (it would be interesting to see a family of ROC curves as a function of compression ratios).

As far as the algorithms used for classification (recognition) go, most of the studies use well-known subspace methods, such as PCA, LDA or ICA. More classification algorithms should be tested to further support the claim that it is safe to use compression in face recognition. Again, with the exception of (Delac et al., 2007a), there are no studies that would compare JPEG and JPEG2000 effects in the same experimental setup. JPEG2000 studies are scarce and we believe that possibilities of using JPEG2000 in a face recognition system should be further explored.

3. Transform (compressed) domain

Before going to individual paper analysis in this section, we would like to introduce some terminology needed to understand the rest of the text. Any information that is extracted from completely compressed data (all the steps in transform coding process were done) is considered to reside in a fully compressed domain (Seales et al., 1998). Thus, fully compressed domain would be the point D in Fig. 1. Papers that we shall review here deal with the semi-compressed domain of simply compressed domain, meaning that some of the steps in decompression procedure were skipped and the available data (most often the transformed coefficients) were used for classification (face recognition in our case). Looking

at Fig. 1, we can say that those are points B and C in the decompression chain, and this is exactly what most of the papers described here use.
An important issue that comes to mind when thinking about face recognition algorithms that would operate in compressed domain is the face detection. We shall here just say that face detection in compressed domain is possible and that some work has been done on this. An interested reader can refer to (Lou & Eleftheriadis, 2000; Fonseca & Nesvadha, 2004) for a good example of research done in this area.

3.1 JPEG (DCT coefficients)

One of the first works done on face recognition in compressed domain was done by Shneier and Abdel-Mottaleb (Shneier & Abdel-Mottaleb, 1996). In their work, the authors used binary keys of various lengths, calculated from DCT coefficients within the JPEG compression scheme. Standard JPEG compression procedure was used, but exact compression rate was not given. Thus, there is no analysis on how compression affects the results. Experimental setup included entropy decoding before coefficients were analyzed. Even though the paper is foremost on image retrieval, it is an important study since authors use face recognition to illustrate their point. Unfortunately, there is little information on the exact face recognition method used and no information on face image database.
Seales et al. (Seales et al., 1998) gave a very important contribution to the subject. In the first part of the paper, they give a detailed overview of PCA and JPEG compression procedure and propose a way to combine those two into a unique recognition system working in compressed domain. Then they provide an interesting mathematical link between Euclidean distance (i.e. similarity - the smaller the distance in feature space, the higher the similarity in the original space) in feature space derived from uncompressed images, feature space derived from compressed images and correlation of images in original (pixel) space. Next, they explore how quantization changes the resulting (PCA) feature space and they present their recognition results (the achieved recognition rate) graphically as a function of JPEG quality factor and the number of eigenvectors used to form the feature space. The system was retrained for each quality factor used. In their analysis at the end of the papers, the authors argue that loading and partly decompressing the compressed images (i.e. working in compressed domain) is still faster than just loading the uncompressed image. The recognition rate is significantly deteriorated only when just a handful of eigenvectors are used and at very low quality factors.
Eickeler et al. (Eickeler e al., 1999; Eickeler et al., 2000) used DCT coefficients as input to Hidden Markov Models (HMM) for classification. Compressed image is entropy decoded and inversely quantized before features are extracted from the coefficients. Fifteen DCT coefficients are taken from each 8×8 block in a zigzag manner ($u + v \leq 4$; $u, v = 0, 1, \ldots, 7$) and those coefficients are rearranged in a 15×1 feature vector. Thus, the features (extracted from one image) used as input to HMM classification make a $15 \times n$ matrix, where n is the total number of 8×8 blocks in an image. The system is tested on a database of images of 40 persons and results are shown as a function of compression ratio (Fig. 3). Recognition rates are practically constant up to compression ratio of 7.5 : 1 (1.07 bpp). At certain compression ratios, authors report a 5.5 % increase in recognition ratio compared to results obtained in the same experiment with uncompressed images. Recognition rate drops significantly only after compression ratio of 12.5 : 1 (0.64 bpp).

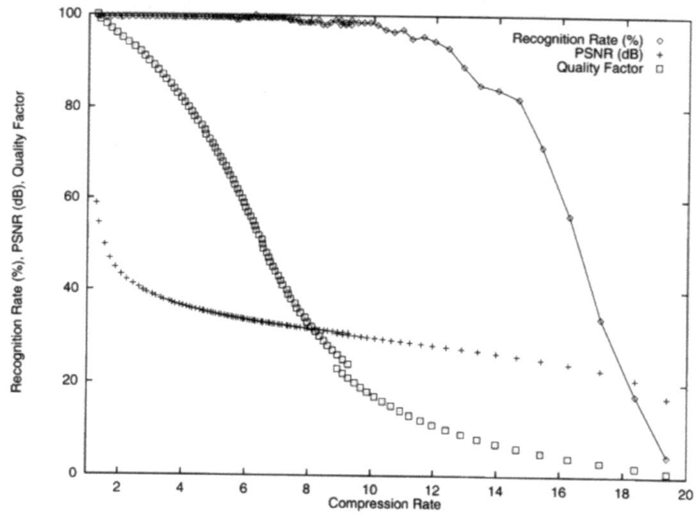

Fig. 3. A plot of recognition ratio vs. compression ratio from Eickeler et al. experiments (Eickeler et al., 2000)

Hafed and Levine (Hafed & Levine, 2001) performed related research using DCT, but they did not follow standard JPEG compression scheme. Instead, they performed DCT over the whole image and kept top 49 coefficients to be used in a standard PCA recognition scenario. The principle on which they choose those 49 coefficients is not given. In their experiment, compared to using uncompressed images, they report a 7 % increase in recognition rate. The experiment was performed on a few small databases and the results are given in tables for rank 1 and in form of a CMS curves for higher ranks.

Ngo et al. (Ngo et al., 2001) performed another related study, originally concerned with image indexing rather than face recognition. The authors took the first 10 DCT coefficients (in a zigzag order) of each 8 × 8 block and based on those 10 DCT coefficients they calculate different statistical measures (e.g. color histograms). Actual indexing is performed using covariance matrices and Mahalanobis distance. With their approach, they achieved an increase in computational speed of over 40 times compared to standard image indexing techniques. At the end of their paper the authors also report how they increased texture classification results by describing textures with variance of the first 9 AC DCT coefficients.

Inspired by human visual system, Ramasubramanian et al. (Ramasubramanian et al., 2001) joined DCT and PCA into a face recognition system based on the transformation of the whole image (since there is no division of the image into blocks, there is no real relation to JPEG). In the first experiment, all available coefficients were used as input to PCA and the yielded recognition rate was used as a benchmark in the following experiments. In the following experiments, they reduce the number of coefficients (starting with higher frequency coefficients). Analyzing the overall results, they conclude that recognition rates increase with the number of available coefficients used as input to PCA. This trend continues up to 30 coefficients. When using more than 30 coefficients the trend of recognition rate increase stops. They use their own small database of 500 images.

Tjahyadi et al. (Tjahyadi et al., 2004) perform DCT on 8 × 8 blocks and then calculate energy histograms over the yielded coefficients. They form several different feature vectors based

on those histograms and calculate Euclidean distance between them as a means of classifying images. They test their system on a small database (15 persons, 165 images) and get an average recognition rate increase of 10 % compared to standard PCA method. In their conclusion, they propose combining their energy histogram-based features with some standard classification method, such as PCA, LDA or ICA. They argue that such a complex system should further increase recognition rate.
Chen et al. (Chen et al., 2005) gave a mathematical proof that orthonormal transformation (like DCT) of original data does not change the projection in PCA and LDA subspace. Face recognition system presented in this paper divides the image in 8 × 8 blocks and performs standard DCT and quantization on each block. Next, feature vectors are formed by rearranging all the coefficients in a zigzag manner. By using the FERET database and standard accompanying test sets, they showed that recognition rates of PCA and LDA are the same with uncompressed images and in compressed domain. Results remain the same even when only 20 (of the available 64) low frequency coefficients for each block are used as features. Fig. 4 shows the results of their experiments for PCA with *fc* and *dup2* probe sets.

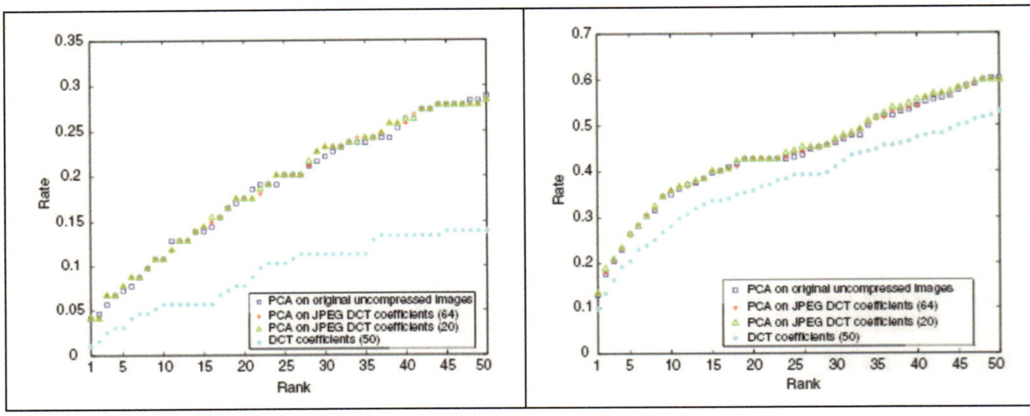

Fig. 4. Performance of PCA in JPEG DCT domain with 20 coefficients and 64 coefficients of each block for the *fc* (left) and *dup2* (right), from (Chen et al., 2005)

They concluded that significant computation time savings could be achieved by working in compressed JPEG domain. These savings can be achieved in two ways: i) by avoiding inverse transformation (IDCT) and ii) by using only a subset of all available coefficients (20 per each 8 × 8 block in this case). Another obvious consequence of their experiments is the fact that storage requirements also drop considerably.
The works presented in (Jianke et al., 2003; Pan et al., 2000) are another example of face recognition in compressed domain, but they are very similar to all the papers already presented in this section. Valuable lessons can be learned from content-based image retrieval (CBIR) research and some good examples from that area can be found in (Lay & Ling, 1999; Jiang et al., 2002; Climer & Bahtia, 2002; Feng & Jiang, 2002; Wu & Liu, 2005; Zhong & Defée, 2004; Zhong & Defée, 2005).

3.2 JPEG2000 (DWT coefficients)

First of all, we would like to point an interested reader to an excellent overview of pattern recognition in wavelet domain that can be found in (Brooks et al., 2001). It would also be worthwhile to mention at this point that most the papers to be presented in this section does not deal with JPEG2000 compressed domain and face recognition in it. They mostly deal with using wavelets as part of the face recognition system, but without any compression or coefficient discarding. They were chose however to be presented here because we believe they form a strong starting point for any work to be done in JPEG2000 domain in future. The work presented in (Delac et al., 2007b) is along those lines of thought.

Sabharwal and Curtis (Sabharwal & Curtis, 1997) use Daubechies 2 wavelet filter coefficients as input into PCA. The experiments are performed on a small number of images and the number wavelet decomposition was increased in each experiment (up to three decompositions). Even though the authors claim that the images were compressed, it remains unclear exactly what they mean since no discarding of the coefficients, quantization or entropy coding was mentioned. The recognition rates obtained by using wavelet coefficients (regardless of the number of decompositions) were in most cases superior to the results obtained with uncompressed images. The observed recognition rate increases were mostly around 2 %. Surprisingly, recognition rates were increasing with the increase of the number of decompositions.

Garcia et al. (Garcia et al., 2000) performed one standard wavelet decomposition on each image from the FERET database. This gave four bands, each of which was decomposed further (not only the approximation band). This way there are 15 detail bands and one approximation. No details on the exact wavelet used were reported. Mean values and variances were calculated for each of the 16 bands and feature vector is formed from those statistical measures. Battacharyya distance was used for classification. The authors did not use standard FERET test sets. They compare their results with the ones obtained using uncompressed (original) images and standard PCA method. The overall conclusion that was given is that face can be efficiently described with wavelets and that recognition rates are superior to standard PCA method with original images.

Similar idea can be found in (Feng e al., 2000) as well. However, in this paper several wavelets were tested (Daubechies, Spline, Lemarie) to finally choose Daubechies 4 to be used in a PCA-based face recognition system. The HH subband after three decompositions was used as input to PCA and recognition rate increase of ≈ 5% was reported.

Xiong and Huang (Xiong & Huang, 2002) performed one of the first explorations of using features directly in the JPEG2000 domain. In their work, they calculate first and second moment of the compressed images and use those as features for content-based image retrieval. Even though this paper does not strictly relate to face recognition, it represents an important step towards fully compressed domain pattern recognition. Authors recognize avoiding IDWT as one of the most important advantages of their approach. In their experiments, the authors used images compressed to 4 bpp (20:1). They observed only a small retrieval success drop on those images and recommend further research of various possible feature extraction techniques in the compressed domain.

Chien and Wu (Chien & Wu, 2002) used two wavelet decompositions to calculate the approximation band, later to be used in face recognition. Their method performed slightly better than standard PCA. Similarly, in (Li & Liu, 2002) Li and Liu showed that using all the DWT coefficients after decomposition as input to PCA yields superior recognition rates compared to standard PCA.

Two decompositions with Daubechies 8 wavelet were used by Zhang et al. (Zhang et al., 2004) with the resulting approximation band being used as input into a neural network-based classifier. By experimenting with several databases (including FERET) significant recognition rates improvements were observed compared to standard PCA in all experiments. Unfortunately, standard FERET test sets were not used so it is hard do compare the results with other studies.

Algs.	DWT coefficients (JPEG2000 at 1 bpp)				DWT coefficients (JPEG2000 at 0.5 bpp)			
	fb	*fc*	*dup1*	*dup2*	*fb*	*fc*	*dup1*	*dup2*
PCA+L1	77.8	49.0	37.1	18.8	79.0	50.0	38.2	18.4
PCA+L2	75.0	19.6	32.4	8.5	75.1	19.6	33.0	9.8
PCA+COS	73.8	19.6	33.9	10.7	73.9	18.6	33.8	10.3
LDA+L1	72.3	18.6	34.6	15.0	72.6	19.6	35.2	15.0
LDA+L2	75.6	22.2	32.7	9.0	75.7	23.2	33.0	9.8
LDA+COS	74.1	21.6	34.1	10.3	74.6	21.1	34.2	10.3
ICA+L1	65.9	18.0	32.4	22.2	65.3	13.9	31.6	21.4
ICA+L2	75.7	45.4	33.7	23.5	75.5	46.4	33.2	22.7
ICA+COS	83.0	68.0	42.9	31.6	82.8	67.5	43.5	31.6

Table 1. Results of the experiments from (Delac et al. 2007b). The numbers in the table represent rank 1 recognition rate percentages.

By using Daubechies 4 wavelet and PCA and ICA, Ekenel and Sankur (Ekenel & Sankur, 2005) tried to find the subbands that are least sensitive to changing facial expressions and illumination conditions. PCA and ICA were combined with L1, L2 and COS metrics in a standard nearest neighbor scenario. They combine images from two databases and give no detail on which images were in the training, gallery and probe sets. An important contribution of this paper lays in the fact this study is performed in a very scientifically strict manner since the same recognition method is used once with uncompressed pixels as input (what we so far referred to as standard PCA method) and once with DWT coefficients as input. In the experiment with images of different expressions, no significant difference in recognition results using uncompressed images and DWT coefficients was observed. In the experiment with images with different illumination conditions, a considerable improvement was observed when DWT coefficients were used instead of pixels (over 20% higher recognition rate for all tested methods).

In (Delac et al., 2007b) the authors showed that face recognition in compressed JPEG2000 domain is possible. We used standard JPEG2000 scheme and stopped the decompression process at point B (right before the inverse DWT). We tested three well-known face recognition methods (PCA, LDA and ICA) with three different metrics, yielding nine different method-metric combinations. FERET database was used along with its standard accompanying protocol. No significant performance drops were observed in all the experiments (see Table 1). The authors therefore concluded that face recognition algorithms can be implemented directly into the JPEG2000 compressed domain without fear of deleterious effect on recognition rate. Such an implementation would save a considerable amount of computation time (due to avoiding the inverse DWT) and storage and bandwidth requirements (due to the fact that images could be compressed). Based on our research we also concluded that JPEG2000 quantization and entropy coding eliminate DWT coefficients not essential for discrimination. Earlier studies confirm that information in low spatial frequency bands plays a dominant role in face recognition. Nastar et al. (Nastar & Ayach, 1996) have investigated the relationship between variations in facial appearance and their deformation spectrum. They found that facial expressions and small occlusions affect the intensity manifold locally. Under frequency-based representation (such as wavelet transform), only high frequency spectrum is affected. Another interesting result that needs to be emphasized is the improvement in recognition rate for PCA and LDA algorithms for the *fc* probe set. This further justifies research into possible implementation of face recognition algorithms directly into JPEG2000 compressed domain, as it could (as a bonus benefit) also improve performance for different illumination task.

3.3 Analysis

From the papers reviewed in this section, one can draw similar conclusion as in previous section: working in compressed domain does not significantly deteriorate recognition accuracy. However, it is important to mention that this claim is somewhat weaker than the one about compression effects when using decompressed images (previous section) since many of the papers surveyed here do not directly use JPEG or JPEG2000 domain. Those that do, however, still agree that working in compressed domain does not significantly deteriorate recognition accuracy. Additionally, most of the papers presented report a slight (sometimes even significant) increase in recognition rates. Although we only presented a short description of each of the papers, when analyzing them in more depth it is interesting to notice that most of them stopped the decompression process at points B or C (Fig. 1). We found no papers that would use entropy-coded information.

We already mentioned that main advantages of working in compressed domain are computational time savings. Inverse discrete cosine transform (IDCT) in JPEG and inverse discrete wavelet transform (IDWT) in JPEG2000 are computationally most intensive parts of the decompression process. Thus, any face recognition system that would avoid IDCT would theoretically save up to $O(N^2)$ operations, where N is the number of pixels in an image. If DCT is implemented using FFT, the savings would be up to $O(N\log N)$. Theoretical savings by avoiding IDWT are up to $O(N)$.

Looking at the papers presented here and analyzing what was done so far, we can conclude that this area is still quite unexplored. There are currently only a handful of papers that deal with JPEG compressed domain and just one paper that deals with face recognition in JPEG2000 domain (Delac et al., 2007b). Additional encouragement to researchers to further explore this area can be found in the success of compressed domain algorithms in other areas, most obviously in CBIR (Mandal et al., 1999).

4. Conclusions

In this chapter we have presented an extensive literature survey on the subject of image compression applications in face recognition systems. We have categorized two separate problems: i) image compression effects on face recognition accuracy and ii) possibilities of performing face recognition in compressed domain. While there are a couple of papers dealing with the former problem strictly connected to JPEG and JPEG2000 compression, the latter problem is up to now only superficially researched. The overall conclusion that can be drawn from research done so far is that compression does not significantly deteriorate face recognition accuracy, neither in spatial domain nor in compressed domain. In fact, most of the studies show just the opposite: compression helps the discrimination process and increases (sometimes only slightly, sometimes significantly) recognition accuracy.

We have also identified a couple important issues that need to be addressed when doing research on compression in face recognition: experimental setup to mimic the expected real life scenario and the problem of results representation. For instance, quality factor in JPEG should be avoided as it will yield different compression ratios for each image, dependent on the contents on the image. There seems to be a need for a consensus on results presentation. Having in mind that the number of bits per pixel (bpp) is the only precise measure of compression, all results should be presented as a function of bpp and compared to results from pixel domain in the same experimental setup.
There is still a lot of work to be done but given that face recognition is slowly entering our everyday lives and bearing in mind the obvious advantages that compression has (reducing storage requirements and increasing computation speed when working in compressed domain), further research of this area seems inevitable.

5. References

Biometric Data Interchange Formats - Part 5: Face Image Data, *ISO/IEC JTC1/SC37 N506, ISO/IEC IS 19794-5*, 2004

Face Recognition Format for Data Interchange, *ANSI INCITS 385-2004*, American National Standard for Information Technology, New York, 2004.

Blackburn D.M., Bone J.M., Phillips P.J., FRVT 2000 Evaluation Report, 2001, available at: http://www.frvt.org/FRVT2000/documents.htm

Brooks R.R., Grewe L., Iyengar S.S., Recognition in the Wavelet Domain: A Survey, *Journal of Electronic Imaging*, Vol. 10, No. 3, July 2001, pp. 757-784

Chen W., Er M.J., Wu S., PCA and LDA in DCT Domain, *Pattern Recognition Letters*, Vol. 26, Issue 15, November 2005, pp. 2474-2482

Chien J.T., Wu C.C., Discriminant Waveletfaces and Nearest Feature Classifiers for Face Recognition, *IEEE Trans. on Pattern Analysis and Machine Intelligence*, Vol. 24, No. 12, December 2002, pp. 1644-1649

Climer S., Bhatia S.K., Image Database Indexing using JPEG Coefficients, *Pattern Recognition*, Vol. 35, No. 11, November 2002, pp. 2479-2488

Delac K., Grgic M., A Survey of Biometric Recognition Methods, *Proc. of the 46th International Symposium Electronics in Marine, ELMAR-2004*, Zadar, Croatia, 16-18 June 2004, pp. 184-193

Delac K., Grgic M., Grgic S., Effects of JPEG and JPEG2000 Compression on Face Recognition, *Lecture Notes in Computer Science - Pattern Recognition and Image Analysis*, Vol. 3687, 2005, pp. 136-145

Delac, K., Grgic, M. (eds.), *Face Recognition*, I-Tech Education and Publishing, ISBN 978-3-902613-03-5, Vienna, July 2007, 558 pages

Delac K., Grgic M., Grgic S., Image Compression Effects in Face Recognition Systems, In: *Face Recognition*, Delac, K., Grgic, M. (Eds.), I-Tech Education and Publishing, ISBN 978-3-902613-03-5, Vienna, July 2007, pp. 75-92

Delac, K., Grgic, M., Grgic, S., Towards Face Recognition in JPEG2000 Compressed Domain, *Proc. of the 14th International Workshop on Systems, Signals and Image Processing (IWSSIP) and 6th EURASIP Conference focused on Speech & Image Processing, Multimedia Communications and Services (EC-SIPMCS)*, Maribor, Slovenia, 27-30 June 2007, pp. 155-159

Eickeler S., Muller S., Rigoll G., High Quality Face Recognition in JPEG Compressed Images, *Proc. of the 1999 International Conference on Image Processing*, ICIP'99, Vol. 1, Kobe, Japan, 24-28 October 1999, pp. 672-676

Eickeler S., Muller S., Rigoll G., Recognition of JPEG Compressed Face Images Based on Statistical Methods, *Image and Vision Computing*, Vol. 18, Issue 4, March 2000, pp. 279-287
Ekenel H.K., Sankur B., Multiresolution Face Recognition, *Image and Vision Computing*, Vol. 23, Issue 5, May 2005, pp. 469-477
Elad, M., Goldenberg, R., Kimmel, R., Low Bit-Rate Compression of Facial Images, *IEEE Trans. on Image Processing*, Vol. 16, No. 9, 2007, pp. 2379-2383
Feng G., Jiang J., JPEG Compressed Image Retrieval via Statistical Features, *Pattern Recognition*, Vol. 36, No. 4, April 2002, pp. 977-985
Feng G.C., Yuen P.C., Dai D.Q., Human Face Recognition Using PCA on Wavelet Subband, *Journal of Electronic Imaging*, Vol. 9, No. 2, April 2000, pp. 226-233
Fonseca, P.; Nesvadha, J., Face detection in the compressed domain, *Proc. of the 2004 International Conference on Image Processing*, Vol. 3, 24-27 Oct. 2004, pp. 2015- 2018
Funk, W., Arnold, M., Busch, C., Munde, A., Evaluation of Image Compression Algorithms for Fingerprint and Face Recognition Systems, *Proc. from the Sixth Annual IEEE Systems, Man and Cybernetics (SMC) Information Assurance Workshop*, 2005, pp. 72-78
Garcia C., Zikos G., Tziritas G., Wavelet Packet Analysis for Face Recognition, *Image and Vision Computing*, Vol. 18, No. 4, March 2000, pp. 289-297
Hafed Z.M., Levine M.D., Face Recognition Using the Discrete Cosine Transform, *International Journal of Computer Vision*, Vol. 43, No. 3, July 2001, pp. 167-188
Jiang J., Armstrong A., Feng G.C., Direct Content Access and Extraction from JPEG Compressed Images, *Pattern Recognition*, Vol. 35, Issue 11, November 2002, pp. 2511-2519
Jianke Z., Mang V., Un M.P., Face Recognition Using 2D DCT with PCA, *Proc. of the 4th Chinese Conference on Biometric Recognition (Sinobiometrics'2003)*, 7-8 December 2003, Beijing, China, available at: http://bbss.eee.umac.mo/bio03.pdf
Lay J.A., Ling, G., Image Retrieval Based on Energy Histograms of the Low Frequency DCT Coefficients, *Proc. IEEE Int. Conf. On Acoustics, Speech and Signal Processing, ICASSP'99*, Vol. 6, Phoenix, AZ, USA, 15-19 March 1999, pp. 3009-3012
Li B., Liu Y., When Eigenfaces are Combined with Wavelets, *Knowledge-Based Systems*, Vol. 15, No. 5, July 2002, pp. 343-347
Li S.Z., Jain A.K., ed., *Handbook of Face Recognition*, Springer, New York, USA, 2005
Luo H., Eleftheriadis A., On Face Detection in the Compressed Domain, *Proc. of the 8th ACM International Conference on Multimedia*, Marina del Rey, CA, USA, 30 October - 3 November 2000, pp. 285-294
Mandal M.K., Idris F., Panchanathan S., A Critical Evaluation of Image and Video Indexing Techniques in the Compressed Domain, *Image and Vision Computing*, Vol. 17, No. 7, May 1999, pp. 513-529
Mascher-Kampfer, A., Stoegner, H., Uhl, A., Comparison of Compression Algorithms' Impact on Fingerprint and Face Recognition Accuracy, *Visual Communications and Image Processing 2007 (VCIP'07), Proc. of SPIE 6508*, 2007, Vol. 6508, 650810, 12 pages
Matschitsch, S., Tschinder, M., Uhl, A., Comparison of Compression Algorithms' Impact on Iris Recognition Accuracy, *Lecture Notes in Computer Science - Advances in Biometrics*, Vol. 4642, 2007, pp. 232-241
McGarry D.P., Arndt C.M., McCabe S.A., D'Amato D.P., Effects of Compression and Individual Variability on Face Recognition Performance, *Proc. of SPIE*, Vol. 5404, 2004, pp. 362-372
Moon H., Phillips P.J., "Computational and Performance Aspects of PCA-based Face-recognition Algorithms", *Perception*, Vol. 30, 2001, pp. 303-321
Nastar C., Ayach N., Frequency-based Nonrigid Motion Analysis, *IEEE Trans. on Pattern Analysis and Machine Intelligence*, Vol. 18, pp. 1067-1079, 1996

Ngo C.W., Pong T.C., Chin R.T., Exploiting Image Indexing Techniques in DCT Domain, *Pattern Recognition*, Vol. 34, No. 9, September 2001, pp. 1841-1851

Pan Z., Adams R., Bolouri H., Dimensionality Reduction of Face Images Using Discrete Cosine Transforms for Recognition, *Technical Report*, Science and Technology Research Centre (STRC), University of Hertfordshire, 2000

Rakshit, S., Monro, D.M., An Evaluation of Image Sampling and Compression for Human Iris Recognition, *IEEE Trans. on Information Forensics and Security*, Vol. 2, No. 3, 2007, pp. 605-612

Ramasubramanian D., Venkatesh Y.V., Encoding and recognition of faces based on the human visual model and DCT, *Pattern Recognition*, Vol. 34, No. 12, September 2001, pp. 2447-2458

Sabharwal C.L., Curtis W., Human Face Recognition in the Wavelet Compressed Domain, *Smart Engineering Systems, ANNIE 97*, St. Louis, Missouri, USA, Vol. 7, November 1997, pp. 555-560

Seales W.B., Yuan C.J., Hu W., Cutts M.D., Object Recognition in Compressed Imagery, *Image and Vision Computing*, Vol. 16, No. 5, April 1998, pp. 337-352

Shneier M., Abdel-Mottaleb M., Exploiting the JPEG compression Scheme for Image Retrieval, *IEEE Trans. on Pattern Analysis and Machine Intelligence*, Vol. 18, No. 8, August 1996, pp. 849-853

Skodras A., Christopoulos C., Ebrahimi T., The JPEG 2000 Still Image Compression Standard, *IEEE Signal Processing Magazine*, Vol. 18, No. 5, September 2001, pp. 36-58

Tjahyadi R., Liu W., Venkatesh S., Application of the DCT Energy Histogram for Face Recognition, Proc. *of the 2nd International Conference on Information Technology for Applications, ICITA 2004*, 2004, pp. 305-310

Wallace G.K., The JPEG Still Picture Compression Standard, *Communications of the ACM*, Vol. 34, Issue 4, April 1991, pp. 30-44

Wat K., Srinivasan S.H., "Effect of Compression on Face Recognition", *Proc. of the 5th International Workshop on Image Analysis for Multimedia Interactive Services*, WIAMIS 2004, 21-23 April 2004, Lisboa, Portugal

Wijaya S.L., Savvides M., Vijaya Kumar B.V.K., "Illumination-tolerant face verification of low-bit-rate JPEG2000 wavelet images with advanced correlation filters for handheld devices", *Applied Optics*, Vol. 44, 2005, pp. 655-665

Wu Y.G., Liu J.H., Image Indexing in DCT Domain, *Proc. of the Third International Conference on Information Technology and Applications, ICITA 2005*, Vol. 2, July 2005, pp. 401- 406

Xiong Z., Huang T.S., Wavelet-based Texture Features can be Extracted Efficiently from Compressed-domain for JPEG2000 Coded Images, *Proc. of the 2002 International Conference on Image Processing, ICIP'02*, Vol. 1, Rochester, New York, 22-25 September 2002, pp. 481-484

Zhang B.L., Zhang H., Ge S.S., Face Recognition by Applying Wavelet Subband Representation and Kernel Associative Memory, *IEEE Trans. on Neural Networks*, Vol. 15, Issue 1, January 2004, pp. 166-177

Zhao W., Chellappa R., Rosenfeld A., Phillips P.J., Face Recognition: A Literature Survey, *ACM Computing Surveys*, Vol. 35, Issue 4, December 2003, pp. 399-458

Zhong D., Defée I., Pattern Recognition in Compressed DCT Domain, *Proc. of the 2004 International Conference on Image Processing, ICIP'04*, Vol. 3, Singapore, 24-27 October 2004, pp. 2031-2034

Zhong D., Defée I., Pattern Retrieval Using Optimized Compression Transform, *Proc. of SPIE*, Vol. 5960, 2005, pp. 1571-1578

2

New Parallel Models for Face Recognition

Heng Fui Liau, Kah Phooi Seng, Li-Minn Ang and Siew Wen Chin
University of Nottingham Malaysia Campus
Malaysia

1. Introduction

Face recognition has gained much attention in the last two decades due to increasing demand in security and law enforcement applications. Face recognition methods can be divided into two major categories, appearance-based method and feature-based method. Appearance-based method is more popular and achieved great success.

Appearance-based method uses the holistic features of a 2-D image. Generally face images are captured in very high dimensionality, normally is more than 1000 pixels. It is very difficult to perform face recognition based on original face image without reducing the dimensionality by extracting the important features. Kirby and Sirovich (Kirby & Sirovich, 1990) first used principal component analysis (PCA) to extract the features from face image and used them to represent human face image. PCA seeks for a set of projection vectors which project the image data into a subspace based on the variation in energy. In 1991, Turk and Pentland (Turk & Pentland, 1991) introduced the well-known eigenface method. Eigenface method incorporates PCA and showed promising results. Another well-known method is Fisherface (Belhumeur, 1997). Fisherface incorporates linear discriminant analysis (LDA) to extract the most discriminant features and to reduce the dimensionality. In general, LDA-based methods outperform PCA-based methods because LDA optimizes the low- dimensional representation of face images with the focus on the most discriminant features extraction. LDA seeks for a set of projection vectors which form the maximum between-class scatter and minimum within-class scatter matrix simultaneously (Chen et al, 2000).

More recently, frequency domain analysis methods such as discrete Fourier transform (DFT), discrete wavelet transform (DWT) and discrete cosine transform (DCT) have been widely adopted in face recognition. Frequency domain analysis methods transform the image signals from spatial domain to frequency domain and analyze the features in frequency domain. Only limited low-frequency components which contain high energy are selected to represent the image. Unlike PCA and LDA, frequency domain analysis methods are data independent. They analyze image independently and do not require training images. Furthermore, fast algorithms are available for the ease of implementation and have high computation efficiency.

In this chapter, new parallel models for face recognition are presented. Feature fusion is one of the easy and effective ways to improve the performance. Feature fusion method is performed by integrating multiple feature sets at different levels. However, feature fusion method does not guarantee better result. One major issue is feature selection. Feature selection plays a very important role to avoid overlapping features and information redundancy. We propose a new parallel model for face recognition utilizing information from frequency and spatial domains. Both features are processed in parallel way. It is well-known that image can be analyzed in spatial and frequency domains. Both domains describe the image in very different ways. The frequency domain features are extracted using DCT, DFT and DWT methods respectively. By utilizing these two very different features, a better performance is guaranteed.

Feature fusion method suffers from the problem of high dimensionality because of the combined features. It may also contain redundant and noisy data. To solve this problem, LDA is applied on the features from frequency and spatial domains to reduce the dimensionality and extract the most discriminant information. However, LDA has a big drawback. If the number of samples is smaller than the dimensionality of the samples, the sample scatter matrix may become singular or close to singular, leading to computation difficulty. This problem is called small sample size (SSS) problem. Several variants of LDA have been developed to counter SSS problem such as, Liu LDA (Liu et al, 1992), Chen LDA (Chen et al, 2000), D-LDA (Hu & Yang, 2001) and modified Chen LDA. These modified LDA techniques will be presented and discussed. Different variants of our parallel model face recognition with different frequency domain transformation techniques and variants of LDA algorithms are proposed. The strategy of integrating the multiple features is also discussed. A weighting function is proposed to ensure the features from spatial and frequency domains contribute equal weight in the matching score level.

ORL and FERET face databases were chosen to evaluate the performance of our system. The results showed that our system outperformed most of the conventional methods.

2. Frequency domain analysis methods

Frequency domain analysis method has been widely used in modern image processing. In this section, DFT, DCT and DWT are presented.

2.1 Discrete fourier transform

Fourier Transform is a classical frequency domain analytical method. For an $1 \times N$ input signal, $f(n)$. DFT is defined as

$$F(k) = \int_{n=1}^{N} f(n) e^{-j2\pi(k-1)(\frac{n-1}{N})} \, dt \qquad 1 \leq k \leq N \qquad (1)$$

The 2D face image is first converted to 1D vector, $f(n)$ by cascading each column together and transforming them into frequency domain. Only low frequency coefficients are selected because most of the signal's energy is located in the low frequency band. In this chapter, 300 coefficients (from k=1 until k=300) are selected. As a matter of fact, human visual system is more sensitive to variation in the low-frequency band [10].

2.2 Discrete cosine transform

DCT possesses some fine properties, such as de-correlation, energy compaction, separability, symmetry and orthogonality. According to the JPEG image compression standard, the image is first divided into 8×8 blocks for the purpose of computation efficiency. Then, two dimensional DCT (2D-DCT) is applied independently on each block.

The DCT coefficients are scanned in a zigzag manner starting from the top left corner of each block as shown in Fig. 1 because DCT coefficients with large magnitude are mainly located at the upper left corner. The first coefficient is called DC-coefficient. The remaining coefficients are referred to as AC coefficients. The frequency of the coefficients increases from left to right and from top to bottom. The DCT coefficients at the most upper-left corner of each 8×8 block are selected and merged to a 1D vector. For an $N \times N$ image, the 2D DCT is defined as

$$C(u,v) = \alpha(u)\alpha(v)\sum_{x=0}^{N-1}\sum_{y=0}^{N-1} f(x,y)\cos\frac{\pi(2x+1)u}{2N}\cos\frac{\pi(2y+1)}{2N} \qquad (2)$$

For υ , v = 0,1,2,...N-1 and $\alpha(u)$ and $\alpha(v)$ are defined as follow: $\alpha(u) = \sqrt{\frac{2}{N}}$ for υ=0 , and

$\alpha(v) = \sqrt{\frac{2}{N}}$ for $v \neq 0$.

Based on (Lay and Guan, 1999) and (Tjahyadi et al, 2007) works, *DC* and AC01, AC10, AC11 which are located at the top-left corner of the block are selected because they give the best result. LDA is further applied to the selected coefficient to extract the most discriminant features for the ease of computation and storage.

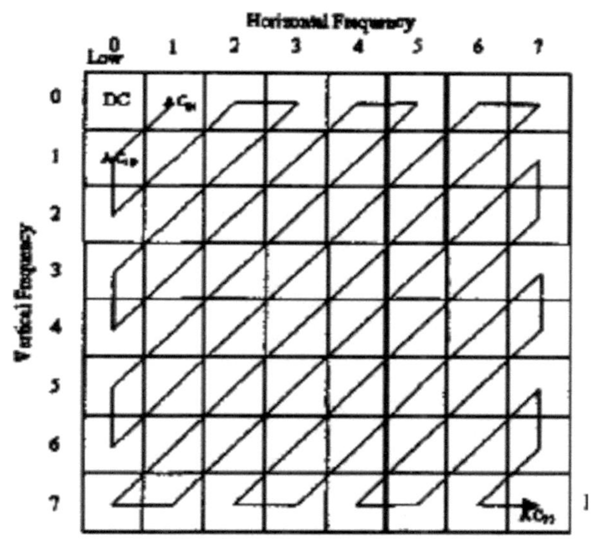

Fig. 1. The zigzag scanning pattern in DCT block

2.3 Discrete wavelet transform

DWT has been widely employed for noise reduction and compression in modern image processing. DWT operates by performing convolution on a target signal with wavelet kernel. There are several well-known wavelets such as coif (3), Haar and etc. DWT decomposes a signal into a sum of shifted and scaled wavelets. The continuous wavelet transform between a signal $f(t)$ and a wavelet $\varphi(n)$ is defined as

$$c(a,b) = \frac{1}{\sqrt{a}} \int f(t) \varphi \left(\frac{t-b}{a} \right) dt \tag{3}$$

where a is the scale and t is the time, and b is the shift. For DWT, the scale, a is restricted to powers of 2 and the position, b, is restricted to the integers multiples of the scales. DWT is defined as

$$c_{j,k} = \int_{-\infty}^{\infty} x(t) \varphi_{j,k} dt \tag{4}$$

where j and k are integers and $\varphi_{j,k}$ are orthogonal baby wavelets defined as

$$\varphi_{j,k} = 2^{\frac{j}{2}} \varphi(2^j t - k) \tag{5}$$

Baby wavelets $\varphi_{j,k}$ have an associated baby scaling function defined as

$$\emptyset_{j,k}(t) = 2^{\frac{j}{2}} \emptyset(2^j t - k) \tag{6}$$

The scaling function can be expressed in terms of low-pass filter coefficients $h_0(n)$ as shown below:

$$\emptyset(t) = \sum_n h_1(n) \sqrt{2} \emptyset(2t - n) \tag{7}$$

The wavelet function can be expressed in term of high-pass filter coefficients $h_1(n)$ as below

$$\varphi(t) = \sum_n h_1(n) \sqrt{2} \emptyset(2t - n) \tag{8}$$

Hence, the signal $f(t)$ can be rewritten as below:

$$f(t) = \sum_k cA_1(k) \emptyset_{j-1,k}(t) + \sum_k cD_1(k) \varphi_{j-1,k}(t) \tag{9}$$

Where $cA_1(k)$ and $cD_1(k)$ represent the approximation coefficients and detail coefficients level 1 respectively. Similarly, the approximation and detail coefficient can be expressed in term of low-pass filter coefficients, $h_0(n)$ and high-pass filter coefficients, $h_1(n)$.

$$cA_1(k) = \sum_n cA_0(n) h_0(n - 2k) \tag{10}$$

$$cd_1(k) = \sum_n cA_0(n) h_1(n - 2k) \tag{11}$$

2-D DWT is implemented by first computing the one-dimensional DWT along the rows and then columns of the image (Meada et al, 2005) as shown in Fig. 2. Features in LL sub-band are corresponding to low-frequency coefficients along the rows and columns and all of them are selected to represent the face image.

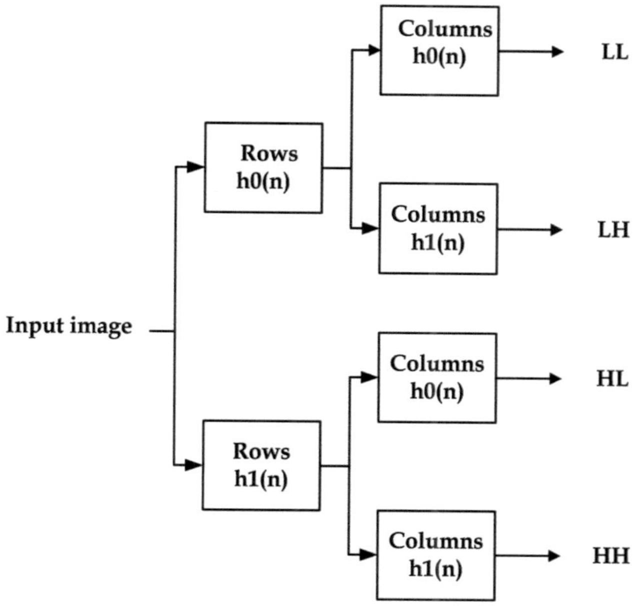

Fig. 2. Two-dimensional discrete cosine transform

3. Linear discriminant analysis

As mentioned in the previous section, feature fusion method suffers from the problem of high dimensionality. Our proposed method incorporates LDA to reduce the dimensionality of the features from frequency and spatial domains. Conventional LDA seeks for a set of projection vectors, W which form the maximum between-class scatter, S_b and minimum within-class scatter matrix, S_w simultaneously (Chen et al, 2000). The function of W is given in Eq. (14).

$$S_W = \sum_{j=1}^{K}\sum_{i=1}^{M}(x_i^j - m_j)(x_i^j - m_j)^T \tag{12}$$

$$S_B = \sum_{j=1}^{K}(m_j - m)(m_j - m)^T \tag{13}$$

$$W = \arg\max \frac{W^t S_b W}{W^t S_w W} \tag{14}$$

For a database which contains K classes and each class has M samples, each sample is represented by n-dimensional vector. The rank of S_w is defined as in Eq. (12). LDA algorithm has a big drawback which is SSS problem. Liu et al, Yang et al and Chen et al proposed different approaches to handle the SSS problem.

If the rank of $S_w \neq n$, then S_w is singular. Liu et al modified the traditional LDA algorithm by replacing S_w in Eq. (14) with total scatter matrix, S_t. S_t is the sum of within-class scatter matrix and between-class scatter matrix. The new projection vector set is defined as in Eq.

(17). The rank of S_t is defined as in Eq. (16) as shown in (Chen et al, 2000).If $S_t \neq n$, S_t is non-singular. Under this circumstance, the LDA criteria will be fulfilled if $W^t S_w W=0$ and $W^t S_b W \neq 0$. Although KM-1> $K(M$-1) , this does not guarantee that S_t is always not equal to n.

$$rank(S_w) = \min(n, K \times (M-1)) \tag{15}$$

$$rank(S_t) = \min(n, KM-1) \tag{16}$$

$$W = \arg\max \frac{W^t S_b W}{W^t S_w W + W^t S_b W} \tag{17}$$

Yang et al proposed a solution called D-LDA to solve the small sample size problem. Unlike conventional LDA, D-LDA starts by diagonalizing the between-class scatter matrix S_b. All of the eigenvectors of which the corresponding eigenvalues are equal to zero or close to zero are discarded because they do not carry any discriminative power (Hu and Yang, 2001). The remaining eigenvectors and the corresponding eigenvalues are chosen to form D_b and V_b respectively. Then, the within-class scatter matrix S_w is transformed to S_{ww}. S_{ww} is defined as below:

$$S_{ww} = \left(D_b V_b^{-\frac{1}{2}}\right) S_w \left(D_b V_b^{-\frac{1}{2}}\right) \tag{18}$$

The projection vector that can satisfy the objective of an LDA process is the one that can maximize the between-class scatter matrix. Only the smallest eigenvalues and the corresponding eigenvalues are chosen to form V_W and D_W respectively. The most discriminant vector set for D-LDA is given by

$$U = D_w^{-\frac{1}{2}} (D_b V_b)^T (D_w)^T \tag{19}$$

Chen LDA used a different approach to counter the problem. Chen LDA starts by calculating the projection vector in the null space of the S_w. This is done by performing singular value decomposition on S_w. Then a set of eigenvectors, of which corresponding eigenvalues are equal to zero, are chosen to form the projection vector. The projection vector set projects S_b to another subspace and the new S_b is $\widetilde{S_b}$. Singular value decomposition is performed on $\widetilde{S_b}$. A set of projection vector, in which corresponding eigenvalues are the largest are chosen. Now, there are two set of eigenvectors. A set of eigenvectors is derived from the null space of S_w. Another set of eigenvectors is derived from S_b, in which the corresponding eigenvalues are the largest. With both set of eigenvectors, the objective of LDA is fulfilled. Chen LDA is summarized as below:

Step 1, Perform the singular value decomposition of S_w. Choose a set of eigenvectors, in which the corresponding eigenvalues are zero to form Q.

Step 2, Compute S_{bb}, where $S_{bb}=QQ^t S_b (QQ^t)^t$. S_b is the between-class scatter matrix.

Step 3, Perform the singular value decomposition of S_{bb}. Choose a set of eigenvectors, in which the corresponding eigenvalues are the largest, to form U. U is the most discriminant vector set for LDA.

In this chapter, Chen LDA algorithm is modified. Instead of only choosing the eigenvectors which the corresponding eigenvalues are equal to zero in the *step 1*, we further includes those eigenvectors which the corresponding eigenvalues are close to zero. We deduced that the most discriminant features are not only located in null space of S_w but also eigenvalues that close to zero. By selecting more eigenvectors, the most discriminant information in S_w is preserved.

4. Parallel models for face recognition

As mentioned in previous section, LDA is applied on the features extracted from frequency and spatial domains. There are two set of features. One carries the important information of the face image which is derived from the spatial domain and the other one from frequency domain. Both sets of feature describe the face images in very different way. Here, both feature sets are assumed to be equally important. In order to make both features from spatial and frequency domains give equal weight in total matching score, a weighting function is applied to the feature set from spatial domain. The weighting function is given in Eq. (20).

$$\omega = \frac{\sum_{i=1}^{n} s_i}{\sum_{i=1}^{n} f_i} \tag{20}$$

Given that S is the feature from spatial domain and f is the feature from frequency domain. The sizes of both features are 1×n. The weighting function is applied to the spatial domain features. The feature vectors from both domains are merged into 1-D vectors [f1,f2,…fn, ωs1, ωs2,…, ωsn].

In section 3, the problem of LDA had been discussed. Chen LDA, D-LDA and modified Chen LDA are capable to counter SSS problem. But Chen LDA and modified Chen LDA do not perform well when S_W is non-singular. Liu LDA cannot counter SSS problem when Eq. (16) equal to n. D-LDA can perform well regardless the condition of S_w because D-LDA starts calculating S_b instead of S_w. Our results in section 5 showed that Liu LDA and D-LDA are equally good when S_w is non-singular. Modified Chen LDA gave the best result when S_w is singular. Based on the simulation result in section 5, three variants of our parallel model face recognition system as shown in Figure 3 are developed. The selection of LDA algorithm is based on the choice of feature domain. The selected DCT features from DCT domain in ORL database in small and the corresponding S_w is non-singular. Hence, D-LDA is incorporated to extract the most discriminant features and to further reduce the dimensionality. D-LDA has advantage over Liu LDA in term of computation because D-LDA does not involve matrix inversion. For DWT and DFT, the feature sets are relatively large and S_w is singular. Modified Chen LDA is employed to extract the most discriminant features because it gave the best result when S_w is singular.

5. Simulation results

The Olivetti Research Laboratory (ORL) and FERET databases were chosen to evaluate the performance of our proposed system. ORL database contains 400 pictures from 40 persons, each person has 10 different images. For each person, 5 pictures are randomly chosen as the training images. The remaining 5 pictures serve as the test images. The similarity between

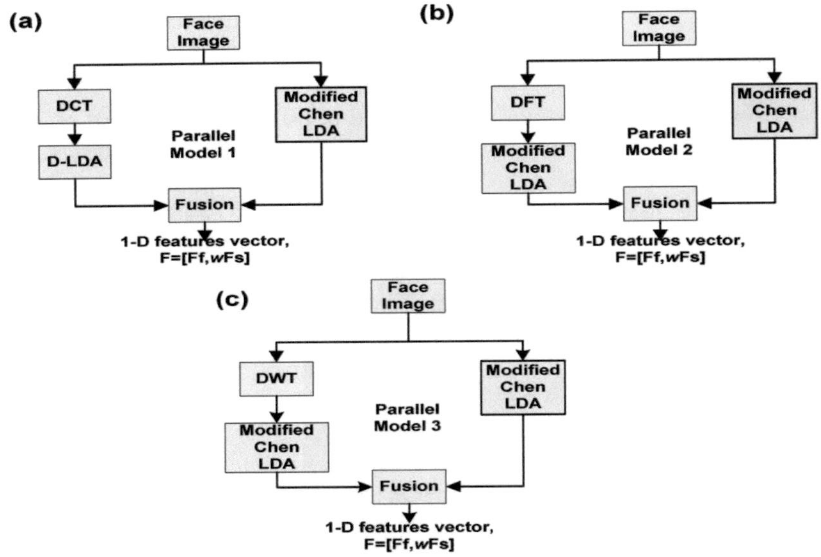

Fig. 3. Parallel models for face recognition

two images is measured using Euclidean Distance. Shorter distance implies higher similarity between two face images. *fb* probe set from FERET database was chosen to evaluate the proposed methods. The training set consists of 165 frontal images from 55 people. Each person has 3 different frontal images.

5.1 Spatial domain result

The dimensionality of the face image was 32×32. ORL database is chosen to evaluate the performance. According to Eq. (15) and Eq. (16), S_w and S_t are singular. Hence, Liu LDA cannot solve the problem. Chen LDA, modified Chen LDA and D-LDA are employed to extract the most discriminant information and further reduce the dimensionality of the feature set from spatial domain. PCA result is included for comparison purpose. The performance for each system is shown in Table 1.

Method	Recognition Rate (%)
PCA	89.5
Chen LDA	90.5
D-LDA	89.5
Modified Chen LDA	91.5

Table 1. Spatial domain result

As shown above, the modified Chen LDA gave the best result. We deduced that modified Chen LDA gave the best result because it preserved more discriminant information of S_w compared to Chen LDA. Hence, modified Chen LDA will be employed to extract the feature when the sample encounter SSS problem.

5.2 Frequency domain result

Since there were only 4 coefficients selected from each block, the total number of coefficients was 64. According (3) and (4), S_w and S_t are non-singular and LDA can be performed in DCT

domain without difficulty. Liu LDA and D-LDA were employed to extract the most discriminant features. For DFT and DWT, the number of selected features that represent face image is 300 and 400 respectively. Therefore, Chen LDA, modified Chen LDA and D-LDA are incorporated to extract the most discriminant features.
From Table 2, it can be seen that Liu LDA and D-LDA gave equally good result in DCT domain which the sample does not suffer SSS problem. They achieved 94% recognition rate. For DFT and DWT which both S_w were singular, modified Chen LDA gave the best result. It scores 96.5% and 94% in DFT domain and DWT domain respectively. Among the frequency domain analysis method, DFT gave better result compared to others. DFT + modified Chen LDA gave the best result.

Method	Recognition rate (%)
DCT+ Liu LDA	94
DCT+D-LDA	94
DFT+Chen LDA	94
DFT+modified Chen LDA	96.5
DFT+ D-LDA	92
DWT+Chen LDA	91
DWT+modified Chen LDA	93.5
DWT+ D-LDA	90.5

Table 2. Frequency domain result

5.3 Parallel models for face recognition result

All parallel models outperformed most of the conventional methods as shown in Table 3. Parallel model 2 gave the best result. Both of them achieved 99% recognition rate in ORL database. Parallel model 2 outperformed parallel model 2 and 3 because the corresponding frequency domain features gave better result. Parallel model 2 and 3 only achieved 97.5% and 96.5% recognition rate respectively.

Method	Recognition rate (%)
Parallel Model 1	97.5
Parallel Model 2	99
Parallel Model 3	96.5
D-LDA (Hu and Yang, 2001)	94
DWT+SHMN (Amira et al, 2007)	97
FD-LDA (Lu et al, 2003)	96

Table 3. Comparison of recognition rate of other face recognition methods

The performances of the proposed parallel models are further evaluated using *fb* probe set of FERET database. Fig. 5. shows the recognition rate of the proposed methods under different number of features. Fig. 6. shows the cumulative matching score (CMS) curve of the proposed methods. Since there are 165 classes, the number of output features of LDA is

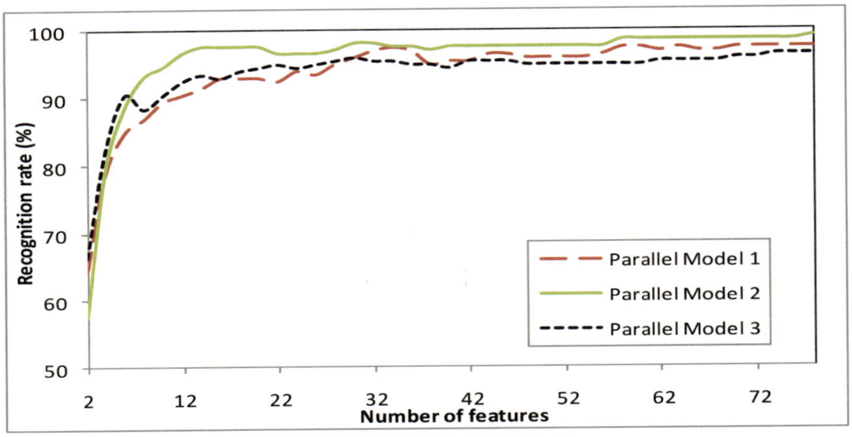

Fig. 4. ORL database result

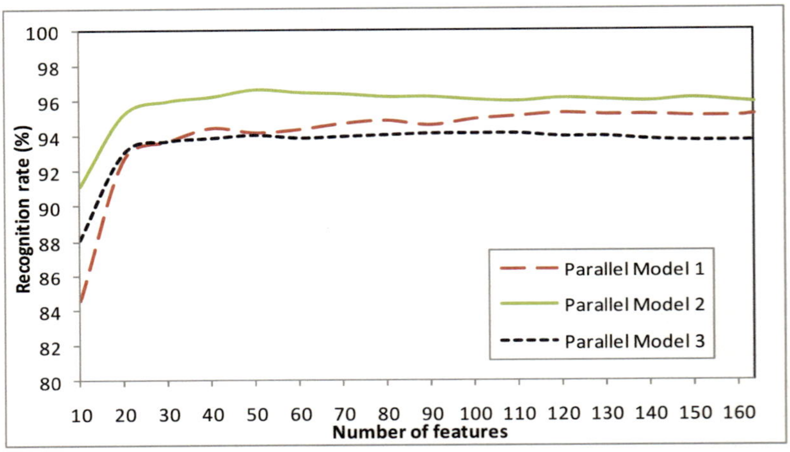

Fig. 5. FERET result

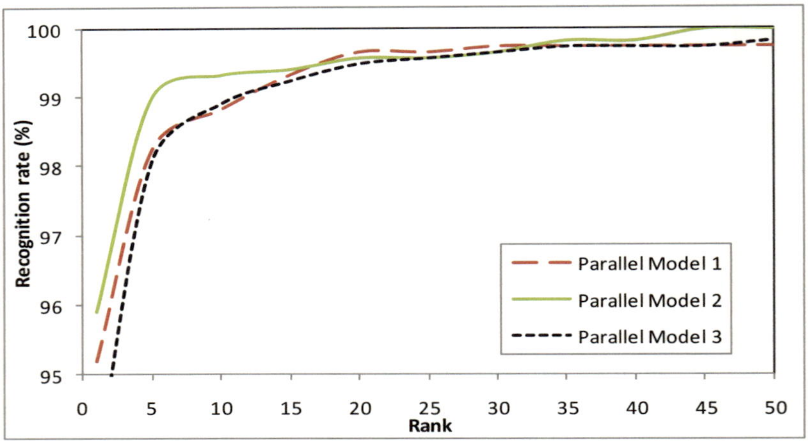

Fig. 6. CMS curve

164. Therefore, the number of selected coefficients from DCT domain is increased from 64 to 192 for parallel model 1.

Similar to ORL database's result, parallel model 2 gave the best result. It achieved 96.7% recognition rate when the number of features was 50. It also gave the best result in CMS. It achieved 100% recognition rate when the rank was 45 and above.

6. Conclusion

In this paper, a new parallel model for face recognition is proposed. There are three variants of parallel model which incorporate different variants of LDA. The proposed utilizing information form frequency and spatial domains. Both features are processed in parallel way. LDA is subsequently applied on the features to counter high dimensionality problem that encounter by feature fusion method. The high recognition rate that is achieved by the proposed methods shows that features of both domains contribute valuable information to the system. Parallel model 1 and 2 gave the best result. Parallel model 2 achieved 99% and 96.7% recognition rate in ORL and FERET database respectively.

7. References

Belhumeur, P.N.; Hespanha, J.P. & Kriegman, D.J. (1997) Eigenface vs. Fisherfaces: Recognition using class specific linear projection, *IEEE Trans. Pattern Anal. Machine Intell*, vol.19, pp.711-720, May 1997.

Chen, L.F.; Mark Liao, H.Y.; Ko, M.T.; Lin, J.C. & Yu, G.J. (2000) A new LDA-based face recognition system which can solve the small space size problem, *Pattern Recognition*, vol.33, pp.1703-1726, 2000.

Kirby, M. & Sirovich, L. (1990) Application of the Karhunen-Loeve procedure of the characteristic of human faces, *IEEE Trans. Pattern Anal.Machine Intell*, vol.12,pp 103-108, Jan,1990.

Lay, J.A. & Guan, L. (1999) Image Retrieval based on energy histogram of the low frequency DCT coefficients, *IEEE International Conference on Acoustics Speech and Signal Processing*, 6:3009-3012, 1999.

Liu, K.; Cheng, Y. & Yang, J. (1992) A generalized optimal set of discriminant vectors, *Pattern Recognition* vol. 25, no. 7, pp. 731-739, 1992.

Lu, J.; Plataniotis, K.N. & Venetsanopoulos, A. N. (2003) Face Recognition Using LDA-based Algorithm", *IEEE trans.Neural Network*, vol.14, No 1, pp.195-199, January 2003.

Meada, M.; Sivakumar, S.C. & Phillips, W.J. (2005) Comparative performance of principal component analysis, Gabor wavelets and discrete wavelet transforms for face recognition", Can. J. Elect. Comput. Eng, vol. 30, No. 2, 2005.

Nicholl, P.; Amira, A.; Bouchaffra, D. & Perrott, R.H. (2007) Multiresolution Hybrid Approaches for Automated Face Recognition, *AHS*, 2007.

Tjahyadi, R.; Liu, W.; An, S. & Venkatesh, S. (2007) Face Recognition via the Overlapping Energy Histogram, *IJCAI*, pp.2891-2896, 2007.

Turk, M. & Pentland, A. (1991) Eigenfaces for recognition, *Journal of Cognitive Neuroscience*, vol. 3, no. 1, pp. 71-86, Mar 1991.

Yu, Hu. & Yang, J. (2001) A Direct LDA algorithm for high-dimension data with application to face recognition, *Pattern Recognition*, vol.34, pp. 2067-2070, 2001.

3

Robust Face Recognition System Based on a Multi-Views Face Database

Dominique Ginhac[1], Fan Yang[1], Xiaojuan Liu[2], Jianwu Dang[2] and Michel Paindavoine[1]
[1]LE2I – University of Burgundy
[2]School of Automation, Lanzhou Jiatong University
[1]France
[2]China

1. Introduction

Biometry is currently a very active area of research spanning several sub-disciplines such as image processing, pattern recognition, and computer vision. The main goal of biometry is to build systems that can identify people from some observable characteristics such as their face, fingerprints, iris, etc. Facial recognition is the identification of humans by the unique characteristics of their faces. It has become a specialized area within the large field of computer vision. It has attracted a lot of attention because of its potential applications. Indeed, vision systems that automate face recognition process appear to be promising in various fields such as law enforcement applications, secure information systems, multimedia systems, and cognitive sciences.

The interest into face recognition is mainly focused on the identification requirements for secure information systems, multimedia systems, and cognitive sciences. Interest is still on the rise, since face recognition is also seen as an important part of next-generation smart environments (Ekenel & Sankur, 2004).

Different techniques can be used to track and process faces (Yang et al, 2001), e.g., neural networks approaches (Férand et al., 2001, Rowley et al., 1998), eigenfaces (Turk & Pentland, 1991), or Markov chains (Slimane et al., 1999). As the recent DARPA-sponsored vendor test showed, much of the face recognition research uses the public 2-D face databases as the input pattern (Phillips et al., 2003), with a recognition performance that is often sensitive to pose and lighting conditions. One way to override these limitations is to combine modalities: color, depth, 3-D facial surface, etc. (Tsalakanidou et al., 2003, Beumier & Acheroy, 2001, Hehser et al., 2003, Lu et al., 2004, Bowyer et al., 2002). Most 3-D acquisition systems use professional devices such as a traveling camera or a 3-D scanner (Hehser et al., 2003, Lu et al., 2004). Typically, these systems require that the subject remain immobile during several seconds in order to obtain a 3-D scan, and therefore may not be appropriate for some applications such as human expression categorization using movement estimation. Moreover, many applications in the field of human face recognition such as human-computer interfaces, model-based video coding, and security control (Kobayashi, 2001, Yeh & Lee, 1999) need to be high-speed and real-time, for example, passing through customs quickly while ensuring security. Furthermore, the cost of systems based on sophiticated 3-D scanners can easily make such an approach prohibitive for routine applications.

In order to avoid using expensive and time intensive 3-D acquisition devices, some face recognition systems generate 3-D information from stereo-vision (Wang, et al., 2003). Complex calculations, however, are necessary in order to perform the self-calibration and the 2-D projective transformation (Hartly et al., 2003). Another possible approach is to derive some 3-D information from a set of face images, but without trying to reconstitute the complete 3-D structure of the face (Tsalakanidou et al., 2003; Liu & Chen, 2003).

In this chapter, we describe a new robust face recognition system base on a multi-views face database that derives some 3-D information from a set of face images. We attempt to build an approximately 3-D system for improving the performance of face recognition. Our objective is to provide a basic 3-D system for improving the performance of face recognition. The main goal of this vision system is 1) to minimize the hardware resources, 2) to obtain high success rates of identity verification, and 3) to cope with real-time constraints.

Our acquisition system is composed of five standard cameras, which can take simultaneously five views of a face at different angles (frontal face, right profile, left profile, three-quarter right and three-quarter left). This system was used to build the multi-views face database. For this purpose, 3600 images were collected in a period of 12 months for 10 human subjects (six males and four females).

Research in automatic face recognition dates back to at least the 1960s. Most current face recognition techniques, however, date back only to the appearance-based recognition work of the late 1980s and 1990s (Draper et al., 2003). A number of current face recognition algorithms use face representations found by unsupervised statistical methods. Typically these methods find a set of basis images and represent faces as a linear combination of those images. Principal Component Analysis (PCA) is a popular example of such methods. PCA is used to compute a set of subspace basis vectors (which they called "eigenfaces") for a database of face images, and project the images in the database into the compressed subspace. One characteristic of PCA is that it produces spatially global feature vectors. In other words, the basis vectors produced by PCA are non-zero for almost all dimensions, implying that a change to a single input pixel will alter every dimension of its subspace projection. There is also a lot of interest in techniques that create spatially localized feature vectors, in the hopes that they might be less susceptible to occlusion and would implement recognition by parts. The most common method for generating spatially localized features is to apply Independent Component Analysis (ICA) in order to produce basis vectors that are statistically independent.

The basis images found by PCA depend only on pair-wise relationships between pixels in the image database. In a task such as face recognition, in which important information may be contained in the high-order relationships among pixels, it seems reasonable to expect that better basis images may be found by methods sensitive to these high order statistics (Bartlett et al., 2002). Compared to PCA, ICA decorrelates high-order statistics from the training signals, while PCA decorrelates up to second-order statistics only. On the other hand, ICA basis vectors are more spatially local than the PCA basis vectors, and local features (such as edges, sparse coding, and wavelet) give better face representations (Hyvarinen, 1999). This property is particularly useful for face recognition. As the human face is a non-rigid object, local representation of faces will reduce the sensitivity of the face variations due to different facial expressions, small occlusions, and pose variations. That means some independent components are less sensitive under such variations (Hyvarinen & Oja, 2000).

Using the multi-views database, we address the problem of face recognition by evaluating the two methods PCA and ICA and comparing their relative performance. We explore the issues of subspace selection, algorithm comparison, and multi-views face recognition performance. In order to make full use of the multi-views property, we also propose a strategy of majority voting among the five views, which can improve the recognition rate. Experimental results show that ICA is a promising method among the many possible face recognition methods, and that the ICA algorithm with majority-voting is currently the best choice for our purposes.

The rest of this chapter is organized as following: Section 2 describes the hardware acquisition system, the acquisition software and the multi-views face database. Section 3 gives a brief introduction to PCA and ICA, and especially the ICA algorithms. Experimental results are discussed in Section 4, and conclusions are drawn in Section 5.

Fig. 1. Acquisition system with the five Logitech cameras fixed on their support

2. Acquisition and database system presentation

Our acquisition system is composed of five Logitech 4000 USB cameras with a maximal resolution of 640×480 pixels. The parameters of each camera can be adjusted independently. Each camera is fixed on a height-adjustable sliding support in order to adapt the camera position to each individual, as depicted on Fig. 1.

The human subject sits in front of the acquisition system, directly facing the central camera. A specific acquisition program has been developed in order to simultaneously grab images from the 5 cameras. The five collected images are stored into the PC hard disk with a frame data rate of 20×5 images per second. As an example, a software screenshot is presented on the Fig. 2.

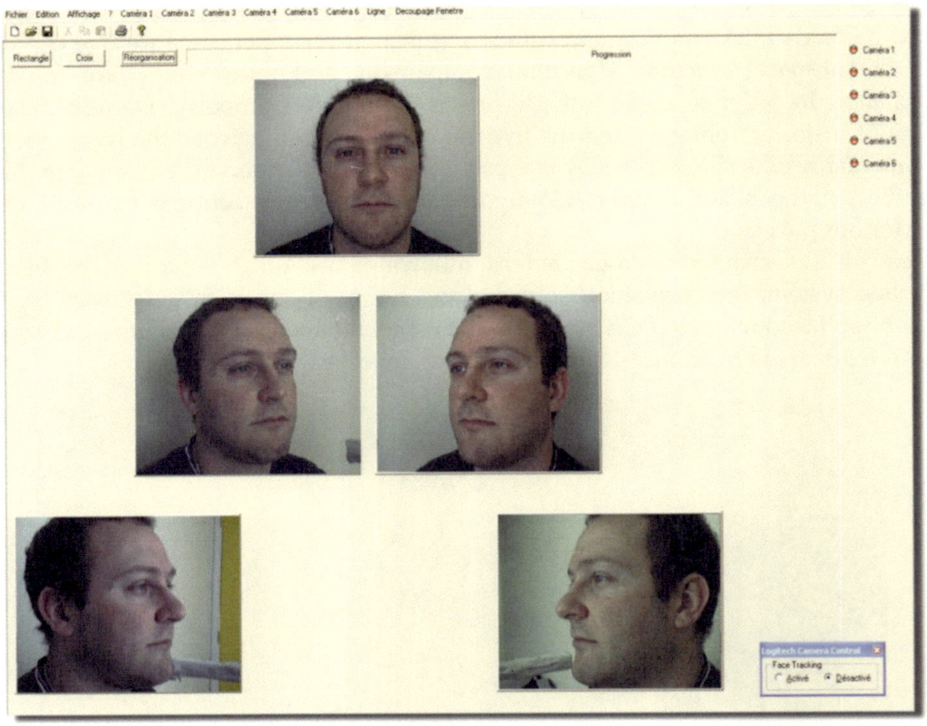

Fig. 2. Example of five images collected from a subject by the acquisition software.

The multi-views face database was built using the described acquisition system of 5 views. This database collected 3600 images taken in a period of 12 months for 10 human subjects (six males and four females). The rate of acquisition is 6 times per subject and 5 views for every subject at each occasion. The hairstyle and the facial expression of the subjects are different in every acquisition. The five views for each subject were made at the same time but in different orientations. **Face, ProfR, ProfL, TQR** and **TQL,** indicate respectively the frontal face, profile right, profile left, three-quarter right and three-quarter left images.
The Fig. 3 shows some typical images stored in the face database.
This database can also been expressed as following:

1. Total of 3600 different images (5 orientations × 10 people × 6 acquisitions × 12 months),
2. Total of 720 visages in each orientation (10 people × 6 acquisitions × 12 months),
3. Total of 360 images for each person (5 orientations × 6 acquisitions × 12 months).

3. Algorithm description: PCA and ICA

3.1 Principal component analysis

Over the past 25 years, several face recognition techniques have been proposed, motivated by the increasing number of real-world applications and also by the interest in modelling human cognition. One of the most versatile approaches is derived from the statistical technique called Principal Component Analysis (PCA) adapted to face images (Valentin et al., 1994; Abdi, 1988). In the context of face detection and identification, the use of PCA was first proposed by Kirby and Sirovich. They showed that PCA is an optimal

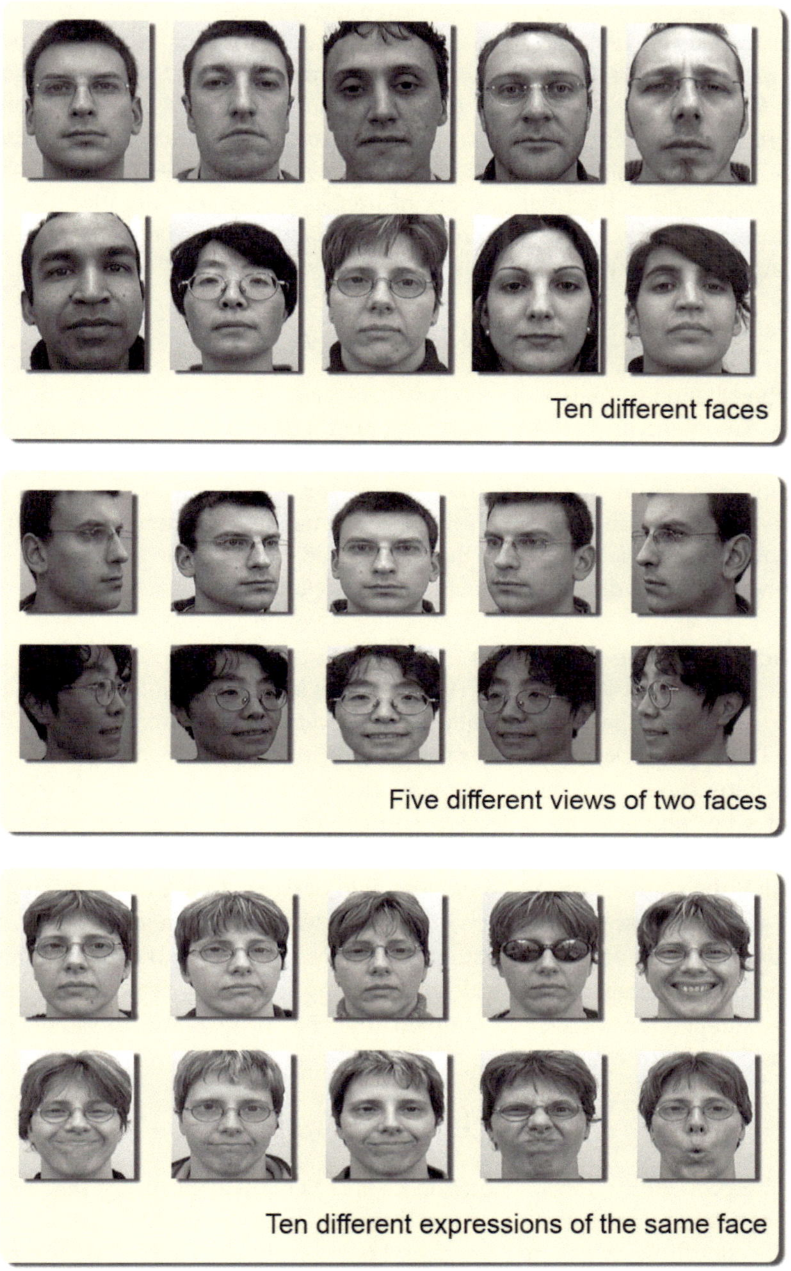

Fig. 3. Different views of the face database: the ten subjects (top), the five views of two subjects (middle), and different expressions of the frontal view of one subject (bottom).

compression scheme that minimizes the mean squared error between the original images and their reconstructions for any given level of compression (Sirovich & Kirby, 1987; Kirby & Sirovich, 1990). Turk & Pentland (1991) popularized the use of PCA for face recognition. PCA is based on the idea that face recognition can be accomplished with a small set of features that best approximates the set of known facial images. Application of PCA for face recognition proceeds by first performing PCA on a set of training images of known human faces. From this analysis, a set of principal components is obtained, and the projection of the test faces on these components is used in order to compute distances between test faces and the training faces. These distances, in turn, are used to make predictions about the test faces. Consider the DxK-dimensional face data matrix $\boldsymbol{X}$, where $\boldsymbol{D}$ represents the number of pixels of the face images and $\boldsymbol{K}$ the total number of images under consideration. $\boldsymbol{XX^T}$ is then the sample covariance matrix for the training images, and the principal components of the covariance matrix are computed by solving the following equation:

$$R^T\left(XX^T\right)R = \Lambda \tag{1}$$

where Λ is the diagonal matrix of eigenvalues and $\boldsymbol{R}$ is the matrix of orthonormal eigenvectors. Geometrically, $\boldsymbol{R}$ is a rotation matrix that rotates the original coordinate system onto the eigenvectors, where the eigenvector associated with the largest eigenvalue is the axis of maximum variance; the eigenvector associated with the second largest eigenvalue is the orthogonal axis with the second maximum variance, etc. Typically, only the $\boldsymbol{M}$ eigenvectors associated with the $\boldsymbol{M}$ largest eigenvalues are used to define the subspace, where M is the desired subspace dimensionality.

3.2 Independent component analysis

Independent Component Analysis (ICA) is a statistical signal processing technique. It is very closely related to the method called Blind Source Separation (BSS) or Blind Signal Separation. The basic idea of ICA is to represent a set of random variables using basis functions, where the components are statistically independent or as independent as possible. Let $\boldsymbol{s}$ be the vector of unknown source signals and $\boldsymbol{x}$ be the vector of observed mixtures. If $\boldsymbol{A}$ is the unknown mixing matrix, then the mixing model is written as: $\boldsymbol{x} = \boldsymbol{As}$. It is assumed that the source signals are independent of each other and the mixing matrix $\boldsymbol{A}$ is invertible. Based on these assumptions and the observed mixtures, ICA algorithms try to find the mixing matrix $\boldsymbol{A}$ or the separating matrix $\boldsymbol{W}$ such that $\boldsymbol{u} = \boldsymbol{Wx} = \boldsymbol{WAs}$ is an estimation of the independent source signals (Cardoso, 1997).

Technically, independence can be defined by the probability densities. Signals are statistically independent when:

$$f_u(u) = \prod_i f_{u_i}(u_i) \tag{2}$$

where f_u is the probability density function of $\boldsymbol{u}$. It is equivalent to say that the vector $\boldsymbol{u}$ is uniformly distributed. Unfortunately, there may not be any matrix $\boldsymbol{W}$ that fully satisfies the independence condition, and there is no closed form expression to find $\boldsymbol{W}$. Instead, there are several algorithms that iteratively approximate $\boldsymbol{W}$ so as to indirectly maximize independence.

Since it is difficult to maximize directly the independence condition above, all common ICA algorithms recast the problem in order to iteratively optimize a smooth function whose global optima occurs when the output vectors $\boldsymbol{u}$ are independent. For example, the algorithm of InfoMax (Bell & Sejnowski, 1995) relies on the observation that independence is maximized when the entropy $\boldsymbol{H(u)}$ is maximized, where:

$$H(u) = -\int f_u(u)\log f_u(u)du \tag{3}$$

The algorithm of InfoMax performs gradient ascent on the elements so as to maximize ***H(u)*** (Sirovich & Kirby, 1987). It gets its name from the observation that maximizing ***H(u)*** also maximizes the mutual information between the input and the output vectors.
The algorithm of FastICA is arguably the most general, maximizing:

$$J(y) \approx c\left[E\{G(y)\} - E\{G(v)\}\right]^2 \tag{4}$$

where G is a non-quadratic function, v is a Gaussian random variable, and c is any positive constant, since it can be shown that maximizing any function of this form will also maximize independence (Hyvarinen, 1999).
InfoMax and FastICA all maximize functions with the same global optima. As a result, the two algorithms should converge to the same solution for any given data set. In practice, the different formulations of the independence constraint are designed to enable different approximation techniques, and the algorithms find different solutions because of differences among these techniques. Limited empirical studies suggest that the differences in performance between the algorithms are minor and depend on the data set (Draper et al., 2003).

4. Experiments and discussions

4.1 Experimental setup

We carried out experiments on the multi-views face database. Again there are 10 individuals, each having 360 images taken simultaneously at five orientations, with different expressions, different hairstyles, and at different times, making a total of 3600 images (see Section 2). For each individual in the set, we have three experimental schemes. First, we choose one visage from each acquisition to compose the training sets, all the visages (10 people) selected are aligned in rows in the training matrix, one visage per row. The remaining five visages for each acquisition are used for testing purposes. We call this scheme (1, 5) or "scheme1". Thereby the training matrix has 120 rows, and the testing matrix has 600 rows. The experiments are performed on five views respectively. In the second scheme, we select two visages in each acquisition as training sets, and the left four visages are used for testing. So the training matrix has 240 rows and there are 480 rows in the testing matrix. This scheme is (2, 4) or "scheme2". The third scheme gets three visages in each acquisition as training sets and the others as testing sets. This is (3, 3) or "scheme3'. Note that the training and testing sets were randomly chosen.
Based on these three schemes, we perform the experiments on two ICA algorithms (InfoMax and FastICA) and PCA according to only one criterion: recognition rate. The purpose is to verify and compare the performance of ICA and PCA on our multi-views face database.
Face recognition performance is evaluated by a nearest neighbor algorithm, using cosines as the similarity measure. Since ICA basis vectors are not mutually orthogonal, the cosine distance measure is often used to retrieve images in the ICA subspaces (Bartlett, 2001).

4.2 Experimental results

The experimental results presented in this section are composed of three parts. The first part analyses the relationship between subspace dimensions and the recognition rate. The second part gives a brief comparison of the three algorithms as applied to a face recognition task. Finally we will report systematically the multi-views performance.

We carry out the experiments using the publicly available MATLAB code written by Tony Bell and Marian Stewart Bartlett and revised in 2003 (InfoMax) and realized by Hugo Gavert, Jarmo Hurri, Jaakko Sareal, and Aapo Hyvarinen, version 2005 (FastICA).

When using ICA in facial identity tasks, we usually perform PCA as a preprocessing, and then load the principal component eigenvectors into rows of input matrix and run ICA on it. The problem that we first meet is the selection of subspace dimensions. We need not use all possible eigenvectors, since in PCA only the M eigenvectors associated with the M largest eigenvalues are used to define the subspace, where M is the desired subspace dimensionality.

We chose the subspace dimensions in proportion to the maximum in different schemes and performed the experiments using two ICA algorithms on our multi-views database. Fig. 4 gives one result of FastICA algorithm using Face images on the three schemes. By the way, although not presented here, we also tested this using the InfoMax algorithm, and the result is similar.

In the Fig. 4, *D1, D2, D3, D4, D5, D6* presents respectively six selected dimensions. For scheme1, there are 120 images in the training set, so the maximum dimension is 120, *D1-D6* are 20-120, i.e. recognition rate were measured for subspace dimensionalities starting at 20 and increasing by 20 dimensions up to a total of 120. For scheme2, there are 240 images in training set, thereby, *D1-D6* changed from 40 to 240 increasing by 40 dimensions. For scheme3, there are 360 images in training set, and *D1-D6* varied from 60 to 360 increasing by 60 dimensions.

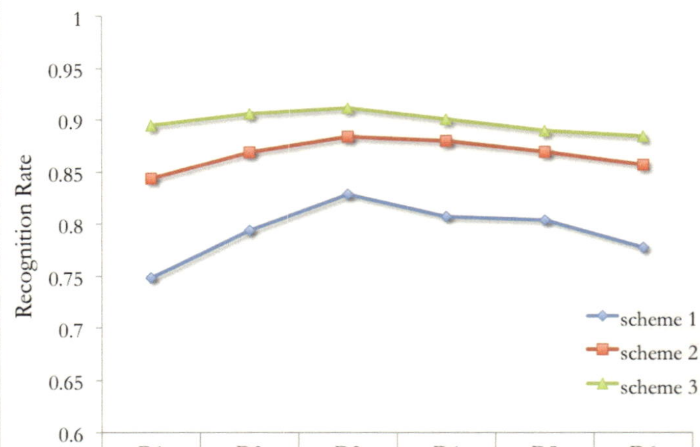

	D1	D2	D3	D4	D5	D6
scheme 1	0.7484	0.7934	0.8284	0.8067	0.8033	0.7767
scheme 2	0.8438	0.8688	0.8834	0.8792	0.8688	0.8563
scheme 3	0.8945	0.9056	0.9111	0.9	0.8889	0.8834

Fig. 4. Relationship between recognition rate and subspace dimensions.

It can be observed from this figure that the desired subspace dimension occurs in the half of the maximum. So, the subspace dimensions we used later are all at the half value of the maximum. Selecting subspace dimensions can simplify and reduce the computation process, which is useful for our future real time application.

After deciding the number of subspace dimensions, it is also interesting to compare the performance of the three face representation algorithms. These experiments were performed on our multi-views database. The results using frontal view are shown in Fig. 5.

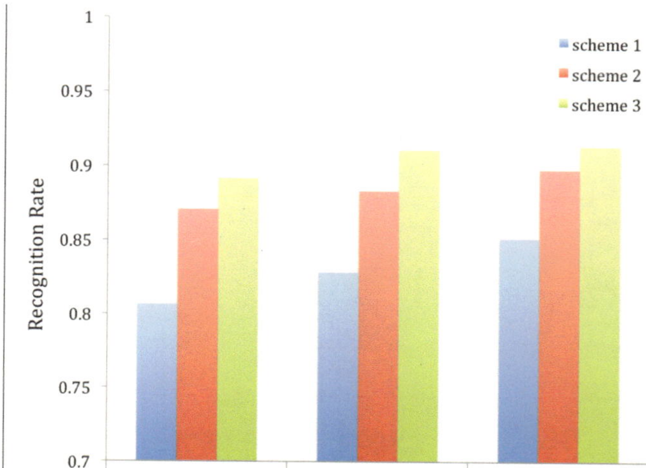

	PCA	FastICA	InfoMax
scheme 1	0.8067	0.8284	0.8517
scheme 2	0.8709	0.8834	0.898
scheme 3	0.8917	0.9111	0.9139

Fig. 5. Comparison of the three algorithms PCA, FastICA, and InfoMax.

4.3 Multi-views system performances

In order to fully explore our multi-views database, we also perform the majority-voting procedure among the five views. Fig. 6, Fig. 7 and Table 1 present the experimental results of this part.

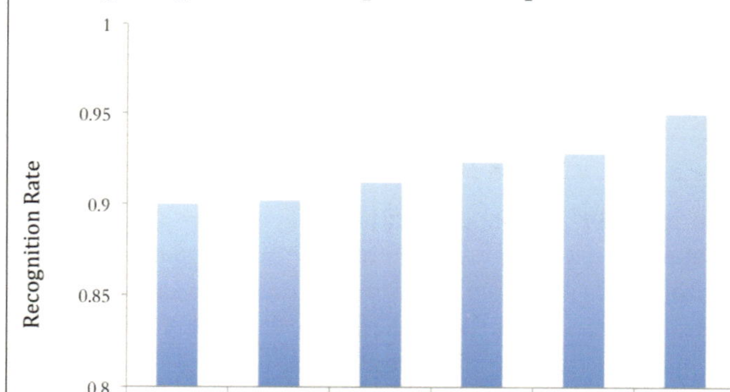

	TQL	TQR	Face	ProfR	ProfL	Vote
Data	0.9	0.902	0.912	0.923	0.928	0.95

Fig. 6. Multi-views performance using the FastICA algorithm.

Fig. 6 gives results of multi-views face recognition performance comparison, using the FastICA algorithm as an example. Fig. 7 illustrates "**VOTE**" and "**Face**" performance for three algorithms. The multi-views face recognition rates for PCA, InfoMax, and FastICA increase respectively by 5.35%, 5.56%, and 5.53% in comparison with frontal face recognition.

In Table 1, **Face, ProfR, ProfL, TQR** and **TQL,** indicate respectively the frontal face, profile right, profile left, three-quarter right and three-quarter left images. **VOTE** presents the results of the majority-voting procedure. (1, 5), (2, 4), and (3, 3) express respectively the number of training and testing sets which we have presented before. We performed several tests for each case and the results in the table are the averaged results.

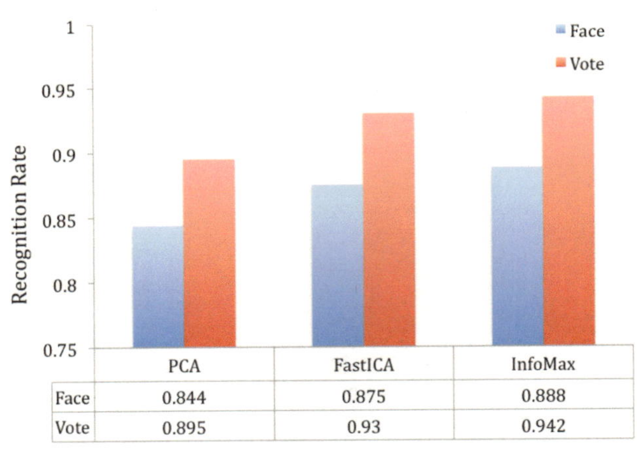

Fig. 7. Face and VOTE performance.

Algorithms	InfoMax			FastICA			PCA		
(train, test)	(1,5)	(2 ,4)	(3,3)	(1,5)	(2 ,4)	(3,3)	(1,5)	(2 ,4)	(3,3)
Face	0.8517	0.8980	0.9139	0.8284	0.8834	0.9111	0.8067	0.8709	0.8917
ProfR	0.9000	0.9313	0.9417	0.8450	0.8923	0.9222	0.8650	0.8958	0.9167
ProfL	0.9017	0.9334	0.9333	0.8683	0.9208	0.9278	0.8600	0.9125	0.9167
TQR	0.8484	0.8833	0.9361	0.8334	0.8480	0.9028	0.8250	0.8438	0.8750
TQL	0.8688	0.8915	0.9111	0.8483	0.8792	0.9000	0.8284	0.8500	0.8611
VOTE	0.9234	0.9479	0.9584	0.9084	0.9313	0.9500	0.8334	0.8875	0.9389

Table 1. Recognition rates for ICA and PCA using the multi-views face database

One can observe from Table 1 that, no matter which view and algorithm we use, the recognition rate always improves as the number of training samples is increased, and it is very interesting that the best performance occurs in **ProfR** or **ProfL**, i.e. the right profile or left profile images, not in **Face**, i.e. the frontal face images. On our opinion, the profile images maybe have more information than frontal face images.

Our results are accordance with the Draper's (Draper et al, 2003) on the FERET face data set that the relative performance of PCA and ICA depends on the task statement, the ICA architecture, the ICA algorithm, and (for PCA) the subspace distance metric, and for the facial identity task, ICA performs well than PCA.

5. Conclusion

In this chapter, we proposed a new face image acquisition system and multi-views face database. Face recognition using PCA and ICA were discussed. We evaluated the performance of ICA according to the recognition rate on this new multi-views face database. We explored the issues of subspace selection, algorithm comparison, and multi-views performance. We also proposed a strategy in order to improve the recognition performance, which performs the majority-voting using five views of each face. Our results are, in

accordance with most other literature that ICA is an efficient method in the task of face recognition, especially in face images with different orientations.
Moreover, based on our multi-views face database, we have the following conclusions:

1. For face recognition task, the algorithms based on statistic analysis method, such as FastICA, InfoMax, and PCA, InfoMax gives the best performance.
2. The desired subspace dimension occurs in the half of the maximum according to our experiments. Selection of subspace dimensions can simplify and reduce the computation process.
3. For every individual, different views have different recognition results. In our system, among five views, the highest recognition rate occurs in **ProfR** or **ProfL**, i.e the profile images, not in **Face**, i.e. the frontal face images. This is very interesting and we think that this is because of the profile images give more face features than frontal images.
4. Majority-voting procedure is a good method for improving the face recognition performance.

Our future work will focus on the multi-views face recognition application in real time systems. We will explore the new methods recently introduced in some literature, such as ensemble learning for independent component analysis using Random Independent Subspace (RIS) in Cheng et al. (2006), Kernel ICA algorithm in Yang et al. (2005), and Common Face method by using Common Vector Approach (CVP) introduced in He et al. (2006). We also will use more information fusion methods to obtain high recognition performance. Our purpose is to study an efficient and simple algorithm for later hardware implementation.

6. References

Abdi, H. (1988). A generalized approach for connectionist auto-associative memories: interpretation, implications and illustration for face processing, in *Artificial Intelligence and Cognitive Sciences*, J. Demongeot (Ed.), Manchester Univ. Press.

Bartlett, M.; Movella, J. & Sejnowski, T. (2002). Face Recognition by Independent Component Analysis, *IEEE Transactions on neural networks*, Vol. 13, No. 6, pp. 1450-1464.

Bartlett, M. (2001). *Face Image Analysis by Unsupervised Learning*, Kluwer Academic, ISBN:0792373480, Dordrecht.

Bell, A. & Sejnowski, T. (1995). An information-maximization approach to blind separation and blind deconvolution, *Neural Computation*, Vol. 7, No. 6, pp.1129-1159.

Beumier, C. & Acheroy, M. (2001). Face verification from 3D and grey level clues, *Pattern Recognition Letters*, Vol. 22, No. 12, pp. 1321–1329.

Bowyer, K.; Chang, K. & Flynn, P. (2002). A survey of 3D and multi-modal 3D+2D face recognition, *Proceedings of the 16th International Conference on Pattern Recognition*, pp. 358–361, Quebec, Canada.

Cardoso, J.-F. (1997). Infomax and Maximum Likelihood for Source Separation, *IEEE Signal Processing Letters*, Vol. 4, No. 4, pp.112-114.

Cheng, J.; Liu, Q.; Lu, H. & Chen, Y. (2006). Ensemble learning for independent component analysis, *Pattern Recognition*, Vol. 39, No. 1, pp.81-88.

Draper, B.; Baek, K.; Bartlett, M. & Beveridge, R. (2003). Recognition faces with PCA and ICA, *Computer Vision and Image Understanding*, Vol. 91, pp.115-117.

Ekenel, H. & Sankur, B. (2004). Feature selection in the independent component subspace for face recognition, *Pattern Recognition Letters*, Vol. 25, No. 12, pp. 1377-1388.

Féraud, R.; Bernier, O. J.; Viallet, J. & Collobert, M. (2001). A fast and accurate face detector based on neural networks, *IEEE Trans. Pattern Anal. Mach. Intell.*, Vol. 23, No. 1, pp. 42–53.

Hartly, R. & Zisserman, A. (2003). *Multiple View Geometry in Computer Vision*, 2nd ed., Cambridge Univ. Press

He, Y.; Zhao, L. & Zou, C. (2006). Face recognition using common faces method, *Pattern Recognition*, Vol. 39, No. 11, pp.2218-2222.

Hehser, C.; Srivastava, A. & Erlebacher, G. (2003). A novel technique for face recognition using range imaging, *Proceedings of 7th International Symposium On Signal Processing and Its Applications (ISSPA)*, pp. 201-204, Tallahassee, FL, USA.

Hyvarinen, A. (1999). The Fixed-point Algorithm and Maximum Likelihood Estimation for Independent Component Analysis, *Neural Processing Letters*, Vol. 10, No. 1, pp. 1-5.

Hyvarinen, A. (1999). Survey on Independent Component Analysis, *Neural Computing Surveys*, Vol. 2, pp. 94–128

Hyvarinen, A. & Oja, E. (2000). Independent Component Analysis: Algorithms and Applications, *Neural Networks*, Vol. 13, No. 4-5, pp.411- 430.

Kirby, M. & Sirovich, L. (1990). Application of the Karhunen-Loeve procedure for the characterization of human faces, *IEEE Transactions on Pattern Analysis and Machine Intelligence*, Vol. 12, No. 1, pp. 103-107.

Kobayashi, K. (2001). Mobile terminals and devices technology for the 21st century, *NEC Research Development*, Vol. 42, No. 1, pp. 15-24.

Liu, X. & Chen, T. (2003). "Geometry-assisted statistical modeling for face mosaicing", *Proceedings of the International Conference. on Image Processing (ICIP)*, Vol.2, pp. 883–886, Barcelona (Spain).

Lu, X.; Colbry, D. & Jain, A. (2004). Three-dimensional model based face recognition, *Proceedings of the 17th International Conference on Pattern Recognition (ICPR)*, Vol. 1, pp. 362–366.

Phillips, P.; Grother, P.; Micheals, R.; Blackburn, D.; Tabassi, E. & Bone, J. (2003). Face recognition vendor test 2002, *Proceedings of the IEEE International Workshop on Analysis and Modeling of Faces and Gestures (AMFG)*, pp. 44.

Rowley, H.; Baluja, S. & Kanade, T. (1998). Neural network-based face detection, *IEEE Transactions on Pattern Analysis and Machine Intelligence*, Vol. 20, No. 1, pp. 23–38.

Sirovich, L. & Kirby, M. (1987). A low-dimensional procedure for the characterization of human face, *Journal of the Optical Society of America A*, Vol. 4, No. 3, pp.519-524.

Slimane, M.; Brouard, T.; Venturini, G. & Asselin de Beauville, J. P. (1999). Unsupervised learning of pictures by genetic hybridization of hidden Markov chain, *Signal Processing*, Vol. 16, No. 6, pp. 461–475.

Tsalakanidou, F.; Tzovaras, D. & Strintzis, M. (2003). Use of depth and colour eigenfaces for face recognition, *Pattern Recognition Letters*, Vol. 24, No. 9-10, pp. 1427–1435.

Turk, M. & Pentland, A. (1991). Eigenfaces for recognition, *Journal of Cognitive Neuroscience*, Vol. 3, No. 1, pp 71–86.

Valentin, D.; Abdi, H.; O'Toole, A. & Cottrell, G. (1994). Connectionist models of face processing: a survey, *Pattern Recogn.* vol 27, pp 1208–1230.

Wang, J.; Venkateswarlu, R. & Lim, E. (2003). Face tracking and recognition from stereo sequence, *Proceedings of the International conference on Audio and Video-based Biometric Person Authentification (AVBPA)*, pp.145–153, Guilford (UK).

Yang, J.; Gao, X.; Zhang, D. & Yang, J. (2005). Kernel ICA: An alternative formulation and its application to face recognition, *Pattern Recognition*, Vol. 38, No. 10, pp.1784-1787.

Yang, M.; Kriegman, D. & Ahuja, N. (2001). Detecting faces in images: A survey, *IEEE Transactions on Pattern Analysis and Machine Intelligence*, Vol. 23, No. 1, pp. 34-58.

Yeh, Y. & Lee, C. (1999). Cost effective VLSI architectures and buffer size optimization for full search block matching algorithms, *IEEE Transactions on VLSI Systems*, Vol. 7, No. 3, pp. 345–358.

4

Face Recognition by Discriminative Orthogonal Rank-one Tensor Decomposition

Gang Hua
Microsoft Live Labs Research,
One Microsoft Way, Redmond, WA 98052,
U.S.A.

1. Introduction

Discriminative subspace analysis has been a popular approach to face recognition. Most of the previous work such as Eigen-faces (Turk & Pentlend, 1991), LDA (Belhumeur et al., 1997), Laplacian faces (He et al., 2005a), as well as a variety of tensor based subspace analysis methods (He et al., 2005b; Chen et al., 2005; Xu et al., 2006; Hua et al., 2007), can all be unified in the graph embedding framework (Yan et al., 2007). In this Chapter, we investigate the effects of two types of regularizations on discriminative subspace based face recognition techniques: a new 2D tensor representation for face image, and an orthogonal constraint on the discriminative tensor projections.

Given a face image, the new tensor representation firstly divides it into non-overlapping blocks. Then following the raster-scan order, the raster-scanned pixel vectors of each of the image blocks are put into the columns of a new 2D tensor. It is easy to figure out that the row vectors of the new 2D tensor are in essence different down-sampled images of the original face images. Pursuing discriminative 2D tensor projections with the new tensor representation is of special interest, because the left projection indeed functions as local filters in the original face image and the right projection reveals to us that which local block is more important for recognition.

This new representation puts concrete physical meanings to the left and right projections of the discriminative tensor projections. While the 2D tensor representation using the original images does not present any meaningful physical explanations on column and row pixel vectors. We call this new tensor representation Global-Local representation (Chen et al., 2005; Hua et al., 2007).

On the other hand, we reveal a very important property regarding the orthogonality between two tensor projections, and thus present a novel discriminative orthogonal tensor decomposition method for face recognition. To the best of our knowledge, this method, firstly introduced in (Hua et at., 2007), is the first discriminative orthogonal tensor decomposition method ever proposed in the literature.

Both of the two regularization techniques put additional constraints on the capacity (a.k.a., the VC-dimension) of the discriminative projections and thereby improve the generalization ability of the learned projections. We perform empirical analysis and comparative study on widely adopted face recognition bench-mark such as Yale, ORL, YaleB and PIE databased to

better understand the behaviours of the two. Note most of our results are adopted from (Hua et al., 2007) but we provide more analysis and discussions in this Chapter.
The rest of the Chapter is organized as follows: Section 2 defines some terminologies and mathematic notations on tensor analysis, as well as a very important property of orthogonal tensor projections, which will be used across the Chapter. Section 3 reviews the Global-Local tensor representation with its benefits discussed. Then, in Section 4, we present the new method for discriminative orthogonal rank-one tensor decomposition. Section 5 will discuss the experimental results on bench-mark face databases. Section 6 highlights some general remarks regarding the orthogonal rank-one tensor decomposition method for the task of face recognition. We conclude this Chapter in Section 7.

2. Introduction to tensor analysis

In multi-dimensional linear algebra, a tensor of order n or a nD tensor is a multiple dimensional array $\mathbf{X} \in \mathbf{R}^{n_0 \times n_1 \times \ldots \times n_n}$. We denote the element at position $(i_1, i_2, \ldots, i_n)$ to be $x_{i_1 i_2 \ldots i_n}$. For example, a matrix is a tensor of order 2 or 2D tensor, and x_{ij} denotes its element at the ith row and j^{th} column. In the following we introduce several definitions in tensor analysis, which is essential to present the discriminative orthogonal tensor decomposition method. Similar definitions are also adopted in (Hua et al., 2007).
The first definition we introduce here is the concept of k-mode product for a tensor and a matrix (a.k.a, an order 2 tensor). Following the tensor algebra literature (Kolda, 2001), we have:
Definition 1: The k-mode product of a tensor $\mathbf{X} \in \mathbf{R}^{n_1 \times n_2 \times \ldots \times n_k \times \ldots \times n_n}$ and a matrix $\mathbf{B} \in \mathbf{R}^{n_k \times m_k}$ is a $\mathbf{X} \in \mathbf{R}^{n_1 \times n_2 \times \ldots \times n_k \times \ldots \times n_n} \rightarrow \mathbf{Y} \in \mathbf{R}^{n_1 \times n_2 \times \ldots \times m_k \times \ldots \times n_n}$ mapping, such that

$$y_{i_1 i_2 \ldots i_{k-1} i'_k i_{k+1} \ldots i_n} = \sum_{j=1}^{n_k} x_{i_1 i_2 \ldots i_{k-1}\, j i_{k+1} \ldots i_n}\, b_{j i'_k}\,. \tag{1}$$

The k-mode product is generally denoted as $\mathbf{Y} = \mathbf{X} \times_k \mathbf{B}$.
The second definition we introduce here is the rank-one tensor. In general, a tensor is said to be of rank one, if it can be decomposed as the tensor product of a set of vectors.
Definition 2: A tensor $\mathbf{X} \in \mathbf{R}^{n_1 \times n_2 \times \ldots \times n_n}$ of order n is said to be with rank one, if and only if there exists a vector set $\hat{X} = \{\hat{\mathbf{x}}_1, \hat{\mathbf{x}}_2, \ldots \ldots, \hat{\mathbf{x}}_n\}$ where each $\hat{\mathbf{x}}_i$ is a vector of dimension n_i, and its jth element is denoted as $\hat{x}_{ij}$, such that

$$x_{i_1 i_2 \ldots i_n} = \prod_{j=1}^{n} \hat{x}_{j i_j}. \tag{2}$$

The tensor $\mathbf{X}$ is called the reconstruction rank one tensor of $\hat{X}$, and $\hat{X}$ is said to be the reconstruction vector set.
Based on the definitions above, we introduce the definition of rank one tensor projection:
Definition 3: Given an order n tensor $\mathbf{X}$, a rank one projection is an $\mathbf{X} \in \mathbf{R}^{n_1 \times n_2 \times \ldots \times n_n} \rightarrow y \in \mathbf{R}$ mapping, which is defined by a projection vector set $\hat{P} = \{\mathbf{p}_1, \mathbf{p}_2, \ldots \ldots, \mathbf{p}_n\}$ where each $\mathbf{p}_i$ is a column vector of dimension n_i. Let p_{ij} be the jth element of the vector $\mathbf{p}_i$, we have

$$y = \sum_{i_1, i_2 \ldots i_n} x_{i_1 i_2 \ldots i_n} \times p_{1 i_1} \times p_{2 i_2} \times \ldots \times p_{n i_n} \tag{3}$$

Let $\mathbf{P} \in \mathbf{R}^{n_1 \times n_2 \times \ldots \times n_n}$ be the reconstruction rank one tensor of $\hat{P}$, we have

$$y = \sum_{i_1, i_2 \ldots i_n} x_{i_1 i_2 \ldots i_n} \times p_{i_1 i_2 \ldots i_n}. \tag{4}$$

For ease of presentation, we denote the rank one projection using $\circledast$, i.e., $y = \hat{P} \circledast \mathbf{X}$ or $y = \mathbf{P} \circledast \mathbf{X}$. Obviously, using the k-mode product notation, if we treat each $\mathbf{p}_\mathrm{i}$ as a $n_i \times 1$ matrix, we also have

$$y = \mathbf{X} \times_1 \mathbf{p}_1 \times_2 \mathbf{p}_2 \times_3 \ldots \times_\mathrm{n} \mathbf{p}_\mathrm{n}. \tag{5}$$

Indeed, a rank one tensor projection can be deemed as a constrained linear projection. To understand it, we introduce the definition of *unfolding vector*.

Definition 4: The unfolding vector of an order n tensor $\mathbf{X} \in \mathbf{R}^{n_1 \times n_2 \times \ldots \times n_n}$ is a vector $\tilde{\mathbf{x}} \in \mathbf{R}^\mathrm{k}$, where $k = n_1 n_2 \ldots n_n$, such that $\tilde{x}_i = x_{i_1 i_2 \ldots i_n}$, where $i_j = \left\lfloor \frac{i - \sum_{k=1}^{j-1} [i_k \prod_{l=k+1}^{n} n_l]}{\prod_{l=j+1}^{n} n_l} \right\rfloor$ can be obtained recursively for $j = 1 \ldots n$. Note that here $\lfloor a \rfloor$ means the largest integer that is not larger than a.

Given the vector set representation $\hat{P} = \{\mathbf{p}_1, \mathbf{p}_2, \ldots \ldots, \mathbf{p}_\mathrm{n}\}$ of a rank-one tensor projection $\mathbf{P} \in \mathbf{R}^{n_1 \times n_2 \times \ldots \times n_n}$, it is easy to figure out that the unfolding vector $\tilde{\mathbf{p}}$ can be obtained by

$$\tilde{\mathbf{p}} = \mathbf{p}_n \otimes \mathbf{p}_{n-1} \otimes \ldots \otimes \mathbf{p}_1, \tag{6}$$

where $\otimes$ is the matrix Kronecker product. It is straightforward to figure out the following properties for rank one tensor projection, i.e.,

$$\hat{P} \circledast \mathbf{X} = \tilde{\mathbf{p}}^T \tilde{\mathbf{x}}\,. \tag{7}$$

It is because of this equivalence that a rank-one tensor projection can be regarded as a parameter constrained vector space linear projection. With the concept of unfolding vector, we finally define orthogonal rank-one tensor projections.

Definition 5: Two rank-one tensor projections $\hat{P}$ and $\hat{Q}$ are said to be orthogonal if and only if their corresponding unfolding vectors $\tilde{\mathbf{p}}$ and $\tilde{\mathbf{q}}$ are orthogonal to each other. Mathematically, we have

$$\hat{P} \perp \hat{Q} \Leftrightarrow \tilde{\mathbf{p}} \perp \tilde{\mathbf{q}} \tag{8}$$

This definition essentially relates orthogonal rank-one tensor projections with orthogonal vector projections. Note Definition 5 of orthogonal rank-one tensor projection is equivalent to the definition of orthogonal rank-one tensors in (Kolda, 2001).

We end the section by presenting a sufficient and necessary condition for orthogonal rank-one tensor projections, along with its proof (Hua et al., 2007).

Theorem 1: Given two rank-one tensor projections $\hat{P} = \{\mathbf{p}_1, \mathbf{p}_2, \ldots \ldots, \mathbf{p}_\mathrm{n}\}$ and $\hat{Q} = \{\mathbf{q}_1, \mathbf{q}_2, \ldots \ldots, \mathbf{q}_\mathrm{n}\}$, where $\mathbf{p}_i$ and $\mathbf{q}_i$ have the same dimensionality $\mathrm{n_i}$, they are orthogonal if and only if $\mathbf{p}_i \perp \mathbf{q}_i$ held at least for one of the dimension i. Or in short, we have

$$\hat{P} \perp \hat{Q} \Leftrightarrow \exists i, \text{such that } \mathbf{p}_i \perp \mathbf{q}_i$$

Proof: Let $\tilde{\mathbf{p}}$ and $\tilde{\mathbf{q}}$ be the unfolding vectors of $\hat{P}$ and $\hat{Q}$, it is easy to figure out that $\tilde{\mathbf{p}}^T \tilde{\mathbf{q}} = \prod_{\mathrm{i}=1}^{\mathrm{n}} \mathbf{p}_i^T \mathbf{q}_i$ based on the property of Kronecker product (See Definition 4).

"$\Rightarrow$": if $\hat{P} \perp \hat{Q}$, by Definition 5, we have $\tilde{\mathbf{p}}^T \tilde{\mathbf{q}} = \prod_{\mathrm{i}=1}^{\mathrm{n}} \mathbf{p}_i^T \mathbf{q}_i = 0$. If there does not exists an i, such that $\mathbf{p}_i \perp \mathbf{q}_i$, we would have $\mathbf{p}_i^T \mathbf{q}_i \neq 0$ for all i. Then we would have $\prod_{\mathrm{i}=1}^{\mathrm{n}} \mathbf{p}_i^T \mathbf{q}_i \neq 0$, which is conflicting with the setting. Therefore, there exists at least one i, such that $\mathbf{p}_i^T \mathbf{q}_i = 0$, i.e., $\mathbf{p}_i \perp \mathbf{q}_i$.

"$\Leftarrow$": If there exists one i , such that $\mathbf{p}_i \perp \mathbf{q}_i$, we have $\mathbf{p}_i^T \mathbf{q}_i = 0$. Then we immediately have $\prod_{i=1}^{n} \mathbf{p}_i^T \mathbf{q}_i = 0$. That essentially means that $\tilde{\mathbf{p}}^T \tilde{\mathbf{q}} = 0$, and thus $\hat{P} \perp \hat{Q}$.■

Theorem 1 reveals that for a pair of rank-one tensors to be orthogonal, it is suffice that the two corresponding vectors in one dimension of their reconstruction vector sets to be orthogonal.

3. Global-local tensor representation

Earlier subspace based methods for face recognition normally treat a face image as a vector data, which completely ignores the spatial structure of the 2 dimensional face image. It is until recently that tensor based representation for face images has become popular (He et al., 2005b; Chen et al., 2005; Xu et al., 2006; Hua et al., 2007). In tensor based representation, a face image is either regarded as an order 2 tensor (raw image) or an order 3 tensor (multi-band filter responses).

With the tensor representation, multi-linear (e.g., bilinear for order 2 tensors) are pursued for discriminative subspace analysis. Tensor based representation enjoys several advantages over vector based representation. First, it has the potential to utilize the spatial structure of the face images. Second, it suffers less from the curse-of-dimensionality because the multi-linear projection has much less parameters to estimate than normal linear vector projections. To give a concrete example, for face images of size 32×32, pursuing one discriminative projection for vector based representation needs to estimate $32 \times 32 = 1024$ parameters. While for order 2 tensor representation (raw image), pursuing one bilinear projection only needs to estimate $32 + 32 = 64$ parameters. Thirdly, because multi-linear projection has much less parameters to estimate, it is less likely to over-fit with the training data, especially when we only have small number of training examples.

Nevertheless, the majority of the previous works regard the raw face image as the order 2 tensor. Given a order 2 tensor $\mathbf{X} \in \mathbf{R}^{n_1 \times n_2}$, the rank-one tensor projection $\hat{P} = \{\mathbf{p}_1, \mathbf{p}_2\}$ is also called a bilinear projection such that $y = \mathbf{p}_1^T \mathbf{X} \mathbf{p}_2$, where $\mathbf{p}_1$ and $\mathbf{p}_2$ are named the left projection and right projection, respectively. Essentially the left and right projections of the bi-linear projection are performing analysis on the column pixel space and raw pixel space of the raw images, respectively. It does not really explore much of the spatial structures of the pixels. In the following, we will introduce a new 2D tensor (a.k.a., order 2 tensor) representation, which we call the Global-Local representation. It is firstly proposed by (Chen et al., 2005), and later on advocated by (Hua et al., 2007).

Instead of using the raw images directly as the 2D tensor representation. The Global-Local representation firstly partitions the original raw face image into non-overlapping blocks. Following the raster scan order, each block is then raster-scanned as a column vector and concatenated together to form the new Global-Local representation. This transformation process is illustrated in Figure.1.

The biggest merit of the Global-Local representation is that it explores the spatial structure of the face image pixels in a good fashion. As we can clearly observe in Figure.1, the column vector of the Global-Local 2D tensor representation is the unfolded vectors from the local blocks of the original raw image. On the other hand, it is also easy to see that the row vector of the Global-Local representation is indeed the unfolded vector of smaller images down-sampled from the original image. Why it is better to perform discriminative subspace analysis on this Global-Local tensor representation?

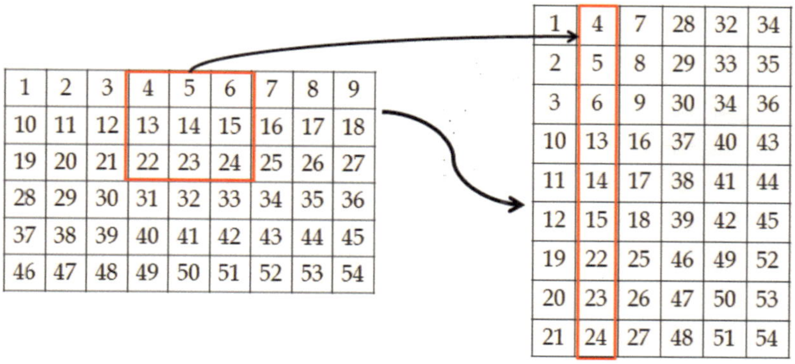

Fig. 1. Original 6×9 2D tensor (left side) and the Glocal-Local Tensor representation of 9×6 (right side) based on 3×3 local blocks.

Let us take a look of the operations of the left projections on the Global-Local tensor representation. By putting it back into the context of the original raw image, it is straightforward to see that the left projection is equivalent to convolute a local filter repeatedly on the different block partitions. Therefore, pursuing discriminative left projections is equivalent to identifying the most discriminative local filters for the original raw image.

On the other hand, the right projection is operating on the row vector of the Global-Local tensor representation. By putting it back into the context of the original raw image, the interpretation could be two-folds: First, by itself the projection is filtering on the down-sampled and shifted version of the original raw face image; on the other hand, coupling with the right projection, it selects which block partition we should weight the most to achieve the highest discriminative power.

Therefore, the combined interpretation of pursuing discriminative bi-linear projection with the Global-Local tensor representation is to seek for the most discriminative local filter and the best weighting scheme for the local pixel blocks. It is more sensible than using the raw face images directly as the 2D tensor representation. It is also clear that the Global-Local representation better utilized the spatial structure of the pixels on the face images.

In the rest of the Chapter, by default all the 2D tensors are with the Global-Local representation. We present here a discriminative orthogonal rank-one tensor decomposition method for face recognition, which is first proposed by (Hua et al., 2007).

4. Discriminative orthogonal rank-one tensor decomposition

In this section, we present the mathematic formulation of the discriminative orthogonal rank one tensor decomposition method followed by the detailed algorithm of how to pursue the tensor decomposition based on a set of labelled training data set. We present all the mathematic formulation under order n tensor but it should be just straightforward to derive from it for order 2 tensors.

We start from a set of training examples $\mathcal{T} = \{\mathbf{X}_i : \mathbf{X}_i \in \mathbf{R}^{n_1 \times n_2 \times \ldots \times n_n}, i = 1,2,\ldots,N\}$ with pair-wise labels $\mathcal{L} = \{l_{ij} : 1 \le i < j \le N, l_{ij} \in \{0,1\}\}$ where $l_{ij} = 1$ if $\mathbf{X}_i$ and $\mathbf{X}_j$ are in the same category (i.e., the faces of the same person under the context of face recognition), and $l_{ij} = 0$ if $\mathbf{X}_i$ and $\mathbf{X}_j$ are in different categories. We denote the k-nearest neighbour of the example $\mathbf{X}_i$

in the original input space to be $\mathcal{N}_k(\mathbf{X}_i)$. Then we define the positive label set and negative label set as $\boldsymbol{\mathcal{S}} = \{(i,j): l_{ij} = 1, 1 \le i < j \le N, \mathbf{X}_i \in \mathcal{N}_k(\mathbf{X}_j) \text{ or } \mathbf{X}_j \in \mathcal{N}_k(\mathbf{X}_i)\}$ and $\boldsymbol{\mathcal{D}} = \{(i,j): l_{ij} = 1, 1 \le i < j \le N, \mathbf{X}_i \in \mathcal{N}_k(\mathbf{X}_j) \text{ or } \mathbf{X}_j \in \mathcal{N}_k(\mathbf{X}_i)\}$, which are the k-nearest neighbour example pairs from the same or different categories, respectively.

For pursuing a discriminative embedding for face recognition, our objective here is to learn a set of orthogonal rank-one tensor projections $\{\hat{P}_1, \hat{P}_2, \dots, \hat{P}_K\}$ such that in the projective embedding space, the distance for those example pairs in $\boldsymbol{\mathcal{S}}$ are minimized while the distance for those example pairs in $\boldsymbol{\mathcal{D}}$ are maximized.

Following similar ideas as in (Duchene & Leclercq, 1988), we optimize a series of locally weighted discriminative cost function to build the discriminative embedding. More formally, suppose that we have already discriminatively pursued $k-1$ orthogonal rank one tensor projections $\{\hat{P}^{(1)}, \hat{P}^{(2)}, \dots, \hat{P}^{(k-1)}\}$, to pursue the kth rank one tensor projections, we solve for the following optimization problem,

$$\max_{\hat{P}^{(k)}} \frac{\sum_{(i,j)\in\boldsymbol{\mathcal{D}}} \omega_{ij} (\hat{P}^{(k)} \circledast \mathbf{X}_i - \hat{P}^{(k)} \circledast \mathbf{X}_j)^2}{\sum_{(i,j)\in\boldsymbol{\mathcal{S}}} \omega_{ij} (\hat{P}^{(k)} \circledast \mathbf{X}_i - \hat{P}^{(k)} \circledast \mathbf{X}_j)^2} \tag{9}$$

$$\text{s.t. } \hat{P}^{(k)} \perp \hat{P}^{(k-1)}, \hat{P}^{(k)} \perp \hat{P}^{(k-2)}, \dots, \hat{P}^{(k)} \perp \hat{P}^{(1)} \tag{10}$$

where ω_{ij} is a weight assigned according to the importance of the example pair $\{\mathbf{X}_i, \mathbf{X}_j\}$. There are different strategies in setting the weight ω_{ij}. In our experiments, we adopted the most popular heat kernel weights, i.e., $\omega_{ij} = \exp\left\{-\left\|\mathbf{X}_i - \mathbf{X}_j\right\|_F^2 / \mathrm{t}\right\}$, where $\|\bullet\|_F$ denotes the Frobenius norm of matrices, and t is a constant heat factor. This weight setting induces heavy penalties to the cost function in Equation (9) for example pairs which are very close in the input space. One more thing to be noticed is that for $k = 1$, we only need to solve for the unconstrained optimization problem in Equation (9).

To solve for the constrained optimization problem in Equation (9~10), we are confronted by two difficulties: First, there is even no closed-form solution for the unconstrained optimization problem in Equation (9). Fortunately, it is well known that this unconstrained problem can be solved by using a sequential iterative optimization strategy. Second, it is in general difficult to keep both the rank-one and orthogonality properties. We address this issue by leveraging the sufficient and necessary conditions for orthogonal rank one tensors in Theorem 1.

In essence, Theorem 1 states that to make two rank one tensors to be orthogonal to each other, we only need to place the orthogonal constraints on one dimension of the rank-one tensors. Therefore, an equivalent set of constraints to the orthogonality constraints is

$$\exists \{j_l : l = 1,2,\dots,k-1; 1 \le j_l \le n\} \;\; s.t. \;\; \mathbf{p}_{j_{k-1}}^{(k)} \perp \mathbf{p}_{j_{k-1}}^{(k-1)}, \mathbf{p}_{j_{k-2}}^{(k)} \perp \mathbf{p}_{j_{k-2}}^{(k-2)}, \dots, \mathbf{p}_{j_1}^{(k)} \perp \mathbf{p}_{j_1}^{(1)}, \tag{11}$$

where $\mathbf{p}_j^{(k)}$ indicates the projection vector corresponding to the jth dimension of the rank one tensor projection $\hat{P}^{(k)}$ which is of order n.

To ease the optimization process, we replace the constraints in Equation (11) with another set of stronger constraints, i.e.,

$$\exists \{j: 1 \le j \le n\} \;\; s.t. \;\; \mathbf{p}_j^{(k)} \perp \mathbf{p}_j^{(k-1)}, \mathbf{p}_j^{(k)} \perp \mathbf{p}_j^{(k-2)}, \dots, \mathbf{p}_j^{(k)} \perp \mathbf{p}_j^{(1)} \tag{12}$$

These constraints are stronger in the sense that it requires all the different j_l in Equation (11) to be same value. It is just trying to put all orthogonal constraints on one dimension of the rank-one tensor projections. With the sufficient condition to ensure the orthogonal property for the rank-one projections in Equation (12), we proceed to derive the solution for the constrained optimization problem in Equation (9~10).

As we have mentioned beforehand, the unconstrained optimization problem in Equation (9) is usually solved numerically in a sequential iterative fashion. That is, at each iteration, we fix $\hat{P}_{-i}^{(k)} = \{\mathbf{p}_1^{(k)}, \mathbf{p}_2^{(k)}, \ldots, \mathbf{p}_{i-1}^{(k)}, \mathbf{p}_{i+1}^{(k)}, \ldots, \mathbf{p}_n^{(k)}\}$ for one of the $1 \le i \le n$, and optimize Equation (9) with respect to $\mathbf{p}_i^{(k)}$. As a matter of fact, once we fixed $\hat{P}_{-i}^{(k)}$, the optimization problem boils down to a problem in a vector space of dimension n_i. To simplify the notation, we denote

$$\mathbf{y}^{(k,i)} = \mathbf{X} \times_1 \mathbf{p}_1^{(k)} \times_2 \mathbf{p}_2^{(k)} \times_3 \ldots \times_{i-1} \mathbf{p}_{i-1}^{(k)} \times_{i+1} \mathbf{p}_{i+1}^{(k)} \times_{i+2} \ldots \times_n \mathbf{p}_n^{(k)} \stackrel{\text{def}}{=} \mathbf{X} \circledast \hat{P}_{-i}^{(k)} \tag{13}$$

which is an n_i dimensional vector. Then it is easy to figure out that the optimization problem in Equation (9) boils down to the following problem

$$\arg\max_{\mathbf{p}_i^{(k)}} \frac{\mathbf{p}_i^{(k)^{\mathrm{T}}} \mathbf{A}_d^i \mathbf{p}_i^{(k)}}{\mathbf{p}_i^{(k)^{\mathrm{T}}} \mathbf{A}_s^i \mathbf{p}_i^{(k)}} \tag{14}$$

where

$$\mathbf{A}_d^i = \textstyle\sum_{(s,t)\in\mathcal{D}} \omega_{st} \left(\mathbf{y}_s^{(k,i)} - \mathbf{y}_t^{(k,i)}\right)\left(\mathbf{y}_s^{(k,i)} - \mathbf{y}_t^{(k,i)}\right)^T \tag{15}$$

$$\mathbf{A}_s^i = \textstyle\sum_{(s,t)\in\mathcal{S}} \omega_{st} \left(\mathbf{y}_s^{(k,i)} - \mathbf{y}_t^{(k,i)}\right)\left(\mathbf{y}_s^{(k,i)} - \mathbf{y}_t^{(k,i)}\right)^T \tag{16}$$

$$\mathbf{y}_o^{(k,i)} = \mathbf{X}_o \circledast \hat{P}_{-i}^{(k)}. \tag{17}$$

It is also well known that the solution to the unconstrained optimization problem in Equation (14) could be obtained by solving a generalized eigenvalue system, i.e.,

$$\mathbf{A}_d^i \mathbf{p} = \lambda \mathbf{A}_s^i \mathbf{p} \tag{18}$$

and the optimal $\mathbf{p}_i^{(k)*}$ is the eigenvector associated with the largest eigenvalue. Equation (15) is solved iteratively over $i = 1,2,\ldots,n$ until convergence. The converged output $\hat{P}^{(k)*} = \{\mathbf{p}_1^{(k)*}, \mathbf{p}_2^{(k)*}, \ldots, \mathbf{p}_i^{(k)*}, \ldots, \mathbf{p}_n^{(k)*}\}$ is regarded to the optimal solution to the unconstrained optimization problem of Equation (9). It only guarantees a local optimal solution, though.

But we are missing the orthogonal constraints Equation (10) here. As we have discussed, the constraints in Equation (12) is a sufficient condition for the constraint in Equation (10). So we need to ensure the constraints in Equation (12). It immediately implies that we only need to ensure the orthogonality for one of the dimension j during the sequential iterative optimization process to ensure the orthogonality of the tensor projections.

That is to say, for $i \neq j$, we only need to solve for an unconstrained optimization problem in Equation (14). But for $i = j$, we essentially need to solve for the following constrained optimization problem,

$$\arg\max_{\mathbf{p}_i^{(k)}} \frac{\mathbf{p}_j^{(k)^{\mathrm{T}}} \mathbf{A}_d^j \mathbf{p}_j^{(k)}}{\mathbf{p}_j^{(k)^{\mathrm{T}}} \mathbf{A}_s^j \mathbf{p}_j^{(k)}} \tag{19}$$

$$s.t.\ \mathbf{p}_j^{(k)^{\mathrm{T}}}\mathbf{p}_j^{(k-1)} = 0, \mathbf{p}_j^{(k)^{\mathrm{T}}}\mathbf{p}_j^{(k-2)} = 0, \dots, \mathbf{p}_j^{(k)^{\mathrm{T}}}\mathbf{p}_j^{(1)} = 0 \tag{20}$$

It is easy to see that it is equivalent to solve for the following constrained optimization problem, i.e.,

$$\arg\max_{\mathbf{p}_i^{(k)}} \mathbf{p}_j^{(k)^{\mathrm{T}}}\mathbf{A}_d^j\mathbf{p}_j^{(k)} \tag{21}$$

$$s.t.\quad \mathbf{p}_j^{(k)^{\mathrm{T}}}\mathbf{A}_s^j\mathbf{p}_j^{(k)} = 1, \mathbf{p}_j^{(k)^{\mathrm{T}}}\mathbf{p}_j^{(k-1)} = 0, \mathbf{p}_j^{(k)^{\mathrm{T}}}\mathbf{p}_j^{(k-2)} = 0, \dots, \mathbf{p}_j^{(k)^{\mathrm{T}}}\mathbf{p}_j^{(1)} = 0. \tag{22}$$

For the constrained optimization problem in Equation (21~22), we show here that the optimal solution can be obtained by solving for the following eigenvalue problem:

$$\widetilde{\mathcal{M}}\mathbf{p}_j^{(k)} = \left(\mathbf{I} - \left(\mathbf{A}_s^j\right)^{-1}\mathcal{A}\mathcal{B}^{-1}\mathcal{A}^T\right)\mathbf{A}_s^{j^{-1}}\mathbf{A}_d^j\mathbf{p}_j^{(k)} = \lambda\mathbf{p}_j^{(k)} \tag{23}$$

where

$$\mathcal{A} = \left[\mathbf{p}_j^{(1)}, \mathbf{p}_j^{(1)}, \dots, \mathbf{p}_j^{(k-1)}\right] \tag{24}$$

$$\mathcal{B} = \mathcal{A}^T\mathbf{A}_s^{j^{-1}}\mathcal{A}\,. \tag{25}$$

The optimal $\mathbf{p}_j^{(k)*}$ is the eigenvector corresponding to the largest eigenvalue of $\widetilde{\mathcal{M}}$. Following similar steps as shown in (Hua et al., 2007; Duchene & Leclercq, 1988), in the following we demonstrate how we derive the solution presented in Equation (23).

We firstly formulate the Lagrangian multipliers out of the constrained optimization problem in Equation (21~23), i.e.,

$$L\left(\mathbf{p}_j^{(k)}, \lambda, \mu_1, \mu_2, \dots, \mu_{k-1}\right) = \mathbf{p}_j^{(k)^{\mathrm{T}}}\mathbf{A}_d^j\mathbf{p}_j^{(k)} - \lambda\left(\mathbf{p}_j^{(k)^{\mathrm{T}}}\mathbf{A}_s^j\mathbf{p}_j^{(k)} - 1\right)$$

$$-\mu_{k-1}\mathbf{p}_j^{(k)^{\mathrm{T}}}\mathbf{p}_j^{(k-1)} - \dots - \mu_2\mathbf{p}_j^{(k)^{\mathrm{T}}}\mathbf{p}_j^{(2)} - \mu_1\mathbf{p}_j^{(k)^{\mathrm{T}}}\mathbf{p}_j^{(1)}. \tag{26}$$

Take the derivative of $L\left(\mathbf{p}_j^{(k)}, \lambda, \mu_1, \mu_2, \dots, \mu_{k-1}\right)$ with respect to $\mathbf{p}_j^{(k)}$, and set it to zero, we have

$$\frac{\partial L\left(\mathbf{p}_j^{(k)}, \lambda, \mu_1, \mu_2, \dots, \mu_{k-1}\right)}{\partial\mathbf{p}_j^{(k)}} = 2\mathbf{A}_d^j\mathbf{p}_j^{(k)} - 2\lambda\mathbf{A}_s^j\mathbf{p}_j^{(k)} - \mu_{k-1}\mathbf{p}_j^{(k-1)} - \dots - \mu_1\mathbf{p}_j^{(1)} = 0 \tag{27}$$

Left multiply both side of Equation (27) by $\mathbf{p}_j^{(k)^{\mathrm{T}}}$, we immediately have

$$\mathbf{p}_j^{(k)^{\mathrm{T}}}\mathbf{A}_d^j\mathbf{p}_j^{(k)} - \lambda\left(\mathbf{p}_j^{(k)^{\mathrm{T}}}\mathbf{A}_s^j\mathbf{p}_j^{(k)} - 1\right) = 0\,. \tag{28}$$

We have

$$\lambda = \frac{\mathbf{p}_j^{(k)^{\mathrm{T}}}\mathbf{A}_d^j\mathbf{p}_j^{(k)}}{\mathbf{p}_j^{(k)^{\mathrm{T}}}\mathbf{A}_s^j\mathbf{p}_j^{(k)}} \tag{29}$$

which is exactly the quantity we want to maximize in Equation (19). Multiply both side of Equation (29) by $\mathbf{p}_j^{(l)^{\mathrm{T}}} \mathbf{A}_s^{j^{-1}}$ for $l = 1,2,\dots,k-1$, and with easy manipulation, we obtain a set of $k-1$ equations, i.e.,

$$\sum_{m=1}^{k-1} \mu_m \mathbf{p}_j^{(1)^T} \mathbf{A}_s^{j^{-1}} \mathbf{p}_j^{(m)} = 2\mathbf{p}_j^{(1)^{\mathrm{T}}} \mathbf{A}_s^{j^{-1}} \mathbf{A}_d^j \mathbf{p}_j^{(k)} \tag{30}$$

$$\sum_{m=1}^{k-1} \mu_m \mathbf{p}_j^{(2)^T} \mathbf{A}_s^{j^{-1}} \mathbf{p}_j^{(m)} = 2\mathbf{p}_j^{(2)^{\mathrm{T}}} \mathbf{A}_s^{j^{-1}} \mathbf{A}_d^j \mathbf{p}_j^{(k)} \tag{31}$$

$$\dots\dots\dots$$

$$\sum_{m=1}^{k-1} \mu_m \mathbf{p}_j^{(k-1)^T} \mathbf{A}_s^{j^{-1}} \mathbf{p}_j^{(m)} = 2\mathbf{p}_j^{(k-1)^{\mathrm{T}}} \mathbf{A}_s^{j^{-1}} \mathbf{A}_d^j \mathbf{p}_j^{(k)}. \tag{32}$$

We can write Equation (30~32) more concisely in matrix form as

$$\begin{bmatrix} \mathbf{p}_j^{(1)^{\mathrm{T}}} \mathbf{A}_s^{j^{-1}} \mathbf{p}_j^{(1)} & \cdots & \mathbf{p}_j^{(1)^{\mathrm{T}}} \mathbf{A}_s^{j^{-1}} \mathbf{p}_j^{(k-1)} \\ \vdots & \ddots & \vdots \\ \mathbf{p}_j^{(k-1)^{\mathrm{T}}} \mathbf{A}_s^{j^{-1}} \mathbf{p}_j^{(1)} & \cdots & \mathbf{p}_j^{(k-1)^{\mathrm{T}}} \mathbf{A}_s^{j^{-1}} \mathbf{p}_j^{(k-1)} \end{bmatrix} \begin{bmatrix} \mu_1 \\ \mu_2 \\ \vdots \\ \mu_{k-1} \end{bmatrix} = 2 \begin{bmatrix} \mathbf{p}_j^{(1)^{\mathrm{T}}} \\ \mathbf{p}_j^{(2)^{\mathrm{T}}} \\ \vdots \\ \mathbf{p}_j^{(k-1)^{\mathrm{T}}} \end{bmatrix} \mathbf{A}_s^{j^{-1}} \mathbf{A}_d^j \mathbf{p}_j^{(k)}. \tag{33}$$

We can further simplify Equation (33) to be

$$\begin{bmatrix} \mathbf{p}_j^{(1)^{\mathrm{T}}} \\ \mathbf{p}_j^{(2)^{\mathrm{T}}} \\ \vdots \\ \mathbf{p}_j^{(k-1)^{\mathrm{T}}} \end{bmatrix} \mathbf{A}_s^{j^{-1}} \begin{bmatrix} \mathbf{p}_j^{(1)} & \mathbf{p}_j^{(2)} & \cdots & \mathbf{p}_j^{(k-1)} \end{bmatrix} \begin{bmatrix} \mu_1 \\ \mu_2 \\ \vdots \\ \mu_{k-1} \end{bmatrix} = 2 \begin{bmatrix} \mathbf{p}_j^{(1)^{\mathrm{T}}} \\ \mathbf{p}_j^{(2)^{\mathrm{T}}} \\ \vdots \\ \mathbf{p}_j^{(k-1)^{\mathrm{T}}} \end{bmatrix} \mathbf{A}_s^{j^{-1}} \mathbf{A}_d^j \mathbf{p}_j^{(k)} \tag{34}$$

Denote $\boldsymbol{\mu} = [\mu_1, \mu_2, \dots, \mu_{k-1}]^T$, and use the notation in Equation (24~25), we can rewrite Equation (34) to be

$$\boldsymbol{\mathcal{B}}\boldsymbol{\mu} = \boldsymbol{\mathcal{A}}^T \left(\mathbf{A}_s^j\right)^{-1} \boldsymbol{\mathcal{A}}\boldsymbol{\mu} = 2\boldsymbol{\mathcal{A}}^T \mathbf{A}_s^{j^{-1}} \mathbf{A}_d^j \mathbf{p}_j^{(k)} \tag{35}$$

Therefore, we have

$$\boldsymbol{\mu} = 2\boldsymbol{\mathcal{B}}^{-1} \boldsymbol{\mathcal{A}}^T \mathbf{A}_s^{j^{-1}} \mathbf{A}_d^j \mathbf{p}_j^{(k)} \tag{36}$$

Multiply both side of Equation (27) by $\mathbf{A}_s^{j^{-1}}$ and rearrange it to be in matrix form, we can easily obtain

$$2\mathbf{A}_s^{j^{-1}} \mathbf{A}_d^j \mathbf{p}_j^{(k)} - 2\lambda \mathbf{p}_j^{(k)} - \mathbf{A}_s^{j^{-1}} \boldsymbol{\mathcal{A}}\boldsymbol{\mu} = 0. \tag{37}$$

Embedding Equation (36) into Equation (37), we obtain

$$2\mathbf{A}_s^{j^{-1}} \mathbf{A}_d^j \mathbf{p}_j^{(k)} - 2\lambda \mathbf{p}_j^{(k)} - 2\mathbf{A}_s^{j^{-1}} \boldsymbol{\mathcal{A}} \boldsymbol{\mathcal{B}}^{-1} \boldsymbol{\mathcal{A}}^T \mathbf{A}_s^{j^{-1}} \mathbf{A}_d^j \mathbf{p}_j^{(k)} = 0\,. \tag{38}$$

Input : $\mathcal{T} = \{\mathbf{X}_i : \mathbf{X}_i \in \mathbf{R}^{n_1 \times n_2 \times \ldots \times n_n}, i = 1,2, \ldots, N\}$

$\mathcal{S} = \{(i,j): l_{ij} = 1, 1 \le i < j \le N, \mathbf{X}_i \in \mathcal{N}_k(\mathbf{X}_j) \text{ or } \mathbf{X}_j \in \mathcal{N}_k(\mathbf{X}_i)\}$

$\mathcal{D} = \{(i,j): l_{ij} = 1, 1 \le i < j \le N, \mathbf{X}_i \in \mathcal{N}_k(\mathbf{X}_j) \text{ or } \mathbf{X}_j \in \mathcal{N}_k(\mathbf{X}_i)\}$

Output : $\widehat{\mathcal{P}} = \{\hat{P}^{(1)}, \hat{P}^{(2)}, \ldots, \hat{P}^{(K)}\}$, a set of K discrimiantive rank one tensor projections.

1. Initialize $k = 0$, and randomly initialize each vector $\mathbf{p}_i^{(k)}$ as a normal vector for $i = 1,2, \ldots, n$. Then sequentially and iteratively solve for the unconstrained discriminative eigenvalue problem in Equation (18) until convergence to obtain the first discriminative rank-one tensor projection $\hat{P}^{(1)}$. Set $k = k + 1$.
2. Randomly initialize each vector$\mathbf{p}_i^{(k)}$ as a normal vector for $i = 1,2, \ldots, n$. Then randomly generate a number j, such that $0 \le j \le n \,\&\, c_k(j) < n_j$ where $c_k(j)$ indicates the number of times that dimension j was picked up prior to this step k.
   2a. For each $i = j, 1,2, \ldots, j-1, j+1, \ldots, n$, fix all the other projection vectors except $\mathbf{p}_i^{(k)}$, i.e., $\hat{P}_{-i}^{(k)} = \{\mathbf{p}_1^{(k)}, \mathbf{p}_2^{(k)}, \ldots, \mathbf{p}_{i-1}^{(k)}, \mathbf{p}_{i+1}^{(k)}, \cdots, \mathbf{p}_n^{(k)}\}$. If $i = j$, then solve for the eigenvalue system in Equation (23) to update $\mathbf{p}_i^{(k)}$. Otherwise, solve for the eigenvalue system in Equation (18) to update $\mathbf{p}_i^{(k)}$. Normalize $\mathbf{p}_i^{(k)}$ after the update.
   2b. Repeat step 2a until convergence, we obtained the kth discriminative rank-one projection $\hat{P}^{(k)}$. Go to step 3.
3. Set $k = k + 1$, if $k < K$, repeat step 2. Otherwise output the final set of discriminative rank-one tensor projection: $\widehat{\mathcal{P}} = \{\hat{P}^{(1)}, \hat{P}^{(2)}, \ldots, \hat{P}^{(K)}\}$.

Fig. 2. Orthogonal rank-one tensor discriminative decomposition.

From Equation (29), it is straightforward to have

$$\left(\mathbf{I} - \mathbf{A}_s^{j^{-1}} \mathcal{A} \mathcal{B}^{-1} \mathcal{A}^T\right) \mathbf{A}_s^{j^{-1}} \mathbf{A}_d^j \mathbf{p}_j^{(k)} = \widetilde{\mathcal{M}} \mathbf{p}_j^{(k)} = \lambda \mathbf{p}_j^{(k)}. \tag{39}$$

Since λ is exactly the quantity we want to maximize, we have the conclusion that the optimal $\mathbf{p}_j^{(k)^*}$ for the constrained optimization problem in Equation (19~20) or Equation (21~22) is the eigenvector corresponding to the largest eigenvalue of the matrix $\widetilde{\mathcal{M}}$.

With all the analysis above, we summarize here a sequential iterative optimization scheme for solving the constrained optimization problem in Equation (9~10), namely discriminative orthogonal rank-one tensor decomposition, as shown in Figure 2. Such a discriminative orthogonal rank-one tensor decomposition method is firstly presented in (Hua et al., 2007). Note when choosing the dimension to reinforce the orthogonal constraint in Step 2 of Figure 2, we cannot choose the same dimension j for more than n_j times because there are at most n_j vector can be orthogonal to each other in a n_j dimensional vector space. In the next section, we present some experimental results on face recognition using our method, and compare them with the state-of-the-art discriminative embedding methods for face recognition, with either vector or tensor based representation.

	Recognition Rate (%)/Dimension of the embedding space			
Method\Dataset	Yale	ORL	YaleB	PIE
SSD baseline	54.4%/1024	88.1%/1024	65.4%/1024	62.1%/1024
PCA	54.8%/ 71	88.1%/ 189	65.4%/ 780	62.1%/1023
LDA	77.5%/ 14	93.9%/ 39	81.3%/ 37	89.1%/ 67
LPP	78.3%/ 14	93.7%/ 39	86.4%/ 76	**89.2%/ 86**
Tensor LPP	76.4%/ 35	**95.8%/ 71**	**92.4%/ 311**	**90.3%/ 68**
OLPP	**82.1%/ 14**	**96.6%/ 41**	**94.3%/ 241**	**93.6%/ 381**
RPAM	**79.1%/ 242**	92.0%/ 219	**92.4%/ 389**	**89.8%/ 399**
2DLDE$_{4\times2}$	**80.7%/ 113**	**95.5%/ 87**	**90.2%/ 88**	88.0%/ 104
ORO	70.2%/ 32	92.8%/ 30	88.1%/ 32	88.1%/ 31
ORO$_{4\times4}$	**80.8%/ 53**	**95.2%/ 58**	89.1%/ 53	**91.5%/ 49**
ORO$_{4\times2}$	**86.8%/ 94** **(82.4%/ 14)**	**97.0%/ 105** **(95.0%/ 41)**	**91.0%/ 108** -------	**93.6%/ 73** -------

Table 1. Face recognition results on Yale, ORL, YaleB and PIE.

5. Experiments and discussions

The proposed method of using discriminative rank-one tensor projections with Global-Local tensor representation are extensively tested on four widely used benchmark face recognition datasets including the Yale dataset (Belhumeur et al., 1997), the Olivetti Research Laboratory (ORL) database (Samaria & Harter 1994), the extended Yale face database B dataset (Georghiades et al., 2001), and the CMU PIE dataset (Sim et al., 2003). We call them Yale, ORL, YaleB, and PIE, respectively.

In all the dataset, we crop the grey scale face images, and align all face images based on their eye positions. The aligned face image is then resized to be 32 × 32 images. No other pre-processing on the image is performed. For each dataset, we randomly split the dataset into training and testing dataset. The average performance over several random splits is reported. Except for Yale dataset, on which we report results with 20 random splits, the results from 50 random splits are aggregated for all the other three dataset. All the results we discuss here are summarized from (Hua et al., 2007). In our experiments, the face recognition is performed based on a 1-Nearest Neighbour classifier based on the Euclidean distance on the embedding space.

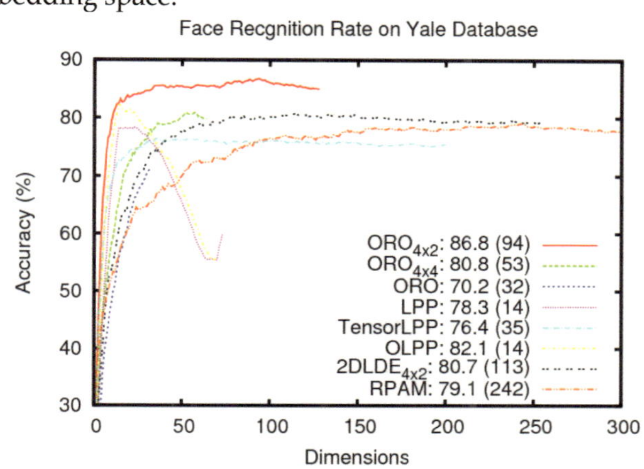

Fig. 3. Face recognition results on the Yale data set (recognition rate v.s. dimensionality).

The discriminative orthogonal rank-one tensor decomposition method is tested with 3 different settings by performing it on: a.) raw image 2D tensors representations; b.) Global-Local tensor representation based on 4×2 block partitions; and c.) Global-Local tensor representation based on 4×4 block partitions. We name them ORO, $ORO_{4\times2}$, and $ORO_{4\times4}$, respectively. We have compared the results from these three settings with almost all the state-of-the-art linear embedding methods such as PCA (Turk & Pentlend, 1991), LDA (Belhumeur et al., 1997), LPP (He et al., 2005a), tensor LPP (He et al, 2005b), orthogonal LPP (Cai et al., 2006), the two dimensional local discriminative embedding with Global-Local representation based on 4×2 blocks ($2DLDE_{4\times2}$) from (Chen et al., 2005), and the Rank-one projection with adaptive margins (RPAM) (Xu et al., 2006).

The recognition accuracies of all the different methods are presented in Table 1. As a baseline, we also present the results of using SSD in the raw image space. For each dataset, the top 5 performed methods are highlighted in the table. In the following subsections, we will discuss in more details of the results dataset by dataset.

Yale Data Set: The Yale data set is indeed a very small face benchmark. It contains 165 faces of 15 different individuals with different facial expressions. The results of the different methods running on this data set are presented in the first column of Table 1. The results reported are the average accuracy over 20 random splits of the data set, with 5 from each person for training and the rest for testing. Therefore, each split utilizes 55 faces for training and 110 for testing.

As we can clearly observe, $ORO_{4\times2}$ achieves the best recognition accuracy of 86.8% with 94 dimensions. Its performance is significantly better than all the other methods. In Figure 3, we present the recognition rates of different methods versus the number of dimensionality of the embedding space. It clearly shows that $ORO_{4\times2}$ outperforms all the other methods. Interestingly, when it goes beyond dimension 14, which is the maximum number of projections LDA can pursue (because there are only 15 different subjects), the recognition accuracy for $ORO_{4\times2}$ continues to go up. The recognition accuracies for both the LPP and the OLPP drop rapidly.

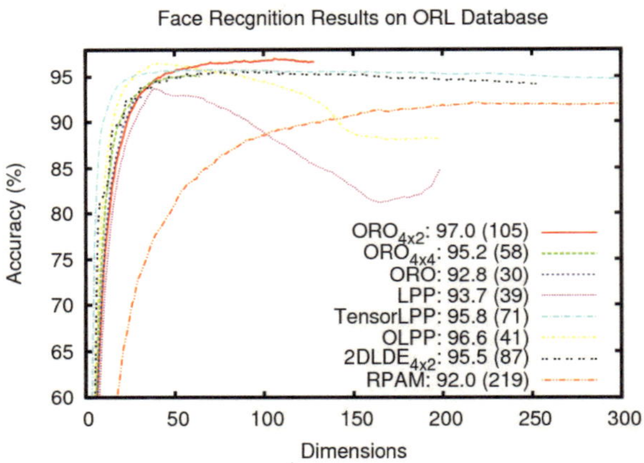

Fig. 4. Face recognition results on the ORL data set (recognition rate v.s. dimensionality).

It is also observed that ORO did not perform as well as the Tensor LPP and RPAM methods. Our intuition is that for small training example set, the orthogonal regularization on the 32×32 rank one tensor projections is too strong. Moreover each rank-one projection only has 64 parameters, which significantly limits the capacity of the rank-one projection.

Without the orthogonal constraints, the Tensor LPP method and RPAM method are able to leverage some additional capacities to achieve higher recognition rate. Last but not least, the effective-ness of the orthogonal constraint regularization can be understood by comparing the result of $ORO_{4\times2}$ with that of $2DLDE_{4\times2}$ since the only difference of the two methods are the orthogonal regularization.

ORL Dataset: the ORL dataset has 40 different subjects. Each has 10 different faces which amount to a total of 400 faces. For each subject, the 10 different faces are taken at different time, under different lighting conditions, and with different facial expressions. In our experiments, 5 images are selected for each person to form the 200 training images, and the rest 200 images are used for testing purpose. The reported results are the aggregated results over 50 random splits.

Again, $ORO_{4\times2}$ leads all the other method, which achieves a recognition rate of 97% with 105 dimensions. This is followed by OLPP with a recognition rate of 96.6% with 41 dimensions. $ORO_{4\times2}$ with 41 dimensions achieves an accuracy of 95%, which is inferior to OLPP. But it is still better than PCA, LDA, LPP and RPAM. It is interesting to observe that with increased number of training examples compared with the Yale data set, the recognition rate of RPAM with 218 dimensions cannot beat that of ORO with only 32 dimensions. Assuming the adaptive margin step poses positive effects, it indicates that with the increased number of training examples, the orthogonal constraint really improves the ability for generalization for the learned rank-one tensor projections. We plot the recognition rate versus dimensionality of the embedding space for all the different methods in Figure 4.

YaleB Dataset: The YaleB dataset contains 21888 face images of 38 different persons under 9 poses and 64 illumination conditions. We choose the subset of 2432 nearly frontal faces (i.e., 64 face images per person). In our evaluation we randomly choose 20 images per person for

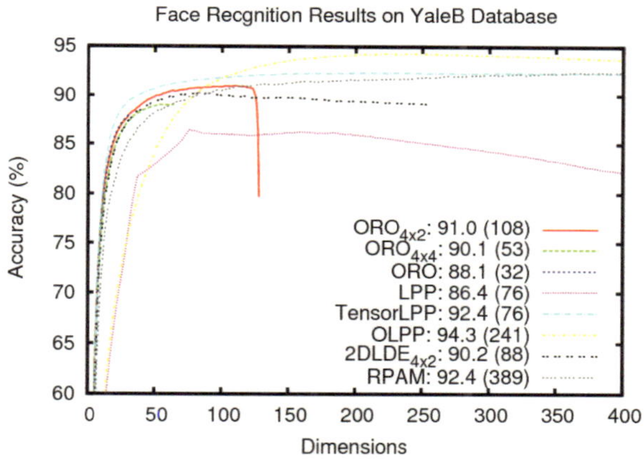

Fig. 5. Face recognition results on the YaleB data set (recognition rate v.s. dimensionality).

training and the rest for testing. Hence there are 760 training face images and 1672 testing faces. This training set is of medium size compared with the raw image dimensionality 1024. We report the results averaged over 50 random splits in the third column of Table 1. The recognition accuracy of $ORO_{4\times2}$ is 91.0% with 108 dimensions, which is better than LDA, lPP and $2DLDE_{4\times2}$, and inferior yet comparable to RPAM, Tensor LPP and OLPP. RPAM is obviously benefiting from the adaptive margin step. Moreover, with more training data, the negative effect of high dimensionality is less severe and thus OLPP may achieve better results. Again, we plot the recognition rate versus dimensionality of all the different methods on this dataset in Figure 5.

PIE Dataset: The PIE database contains 41368 face images of 68 people, which are taken under 13 poses, 43 illumination conditions, and 4 expressions). We use the images of 5 nearly front poses (C05, C07, C09, C27, C29) under all illumination conditions and expressions. This forms a subset of 11560 face images with 170 images per person. For each run, 30 images are randomly picked up for training and the rest 120 images per person are used for testing. Again, the average recognition rate over 50 different runs is summarized in the fourth column of Table 1.
Both the $ORO_{4\times2}$ and OLPP achieves the highest recognition rate of 93.6%. But $ORO_{4\times2}$ achieves this performance using only 73 dimensions while OLPP needs to pick up as high as 381 projection vectors. The red curve in Figure 6 shows how $ORO_{4\times2}$ can greedily pursue the smallest but most discriminative set of orthogonal rank-one projections to achieve the highest recognition rate.

6. Remarks

We highlight some of our general remarks about the performance of the discriminative rank-one tensor projections on the task of face recognition.

- First of all, it is noted in our experiments that the discriminative power (i.e., the largest eigenvalue corresponding to the linear system defined in either Equation (18) or Equation (23)) of consecutively pursued orthogonal rank-one projections is not monotonically decreasing. Therefore, after the final solution set was obtained, we need to sort these orthogonal rank-one tensor projections by their discriminative powers and pick up the top K ones to form the discriminative embedding for the face recognition task.

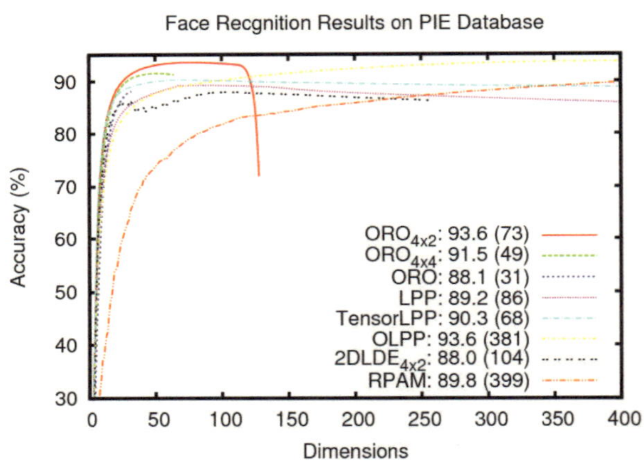

Fig. 6. Face recognition results on the PIE data set (recognition rate v.s. dimensionality).

- As shown in Figure (5~6), on the YaleB and PIE datasets, adding in the last several orthogonal rank-one projections obtained by $ORO_{4\times2}$ dramatically degrades the recognition accuracy. In this case the orthogonal regularization forces these last projections to preserve only non-discriminative information.
- The performance of ORO is limited by the number of orthogonal rank one projections we can obtain from the algorithm presented in Figure 2. However, on YaleB, it achieves the error rate of 11.9% with only 32 dimensions, which is much better than LDA (18.7%

with 37 dimensions) and LPP (13.6% with 76 dimensions). This may be partially due to the tensor based representation, which suffers less from the curse-of-dimensionality.

- The Global-Local tensor representation in general gives an significant boost to the performance. For example, the two methods $ORO_{4\times2}$ and $ORO_{4\times4}$, which adopted the Global-Local tensor representation, are consistently performing better across all the four datasets than ORO, which adopted the naive tensor representation of raw images.
- Posing orthogonal constraints on the discriminative rank-one tensor projections in general helps to improve the performance. This conclusion comes from comparing the recognition results between $ORO_{4\times2}$ and $2DLDE_{4\times2}$. $ORO_{4\times2}$ consistently achieves better recognition accuracy than $2DLDE_{4\times2}$ across all the four face benchmark.
- Overall, the two orthogonal constrained algorithms, $ORO_{4\times2}$ and OLPP achieve the best recognition rate. $ORO_{4\times2}$ outperforms OLPP on Yale and ORL, and achieves equivalent performance to that of OLPP on PIE. It is only inferior to OLPP on the YaleB dataset.
- RPAM (Xu et al., 2006) tends to require more projections to achieve a good performance. This may be due to the adaptive margin step, which seems to be effective according to our experiments.
- On small or medium size face datasets such as Yale and ORL, the discriminative orthogonal rank-one tensor projection method outperforms the other state-of-the-art discriminative embedding methods. On larger size database such as YaleB or PIE, it achieves comparable results to the best state-of-the-art, but uses much less number of projections. This is a very interesting phenomenon we observe. It surely makes it more scalable for face recognition on larger scale face databases.

Nevertheless, further investigation and consolidation of the remarks we summarized above is definitely beneficial to have a deeper understanding of the behaviour of the discriminative rank-one tensor decomposition method presented in this Chapter.

7. Conclusions

This Chapter illustrated two types of regularization methods recently developed in the computer vision literature for robust face recognition (Hua et al, 2007). The first regularization method is a new tensor representation of face images, which we call Global-Local tensor representation. It enables the successive discriminative embedding analysis to better leverage the geometric structure of the face image pixels. It also reinforces physically meaningful interpretation of the different dimensions of the tensor projections.

The second type of regularization method is an orthogonal constraint on discriminative rank-one tensor projections. We reveal a nice property of orthogonal rank-one tensors, which enables a fairly simple scheme to reinforce the orthogonality of the different rank-one projections. A novel, simple yet effective sequential iterative optimization algorithm is proposed to pursue a set of orthogonal rank-one tensor projections for face recognition.

By combining the two regularization methods, our extensive experiments demonstrate that it outperforms previous discriminative embedding methods for face recognition on small scale face databases. When dealing with larger face databases, it achieves comparable results to the best state-of-the-art, but results in more compact embeddings. In other words, it achieves comparable results to the best in the literature while uses much less number projections. This makes it far more efficient to handle larger face databases, in terms of both memory usage and recognition speed.

8. References

Duchene, J. & Leclercq S. (1988). An optimal transformation for discriminant and principal component analysis. *IEEE Trans. Pattern Anal. Mach. Intell.*, Vol.10, No.6, November 1988 (978–983).

Turk M. A. & Pentland A. P. (1991). Face recognition using eigenfaces. *Proceedings of IEEE Conf. on Computer Vision and Pattern Recognition*, pp. 586–591, June 1991.

Samaria, F. & Harter A. (1994). Parameterization of a stochastic model for human face identification. *Proceedings of IEEE Workshop on Applications of Computer Vision*, pp.138–142, Sarasota, FL, USA, December 1994.

Belhumeur, P. N.; Hespanha J. P. & Kriegman D. J. (1997). Eigenfaces vs. Fisherfaces: Recognition using class specific linear projection. *IEEE Trans. Pattern Anal. Mach. Intell.*, Vol. 19, No.7, July 1997 (711–720). Special Issue on Face Recognition.

Kolda T. G.(2001). Orthogonal tensor decompositions. *SIAM Journal on Matrix Analysis and Applications*, Vol.23, NO.1, January, 2001 (243–257).

Georghiades, A. S.; Belhumeur, P. N., & Kriegman, D. J. (2001). From few to many: Illumination cone models for face recognition under variable lighting and pose. *IEEE Trans. Pattern Anal. Mach. Intelli.*, Vol.23, No.6, June 2001 (643–660).

Sim, T. ; Baker, S. ; & Bsat, M. (2003). The cmu pose, illumination, and expression database. *IEEE Trans. on Pattern Anal. Mach. Intelli.*, Vol.25, No.12, December 2003 (1615–1618).

Chen, H.-T.; Liu, T.-L. & Fuh, C.-S. (2005). Learning effective image metrics from few pairwise examples. *Proceedings of IEEE International Conf. on Computer Vision*, pp. 1371–1378, Beijing, China, Octobor 2005.

He, X.F.; Yan S.C.; Hu, X.; Niyogi, P. & Zhang, H.J. (2005a). Face recognition using laplacianfaces. *IEEE Transaction on Pattern Anal Mach. Intell.*, Vol.27, NO.3, March, 2005 (328–340).

He X.F.; Cai D.; & Niyogi P. (2005b). Tensor subspace analysis. *Proceedings of Advances in Neural Information Processing Systems*, Vol18, Vancouver, Canada, December 2005.

Xu D. ; Lin S. ; Yan S.C. & Tang X. (2006). Rank-one projections with adaptive margins for face recognition. *Proceedings of IEEE Conf. on Computer Vision and Patter Recognition*, Vol.1, pp. 175–181, New York City, NY, June 2006.

Cai, D.; He, X.F.; Han, J.; & Zhang, H.-J. (2006). Orthogonal laplacianfaces for face recognition. *IEEE Trans. on Image Processing*, Vol. 15, No.11, November 2006 (3608–3614).

Hua, G.; Viola, P. & Drucker, S. (2007). Face Recognition using Discriminatively Trained Orthogonal Rank One Tensor Projections, *Proceedings of IEEE Conf. on Computer Vision and Pattern Recognition, Minneaplois*, MN, 2007.

Yan, S.C. ; Xu, D. ; Zhang, B. ; Zhang, H.J. ; Yang, Q. & Lin, S. (2007). Graph Embedding and Extensions: A General Framework for Dimensionality Reduction, *IEEE Trans. Pattern Anal. Mach. Intell.*, Vol.29, No.1, January, 2007 (40-51)

5

Intelligent Local Face Recognition

Adnan Khashman
Near East University
Northern Cyprus

1. Introduction

Our faces are complex objects with features that can vary over time. However, we humans have a natural ability to recognize faces and identify persons in a glance. Of course, our natural recognition ability extends beyond face recognition, where we are equally able to quickly recognize patterns, sounds or smells. Unfortunately, this natural ability does not exist in machines, thus the need to simulate recognition artificially in our attempts to create intelligent autonomous machines. Intelligent systems are being increasingly developed aiming to simulate our perception of various inputs (patterns) such as images, sounds...etc. Biometrics, in general, and facial recognition in particular are examples of popular applications for artificial intelligent systems.

Face recognition by machines can be invaluable and has various important applications in real life, such as, electronic and physical access control, national defence and international security. Simulating our face recognition natural ability in machines is a difficult task, but not impossible. Throughout our life time, many faces are seen and stored naturally in our memories forming a kind of database. Machine recognition of faces requires also a database which is usually built using facial images, where sometimes different face images of a one person are included to account for variations in facial features. The development of an intelligent face recognition system requires providing sufficient information and meaningful data during machine learning of a face.

This chapter presents a brief review of known face recognition methods such as Principal Component Analysis (PCA) (Turk & Pentland, 1991), Linear Discriminant Analysis (LDA) (Belhumeur et al., 1997) and Locality Preserving Projections (LPP) (He et al., 2005), in addition to intelligent face recognition systems that use neural networks such as (Khashman, 2006) and (Khashman, 2007). There are many works emerging every year suggesting different methods for face recognition (Delac & Grgic, 2007); these methods are mostly appearance-based or feature-based methods that search for certain global or local representation of a face.

The chapter will also provide a detailed case study on intelligent local face recognition, where a neural network is used to identify a person upon presenting his/her face image. Local pattern averaging is used for face image preprocessing prior to training or testing the neural network. Averaging is a simple but efficient method that creates "fuzzy" patterns as compared to multiple "crisp" patterns, which provides the neural network with meaningful learning while reducing computational expense.

In previous work (Khashman, 2007) an intelligent global face recognition system which considers a person's face and its background was presented, and suggestions were made that a quick human "glance" can be simulated in machines using image pre-processing and global pattern averaging, whereas, the perception of a "familiar" face can also be achieved by exposing a neural network to the face via training. In this work, an intelligent local face recognition system which considers a person's essential face features (eyes, nose and mouth) will be presented, and suggestions are made that a person's face can be recognized regardless of his/her facial expression whether being smiley, sad, surprised…etc. Previous works successfully used local facial features for face recognition purposes (Campadelli et al., 2007), (Matsugu, 2007); and also for recognising the facial expression of a person (Matsugu, 2007), (Pantic & Bartlett, 2007).

The chapter is organized as follows: section 1 contains an introduction to the chapter. Section 2 presents a review on face recognition that includes: available face image databases, difficulties in face recognition, and brief description of available conventional and artificially intelligent face recognition methods. Section 3 presents in details our case study on intelligent local face recognition, including analysis and discussion of the results of implementing this method. The conclusion of this chapter is presented in section 4, which also provides a discussion on the efficiency of intelligent face recognition by machines. Finally, section 5 lists the references used in this chapter, and section 6 lists commonly used online resources for face recognition databases.

2. Reviewing face recognition

This section provides a brief review of face recognition in general. Commonly used face databases will be listed, difficulties with face detection will be discussed and examples of successful face recognition methods will be briefly described.

2.1 Available face image databases

"Face Recognition" can be simply defined as the visual perception of familiar faces or the biometric identification by scanning a person's face and matching it against a library of known faces. In both definitions the faces to be identified are assumed to be familiar or known. Luckily, for researchers we have rich libraries of face images that are usually freely available for developers. Additionally, "own" face image databases can be built and used together with known databases. The commonly used known libraries include (online resources):

- The Color FERET Database, USA
- The Yale Face Database
- The Yale Face Database B
- PIE Database, CMU
- Project - Face In Action (FIA) Face Video Database, AMP, CMU
- AT&T "The Database of Faces" (formerly "The ORL Database of Faces")
- Cohn-Kanade AU Coded Facial Expression Database
- MIT-CBCL Face Recognition Database
- Image Database of Facial Actions and Expressions - Expression Image Database
- Face Recognition Data, University of Essex, UK
- NIST Mugshot Identification Database
- NLPR Face Database
- M2VTS Multimodal Face Database (Release 1.00)

- The Extended M2VTS Database, University of Surrey, UK
- The AR Face Database, Purdue University, USA
- The University of Oulu Physics-Based Face Database
- CAS-PEAL Face Database
- Japanese Female Facial Expression (JAFFE) Database
- BioID Face DB - HumanScan AG, Switzerland
- Psychological Image Collection at Stirling (PICS)
- The UMIST Face Database
- Caltech Faces
- EQUINOX HID Face Database
- VALID Database
- The UCD Colour Face Image Database for Face Detection
- Georgia Tech Face Database
- Indian Face Database

Web links to the above databases are included in section 6: Online Resources. The following section discusses some of the problems that should be accounted for when selecting a certain database or when making one's own database.

2.2 Problems in face detection

Most commonly used databases for developing face recognition systems rely on images of human faces captured and processed in preparation for implementing the recognition system. The variety of information in these face images makes face detection difficult. For example, some of the conditions that should be accounted for, when detecting faces are (Yang et al., 2002):

- Pose (Out-of Plane Rotation): frontal, 45 degree, profile, upside down
- Presence or absence of structural components: beards, mustaches and glasses
- Facial expression: face appearance is directly affected by a person's facial expression
- Occlusion: faces may be partially occluded by other objects
- Orientation (In Plane Rotation)::face appearance directly varies for different rotations about the camera's optical axis
- Imaging conditions: lighting (spectra, source distribution and intensity) and camera characteristics (sensor response, gain control, lenses), resolution

Face Recognition follows detecting a face. Face recognition related problems include (Li & Jain, 2005):

- Face localization
- Aim to determine the image position of a single face
- A simplified detection problem with the assumption that an input image contains only one face
- Facial feature extraction
- To detect the presence and location of features such as eyes, nose, nostrils, eyebrow, mouth, lips, ears, etc
- Usually assume that there is only one face in an image
- Face recognition (identification)
- Facial expression recognition
- Human pose estimation and tracking

The above obstacles to face recognition have to be considered when developing face recognition systems. The following section reviews briefly some known face recognition methods.

2.3 Recognition methods

Much research work has been done over the past few decades into developing reliable face recognition techniques. These techniques use different methods such as the appearancebased method (Murase & Nayar, 1995); where an image of a certain size is represented by a vector in a dimensional space of size similar to the image. However, these dimensional spaces are too large to allow fast and robust face recognition. To encounter this problem other methods were developed that use dimensionality reduction techniques (Belhumeur et al., 1997), (Levin & Shashua, 2002), (Li et al., 2001), (Martinez & Kak, 2001). Examples of these techniques are the Principal Component Analysis (PCA) (Turk & Pentland, 1991) and the Linear Discriminant Analysis (LDA) (Belhumeur et al., 1997).
PCA is an eigenvector method designed to model linear variation in high-dimensional data. PCA performs dimensionality reduction by projecting an original n-dimensional data onto a k (<< n)-dimensional linear subspace spanned by the leading eigenvectors of the data's covariance matrix. Its aim is to find a set of mutually orthogonal basis functions that capture the directions of maximum variance in the data and for which the coefficients are pairwise decorrelated. For linearly embedded manifolds, PCA is guaranteed to discover the dimensionality of the manifold and produces a compact representation. PCA was used to describe face images in terms of a set of basis functions, or "eigenfaces".
LDA is a supervised learning algorithm. LDA searches for the projection axes on which the data points of different classes are far from each other while requiring data points of the same class to be close to each other. Unlike PCA which encodes information in an orthogonal linear space, LDA encodes discriminating information in a linearly separable space using bases that are not necessarily orthogonal. It is generally believed that algorithms based on LDA are superior to those based on PCA. However, some recent work (Martinez & Kak, 2001) shows that, when the training data set is small, PCA can outperform LDA, and also that PCA is less sensitive to different training data sets.
Another linear method for face analysis is Locality Preserving Projections (LPP) (He & Niyogi, 2003) where a face subspace is obtained and the local structure of the manifold is found. LPP is a general method for manifold learning. It is obtained by finding the optimal linear approximations to the eigenfunctions of the Laplace Betrami operator on the manifold. Therefore, though it is still a linear technique, it seems to recover important aspects of the intrinsic nonlinear manifold structure by preserving local structure. This led to a recently developed method for face recognition; namely the Laplacianface approach, which is an appearance-based face recognition method (He et al., 2005).
The main difference between PCA, LDA, and LPP is that PCA and LDA focus on the global structure of the Euclidean space, while LPP focuses on local structure of the manifold, but they are all considered as linear subspace learning algorithms. Some nonlinear techniques have also been suggested to find the nonlinear structure of the manifold, such as Locally Linear Embedding (LLE) (Roweis & Saul, 2000). LLE is a method of nonlinear dimensionality reduction that recovers global nonlinear structure from locally linear fits. LLE shares some similar properties to LPP, such as a locality preserving character. However, their objective functions are totally different. LPP is obtained by finding the optimal linear approximations to the eigenfunctions of the Laplace Beltrami operator on the

manifold. LPP is linear, while LLE is nonlinear. LLE has also been implemented with a Support Vector Machine (SVM) classifier for face authentification (Pang et al., 2005).
Approaches that use the Eigenfaces method (Turk & Pentland, 1991), the Fisherfaces method (Belhumeur et al., 1997) and the Laplacianfaces method (He et al., 2005) have shown successful results in face recognition. However, these methods are appearance-based or feature-based methods that search for certain global or local representation of a face. More recently, other face recognition methods which do not use artificial intelligence within its implementation have also emerged; these include (Dai & Yan, 2007), (Kodate & Watanabe, 2007), (Padilha et al., 2007), and (Park & Paik 2007). On the other hand many face recognition methods, which use artificial intelligence within their intelligent systems, have been suggested; examples of these methods are reviewed in the following section.

2.4 Face recognition and artificial intelligence

Intelligent systems are being increasingly developed aiming to simulate our perception of various inputs (patterns) such as images, sounds…etc. Biometrics is an example of popular applications for artificial intelligent systems. Face recognition by machines can be invaluable and has various important applications in real life. The development of an intelligent face recognition system requires providing sufficient information and meaningful data during machine learning of a face.
The use of neural networks for face recognition has been addressed in (Pang et al., 2005), (Zhang et al., 2004), (Fan & Verma, 2005), (Lu et al., 2003). Recently, Li et al. (Li et al., 2006) suggested the use of a non-convergent chaotic neural network to recognize human faces. Lu et al. (Lu et al., 2006) suggested a semi-supervised learning method that uses support vector machines for face recognition. Zhou et al. (Zhou et al., 2006) suggested using a radial basis function neural network that is integrated with a non-negative matrix factorization to recognize faces. Huang and Shimizu (Huang & Shimizu, 2006) proposed using two neural networks whose outputs are combined to make a final decision on classifying a face. Park et al. (Park et al., 2006) used a momentum back propagation neural network for face and speech verification.
Many more face recognition methods that use artificial intelligence are emerging continually such as; (Abate et al., 2007), (Dominique et al., 2007), and (Hiremath et al., 2007), however, one intelligent face recognition method; namely intelligent local face recognition, will be studied in this chapter, and is described in the following section.

3. Intelligent local face recognition

This case study presents an intelligent face recognition system that uses local pattern averaging of essential facial features (eyes, nose and mouth). Here, multiple face images of a person with different facial expressions are used, where only eyes, nose and mouth patterns are considered. These essential features from different facial expressions are averaged and then used to train a supervised neural network (Khashman, 2006). A real-life application will be presented using local averaging and a trained neural network to recognize the faces of 30 persons.

3.1 Image database

The face images, which are used for training and testing the neural network within the intelligent local face recognition system, represent persons of various ethnicities, age and gender. A total of 180 face images of 30 persons with different facial expressions are used, where 90 images are from the ORL face database (AT&T Laboratories Cambridge, online resources), and 90 images are from our own face database. Our face database was built using face images captured under the following conditions:

- Similar lighting condition
- No physical obstruction
- Head pose is straight without rotation or tilting
- Camera at the same distance from the face

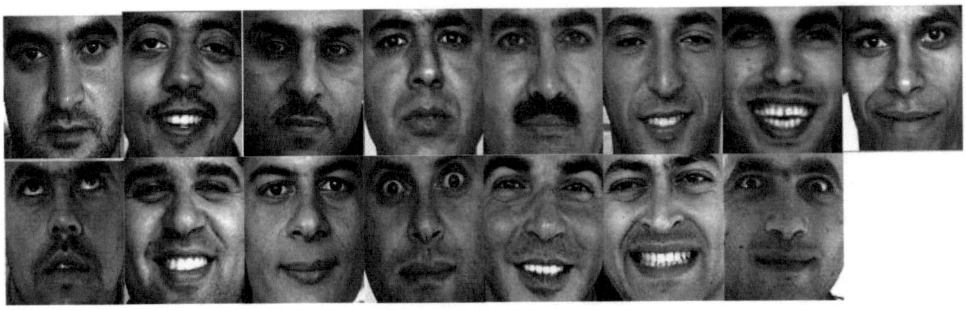

a- Faces of 15 persons (Own Database)

b- Faces of 15 persons (ORL Database (AT&T Laboratories Cambridge, online resources))

Fig. 1. Face Databases for Local Face Recognition

Each person has six different face expressions captured and the image is resized to (100x100) pixels, thus resulting in 90 face images from each face database. Fig. 1 shows the faces of the 30 persons from our face database and the ORL face database, whereas Fig. 2 shows examples of the six facial expressions.

The 180 face images of the 30 persons with different expressions were used for the development and implementation of the intelligent local face recognition system. Approximation or local averaging of four multi-expression faces is applied only during the neural network training phase where the four facial expressions (natural, smiley, sad and surprised) images are reduced to one face image per person by separately averaging the essential features (eyes, nose, and mouth), thus providing 30 averaged face images for training the neural network. Testing the neural network is implemented using the six facial expressions without the averaging process, thus providing 180 face images for testing the trained neural network.

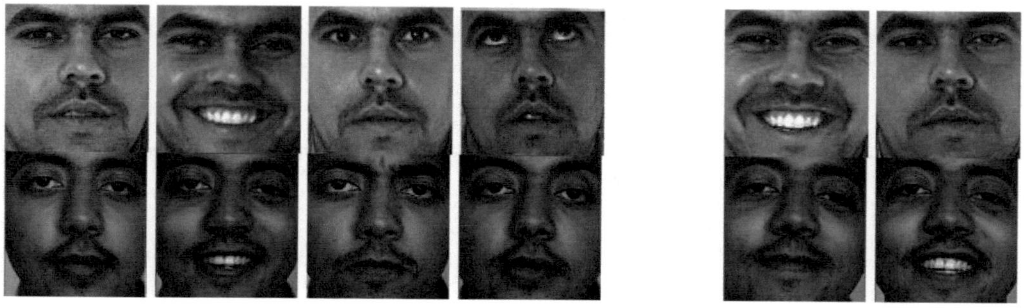

Natural Smiley Sad Surprised Random Expressions

a- Examples of Multi-expression faces from our database

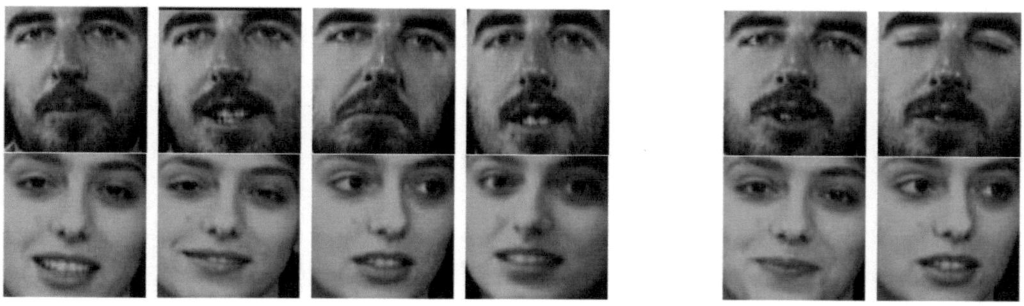

Natural Smiley Sad Surprised Random Expressions

b- Examples of Multi-expression faces from ORL database (AT&T Laboratories Cambridge, online resources)

Fig. 2. Examples of the different facial expressions

3.2 Image pre-processing and local averaging

The implementation of the recognition system comprises the image preprocessing phase and the neural network arbitration phase.

Image pre-processing is required prior to presenting the training or testing images to the neural network. This aims at reducing the computational cost and providing a faster recognition system while presenting the neural network with sufficient data representation of each face to achieve meaningful learning.

The back propagation neural network is trained using approximations of four specific facial expressions for each person, which is achieved by averaging the essential features, and once trained; the neural network is tested using the six different expressions without approximation.

There are 180 face images of 30 persons with six expressions for each. Training the neural network uses 120 images (which will be averaged to 30 images) representing the 30 persons with four specific expressions. The remaining 60 images of the 30 persons with random different expressions are used together with the 120 training images (prior to averaging) for testing the trained neural network, as can be seen in Fig. 3, thus resulting in 180 face images for testing.

The four essential features (eyes, nose and mouth) from four expressions (natural, smiley, sad and surprised) are approximated via local averaging into one single vector that represents the person. Fig. 4 shows the scheme for the intelligent local face recognition system.

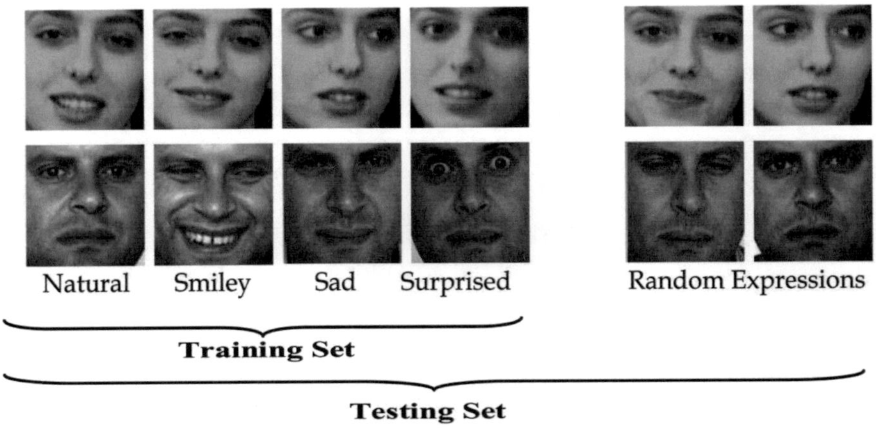

Fig. 3. Examples of training and testing face images

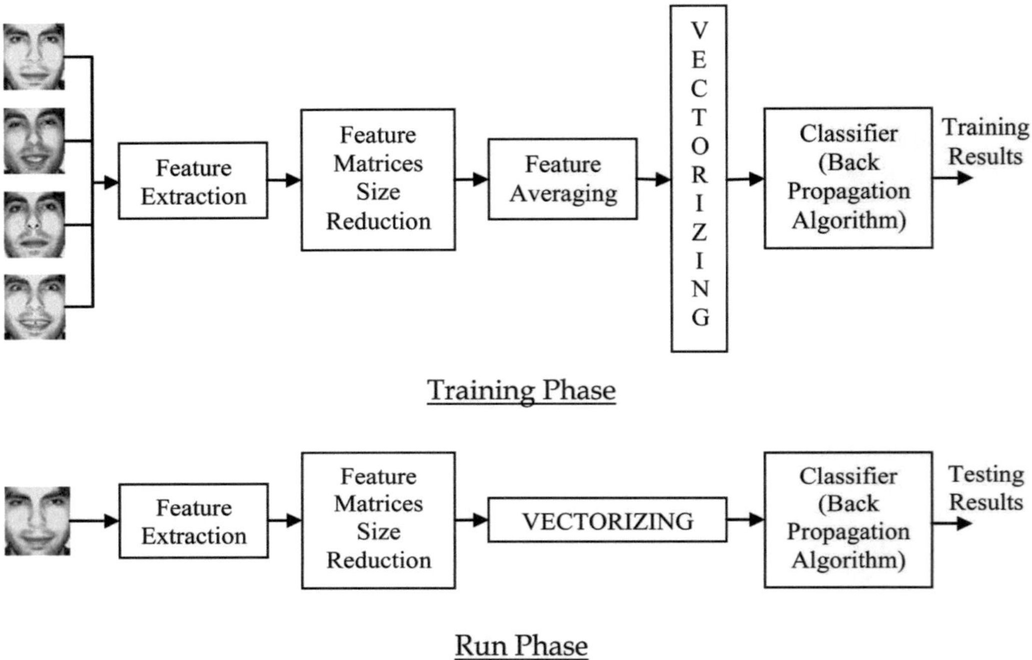

Fig. 4. General architecture of the intelligent local face recognition system

The features are, firstly extracted for each facial expression of each subject as shown in Fig. 5. Feature extraction is manually performed using Photoshop. Secondly, the dimensions of each feature are reduced by interpolation. The right eye, left eye, nose and mouth dimensions are reduced to (5 x 10) pixels, (5 x 10) pixels, (7 x 10) pixels and (6 x 17) pixels respectively.

Thus, the output matrices dimension after interpolation process will be 1/3 of the input matrices; for example, the 15x30 pixels input matrix will be after interpolation 5x10 pixels. Local averaging is then applied where the 120 training images are reduced to 30 averaged images by taking the average for each feature in the four specific expressions for each subject.

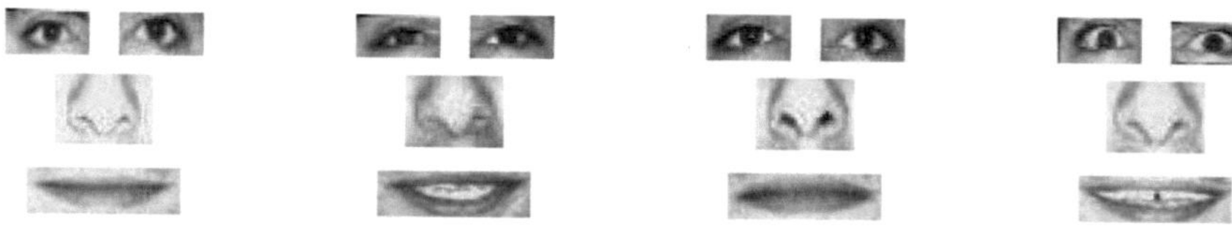

Fig. 5. Extracted local features from four different expressions

The local feature averaging process for each feature can be implemented using the following equation:

$$f_{avg} = \frac{1}{4}\sum_{i=1}^{4} f_i ,$$

where f_{avg} is the feature average vector and f_i is feature in expression i of one person. Finally, the averaged features are represented as (272x1) pixel vectors, which will be presented to the input layer of the back propagation neural network.

3.3 Neural network training

The back propagation algorithm is used for the implementation of the proposed intelligent face recognition system, due to its simplicity and efficiency in solving pattern recognition problems. The neural network comprises an input layer with 272 neurons that carry the values of the averaged features, a hidden layer with 65 neurons and an output layer with 30 neurons which is the number of persons. Fig. 6 shows the topology of this neural network and data presentation to the input layer.

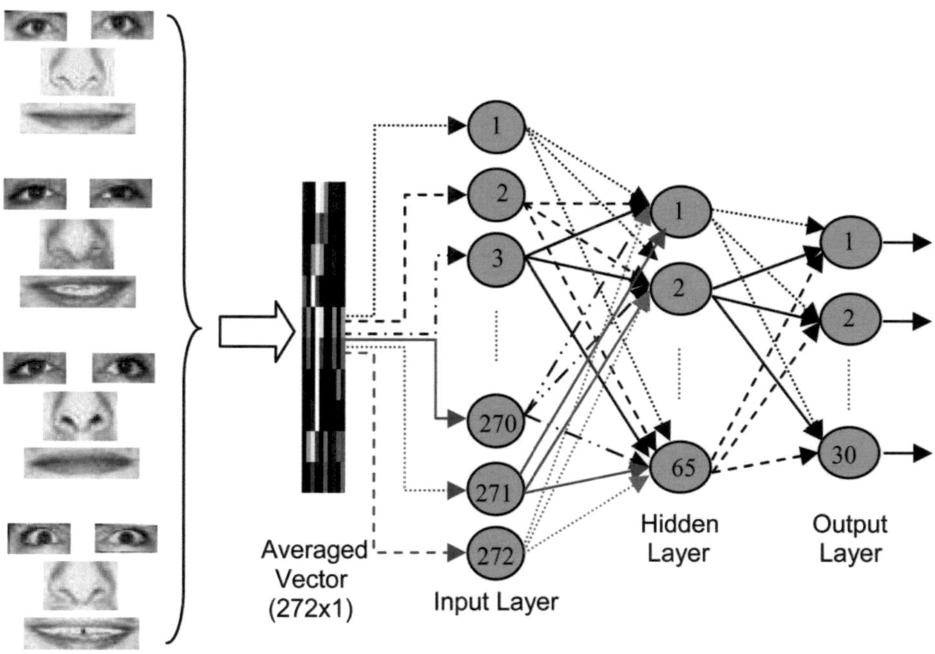

Fig. 6. Local pattern averaging and neural network design

3.4 Results and discussion

The neural network learnt the approximated faces after 3188 iterations and within 265 seconds, whereas the running time for the trained neural network using one forward pass was 0.032 seconds. These results were obtained using a 1.6 GHz PC with 256 MB of RAM, Windows XP OS and Matlab 6.5 software. Table 1 shows the final parameters of the successfully trained neural network. The reduction in training and testing time was achieved by the novel method of reducing the face data via averaging selected essential face features for training, while maintaining meaningful learning of the neural network. The face recognition system correctly recognized all averaged face images in the training set as would be expected.

The intelligent system was tested using 180 face images which contain different face expressions that were not exposed to the neural network before; these comprised 90 images from our face database and 90 images from the ORL database. All 90 face images in our database were correctly identified yielding 100% recognition rate with 91.8 % recognition accuracy, whereas, 84 out of the 90 images from the ORL database were correctly identified yielding 93.3% recognition rate with 86.8% recognition accuracy.

Input Layer Nodes	272
Hidden Layer Nodes	65
Output Layer Nodes	30
Bias Neurons Value	1
Learning Rate	0.0495
Momentum Rate	0.41
Minimum Error	0.001
Iterations	3188
Training Time (seconds)	265
Generalization/Run Time (seconds)	0.032

Table 1. Trained neural network final parameters using local face data

The overall recognition rate for the system was 96.7% where 174 out of the available 180 faces were correctly recognized with an accuracy rate of 89.3%. The recognition rate refers to the percent of correctly recognized faces, whereas the recognition accuracy refers to the classification real output value in comparison to the desired output value of "1", using binary output coding.

The processing time for face image preprocessing and feature averaging was 7.5 seconds, whereas running the trained neural network took 0.032 seconds. The recognition rates and recognition accuracy the trained system are shown in Table 2.

Database	Own	ORL	Total
Recognition Rate	100 %	93.3 %	96.7 %
Recognition Accuracy	91.8 %	86.8 %	89.3 %

Table 2. Recognition Rates, Accuracy and Run Time

Further investigations of the capability of the developed face recognition system were also carried out by testing the trained neural network ability to recognize two subjects with eyeglasses. Fig. 7 shows the two persons with and without glasses; person 1 wears clear eyeglasses whereas, person 2 wears darker eyeglasses.

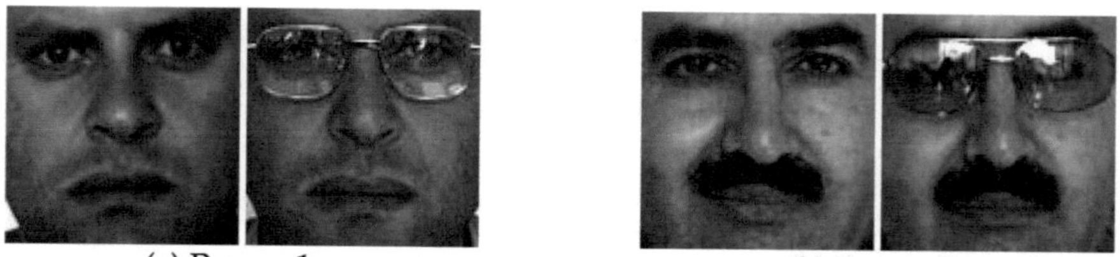

(a) Person 1 (b) Person 2

Fig. 7. (a) Clear eyeglasses (b) Darker eyeglasses

The effect of the presence of facial detail such as glasses on recognition performance was investigated. The neural network had not been exposed to the face images with glasses prior to testing. Correct recognition of both persons, with and without their glasses on, was achieved. However, the recognition accuracy was reduced due to the presence of the glasses. The ability of the trained neural network to recognize these faces despite the presence of eyeglasses is due to training the network using feature approximations or "fuzzy" feature vectors rather than using "crisp" feature vectors. Table 3 shows the accuracy rates for both persons with and without glasses.

Person 1		Person 2	
No Eyeglasses	Clear Eyeglasses	No Eyeglasses	Dark Eyeglasses
96 %	86%	90 %	73 %

Table 3. Recognition Accuracy With and Without Eyeglasses

3.5 Conclusions

This case study, which is based on using local (facial features) data averaging, described another method to intelligent face recognition. The method approximates four essential face features (eyes, nose and mouth) from four different facial expressions (natural, smiley, sad and surprised), and trains a neural network using the approximated features to learn the face. Once trained, the neural network could recognize the faces with different facial expressions. Although the feature pattern values (pixel values) may change with the variations in facial expression, the use of averaged-features of a face provides the neural network with an approximated understanding of the identity and is found to be sufficient for training a neural network to recognize that face with any expression, and with the presence of minor obstructions such as eyeglasses.

The successful implementation of this method was shown throughout a real-life implementation using 30 face images showing six different expressions for each. An overall recognition rate of 96.7% with recognition accuracy of 89.3% was achieved.

The use of feature approximation helped reducing the amount of training image data prior to neural network implementation, and provided reduction in computational cost while maintaining sufficient data for meaningful neural network learning. The overall processing times that include image preprocessing and neural network implementation were 272.5 seconds for training and 0.032 seconds for face recognition.

4. Discussions and conclusion

This chapter presented a review of related works on face recognition in general and on intelligent face recognition in particular. Research work on the later has been increasing lately due to the advancement in Artificial Intelligence and the availability of fast computing power.

The recognition of a face that has been seen before is a natural and easy task that we humans perform everyday. What information we pick from a face during a glance may be mysterious but the result is usually correct recognition. Do we only look at features such as eyes or nose (local recognition) or do we ignore these features and look at a face as a whole (global recognition)? How about the other "input" information in addition to our visual information such as sounds or smell? The brain is an efficient parallel processor that receives enormous amount of data and processes it at incredibly high speeds. Therefore, in real life face recognition, the brain would be processing not only the image of a face, but also gestures, sounds, odor and any other information that might help achieving a quick recognition. Of course, to simulate such a parallel perceiving machine that would use multisenses is yet to be achieved. Meanwhile, we focus on the visual input that is represented as facial images.

Many research works on face recognition attempt to answer the above questions, while scientist differ in their approaches or methods to how face recognition can be simulated in machines. One common concept that is shared by most methods is that the detection of a face requires facial information, which can be obtained locally (using local facial features such as eyes) or globally (using a whole face).

The diversity of the different methods and approaches is more evident when investigating the development of artificial intelligent face recognition systems. These intelligent systems aim to simulate the way we humans recognize faces. Here one can pause for a while and think "What do I really look at when I look at a face?". The answer could be that we all have our own ways which might differ, thus the diversity in simulating intelligent face recognition in machines.

This chapter described one example of intelligent face recognition methods that has been previously suggested. The method uses essential local face features of a person with different facial expression, and is referred to as "Intelligent Local Face Recognition". The artificial intelligent system was implemented using supervised neural networks whose tasks were to simulate the function and structure of a brain that receives visual information.

The local averaging neural network learnt to classify the faces within 265 seconds, whereas the running time for the trained neural network was 0.032 seconds. These time costs can be further reduced by using faster machines, which will inevitably occur in the near future. The local average neural network implementation yielded 100% recognition rate when using the 30 locally averaged face images in the training set. Testing was carried out using 180 face images which contain different face expressions that were not exposed to the neural network before. Here, 174 out of the 180 test images were correctly identified yielding 96.7% recognition rate. Thus, the overall recognition rate was determined as 97.14%.

In conclusion, local averaging can be applied successfully to identify faces with different expressions. Here, the image databases contain only the faces as the method uses essential facial features such as eyes, nose and mouth; therefore the existence of background and occlusions is irrelevant. Although the local feature pattern values (pixel values) may change with the change of facial expression, the use of local averaging of a face provides the neural network with an approximated understanding of the identity and is found to be sufficient for training a neural network to recognize that face with any expression.

Despite successful implementations of artificial intelligent face recognition systems such as the one shown in the case study in this chapter, there are questions that are yet to be

answered before we can completely trust a machine whose intelligence "evolves" in minutes in comparison with our natural intelligence that took thousands of years to evolve. There is no doubt that the advancement in technology provides us with the means to develop artificially intelligent systems, but how intelligent are they really are?
Most of the currently developed intelligent recognition systems are aimed to be used as an aid to human operators. A completely, autonomous system would be our eventual target. The development of more powerful and faster computing systems is continuing, and with this increase in computational power we can design intelligent recognition systems that could perform many recognition tasks at once. So the simulation of our parallel information processing is getting closer albeit slowly and gradually.

5. References

Abate, A.F. ; Ricciardi, S. & Sabatino, G. (2007). 3D Face Recognition in a Ambient Intelligence Environment Scenario, In K. Delac and M. Grgic (Eds.), *Face Recognition*, (1-14), Ch. 1, I-Tech Education and Publishing, Vienna, Austria

Belhumeur, P.N. ; Hespanha, J.P. & Kriegman, D.J. (1997). Eigenfaces vs. Fisherfaces: Recognition Using Class Specific Linear Projection, *IEEE Transactions (PAMI)*, Vol. 19, No. 7, (1997), (711-720)

Campadelli, P. ; Lanzarotti, R. & Lipori, G. (2007). Automatic Facial Feature Extraction for Face Recognition, In K. Delac and M. Grgic (Eds.), *Face Recognition*, (31-58), Ch. 3, Itech Education and Publishing, Vienna, Austria

Dai, D.-Q. & Yan, H. (2007). Wavelets and Face Recognition, In K. Delac and M. Grgic (Eds.), *Face Recognition*, (59-74), Ch. 4, I-Tech Education and Publishing, Vienna, Austria

Delac, K. & Grgic, M. (2007). Face Recognition, I-Tech Education and Publishing, Vienna, Austria.

Dominique, G. ; Fan, Y. and Michel, P. (2007). Design, Implementation and Evaluation of Hardware Vision Systems dedicated to Real-Time Face Recognition, In K. Delac and M. Grgic (Eds.), *Face Recognition*, (123-148), Ch. 8, I-Tech Education and Publishing, Vienna, Austria

Fan, X. & Verma, B. (2005). A Comparative Experimental Analysis of Separate and Combined Facial Features for GA-ANN based Technique, *Proceedings of Conference on Computational Intelligence and Multimedia Applications*, pp. 279-284

He, X. & Niyogi, P. (2003). Locality Preserving Projections, *Proceedings of Conference on Advances in Neural Information Processing Systems*

He, X. ; Yan, S. ; Hu, Y. ; Niyogi, P. & Zhang, H.J. (2005). Face Recognition Using Laplacianfaces, *IEEE Transactions (PAMI)*, Vol. 27, No. 3, (2005), (328-340)

Hiremath, P.S. ; Danti, A. & Prabhakar C.J. (2007). Modelling Uncertainty in Representation of Facial Features for Face Recognition, In K. Delac and M. Grgic (Eds.), *Face Recognition*, (183-218), Ch. 10, I-Tech Education and Publishing, Vienna, Austria

Huang, L.L. & Shimizu, A. (2006). Combining Classifiers for Robust Face Detection. In *Lecture Notes in Computer Science*, (116-121), 3972, Springer-Verlag

Khashman, A. (2006). Intelligent Face Recognition: Local versus Global Pattern Averaging, In *Lecture Notes in Artificial Intelligence*, (956-961), 4304, Springer-Verlag

Khashman, A. (2007). Intelligent Global Face Recognition, In K. Delac and M. Grgic (Eds.), *Face Recognition*, (219-234), Ch. 11, I-Tech Education and Publishing, Vienna, Austria

Kodate, K. & Watanabe, E. (2007). Compact Parallel Optical Correlator for Face Recognition and its Application, In K. Delac and M. Grgic (Eds.), *Face Recognition*, (235-260), Ch. 12, I-Tech Education and Publishing, Vienna, Austria

Levin, A. & Shashua, A. (2002). Principal Component Analysis over Continuous Subspaces and Intersection of Half-Spaces, In *Proceedings of European Conf. Computer Vision.* Vol. 3, (2002), pp. 635-650

Li, G. ; Zhang, J. ; Wang, Y. & Freeman, W.J. (2006). Face Recognition Using a Neural Network Simulating Olfactory Systems. In *Lecture Notes in Computer Science*, (93-97), 3972, Springer-Verlag

Li, S.Z. ; Hou, X.W. ; Zhang, H.J. & Cheng, Q.S. (2001). Learning Spatially Localized, Parts-Based Representation. In *Proceedings of IEEE Conf. Computer Vision and Pattern Recognition*, pp. 207-212

Li, S.Z. & Jain, A.K. (2005). *Handbook Of Face Recognition*, Springer-Verlag

Lu, K. ; He, X. & Zhao, J. (2006). Semi-supervised Support Vector Learning for Face Recognition. In *Lecture Notes in Computer Science*, (104-109), 3972, Springer-Verlag

Lu, X. ; Wang, Y. & Jain, A.K. (2003). Combining Classifiers for Face Recognition, In *IEEE Conference on Multimedia & Expo*, Vol. 3, pp. 13-16

Martinez, A.M. & Kak, A.C. (2001). PCA versus LDA. In *IEEE Transactions (PAMI)*, Vol. 23, No. 2, (2001), (228-233)

Matsugu, M. (2007). Selection and Efficient Use of Local Features for Face and Facial Expression Recognition in a Cortical Architecture, In K. Delac and M. Grgic (Eds.), *Face Recognition*, (305-320), Ch. 16, I-Tech Education and Publishing, Vienna, Austria

Murase, H. & Nayar, S.K. (1995). Visual Learning and Recognition of 3-D Objects from Appearance. In *Journal of Computer Vision*, Vol. 14, (1995), (5-24)

Padilha, A. ; Silva, J. & Sebastiao, R. (2007). Improving Face Recognition by Video Spatial Morphing, In K. Delac and M. Grgic (Eds.), *Face Recognition*, (357-376), Ch. 19, Itech Education and Publishing, Vienna, Austria

Pang, S. ; Kim, D. & Bang, S.Y. (2005). Face Membership Authentication Using SVM Classification Tree Generated by Membership-Based LLE Data Partition. In *IEEE Transactions on Neural Networks*, Vol. 16, No. 2, (2005), (436-446)

Pantic, M. & Bartlett, M.S. (2007). Machine Analysis of Facial Expressions, In K. Delac and M. Grgic (Eds.), *Face Recognition*, (377-416), Ch. 20, I-Tech Education and Publishing, Vienna, Austria

Park, C. ; Ki, M. ; Namkung, J. & Paik, J.K. (2006). Multimodal Priority Verification of Face and Speech Using Momentum Back-Propagation Neural Network. In *Lecture Notes in Computer Science*, (140-149), 3972, Springer-Verlag

Park, C. & Paik, J. (2007). Face Recognition Using Optimized 3D Information from Stereo Images, In K. Delac and M. Grgic (Eds.), *Face Recognition*, (457-466), Ch. 23, I-Tech Education and Publishing, Vienna, Austria

Roweis, S.T. & Saul, L.K. (2000). Nonlinear Dimensionality Reduction by Locally Linear Embedding. In *Science*, No. 290, (2323-2326)

Turk, M. & Pentland, A.P. (1991). Face Recognition Using Eigenfaces, In *Proceedings of IEEE Conference on Computer Vision and Pattern Recognition*, pp. 586-591

Yang, M.H. ; Kriegman, D.J. & Ahuja, N. (2002). Detecting Faces in Images: A Survey. In *IEEE Transactions (PAMI)*, Vol. 24, No. 1, (2002), (34-58)

Zhang, B. ; Zhang, H. & Ge, S. (2004). Face Recognition by Applying Wavelet Subband Representation and Kernel Associative Memory. In *IEEE Transactions on Neural Networks*, Vol.15, (2004), (166-177)

Zhou, W. ; Pu, X. & Zheng, Z. (2006). Parts-Based Holistic Face Recognition with RBF Neural Networks. In *Lecture Notes in Computer Science*, (110-115), 3972, Springer- Verlag

6. Online resources

6.1 Comprehensive face recognition resources

http://www.cbsr.ia.ac.cn/users/szli/FR-Handbook/
http://www.face-rec.org/general-info/
http://www.epic.org/privacy/facerecognition/
http://www.findbiometrics.com/Pages/face_articles/face_2.html

6.2 Fun with face recognition

http://www.myheritage.com/FP/Company/tryFaceRecognition.php
http://faculty.washington.edu/chudler/java/faces.html
http://faculty.washington.edu/chudler/java/facemem.html

6.3 Face databases

The Color FERET Database, USA
http://www.itl.nist.gov/iad/humanid/colorferet/home.html

The Yale Face Database
http://cvc.yale.edu/projects/yalefaces/yalefaces.html

The Yale Face Database B
http://cvc.yale.edu/projects/yalefacesB/yalefacesB.html

PIE Database, CMU
http://www.ri.cmu.edu/projects/project_418.html

Project - Face In Action (FIA) Face Video Database, AMP, CMU
http://amp.ece.cmu.edu/projects/FIADataCollection/

AT&T "The Database of Faces" (formerly "The ORL Database of Faces")
http://www.cl.cam.ac.uk/Research/DTG/attarchive/facedatabase.html

Cohn-Kanade AU Coded Facial Expression Database
http://vasc.ri.cmu.edu/idb/html/face/facial_expression/index.html

MIT-CBCL Face Recognition Database
http://cbcl.mit.edu/software-datasets/heisele/facerecognition-database.html

Image Database of Facial Actions and Expressions - Expression Image Database
http://mambo.ucsc.edu/psl/joehager/images.html

Face Recognition Data, University of Essex, UK
http://cswww.essex.ac.uk/mv/allfaces/index.html

NIST Mugshot Identification Database
http://www.nist.gov/srd/nistsd18.htm

NLPR Face Database
http://nlpr-web.ia.ac.cn/english/irds/facedatabase.htm

M2VTS Multimodal Face Database (Release 1.00)
http://www.tele.ucl.ac.be/PROJECTS/M2VTS/m2fdb.html

The Extended M2VTS Database, University of Surrey, UK
http://www.ee.surrey.ac.uk/Research/VSSP/xm2vtsdb/

The AR Face Database, Purdue University, USA
http://rvl1.ecn.purdue.edu/~aleix/aleix_face_DB.html

The University of Oulu Physics-Based Face Database
http://www.ee.oulu.fi/research/imag/color/pbfd.html

CAS-PEAL Face Database
http://www.jdl.ac.cn/peal/index.html

Japanese Female Facial Expression (JAFFE) Database
http://www.irc.atr.jp/~mlyons/jaffe.html

BioID Face DB - HumanScan AG, Switzerland
http://www.humanscan.de/support/downloads/facedb.php

Psychological Image Collection at Stirling (PICS)
http://pics.psych.stir.ac.uk/

The UMIST Face Database
http://images.ee.umist.ac.uk/danny/database.html

Caltech Faces
http://www.vision.caltech.edu/html-files/archive.html

EQUINOX HID Face Database
http://www.equinoxsensors.com/products/HID.html

VALID Database
http://ee.ucd.ie/validdb/

The UCD Colour Face Image Database for Face Detection
http://ee.ucd.ie/~prag/

Georgia Tech Face Database
http://www.anefian.com/face_reco.htm

Indian Face Database
http://vis-www.cs.umass.edu/~vidit/IndianFaceDatabase/

6

Generating Optimal Face Image in Face Recognition System

Yingchun Li, Guangda Su and Yan Shang
Electronic Engineering Department, Tsinghua University Beijing, China

1. Introduction

Automatic face detection and recognition have been an active research area in the last two decades. There are urgent needs for face recognition in many practical applications, such as security monitoring, surveillance system and biometrics identified system. The majority of research has so far focused on frontal face and neutral expression face recognition. Recognizing faces reliably across changes in pose and expression has proved to be a much harder problem.

The most existing face recognition systems consist of single route image acquisition module with one camera. They follows the strategy of detection face images in complicated background, normalizing the detected face image and transmitting them to recognition module to be recognized. In real surveillance applications, because of the irregular head movement, most of the face images are of various pose and expression. The recognition rate is relatively low in such dynamic system. The evaluation of FRVT shows the level of performance for face verification of the best systems to be on par with face recognition for frontal faces. With increasing of the pose angle, the recognition rate decreases. The recognition rate decreases greatly when the pose angle is larger than 30 degree. This paper proposed a new method to improve the recognition rate by selecting and generating optimal face image from serial face images. Meanwhile, a new face recognition system with three route parallel modules is constructed. In order to get optimal face, it is necessary to estimate face pose and expression from the detected face images.

Pose estimation techniques can be classified into two main categories: model-based approaches and appearance-based approaches. The former use an explicit model of the face and recover the face pose based on the assumed model. A set of feature correspondences are established to estimate face pose. The latter directly use image pixels or features and assume that there exists a mapping relationship between face pose and certain properties of the facial image, which is constructed from a large number of training images. The popular eigenface approach is extended to handle multiple views and compared the performance of a parametric eigenspace with view-based eigenspace. Some researchers used model shape and texture nonlinearities across views in full 180 degree rotations. However, no face recognition experiments were performed. 3D can show face deep and topology information but at the cost of time. It is not suitable for real-time applications.

This paper is organized as follows. Section 2 introduces structure of the new face recognition system with optimal face image generation module. A new system module is built between face detecting module and face recognition module which is called optimal face generation module. The pose estimate method is explained in Section 3. Section 4 give a detailed explanation of the optimal face generation algorithm. Through combining the pose estimate method and adopting three routes parallel detecting system, we can select the optimal face image with little view rotation (when have appropriate view) or generate the face image with frontal view (when have no appropriate view). Experiments and conclusions are given in Section 5. The face recognition rate is improved after applying the proposed method and new system module.

2. The system structure

The proposed method is applied in parallel multi-route surveillance system. Its flow chart is shown in Fig.1. The system consists of four parts: multi-route face image acquisition module, multi-route face image detection module, optimal face generation module and face recognition module.

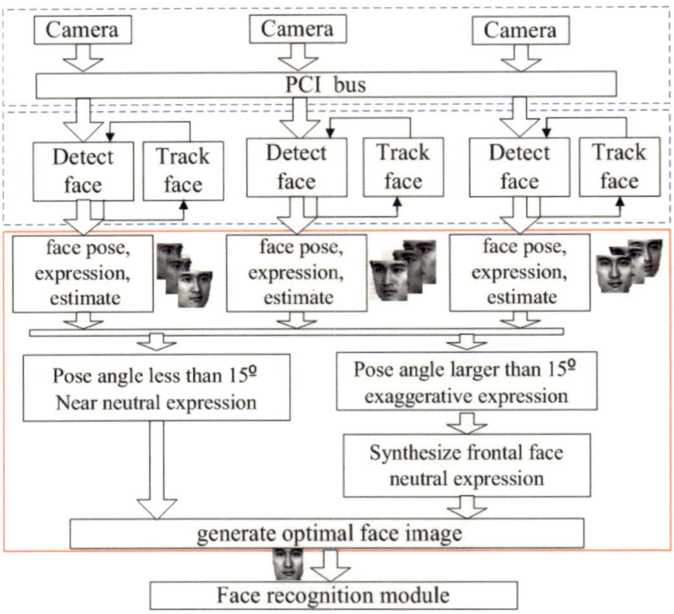

Fig. 1. Face recognition system.

The face image acquisition module consists of three cameras, image collective cards and PCI bus. It utilizes three cameras simultaneously capturing different pose angles from different face views in yaw. The image capturing device is shown in Fig. 2.
The three image streams are transmitted to the face detecting modules. Three cameras arranged in a row with equal intervals can extend detecting views and capture multiple face views in parallel. In Fig.2, we see that camera 1 can capture image with little pose angle even if the head is in a large rotation to camera 2. These performances are in need of real-time robust face detection module. The optimal face generation module is to select or synthesize best fit face to satisfy needs of recognition module by estimating the face pose and expression. FRVT shows that the recognition rate is high when pose angle is between 15° and -15° (Set the frontal view is 0°) and it greatly decreases after the pose angle larger

than 15°. Three cameras can enlarge rotation angles to 45° towards right and left. This structure is able to solve the problem of face recognition with large pose angles.

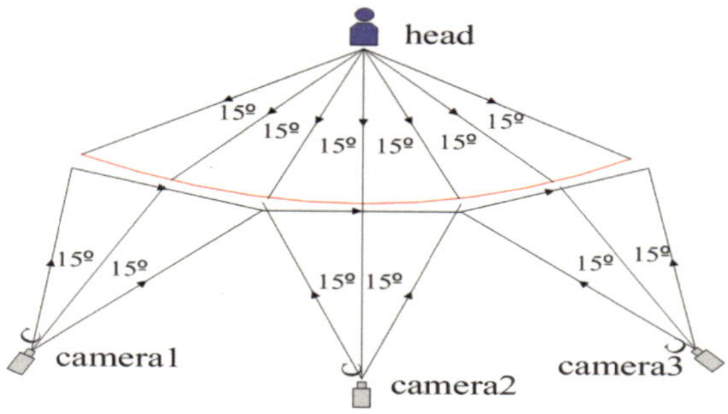

(a)

(b)

Fig. 2. Three-route face images captured device. (a)the configuration of cameras. (b) the image capturing device.

In the meantime, the optimal face generation module selects and synthesizes neutral facial expression from multiple detected face images. At last the optimal face image is acquired to be recognized in the following recognition module. This constructs a new face recognition system.

3. The method of pose estimation

In order to acquire optimal face with optimal face generation module, the first step is to estimate pose of the face images. The face images are preprocessed such as aligned, normalized, selected features. The system can automatically detect face locations of three feature points (two eyes and chin tip) and geometrically aligns the image to candidate poses training and test of the subjects. The examples of training images in TH (Tsinghua)database (built by ourselves) are shown in Fig.3.

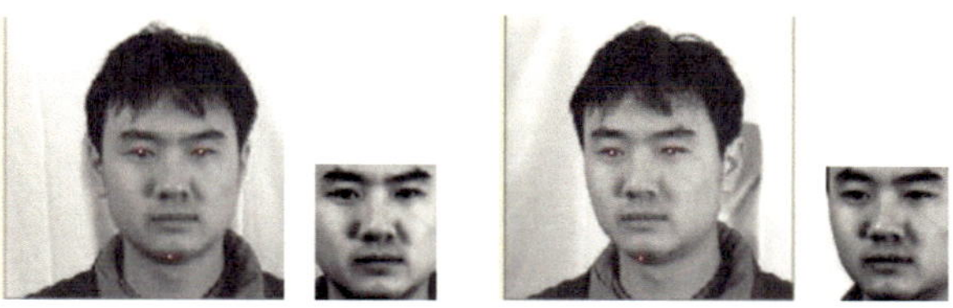

Fig. 3. The training face images in TH database.

It is essential to extract features from images utilizing the composite PCA (principle component analysis) and projecting face images to the eigenspace. Eigenvalue and eigenvector to each class can be calculated.

Given a set of samples $X_i \in \mathbb{R}^N$ represented face images by column vectors. The transformation matrix can be formed by using eigenvectors which normalized to unit matrix T .The projection of X_i into the N-dimensional subspace can be expressed as

$$\alpha = \{\alpha_1, \cdots, \alpha_N\} = X_i^T \cdot T \tag{1}$$

SVM (support vector machine) is a learning algorithm for pattern classification. Its basic principle is to find the optimal linear hyperplane which the expected classification error for unseen test samples is minimized. According to the structural risk minimization principle, a function that classifies the training data accurately will generalize best regardless of the dimensionality of the input space.

Each training sample x_i is associated with conefficient α_i .Those samples whose coefficient α_i is nonzero are Support Vectors

Constructing an optimal hyperplane $W(\alpha)$ is to find all the nonzero α_i . Any vector x_i that corresponds to α_i is a support vector of the optimal hyperplane. $f(x)$ is an optimal classified function. $y_i \in (+1, -1)$.

$$f(x) = \mathrm{sgn}(\sum_{\text{vector}} y_i \alpha_i^* K(x_i, x) + b^*) \tag{2}$$

$$K(x_i, x_j) = \phi(x_i) \cdot \phi(x_j) \tag{3}$$

Where the K is a kernel function. Here we use linear kernel, $\phi(x_i) = x_i$,then $K(x_i, x_j) = x_i \cdot x_j = x_i^T x_j$.

Combining the above PCA and SVM classifier, we can draw better classification results. The samples were projected to eigenspace and the optimal hyperplane that correctly separates data points were found. Then the pose angle will be acquired for each face image.

The shape feature is shown in Fig.4. The feature points can give geometric characteristic. AB is the distance between two eyes when pose angle is 0, A'E is the distance between two eyes when pose angle is β .Set central angle $\alpha = 2\theta$, radius is unit 1, so

$$A'E = 2\sin\theta\cos\beta = \sin(\theta+\beta) + \sin(\theta-\beta) \tag{4}$$

Since distance $AB = 2\sin\theta$, then

$$\beta = \arccos(\frac{\mathrm{A'E}}{\mathrm{AB}}) \tag{5}$$

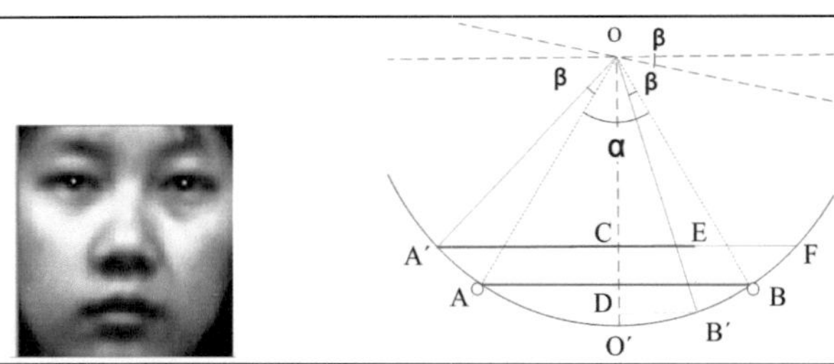

Fig. 4. Shape feature points and the configuration of pose variance.

We set weights of two vectors α and β after two groups of features are gained. The combining PCA is expressed as:

$$\xi = p \cdot \alpha + q \cdot \beta \qquad p + q = 1 \tag{6}$$

Through selecting the suitable coefficient of weights, we get new eigenvector ξ.
Besides pose estimation, the human facial expressions are also estimated. After estimate the pose and expression, we can generate optimal face by multi-linear mappings over a set of vector spaces.

4. Construction of optimal face generation

Tensor is a multidimensional generalization of a matrix. A n-mode SVD (Singular Value Decomposition) can decompose an n-dimensional tensor $\mathbb{F}$ into the n-mode product of N-orthogonal spaces. The notion of tensor can be applied to a face image in the following way. Consider a set of U_{pixels} images of $U_{peoples}$ people's faces, each image in U_p poses, with U_e expressions. The facial image tensor can be decomposed into

$$\mathbb{F} = \mathbb{Z} \times_1 U_{pixels} \times_2 U_{peoples} \times_3 U_p \times_4 U_e \tag{7}$$

Each mode matrix represents a parameter. The columns of U_p and U_e respectively span the space of pose and expression parameters. The columns of U_{pixels} span the image space. These are the eigenfaces obtained by PCA on the whole data set. The core tensor $\mathbb{Z}$ governs the interactions between these mode matrices and represents only the principal axes of variation over all images.
Each person can be represented by the same coefficient vector regardless of pose and expression. It is expressed as

$$\mathbb{F} = \mathbb{S} \times_2 U_{peoples} \tag{8}$$

$$\mathbb{S} = \mathbb{Z} \times_1 U_{pixels} \times_3 U_p \times_4 U_e \tag{9}$$

$\mathbb{S}$ defines different bases for each combination of pose and expression and $U_{peoples}$ contains the coefficients. Tensor $\mathbb{S}$ can be indexed into a particular pose and expression to obtain a subtensor $\mathbb{S}_{p,e}$. Then the subtensor $\mathbb{S}_{p,e(peoples)}$ was flattened along identity (people) mode, which column vectors span the space of images under particular pose and expression. Subtensor $\mathbb{S}_p$, $\mathbb{S}_e$ are in the maximum projection direction of which $\mathbb{S}_{p,e}$ projects in various types of eigenspace. Given an input image, the estimate value is computed by projecting into correlative subtensor such as pose, expression, and then identify them relatively.
The frontal faces or the faces which pose angle is less than 15° (radian is $\pi/12$) are the optimal face with optimal pose. If the pose angle of face image is over 15°, the frontal view can be synthesized by several multi-view face images in morphable model method. The optimal pose view U_{op_p} is expressed as

$$U_{op\_p} = \frac{1}{2}\left\{ U_p \left[\operatorname{sgn}\left(\frac{\pi}{12} - |U_p| \right) + 1 \right] + U_{ps} \left[\operatorname{sgn}\left(|U_p| - \frac{\pi}{12} \right) + 1 \right] \right\} \tag{10}$$

Where sgn is sign function, U_p is pose parameter, U_{ps} is synthesis parameter.

The same idea is also applied in expression estimate. Neutral expressions or little variation expressions are the optimal expression. So the faces with exaggerated expression can be synthesized to normal expression to generate optimal expression U_{op_e}.

The optimal face image is the well-posed (the yaw pose angle is within 15°) image with neutral facial expression or little variation expression. The optimal face B_{op_face} is expressed as

$$B_{op\_face} = \mathbb{Z} \times_1 U_{peoples} \times_3 U_{op\_p} \times_4 U_{op\_e} \tag{11}$$

The optimal face image can reduce high dimensions which caused by the effects of uncertain factors such as pose and expression. It can simplify the design of the classifiers and improve their performance.

5. Experimental results

We used three databases in our system across pose experiments, still face images of TH database, CMU PIE database and video images of TH database. Fig.5 and Fig.6 show parts of results of pose estimation of still images in CMU PIE database and video images in TH database. The comparison results of the three tests are in Table 1.

Database \ Test	images	Correct	Correct rate
TH database	1080	1059	98.1%
CMU_PIE	400	386	96.9%
TH video	395	379	95.9%

Table 1. Comparison of pose estimation in three databases.

Adopting the method of generating optimal face image can acquire a best fit face image among serial images. The recognition rate of still images is higher than that of video images. Because the training images are original from TH database, the quality of still image is better than that of video images. The recognition rate of still images in TH database is higher than that in CMU PIE database. We compare another performance of the proposed system. The test is between three-route parallel face recognition system with optimal face image generation module and single-route face recognition system. The test results are shown in Table 2.

Standard \ Recognition rate	Single route	Three route
TH Standard	82.57%	85.71%
FRVT Standard	78.29%	80.80%

Table 2. Comparison of recognition rates in face system.

We test recognition rates in dynamic face system according to TH standard and FRVT standard respectively. We have tested 656 individuals in pose angle no more than 60°(towards left and right). The experiment results show that three-route parallel system gets higher recognition rate and outgoes single system no matter which standard is adopted. FRVT reported the test in database of 87 individuals which only have pose variance. When the pose view reached 30° or 45°, its recognition rate decreased to 45%. But our proposed method overcomes the problem which large pose angles affect face recognition rate. It helps to increase recognition rate and improve performance of system.

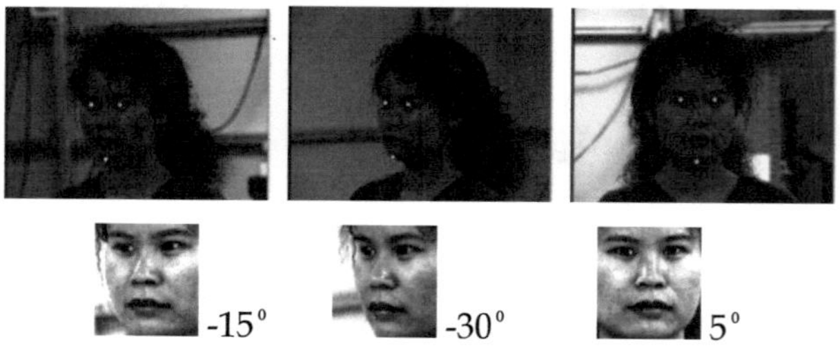

Fig. 5. Pose estimation results in CMU PIE database.

Fig. 6. Pose estimation results in surveillance system.

The key point of face recognition is to acquire optimal face image. The aim of generating optimal face image is to form a fit image for recognition which has minimum pose angle and neutral expression in a serial dynamic face images.

In fact, the optimal face image generation module is a new integrated preprocessing module in face recognition system. Its idea can extend to other factors such as illumination and resolution and so on. The experiment results show that proposed method is feasible and effective. The optimal face image generation module is indispensable in the face recognition system. Future research will focus on improving its calculating speed to meet the needs of the real-time application.

6. Conclusion

The theory about discrimination of 2D optimal face is to improve recognition rate in dynamic system. In order to overcome the effects of face pose, expression, illumination and resolution, it is essential to select a 2D optimal face and transmit it to the dynamic face recognition system to be recognized. The discriminate system of 2D optimal face is built between face detecting and face recognition system. It depends on the facial pose estimate, expression estimate, lighting estimate and the computation of detected facial area.

7. References

Phillips, P.J., Grother, P., Micheal, R., Blackburn, D.M. , Tabassi, E. & Bone, M., (2003). Face Recognition Vendor Test 2002, *Analysis and Modeling of Faces and Gestures*, Arlington, USA. ISBN: 0-7695-2010-3.

Gao, Y., Leung, M. & Wang, W., (2001). Fast face identification under varying pose from a single 2-D model view, *IEE Proceedings of Vision Image Signal Process*. Vol. 148, No.4.

Ji, Q., (2002). 3D Face pose estimation and tracking from a camera, *Image and Vision Computing*, Vol. 20, No.7, pp.499-511.

Turk, M., Pentland, A., (1991). Face Recognition Using Eignefaces, *IEEE Conference on Computer Vision and Pattern Recognition*, pp. 586-591.

Gu, H., Su, G. & Du, C. (2003). Feature Points Extraction from Faces, *Image and Vision Computing*, pp.154-158.

Vapnik, V., (1998) .*Statistical Learning Theory*, John Wiley, New York. ISSN: 0-471-03003-1

Sim, T.,Baker, S. & Bsat, M., (2003). The CMU Pose, Illumination, and Expression Database, *IEEE Transactions on Pattern Analysis and Machine Intelligence*, Vol. 25, No.12, pp.1615-1618. ISSN: 0162-8828.

7

Multiresolution Methods in Face Recognition

Angshul Majumdar[1] and Rabab K. Ward[2]
[1]*MASc student, Dept of Electrical and Computer Engg, University of British Columbia*
[2]*Professor, Dept of Electrical and Computer Engg, University of British Columbia*
Country

1. Introduction

Wavelets have been a prominent image analysis tool over the past decade. Face recognition researchers use it for varied reasons - pre-processing, compression and feature extraction. We refer the reader to [1] for a good review on the theory and applications of wavelets in face recognition. In this chapter we will concentrate on some new transforms that have emerged from the limitations in wavelets. First, we will outline the limitations of wavelets and show how the new image analysis tools overcome them. Next, we review some of the existing work in face recognition that has benefited from using these tools. Finally, we show how these new tools fit into the larger, newly developing arena of signal processing known as Compressive Sampling or Compressed Sensing (CS). We outline how CS can be used for face recognition which certainly will be a new direction in the field of face recognition.

2. The new image analysis tools

The literal meaning of the word 'transform' is 'change'. When we speak of an 'image transform', we refer to an alternate (changed) way of representing an image. Generally an image is represented in the spatial domain by pixels, but there are alternate representations, the most popular being the frequency domain representation obtained by the Fourier transform. However, the Fourier transform of an image is not very informative from the perspective of object recognition. Other transforms like wavelets, curvelets etc. provide alternative image representations (other than pixels or frequency). These transforms represent images in such a way that recognition is facilitated.

In [2], the five 'must-needed' properties of a multiresolution image transform are pointed out:

1. Multiresolution. The transform should allow images to be successively approximated, from coarse to fine resolutions.
2. Localization. The basis elements of the transforms should be localized in both the spatial and the frequency domains.
3. Critical sampling. For some applications (e.g., compression), the transforms should form a basis, or a frame with small redundancy. We will discuss more about it in section 2.2.
4. Directionality. The transform should contain basis elements oriented at a variety of directions, compared with the few directions offered by separable wavelets.

5. Anisotropy. When a physical property changes with direction, that property is said to be anisotropic, e.g. in certain crystals the conductivity of heat is more in horizontal direction than in vertical direction; for such a case, the conductivity is said to be anisotropic. For image transforms, anisotropicity means that the basis elements of the transforms should not be circular (similar in all directions) but may be elliptical (more along the major axis and less along the minor axis).

From the above wish-list, the first three properties are provided by separable wavelets. To cover all the five properties, new transforms are required. This deficit inspired researchers to search for new methods for image representations, including curvelets, contourlets and surfacelets which we discuss below.

2.1 Motivation

In a seminal publication [3], it was shown that the widely accepted belief that an adaptive representation that in some sense 'tracks' the shape of the discontinuity of an image can be used to efficiently represent an otherwise smooth object with discontinuities such as edges, is incorrect. When the geometry of the object is known a priori, an ideal adaptive representation satisfies

$$\| f - \widehat{f}_m \| \propto m^{-2}$$

where f and $\widehat{f}_m$ are the image and its approximation using the m largest valued coefficients respectively. The error between the actual object (f) and the m-largest terms approximation ($\widehat{f}_m$) is reduced quadratically in the number of terms. In practical scenarios, the geometry of the object is never known beforehand, so adaptive schemes like wavelets do not reach the ideal rate. The m-largest term approximation for wavelets satisfies

$$\| f - \widehat{f}_m^W \| \propto m^{-1}.$$

This convergence rate is an order of magnitude smaller than the ideal rate. In [3] the authors proposed a non-adaptive (fixed) curvelet scheme which reached the ideal convergence rate asymptotically

$$\| f - \widehat{f}_m^C \| \propto m^{-2} (\log m)^3$$

The crux of the above discussion is that, for an image, the discontinuities (edges) will be better approximated by curvelets than wavelets, i.e. to capture the edge information fewer curvelet coefficients are needed than wavelet coefficients. Looked at it differently, the same number of curvelet coefficients contain more edge information compared to wavelet coefficients. Since object recognition is driven by edge information, the more efficiently we can use this information, the better the recognition.

The curvelet transform was introduced in 1999 but its application was scarce till 2006. Following similar ideas to curvelets, the contourlet transform [2] was introduced in 2005. The contourlet transform was defined directly in the digital domain (while curvelets were defined in the continuous domain) and can be implemented efficiently through filter-banks. However it lacks the rich operator theory of curvelets and hence is not easily analyzed. The simpler and faster version of curvelets seen today was introduced in 2006 [4]. The problem with curvelets is that they are over-complete and suffer from redundancy (redundancy factor is ~7.2 for 2D, and ~24 for 3D). Moreover, although theoretically it is possible to extend the curvelets to higher dimensions (more than 3), practically it has never been achieved. In 2007, surfacelets, a new transform that can be readily extended to higher dimensions was introduced [5]. Surfacelets are based on the filter-bank representation of contourlets.

Face recognition is mainly carried out using still images or video sequences, i.e. through 2D information. Thus we will discuss the 2D curvelet transform and the contourlet transform (surfacelets can be looked upon as an efficient higher-dimensional extension of contourlets).

2.2 Curvelet transform

Since curvelet transform is the pioneer of all the non-adaptive transforms available today, we will discuss it in a more detail. Once the reader understands the basics of curvelets, it will be easier to understand contourlets.

The core of the curvelet transform [4] is displayed in Fig. 1.

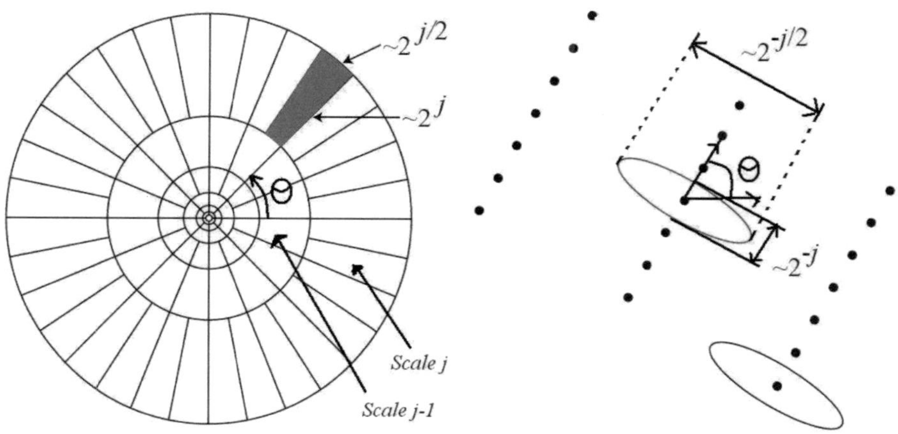

Fig. 1. Curvelet Transform: Fourier Frequency Domain partitioning (left) and Spatial Domain representation of a wedge (right) [4]

In Fig. 1 on the left, the Fourier plane is divided into wedges. The shaded area is one of the wedges. The wedge is formed by partitioning the frequency plane into radial and angular divisions. The radial divisions (concentric circles) are for band-passing the image at different resolution/scales. The angular divisions divide each bandpassed image into different angles. Therefore when we consider each wedge (say the shaded one), we are actually analyzing the bandpassed image at scale j and angle θ.

Property 2 of the aforesaid wish-list requires the transform to be localized both in the frequency and the spatial domain. However, a signal that is perfectly localized in one domain is spread out in the other. So, one can only expect the transform to be approximately localized in both domains. The image on the left of Fig. 1 shows how the Fourier plane is divided into wedges. If a wedge has an abrupt boundary in the frequency domain, it will be spread in the spatial domain. To avoid that, the boundary of the wedge is tapered as shown in Fig. 2.

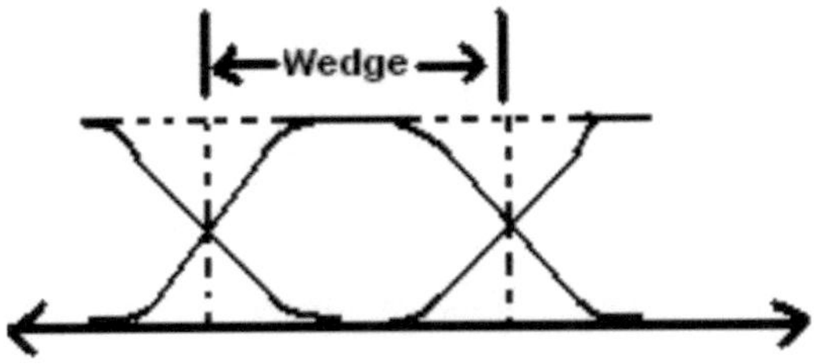

Fig. 2. Boundary of Wedge

The dotted line shows an abrupt wedge boundary, the continuous lines show the actual wedge boundary which is tapered off. This smooth tapering allows for localization in both the frequency and spatial domains.

Let us return to Fig. 1. Once the scale and the angle are defined the wedge (shaded region) is identified. The wedge is inverted to the spatial domain (right side of Fig. 1) by Inverse Fourier transform. The inverse Fourier transform of the wedge are the curvelets corresponding to the wedge (i.e. a particular scale and angle). The curvelets are periodic and repeated infinitely. In Fig. 1 they are shown as ellipses, the centres of the ellipses are shown as dots.

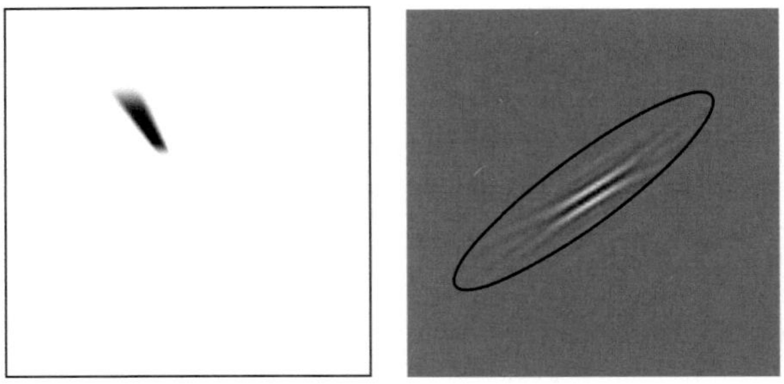

Fig. 3. Fourier Transform (left) and Curvelet in spatial domain (right) [4]

Fig. 3 shows an actual wedge (in the frequency domain) the left, and a curvelet (in spatial domain) corresponding to the wedge on the right. As we can see, the curvelet is not exactly an ellipse as depicted in Fig.1. It is elongated in one direction and wave-like in the other but its effective support is elliptical as shown in the right of Fig. 1 and 3. The relationship between the length of major and minor axes of the ellipse follow a parabolic scaling law, i.e. major axis ≈ minor axis^2. For wavelets, the corresponding shapes would be circular, because they are isotropic.

The curvelet shapes for all images are the same (elliptical). However, the values of the curvelet coefficients are determined by how much the curvelets and the actual image are aligned.

Fig. 4 shows how the curvelet coefficients are determined. The top left shows the image of an arbitrary object. The top right image shows the ideal band-passed image with prominent edges (at a particular concentric ring in Fig. 1). The bottom image shows some curvelets in the spatial domain corresponding to wedges at different orientations i.e. different wedges in the same concentric ring of Fig. 1. In this case, the values of the curvelets that are aligned with the edges will have high values e.g. curvelet c in Fig. 4. Curvelets that are not aligned to the bandpassed image i.e. a and b have very small coefficients. The greater the 'edginess' of the image at a particular location, scale and orientation is, the higher the values of the curvelet coefficients. We will not discuss the exact algorithms for finding the curvelet coefficients. The interested reader can refer to the original paper [4].

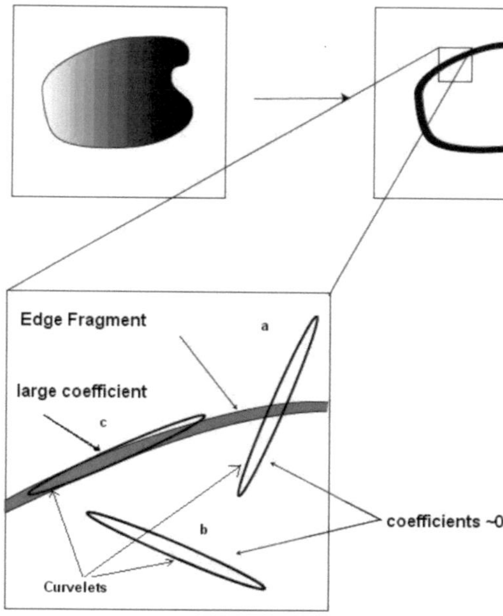

Fig. 4. Curvelet Alignment [6]

In the previous paragraph we qualitatively describe what the curvelet coefficients actually mean. This description applies to other transforms as well. For example, the wavelet representation in the frequency domain is not divided into angular wedges. The Fourier frequency plane is only divided into concentric rings corresponding to different scales. The spatial representation of such concentric rings is circles. When these circles are aligned with the bandpassed image the values of the coefficients is high, otherwise the values are low.
All the five properties of the wish-list are covered by the curvelet transform. Property 1, i.e. the multiresolution property of the curvelet transform, is easily discernible from Fig. 1. In the first step of the transform, the entire frequency plane is divided into concentric rings in order to facilitate bandpassing at multiple resolutions. Fig. 3. refers to property 2, it shows the actual localization related to the curvelets in both spatial and frequency domain. Curvelets do not have a compact support in the spatial domain, but the effective support is elliptical and can be compared with wavelets having infinite vanishing moments. As for property 3 of the wish-list (related to critical sampling) curvelets do not form a basis, but form tight frames[1]. Unlike wavelets, the curvelet transform is redundant having a

---

[1] For a basis, e.g. wavelets, we have $WW^T = W^TW$ = Identity; where W and W^T are the forward and inverse wavelet transform matrices respectively. For tight frames like Curvelets, C^TC = Identity but $CC^T \neq$ Identity; i.e. the forward transform followed by the inverse transform gets back to the original domain, but the reverse order (inverse transform followed by forward transform) does not.

redundancy factor around 7.2. The directionality of the curvelet transform (property 4) is easily discerned in Fig. 1. The entire frequency plane is divided into angular wedges. This allows for analyzing the image at various orientations. As for the last property of the wish-list, from the perspective of image processing, a transform is said to be anisotropic if its basis elements are not circular. Curvelets are elliptical in shape (the major and the minor axes related by a parabolic scaling law), thus they are anisotropic.

2.3 Contourlet transform

So far, our discussion on curvelets was completely for continuous signals. The curvelet literature defines its concepts in this domain and digitizes it during implementation. The algorithms for digital implementations are quite involved [4]. To overcome this (and also for combating the redundancy issues) researchers defined the contourlet transform directly in the digital domain [2]. The contourlet keeps all the desirable properties of curvelets including directionality and anisotropicity and at the same time reduces the redundancy of the curvelets. However, the contourlet transform does not follow the nice properties of operator theory and hence can not be easily analyzed.

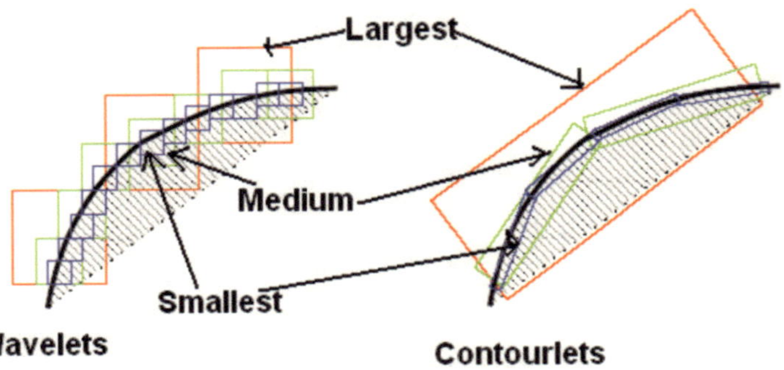

Fig. 5. Wavelets (left) vs Contourlets (right) [2]

As mentioned earlier, the coefficients of the curvelet transform are decided depending on how the curvelets align with the edge at a particular location, scale and orientation; the same argument is in fact true for all other transforms including wavelets and contourlets. In Fig. 5 the shaded area is an image of a portion of an arbitrary object where the blue boundary shows an image edge. Fig. 5 (left) shows how wavelets align with the edge, while the right shows alignment of contourlets with the edge. As mentioned above, in the spatial domain the support of wavelets is circular. In a digital domain the support of wavelets is approximated to be square. To analyze the image by wavelets, we examine how the wavelets align along the edge.

Fig. 5 (left) shows how wavelets arrange themsleves along the edge at different resolutions. The small blue squares represent the wavelets at the finest resolution, the green squares represent intermediate resolution and the red squares represent wavelets at the coarsest resolution. Fig. 5 on the right shows the alignment of contourlets. Notice that the squares are replaced by rectangles. We can see that at each resolution, the edge can be represented by a far less number of contourlets than wavelets. As Wavelets are isotropic they can not take advantage of the underlying geometry of the edge. They approximate the edge as a collection of dots (small squares) so many points are needed to represent an edge, but contourlets are representing the edge as a collection of small needles hence only a few needle shaped line segments can represent the edge).

Very loosely speaking, one contourlet in Fig. 5 may be assumed to be formed by grouping several wavelets at the same resolution. For example at the finest resolution, 4 or 5 consecutive wavelets may be grouped together to form a contourlet, at the next highest resolution, about 3 consecutive wavelets can be grouped to form a contourlet and so on. Based on this simple assumption the contourlet algorithm can be written as:

1. Apply a scale-space decomposition on the image, i.e. find the Laplacian of the image at several scales.
2. At each scale, represent the Laplacian of the image by wavelet elements (small squares as shown in Fig. 5).
3. At each scale, group the wavelet elements in a particular direction to form contourlets.

The filter-bank representation of the above three steps is shown in Fig. 6

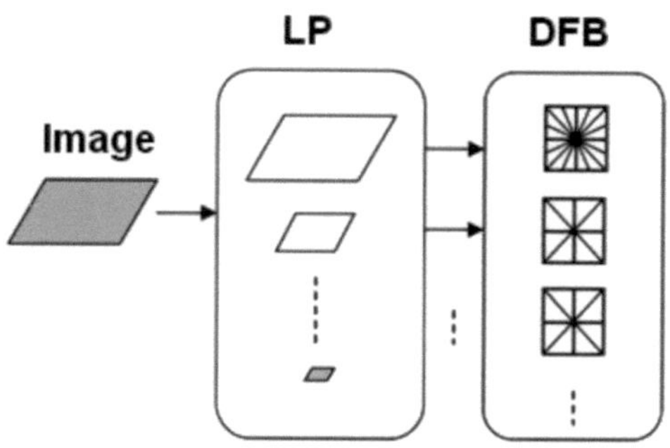

Fig. 6. Flow Filter-bank representation for Contourlets [7]

The image first undergoes a wavelet-like decomposition by a Laplacian Pyramid (LP). In the LP block of Fig. 6, the largest parallelograms represent the decomposition at the finest scale (corresponding to blue squares in Fig. 5). The smaller parallelograms of the LP denote coarser decompositions. Once the image is decomposed into different scales, they are represented by small square wavelet elements. The Directional Filter Bank (DFB) groups the wavelet elements at each scale and groups them into different orientation to form contourlets. The DFB block of Fig. 6 shows that, at the finest scale (corresponding to the largest parallelogram of LP block), DFB decomposes the image into the maximum number of orientations. As the resolution becomes coarser, DFB decomposes the image into a lesser number of orientations.

Although this contourlet implementation is simple to understand, it is not robust to noise; this version of the contourlet transform is implemented in [7]. The original implementation of the contourlet transform which is more robust is described in [2]. From this discussion, it is not clear how the redundancy is reduced in the contourlet implementation (compared to curvelets). We refer the interested reader to the original work in contourlets [2] to pursue the issue. Coarsely speaking, we can say that the contourlet transform uses a smart sub-Nyquist sampling scheme to check the redundancy.

3. Review of previous work

In a classic experiment reported in Nature [8], Field and Olshausen set up a computer experiment for empirically discovering the best representation for a database of 16 by 16 image patches. Although this experiment is limited in scale, they discovered that the best way (in the sense of facilitating vision) to represent these image patches is a collection of needle shaped filters occurring at various scales, locations and orientations. These filters are shown in Fig. 7.

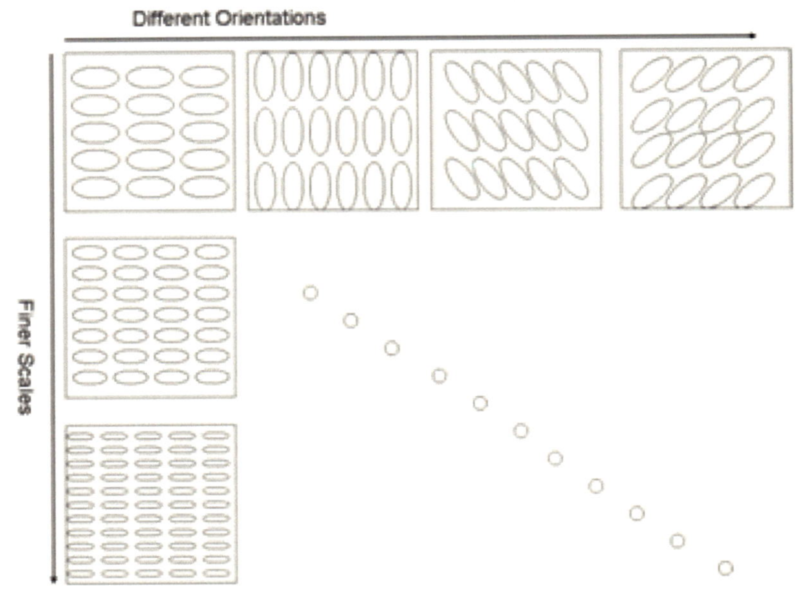

Fig. 7. Field and Olshausen's Filters

In Fig. 7, the first row shows the filters corresponding to the same scale but different orientations in the spatial domain and in first columns shows the filters at the same orientation but different scales. If an edge falls within a filter, the response of the filter is high. Fig. 8 shows the filter response of the filters at different scales for an arbitrary object.

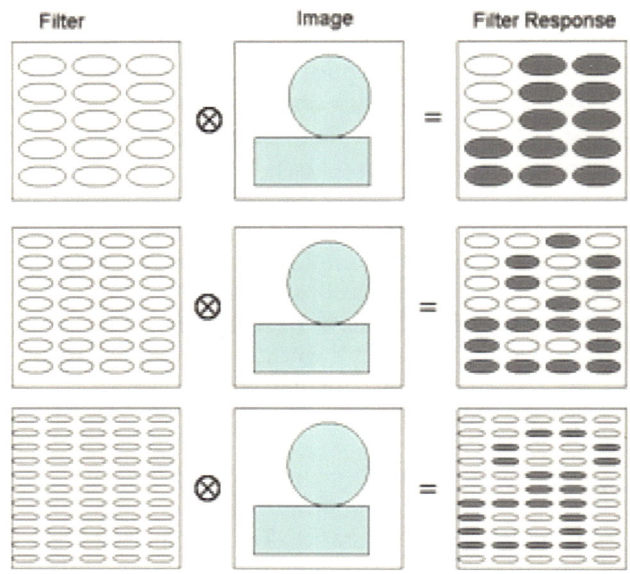

Fig. 8. Convolution of the filter-bank with an image

The researchers [8] found that, the response of such filter-banks facilitate object recognition. The stark similarity between curvelets (Fig. 1, 3 and 4), derived from mathematical analysis, and this empirical filter-bank arising from experiments (Fig. 7 and 8), is pointed out in [9]. The classic experiment [8] discovered that such filter responses (encoding edge information) were very suitable for computer vision tasks. Besides computer vision, human vision is also driven to a large extent by edge information. Neuro-scientists showed that edge processing neurons form the earliest and most fundamental stages of the pipeline upon which mammalian visual processing is built [10].

Face Recognition and other computer vision tasks in general are dependent on edge information. Successful multiresolution transforms mainly try to capture this information. Curvelets and contourlets capture the edge information more efficiently than wavelets. Once the implementation of these transforms were known, researchers in face recognition tried to use them to address different problems, but since the transforms are very new, their full potential is not yet completely achieved.

3.1 Comparative works

In [11] the author compared wavelets and curvelets as feature sets for face recognition. Curvelet and wavelet transform were applied to the images. The approximate coefficients i.e the non-directional transform coefficients (those corresponding to the innermost circle of Fig. 1) were used as features for recognition. It was found empirically that curvelets were better than wavelets for face recognition. A similar comparative empirical study, but between contourlets and wavelets [12] however showed that contourlets were not as good as wavelets for recognition.

A comprehensive empirical study comparing curvelets, contourlets and wavelets [13] decomposed the face images to several resolutions from fine to coarse using the three transforms. At each resolution the recognition accuracy of each of the three transforms were compared. An interesting observation was that the recognition accuracy from wavelets decreased as the scale was made coarser, where as for curvelets and contourlets the accuracy increased.

The studies [11 and 12] do not contradict [13] each other. In [11 and 12] the curvelet, wavelet and the contourlet transform was taken at the finest resolution. The studies showed that curvelet coefficients are the best for face recognition, followed by wavelet coefficients and lastly the contourlet coefficients. However [13] revealed that at coarser resolutions both curvelets and contourlets show better recognition accuracy than wavelets.

3.2 Feature extraction

Researchers have started using curvelet coefficients are used as features for face recognition only in the last few years [14-17]. The simplest application of using curvelets in face recognition can be found in [14]. The face images undergo a curvelet transform, and the approximate curvelet coefficients are used in a Nearest Neighbour classifier for recognition.

Face image is a 2D projection of the actual 3D human face. The 3D information is encoded as change in shade in a 2D image. Researchers in [15], wanted to capture some of this information from the face images. The number of bits in the original 8 bit images was quantized to 4 bit and 2 bit versions. 8 bit images with 256 levels of grayscale allow finer variations in shading. The variations in shading arising out of bit-quantization can be seen from Fig. 9. The 8 bit image shows fine variations in depth resulting in fine edges. The 4 bit image loses some of the finer depth information. The 2 bit image only shows the boldest edges corresponding to large variations in depth. Curvelet transform of the different bit quantized versions encode varying edge information. The curvelet coefficients resulting out of these three versions of the same image were used as features for recognition. This approach was based on the assumption that different types of edge information (finer to coarser) will enhance the recognition accuracy. The recognition results obtained in [15] were better than those obtained in [14].

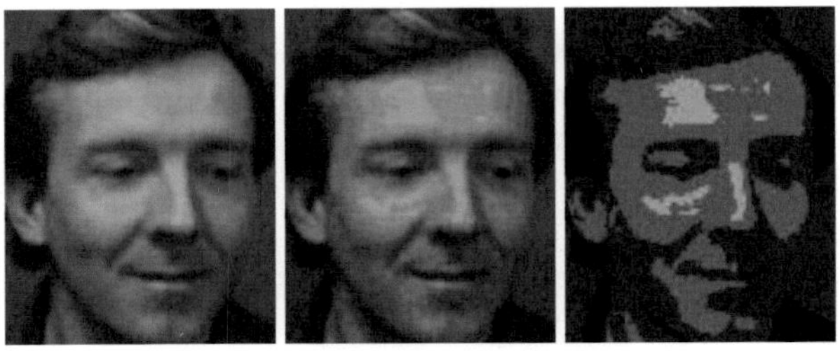

Fig. 9. 8 bit, 4 bit and 2 bit representations (from left to right) [15]

The work in [15] did not use the multiresolution properties of the curvelet transform. The transform was applied to bit-quantized images at a single resolution. Studies following the previous one [15] overcame this shortcoming [16, 17]. Each of the bit-quantized face images were transformed at three resolutions. For three levels of bit-quantization there were a total of nine sets of transform coefficients. These transform coefficients were used by separate classifiers for recognition. Finally the results from all the classifiers were fused using majority voting rule. In [16] the contourlet coefficients were used, and in [17] the same was done using curvelet coefficients. The results in [16, 17] showed that, curvelet and contourlet based schemes were better than wavelet based recognition schemes. The results also showed improvement over the previous approach [15].

The idea of using coefficients at multiple resolutions was probably borrowed from handwriting recognition literature [18-20], where the fine details and the coarse shape of the image are assumed to offer complementary information. The wavelet transform of handwritten characters at different resolutions were used to train neural networks. The outputs from the different neural nets were combined using majority voting. In this manner, very high recognition accuracy on handwritten characters was achieved. In [16, 17] the same idea was implemented on face images, but using curvelet and contourlet transforms instead of wavelets.

Subspace techniques like Eigenface and Fisherface are popular methods in face recognition. Experimental work on subspace techniques in the curvelet domain was carried out in [21]. The Eigenface and Fisherface techniques were applied on the curvelet coefficients. It was shown that such methods applied in the curvelet domain gave better recognition results compared to subspace methods in pixel domain and wavelet domain [22].

The idea of using Principal Component Analysis (PCA) followed by Linear Discriminant Analysis (LDA) for dimensionality reduction of face images is proposed in [23, 24]. The rationale behind this approach is somewhat eluding, but it was empirically shown that better recognition results are obtained by this combination rather than by PCA or LDA alone. The combined approach of PCA and LDA in the curvelet and in the wavelet domain is carried out in [21]. In this work, several standard subspace face recognition approaches are compared, and it is shown that the curvelet based ones always gave better results.

A challenging area in face recognition arises when there is only one image available for training. A recent work in this area used multiresolution transform for addressing this problem [25]. When pixel values or transform coefficients are used to represent a face image, the input vector is very high dimensional. This high dimensional space is called the face-space. In the aforesaid work, it is assumed that, there is a mapping from the high dimensional face-space to a lower dimensional discriminative subspace. If for a certain set of people, such a mapping can be found (by training) then this mapping is assumed be applicable to another set of people as well. The Fisher Linear Discriminant (FLD) was used for such a mapping in [25]. Instead of using pixel values to represent the high dimensional face-space, the image transform coefficients (wavelet/curvelet/contourlet) were used. The application of FLD mapping on the transform coefficients showed better results than previous discriminative subspace based approaches addressing the same problem.
For tackling the problem of having only one single training image for each person, another approach is proposed in [26]. In this paper new face images with varying edge information are generated from the single available image. Since vision is largely edge-driven, it is assumed that varying the edge information will synthesize new image samples that can be used for recognition by standard machine learning tools. In [26] after applying the curvelet transform to the image, a non-linear approximation algorithm is used threshold the transform coefficients. By varying the number of thresholded coefficients, slightly different versions of the original image are obtained. As thresholding the transform coefficients results in the loss of some edge information, the edge information in the synthesized image is thus different from the original one. The results in [26] show better recognition accuracy compared to other algorithms that generate new face images from a single available one in order to address the problem of identifying a person from a single available training image. It also shows better recognition results when compared to [25].

3.3 Pre-processing

The contourlet transform has been used to denoise face images [27]. The main problem in [27] was to transmit face images through wireless channels, and see how the channel affects recognition performance. The contourlet transform was used for denoising the received images. Several thresholding schemes such as Hard Thresholding, Soft Thresholding and Stein's Thresholding were tested. Stein's thresholding gave the best results. However, better denoising schemes other than thresholding are available today - Iterative Soft Thresholding, Basis Pursuit Denoising, Stagewise Orthogonal Matching Pursuit etc. to name a few.
A follow-up of [27] used the same contourlet based denoising scheme for face recognition, but the machine learning algorithm was different [28]. A sophisticated Active Learning framework called Swarm Intelligence was used to recognize faces.

4. Dimensionality reduction: random projection and compressive sampling

Face images are very high dimensional when represented as pixel values or transform coefficients. This makes the classification phase time consuming. In order to reduce the time during classification, a dimensionality reduction/feature extraction algorithm is usually applied to the face image. Standard dimensionality reduction algorithms are Eigenface (using PCA) and Fisherface (using LDA). However, these deterministic dimensionality reduction methods are computationally very complex and consequently time consuming. To reduce the computational complexity, several studies [29-32] applied Random Projections (RP) for dimensionality reduction. In RP, the original high-dimensional data is projected onto a low dimensional subspace using a random matrix whose columns have unit norm. However, RP is instable. In this section we will show how RP can be used to make stable projections of face images.

There are two advantages of RP over conventional dimensionality reduction schemes like PCA and LDA:

- The conventional dimensionality reduction methods are data-dependent. The low dimensional components are chosen from the high dimensional input data by optimizing certain criterion e.g. maximizing variance in PCA. Random projection matrices are independent of the input data and are very easy to compute, they can be constructed just by normalizing the columns of a random matrix.
- RP is computationally simple and efficient to implement. Moreover theoretical results show that such projections approximately preserve pair-wise distances of points in Euclidean space. They also preserve volumes, affine distances and the structure of the data. Such properties make RP especially suitable for machine learning.

There is a problem however with RP and that the projections are not stable. A common practice to overcome this problem is to use multiple random projections so that the low dimensional projections of the input data form many random subspaces. Recognition is carried out in each of these low dimensional sub-spaces. Finally, the results from these multiple random subspaces are fused to arrive at the final decision. This approach is ad hoc. There is no theoretical framework for deciding how many random projections are required to stabilize the results. Moreover making multiple projections add to the computational complexity of the approach.

4.1 Choosing the subspace

In the Eigenface method, the number of principal components is chosen such that most of the energy of the original face image is retained. Formally, we chose the projection matrix P so that the energy is preserved

$$\frac{\| Px \|}{\| x \|} \approx 1 \qquad (1)$$

where x is the original face image.

Unfortunately it is not possible to find a random projection matrix P, so that the above criterion is satisfied. Stability of projection is closely related to its energy conservation. Energy is approximately conserved in PCA projection (Eigenface method), but for RP the ratio (1) is much greater than unity, consequently the RP projections are instable.

In the next sub-section, we will show that an emerging paradigm in signal processing, called Compressive Sampling or Compressed Sensing (either way it is CS in short) attain energy conservation and and keep the advantages of RP. The solution is computationally fast and the recognition results are stable.

4.2 CS dimensionality reduction

The Uniform Uncertainty Principle (UUP) of the CS literature states that for a sparse signal x there exist some matrices $\mathbf{\Psi}$ such that the energy of x and that of Ψx are nearly the same; i.e.

$||\Psi x|| \approx ||x||$. This approximation is quantified by the "restricted orthonormality hypothesis" [33] which states that

$$(1-\delta_x)\,||x||^2 \leq ||\Psi x|| \leq (1+\delta_x)\,||x||^2 \qquad (2)$$

δ_x (<< 1)is the restricted orthonormality constant.

Finding such a projection matrix Ψ deterministically is an NP hard problem. The CS literature however proves that, any random projection matrix will satisfy the restricted orthonormality hypothesis (2) with a very high probability.

When the signal is sparse, the restricted orthonormality hypothesis ensures that RP satisfies the energy conservation criterion approximately. This makes RP a stable dimensionality reduction technique for sparse signals.

The words 'restricted isometry', 'approximate isometry' comes up in compressive sampling frequently. Equation (2) says that the energy of a sparse vector x is conserved after it is projected by Ψ. This shows the near orthogonality of RP matrix with sparse vectors. CS literature provides even stronger property of Ψ and states that Ψ behaves as an identity matrix (isometry), and all the information content of the sparse signal x is preserved in the lower dimensional projection Ψx. The isometry is a stronger property compared to the orthonormality.

Equation (2) can be re-written as

$$\frac{||\Psi x||}{||x||} \approx 1 \pm \delta_x \qquad (3)$$

Equations (1) and (3) are almost the same, i.e. when x is a sparse vector almost all the energy in the original signal is conserved by both RP (3) and the Eigenspace projection (1). This relation does not hold for dense signals. In the following table we show the simulation results we carried out to give the reader a feel of the numerical values involved in the discussion.

Length of signal	Number of non-zero coefficients		Length of Ψx	$\|\|\Psi x\|\|/\|\|x\|\|$ for sparse vector	$\|\|\Psi x\|\|/\|\|x\|\|$ for dense vector
	Sparse	Dense			
1000	50	1000	100	1.0056	3.5074
			200	0.9982	2.2744
			400	1.0022	4.0653
			800	0.9997	4.2277
	100		200	1.0034	2.7935
			400	1.0006	5.1309
			800	0.9999	3.9024
10000	500	10000	1000	0.9965	4.4473
			2000	1.0005	4.2946
	1000		2000	0.9994	3.9333

Table 1. Ratio between norms after and before projection

The results in column 5 in Table 1 were generated by creating sparse signals. The positions and amplitudes of the non-zero elements in the sparse signal were at random. An i.i.d

Gaussian matrix, with the columns normalized to unity, was used as the projection matrix. For the results in the last column of Table 1, the projection matrix remained the same, but the signal was dense. The dense signal was generated at random. The results shown in Table 1, are obtained by averaging the results of 100 test runs.

Table 1, is an experimental verification of compressive sampling. It demonstrates the theoretical result that for sparse vectors, the RP behaves as a restricted isometry.

We conclude that, if the input vector is sparse, we could rely on RP for dimensionality reduction. This dimensionality reduction has two advantages

1. RP is stable because the energy is conserved during projection. For dense vectors this condition was satisfied by PCA but not by RP.
2. RP is computationally efficient. The computational cost for PCA is $O(n^3) + O(nd)$, while for RP is it only O(nd), where n denotes the length of the vector and d is the number of projections.

But, for our signal, the input face image is not sparse.

We now relate how the multiresolution analysis methods are related to CS (and RP) dimensionality reduction. Face images are not sparse in the pixel domain. However, their representation using the multiresolution transforms like wavelets, curvelets and contourlets are sparse. The following figure shows the sparsity of these transforms.

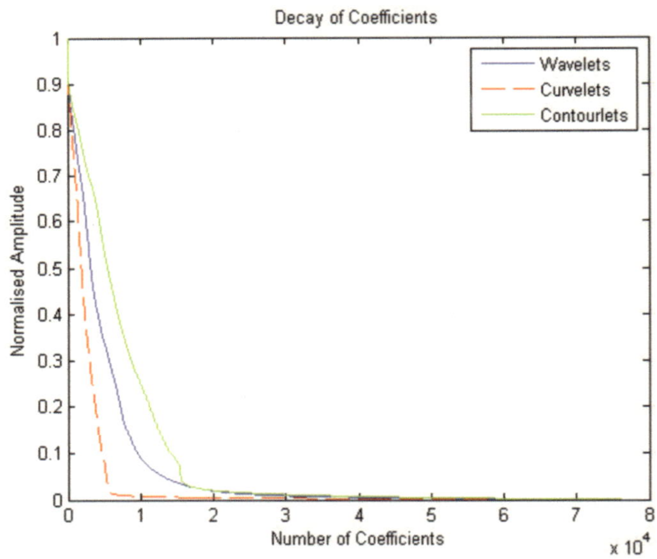

Fig. 10. Decay of Transform coefficients

In Fig. 10, in order to see how sparse the coefficients of this transforms are, the amplitude of the coefficients are normalized and plotted in descending order. The sparser the result of a transform is, the lesser is the number of high valued coefficients. Fig. 10 shows the decay of the transform coefficients. The results are from the ORL face database and are averaged over 400 images in the database. In the pixel domain each face images were of 256X256 resolution leading to 65,536 pixel values. From the figure, we can see that curvelets give the sparsest representation followed by wavelets and lastly contourlets.

A sparse representation of the image *I*, *x* can be obtained by a linear operation i.e. $x = \Phi I$, where Φ, can be any of the aforesaid three transforms.

We now quantify the limits of dimensionality reduction. Compressive Sampling (CS) states that if an n dimensional signal is s sparse then m projections are required where,

$$m = C \cdot s \cdot \mu^2_{\Phi,\Psi} \cdot \log(n) \tag{4}$$

C is a constant (between 2 and 5) and $\mu_{\Phi,\Psi}$ ($\in [1, \sqrt{n}]$) is the measure of coherence between the sparsifying transform Φ and the random sampling matrix Ψ.
From equation (4), it is deduced that smaller the μ i.e. the coherence between Φ and Ψ, lower will is the number of projections (dimensionality) m. In [33] it is shown that for Gaussian projection matrices are minimally coherent with wavelet, curvelet or contourlet basis. Hence whatever be the choice of Φ (wavelet/curvelet/contourlet), Ψ can be a Gaussian random matrix with columns normalized to unity. Other projection matrices like random permutations of the Fourier matrix and Bernoulli matrices (whose entries are formed by randomly placed 1 and -1) can be used instead of Gaussian projection matrix, but Gaussian projection matrices have been proven to be minimally coherent.
Equation (4) is derived for signal reconstruction and not for recognition. For the case of face recognition, the estimate m is pessimistic, i.e. we can afford to be greedy and can get good recognition accuracy with far less number of projections than indicated by (4). A study [34] showed that good recognition accuracy can be achieved by CS dimensionality reduction, but with far less number of samples that suggested by (4). However, there are no theoretical bounds for deciding the number of CS projections needed for recognition.

4.3 Some results

To apply CS dimensionality reduction in face recognition we need to follow three steps:
1. Sparsify the images using wavelets, curvelets or contourlets.
2. Create random projection matrices. These can be Gaussian, Bernoulli or Fourier.
3. Use the random projections of the sparse vectors as features in the classification stage.

In the following table, we show the results for CS dimensionality reduction and normal RP dimensionality reduction. A new classification framework proposed in [32] is used.

Method	Number of Projections	Dimensionality Reduction Ratio					
		1:1	2:1	4:1	8:1	16:1	32:1
RP applied to original image	1	0.08	0.09	0.095	0.085	0.145	0.21
	3	-	0.085	0.08	0.085	0.075	0.125
	5	-	0.085	0.085	0.085	0.075	0.105
RP applied to sparse wavelet coefficients	1	0.08	0.08	0.08	0.085	0.085	0.095

Table 2. Error Rates on ORL Face Database

The first column denotes the type of dimensionality reduction method used. The second column of the table shows, how many RPs were taken. As mentioned earlier RP on dense inputs results in instability. To counter the instability, multiple random projections need to be taken. RP applied to sparse vectors (wavelet coefficients) is stable and does not require multiple projections. The rest of the columns (from third to last) shows error rates for different dimensionality reduction ratios.

5. Conclusion

This chapter starts with discussion on curvelets and contourlets. These transforms are new and the research studies that make use of these transforms provide a formal mathematical description. This chapter gives a qualitative intuitive understanding of these transforms. Readers from areas of image processing other than pattern recognition may also find this section interesting. In section 2, a complete up-to-date summary of the different applications of these transforms in the face recognition area is provided. Current research in face recognition is yet to utilize the full potential of these transforms. Previous work only used the approximate transform coefficients of the transforms. The rich orientation information of the detail coefficients has yet to be used in feature extraction.

In the final section we relate state-of-the-art signal processing techniques to traditional feature extraction methods. Compressive Sampling is a new paradigm in signal processing with many promising prospects [35]. Current literature in CS mainly deals with signal reconstruction. CS's potential in signal recognition has not yet been studied. Investigating CS techniques in face recognition will be an exciting area of research.

6. References

D. Q. Dai and H. Yan, "Wavelets and Face Recognition" in Face Recognition, K. Delac and M. Grgic ed., I-TECH Education and Publishing, Vienna, 2007.

M. N. Do and M. Vetterli, "The contourlet transform: an efficient directional multiresolution image representation", IEEE Transactions Image on Processing, Vol. 14 (12), pp. 2091-2106, 2005.

E. J. Candès and D. L. Donoho. Curvelets - a surprisingly effective nonadaptive representation for objects with edges. Curves and Surfaces, L. L. Schumaker et al. (eds), Vanderbilt University Press, Nashville, TN

E. J. Candès, L. Demanet, D. L. Donoho and L. Ying, "Fast discrete curvelet transforms", Multiscale Model. Simul., Vol. 5 pp. 861-899, 2006.

Y. M. Lu and M. N. Do, "Multidimensional directional filter banks and surfacelets", IEEE Transactions on Image Processing, Vol. 16 (4), pp. 918-931, Apr. 2007.

E.J. Candès and D. L. Donoho, "New tight frames of curvelets and optimal representations of objects with piecewise-C2 singularities", Comm. Pure Appl. Math., Vol. 57, pp. 219-266, 2002.

R. Eslami and H. Radha, "The Contourlet Transform for Image De-noising Using Cycle Spinning", Signals, Thirty-Seventh Asilomar Conference on Systems and Computers, Vol.2, pp. 1982-1986, 2003.

B. A. Olshausen and D. J. Field, "Emergence of simple-cell receptive field properties by learning a sparse code for natural images," Nature, vol. 38, pp. 607–609, 1996.

E.J. Candes and F. Guo. "New multiscale transforms, minimum total variation synthesis: Applications to edge-preserving image reconstruction," Signal Processing, Vol. 82 (2), pp. 1519-1543,2002.

H. Moravec, ROBOT: Mere Machine to Transcendent Mind, Oxford University Press, 1998

A. Majumdar, "Curvelets: A New Approach to Face Recognition", Proceedings of National Conference on Knowledge Based Frontier Technologies, National conference on Knowledge Based Computing Systems and Frontier Technologies, pp. 197-205, 2007.

A. Majumdar and J.N. Mazumdar, "Wavelets or Contourlets: Which is a better descriptor for Pattern Recognition?" Proceedings of INDIACom pp. 405-411, 2007.

A. Majumdar and A. Bhattacharya, "A Comparative Study in Wavelets, Curvelets and Contourlets as Feature Sets for Pattern Recognition", International Arab Journal of Information Technology (In Print).

Z. Jiulong, Z. Zhiyu, H. Wei, L. Yanjun and W. Yinghui, "Face Recognition Based on Curvefaces," Third International Conference on Natural Computation, Vol.2, pp.627-631, 2007.

T. Mandal, A. Majumdar and J. Hu, " Face Recognition Via Curvelet Based feature Extraction", International Conference on Image Analysis and Recognition, pp. 806-817, 2007.

A. Majumdar, S. Ray and A. Bhattacharya, "Face Recognition by Contourlet Based Feature Extraction" Indian International Conference on Artificial Intelligence, pp. 2010-2026, 2007.

A. Majumdar and A. Bhattacharya, "Face Recognition by Multiresolution Curvelet Transform on Bit Quantized Facial Images", IEEE International Conference on Computational Intelligence and Multimedia Applications, pp. 209-213, 2007.

A. Majumdar and B. B. Chaudhuri, "Curvelet-Based Multi SVM Recognizer for Offline Handwritten Bangla: A Major Indian Script", IEEE International Conference on Document Analysis and Research, Vol. 1, pp.491-495, 2007.

U. Bhattacharya and B. B. Chaudhuri, "Fusion of Combination Rules of an Ensemble of MLP Classifiers for Improved Recognition Accuracy of Handprinted Bangla Numerals", IEEE International Conference on Document Analysis and Research, Vol. 1, pp.322-326, 2005.

U. Bhattacharya and B. B. Chaudhuri, "A Majority Voting Scheme for Multiresolution Recognition of Handprinted Numerals IEEE International Conference on Document Analysis and Research, Vol. 1, pp.16-20, 2003.

T, Mandal, "A New Approach to Face Recognition Using Curvelet Transform", MASc Thesis, University of Windsor, ON, Canada.

H. K. Ekenel and B. Sankur, "Multiresolution face recognition." Image. Vision Comput., Vol. 23 (5), pp. 469–477, 2005.

G.L. Marcialis and F. Roli, "Fusion of LDA and PCA for Face Verification", Workshop on Biometric Authentication, pp. 30-37, 2002.

G.L. Marcialis and F. Roli, "Fusion of LDA and PCA for Face Recognition", Workshop on Machine Vision and Perception, Italian Association for Artificial Intelligence, pp. 215-227, 2002.

A. Majumdar and R. K. Ward, "Pseudo-Fisherface Method for Single Image per Person Face Recognition", International Conference on Acoustics, Speech, and Signal Processing, pp. 989-992, 2008.

A. Majumdar and R. K. Ward, "Single Image per Person Face Recognition with Images Synthesized by Non-Linear Approximation", accepted at International Conference on Image Processing (ICIP08).

Y. Yan and L. A. Osadciw, "Contourlet Based Image Recovery and De-noising Through Wireless Fading Channels",Annual Conference on Information Sciences and Systems, John Hopkins Unversity, 2005

R. Muraleedharan, Y. Yan and L. A. Osadciw, "Constructing an Efficient Wireless Face Recognitions System by Swarm intelligence", Academic Graduate Excellence Symposium Program (AGEP 2007), Syracuse University, New York, June 2007.

N. Goel, G. Bebis and A. V. Nefian, "Face recognition experiments with random projections", SPIE Conference on Biometric Technology for Human Identification, pp. 426-437, 2005.

T. A. B. Jin and T. Y Chong, "Cancelable Biometrics Realization With Multispace Random Projections," IEEE Transactions on Systems, Man, and Cybernetics, Part B, Vol.37 (5), pp.1096-1106, 2007.

Y. H. Pang and A. T. B. Jin, "Random Projection with Robust Linear Discriminant Analysis Model in Face Recognition", Computer Graphics, Imaging and Visualization, pp. 11-15, 2007.

J. Wright, A. Y. Yang, A. Ganesh, S. Sastry, and Y. Ma. Robust face recognition via sparse representation. To appear in PAMI, 2008.

E. J. Candes, and T. Tao. "Decoding by linear programming", IEEE Transactions on Information Theory, Vol. 51(12), pp. 4203-4215, 2006.

J. Haupt, R. Castro, R. Nowak, G. Fudge, and A. Yeh, "Compressive Sampling for Signal Classification," Asilomar Conference on Signals, Systems and Computers, pp.1430-1434, 2006.

"IEEE Signal Processing Magazine [Sensing, Sampling, and Compression]," Signal Processing Magazine, IEEE , Vol.25 (2), pp.c1-c1, March 2008

8

Illumination Normalization using Quotient Image-based Techniques

Masashi Nishiyama, Tatsuo Kozakaya and Osamu Yamaguchi
Corporate Research & Development Center, Toshiba Corporation
Japan

1. Introduction

This chapter focuses on correctly recognizing faces in the presence of large illumination variation. Our aim is to do this by synthesizing an illumination normalized image using Quotient Image-based techniques (Shashua et al., 2001, Wang et al., 2004, Chen et al., 2005, Nishiyama et al., 2006, Zhang et al., 2007, and An et al., 2008). These techniques extract an illumination invariant representation of a face from a raw facial image.
To discuss the variation of facial appearances caused by illumination, the appearances are classified into four main components: diffuse reflection, specular reflection, attached shadow and cast shadow (see Figure 1) as described in (Shashua, 1999).

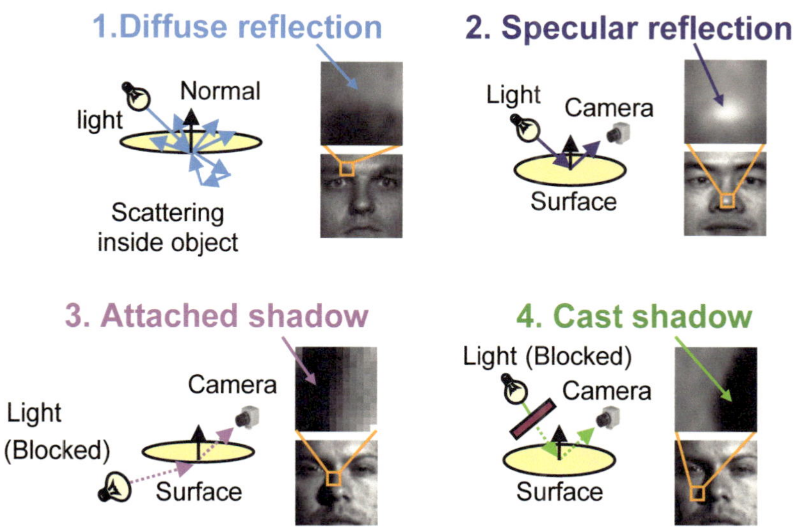

Fig. 1. Facial appearance classified into four main components: diffuse reflection, specular reflection, attached shadow and cast shadow. Diffuse reflection occurs when the incident light is scattered by the object. The pixel value of diffuse reflection is determined by albedo that is invariance (see Equation (2)). Specular reflection occurs when the incident light is cleanly reflected by the object. Attached shadow occurs when the object itself blocks the incident light. Cast shadow occurs when a different object blocks the incident light.

The Self-Quotient Image (SQI) (Wang et al., 2004) of a pixel is defined as the ratio of the albedo of that pixel to a smoothed albedo value of local pixels. The SQI however is neither synthesized at the boundary between a diffuse reflection region and a shadow region, nor at the boundary between a diffuse reflection region and a specular reflection region. This problem is not addressed in the Total Variation Quotient Image (Chen et al., 2005, An et al., 2008) and the Morphological Quotient Image (Zhang et al., 2007). Determining the reflectance type of an appearance from a single image is an ill-posed problem.
Our technique exploits a learned statistical model to classify the appearances accurately. Our statistical model is defined by a number of basis images representing diffuse reflection on a generic face. These basis images are trained on faces that are completely different to those later registered for identification. Synthesized images using our model are called the Classified Appearance-based Quotient Images (CAQI). The effectiveness of CAQI is demonstrated on the Yale Face Database B and a real-world database (see Section 4). We compare CAQI with SQI, Retinex (Jobson et al., 1997) images produced by an equation similar to SQI, and conventional histogram equalization for illumination normalization. From these results, we see a significant improvement by classifying appearances using our Quotient Image-based technique.

1.1 Background

A method for synthesizing illumination normalized images without an explicit appearance model has been proposed in (Belhumeur et al., 1997, Nishiyama et al., 2005), where the variation caused by illumination is regarded as an intra-class variation. An illumination normalized image is synthesized by projection onto a subspace that is insensitive to the intra-class variation due to illumination, but sensitive to the interclass variation representing changes in appearance between individuals. However, in the case of different lighting conditions amongst training images for the subspace, an illumination normalized image cannot be synthesized since the subspace cannot estimate a novel appearance that is not included in the training images.
In order to apply an explicit appearance model for illumination, the basis images method has been proposed in (Shashua et al., 2001, Okabe et al, 2003), which is suitable for modelling the variation in facial appearance caused by diffuse reflection. This model is advantageous in that a registration system stores only a few images and fitting a face image to the model is simple. Shashua et al. have proposed the Quotient Image technique (QI) (Shashua et al., 2001), which is the ratio of albedo between a face image and linear combination of basis images, for each pixel. This ratio of albedo is illumination invariant. However, the QI assumes that a facial appearance includes only diffuse reflection. Okabe et al. synthesized a normalized image consisting of diffuse reflection and attached shadow, removing specular reflection and cast shadow from a face image (Okabe et al, 2003). This method estimates diffuse reflection and attached shadow using basis images and random sample consensus. Basis images are generated from three face images acquired under fixed pose and a moving point light source (Shashua, 1999), or from four face images acquired under a moving pose and a fixed point light source (Nakashima et al., 2002). Therefore, these methods (Shashua et al., 2001, Okabe et al, 2003) require multiple face images for each individual in the registration stage of training. This requirement is an important limitation for practical applications. In the case that there is only one training image available per person, these methods cannot be applied.

2. Obtaining invariance with respect to diffuse reflection

2.1 Self-Quotient Image (SQI)

The SQI technique (Wang et al., 2004) has been proposed for synthesizing an illumination normalized image from a single face image. The SQI is defined by a face image $I(x,y)$ and a smoothed image $S(x,y)$ as

$$Q(x,y) = \frac{I(x,y)}{S(x,y)} = \frac{I(x,y)}{F(x,y) * I(x,y)}, \tag{1}$$

where $F(x,y)$ is a smoothing filter; $*$ is the convolution operation. In the case that a smoothing filter is an isotropic Gaussian filter $G(x,y)$, Equation (1) is equivalent to the center/surround retinex transform described in (Jobson et al., 1997). However, in the case of the SQI technique, an anisotropic, weighted Gaussian filter $W(x,y)G(x,y)$ is used.

As described in (Wang et al., 2004), $Q(x,y)$ is illumination invariant if certain assumptions are met (see assumptions (a) and (b)). The diffuse reflection is defined by the Lambertian model as

$$i = \max(al\mathbf{n}^T\mathbf{s}, 0), \tag{2}$$

where i is pixel value of $I(x,y)$; a and $\mathbf{n}$ are the albedo and the normal of the object surface; l and $\mathbf{s}$ are the strength and direction of the light source. The lengths of $\mathbf{n}$ and $\mathbf{s}$ are normalized. Attached shadow appears in the case where the dot-product between $\mathbf{n}$ and $\mathbf{s}$ is negative. We make two assumptions in a local region: that (a) l, $\mathbf{n}$, and $\mathbf{s}$ are uniform and (b) all observed appearance is diffuse reflection. Then the ratio of albedo is extracted as

$$Q(x,y) = \frac{a(x,y)l\mathbf{n}^T\mathbf{s}}{F(x,y) * a(x,y)l\mathbf{n}^T\mathbf{s}} = \frac{a(x,y)}{F(x,y) * a(x,y)}. \tag{3}$$

Under multiple light sources, the ratio of albedo is also obtained using additivity $\mathbf{s} = \sum_{k=1}^{n} \mathbf{s_k}$.

2.2 Problems caused by effects other than diffuse reflection

Equation (3) works well for a local region such as Figure 2 (i) that includes the low albedo region of the eyebrow and the middle albedo region of the forehead. The assumptions of Section 2.1 are valid in this local region where only diffuse reflection is observed. However, the assumptions are violated in Figure 2 (ii) and (iii) where cast shadow, or specular reflection, is partially observed. In the specular reflection region, diffuse reflection pixel values cannot be extracted because the pixel values are saturated. Then, we need to estimate diffuse reflection pixel values from the pixels that are in the specular reflection region. In a cast shadow region, light parameters, l and s, are different from those of diffuse reflection because there is an obstruction between the light source and the facial region of interest. The same is true of the attached shadow regions. In these regions, diffuse reflection can be sometimes observed because the region is illuminated by another light source e.g. ambient light. Then, we need to determine a local region that is all subject to the same lighting conditions for Equation (3) to work well.

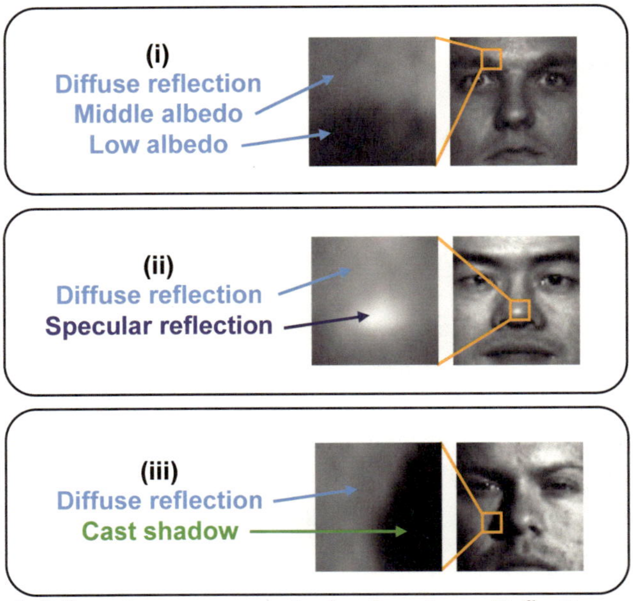

Fig. 2. Examples of different appearances in local regions. Reflections other than diffuse reflection are also observed in local regions (ii) and (iii). This means that, using the QI technique, an illumination invariant feature cannot be extracted from these local regions.

2.3 Weight function for synthesizing the SQI

The weight function $W(x,y)$ of the SQI is designed for each pixel to prevent halo effects either side of the edges in the image. The weight function divides a local region into two subregions M_1 and M_2 . If $I(x,y) \in M_1$ then $W(x,y)=1$ else $W(x,y)=0$. The subregion is determined by a threshold τ that is the average of pixel values in the local region. The subregion with the larger number of pixels is set to M_1, the other is set to M_2. However, the weight function is unable to discriminate between shadow and low albedo regions, e.g. eyes and eyebrows. Illumination invariant features can only be extracted from a local region containing an edge between a middle albedo region and a low albedo region such as Figure 2(i). This inability of the SQI to discriminate between shadow and low albedo region results important information representing identity being neglected. Another problem is that a region is not simply divided where pixel values change smoothly, e.g. soft shadow is observed on the edge of the cast shadow.

3. Classified Appearance-based Quotient Image (CAQI)

In this section we introduce a new method for extracting the ratio of albedo from a face image that includes specular reflection and shadow. In this method the weight function for the weighted Gaussian filter is calculated by classifying the appearance of each pixel.

3.1 Classification of appearance caused by illumination using photometric linearization

To classify surface appearance into diffuse reflection, specular reflection, attached shadow and cast shadow, we utilize photometric linearization (Mukaigawa et al., 2001). Photometric linearization transforms a face image into a linearized image consisting of only diffuse reflection. A linearized image $\widetilde{I}(x,y)$ is defined by a model (Shashua, 1999) in which arbitrary images with only diffuse reflection are represented by a linear combination of three basis images $I_i(x,y)(i=1,2,3)$ taken under point light sources in linearly independent directions as

$$\widetilde{I}(x,y)=\sum_{i=1}^{3}c_iI_i(x,y). \tag{4}$$

To estimate coefficients c_i from a face image including specular reflection and shadow, photometric linearization uses random sampling of pixels. By random sampling we calculate candidates of c_i. The final c_i is determined from the distribution of candidates by iterating between outlier elimination and recomputation of the mean. The appearance is classified using a difference image $I'(x,y)$, defined as

$$I'(x,y)=I(x,y)-\widetilde{I}(x,y). \tag{5}$$

As in (Mukaigawa et al., 2001) a pixel having a negative value in $I'(x,y)$ is classified as cast shadow. A pixel having a value greater than the threshold in $I'(x,y)$ is classified as specular reflection. A pixel having a negative value in $\widetilde{I}(x,y)$ is classified as attached shadow. To estimate diffuse reflection for a pixel that has specular reflection, we replace the pixel value $I(x,y)$ with $\widetilde{I}(x,y)$.

3.2 Generation of basis images

Since we do not acquire basis images $I_i(x,y)$ for each individual in the training stage, we generate basis images using different individuals from those in the training stage. For this purpose, we acquire images under fixed pose and a moving point light source. These images do not exhibit specular reflection or shadow. The point light source is moved so as to make each basis image linearly independent. We apply Singular Value Decomposition (SVD) using all the acquired images. The vectors, selected in descending order of singular value, are the basis images. We assume that the basis images represent the diffuse reflection on a generic face. However, retaining the first three basis images, the estimated c_i in Equation (4) has an error induced by the difference between a generic face and an individual face. For fitting basis images to various individuals, we select more than four vectors in descending order of singular value. These vectors represent the principal component of the variation in appearance in a diffuse reflection of the individuals.

3.3 Calculation of the weighted function using classified appearance

To calculate the weight function for the weighted Gaussian filter, we utilize a difference image $I'(x,y)$ representing the difference of the appearance. We aim to extract the ratio of albedo from a local region in which similar appearance is observed. For example, if the center of a local region is classified as diffuse reflection, we give a large weight to diffuse reflection of the surrounding area of the center and small weight to areas in shadow. The weight function $W(x,y)$ is defined by comparing the center of a Gaussian filter with its surrounding area as follows:

$$W(x,y) = \frac{1}{1+\alpha\left|I'(x,y) - I'(x_0,y_0)\right|}, \tag{6}$$

where (x_0, y_0) is the center pixel of the Gaussian filter; α is constant $(\alpha > 0)$. If $I'(x,y)$ is greater than $I'(x_0,y_0)$, then $I'(x,y)$ has a different appearance to $I'(x_0,y_0)$, and a small weight is given to $I'(x,y)$.

3.4 Algorithm for synthesizing the CAQI

We now explain the algorithm for synthesizing the Classified Appearance-based Quotient Image (CAQI). The flow diagram of the algorithm is shown in Figure 3. First, a face image is aligned from the positions of the pupils and the nostrils. Next, appearance is classified using photometric linearization. Then, the specular reflection is replaced with the estimated diffuse reflection.

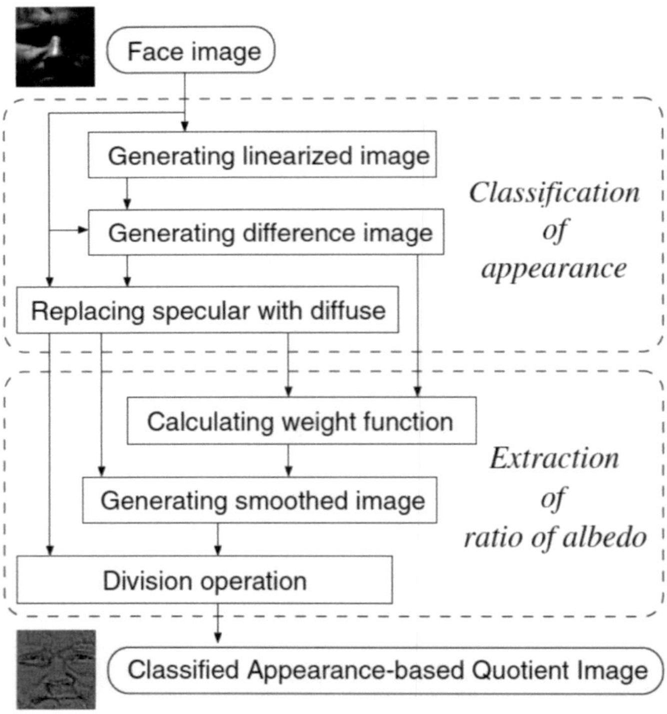

Fig. 3. Flow of synthesizing the CAQI.

For calculating the ratio of the albedo, we need to determine the size of a local region in order to obtain a uniform surface normal $\mathbf{n}$. However, searching for a suitable size is difficult since there is an ambiguity in the computation of $\mathbf{n}$ for basis images that are generated by unknown l and $\mathbf{s}$ (Hayakawa, 1994). Therefore we use multiple sizes as in

(Jobson et al., 1997, Wang et al., 2004). The size is defined by the standard deviation σ of the Gaussian filter used in the smoothing operation. We calculate the weight function $W_j(x,y)$ for each $\sigma_{j:}(j=1,...,N)$. Finally, the illumination normalized image $Q(x,y)$ is synthesized as

$$Q(x,y)=\sum_{j=1}^{N} f\left(\frac{I(x,y)}{W_j(x,y)G_j(x,y)*I(x,y)}\right). \tag{7}$$

Note that we assume $\int\int W_j(x,y)G_j(x,y)dxdy=1$. As in (Jobson et al., 1997, Wang et al., 2004) we use f in Equation (7). The function f prevents asymptotic approach to infinity when the term $W_j(x,y)G_j(x,y)*I(x,y)$ tends to zero in shadowed regions.

4. Empirical evaluation

4.1 Performance for varying illumination

4.1.1 Experimented conditions

To illustrate the performance of our method, we have conducted face identification experiments using the Yale Face Database B (Georghiades et al., 2001). The database consists of images taken under 64 different lighting conditions, which are divided into 5 subsets. In Figure 4, we show examples of face images in each subset. We used 640 images in total taken of 10 individuals in a frontal pose. We located a 64×64 pixels face image from the positions of the pupils and the nostrils, obtained manually. In our experiments we use a single face image of each individual for training, where the lighting conditions are the same for all subjects. This is different from (Wang et al., 2004) which used multiple images for training. The images taken under the remaining 63 lighting conditions are used for testing.
For the generation of basis images, we used the CMU PIE (Sim et al., 2003) consisting of different individuals from the Yale Face Database B. We selected images taken from a frontal pose (c27) under light sources (f06, f07, f08, f09, f11, f12, f20, f21). We applied SVD to all the images of 68 individuals and selected the 7 basis images shown in Figure 5.

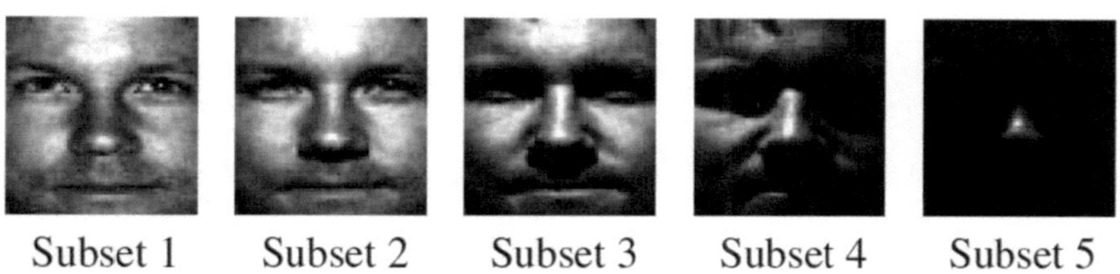

Fig. 4. Examples from the Yale face database B.

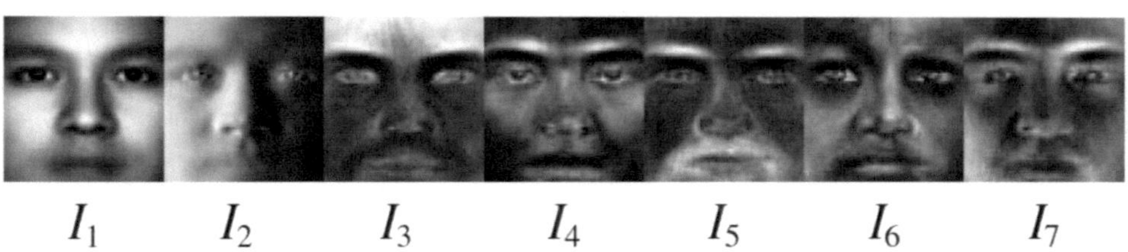

Fig. 5. Basis images generated from the 68 CMU-PIE individuals under 8 lighting conditions.

4.1.2 Identification performance

We compared the performance of the CAQI with the gray-scale image (GS), the histogram equalized image (HE), the Multi-scale Center/Surround Retinex image (MSR) (Jobson et al., 1997) and the SQI (Wang et al., 2004). For GS, we used the face image directly. For HE, we used the histogram equalization of face image. For MSR, SQI and CAQI, we used multiple Gaussian filters, σ_i were set to 1.0, 2.0, 3.0, and f in Equation (7) was chosen as the logarithmic function. For CAQI, we sampled 20,000 candidates to estimate c_i and α was set to 0.1. The synthesized image was transformed to a vector by raster-scanning of the image and the length of the vector was normalized. Then, we calculated the similarity between the training vector and the testing vector using normalized correlation.
Table 1 shows the evaluation results for each method in terms of the correct recognition rate (RR). RR is the probability that a face image of the right person is accepted correctly when using nearest neighbor classification. We show the average of the RR for each subset in the table. The performance of the MSR is superior to that of the SQI. Heusch et al. reported a similar result for a different database (Heusch et al., 2005). For this reason, we infer that the weight function for the SQI causes the problem that the center pixel of Gaussian filter is not included in the subregion M_1. Since the appearance differs between the center pixel and the subregion, the assumptions for Equation (3) are invalid. From the table we can see that the performance of CAQI is superior to that of the others. In particular, the performance in subset 5 where faces are mostly shadowed is improved significantly.

Subset (Training)	Method				
	GS	HE	MSR	SQI	CAQI
1	68	71	93	87	96
2	64	68	91	82	95
3	54	58	82	71	88
4	39	43	79	68	84
5	25	42	79	75	91

Table 1. RR (%) on the Yale Face Database B. Images taken under one lighting condition were used for training set. Images taken under 63 different lighting conditions were used for test set.

4.1.3 Comparison of synthesized images

Figure 6 shows the synthesized center/surround retinex image, SQI and CAQI. To synthesize these images we used a single σ = 1.0. In the case of the synthesized images in subset 4, features hidden by shadow around the eyes in the gray-scale image appear in the center/surround retinex image, SQI, and CAQI. It can clearly be observed that the influence of cast shadows is reduced in the CAQI. This is particularly evident at the edge of the shadowed region and in the region of specular reflection on the nose.

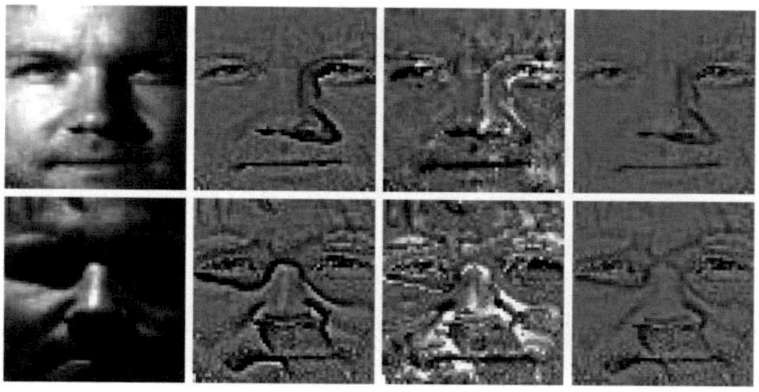

Fig. 6. Examples of an image synthesized by each method. (The upper row is subset 3 and the lower row is subset 4)

4.1.4 Identification performance in the case of basis images for each individual

We compared the identification performance using basis images of each individual (CAQI-same) and using basis images of others (CAQI-other). In CAQI-other, we used basis images of CMU-PIE shown in Figure 5. In CAQI-same, basis images for each individual in a training set were generated using 7 face images in subset 1. We selected three basis images in descending order of singular value. Images taken under one lighting condition in subset 1 were used for training set. Images taken under 63 different lighting conditions were used for the test set. Table 2 shows the evaluation result in terms of RR. CAQI-other and CAQI-same are superior to the SQI. However, CAQI-same is superior to CAQI-other. For this reason, we presume that the albedo and the surface normal of faces in the test set are different from those for individuals included in CMU-PIE. To increase performance further, we are considering developing a method of deforming basis images from generic basis images without requiring more than one training image per person.

Method	Subset (Input)				
	1	2	3	4	5
SQI	100	97	91	76	70
CAQI-other	100	97	97	93	93
CAQI-same	100	99	99	95	94

Table 2. Comparison of identification performance using basis images of each individual versus basis images of others. Images taken under one lighting condition in subset 1 were used for the training set.

4.2 Performance assessment on a real-world database

We also evaluated the methods using a database collected under two lighting conditions for 100 individuals. We assumed a practical application of face recognition, namely to passport-based identification. The lighting conditions are (I) no shadow on the facial appearance by using a flash attached to the camera, and (II) face shadowed by a single spotlight mounted on the ceiling as shown in Figure 7. We collected a single face image for each individual and each lighting condition when the ceiling fluorescent lamps were on. The parameters of Section 4.1 remained unchanged. We show the RR (%) in Table 3 for the condition that (I) is the training set and (II) is the testing set, and vice versa.

We can see that the method using the CAQI is superior to the other methods. In particular, the CAQI is effective when images containing cast shadow regions, as in (II), are used as training examples. However, an error in the photometric linearization arose since a single set of c_i does not fully represent the diversity of illumination under multiple light sources. To improve the performance, we are considering developing a method of estimating multiple sets of c_i under multiple light sources.

Fig. 7. Examples of a real-world database.

Training image	GS	HE	MAR	SQI	CAQI
(I)	30	16	78	65	82
(II)	33	25	73	29	80

Table 3. RR (%) on a real-world database.

5. Conclusion

This chapter discussed a method of synthesizing an illumination normalized image using Quotient Image-based techniques. Facial appearance contains diffuse reflection, specular reflection, attached shadow and cast shadow. Our Quotient Image-based technique classifies facial appearance into four components using basis images representing diffuse reflection on a generic face. Our method is able to obtain high identification performance on the Yale Face Database B and on a real-world database, using only a single image for each individual in training.

6. Acknowledgements

We would like to thank Mr. Masahide Nishiura, Dr. Paul Wyatt, Dr. Bjorn Stenger, and Mr. Jonathan Smith for their significant suggestions and comments.

7. References

An, G.; Wu, J. & Ruan, Q. (2008). Kernel TV-Based Quotient Image Employing Gabor Analysis and Its Application to Face Recognition, *IEICE Transactions on Information and Systems*, Vol. E91-D, No. 5, pp. 1573-1576

Belhumeur, P. N.; Hespanha, J. P. & Kriegman, D. J. (1997). Eigenfaces vs. fisherfaces: Recognition using class specific linear projection, *IEEE Transactions Pattern Analysis and Machine Intelligence*, Vol. 19, No. 7, pp. 711 - 720

Chen, T.; Yin, W.; Zhou, X. S.; Comaniciu, D. & Huang, T. S. (2005). Illumination Normalization for Face Recognition and Uneven Background Correction Using Total Variation Based Image Models, *Proceedings of IEEE Computer Society Conference on Computer Vision and Pattern Recognition*, Vol. 2, pp. 532 - 539

Georghiades, A. S.; Belhumeur, P. N. & Kriegman D. J. (2001). From few to many: Illumination cone models for face recognition under variable lighting and pose, *IEEE Transactions on Pattern Analysis and Machine Intelligence*, Vol. 23, No. 6, pp. 643 - 660

Hayakawa, H. (1994). Photometric stereo under a light source with arbitrary motion, *The Journal of the Optical Society of America A*, Vol. 11, No. 11, pp. 3079 - 3089

Heusch, G.; Cardinaux, F. & Marcel, S. (2005). Lighting normalization algorithms for face verification. *IDIAP-Com 05-03*

Jobson, D. J. ; Rahman, Z. & Woodell, G. A. (1997). A multi-scale retinex for bridging the gap between color images and the human observation of scenes, *IEEE Transactions on Image Processing*, Vol. 6, No. 7, pp. 965 - 976

Mukaigawa, Y.; Miyaki, H. ; Mihashi, S. & Shakunaga, T. (2001). Photometric image-based rendering for image generation in arbitrary illumination, *IEEE International Conference on Computer Vision*, Vol. 2, pp. 652 - 659

Nakashima, A.; Maki, A. & Fukui, K. (2002). Constructing illumination image basis from object motion, *Proceedings of 7th European Conference on Computer Vision*, Vol. 3, pp. 195 - 209

Nishiyama, M. ; Yamaguchi O. & Fukui, K. (2005). Face recognition with the multiple constrained mutual subspace method, *Proceedings of 5th International Conference on Audio- and Video-based Biometric Person Authentication*, pp. 71 - 80

Nishiyama, M. & Yamaguchi, O. (2006). Face Recognition Using the Classified Appearance-based Quotient Image, *Proceedings of 7th IEEE International Conference on Automatic Face and Gesture Recognition*, pp. 49 - 54

Okabe, T. & Sato, Y. (2003). Object recognition based on photometric alignment using ransac, *IEEE Proceeding Conference on Computer Vision and Pattern Recognition*, Vol.1, pp. 221 -228

Shashua, A. (1999). Geometry and photometry in 3d visual recognition, *Ph. D. Thesis*

Shashua, A. & Riklin-Raviv, T. (2001). The quotient image: Classbased re-rendering and recognition with varying illuminations, *IEEE Transactions Pattern Analysis and Machine Intelligence*, Vol. 23, No. 2, pp. 129 - 139

Sim, T.; Baker, S. & Bsat, M. (2003). The cmu pose, illumination, and expression database, *IEEE Transactions on Pattern Analysis and Machine Intelligence*, Vol. 25, No. 12, pp. 1615 - 1618

Wang, H.; Li, S. Z. & Wang, Y. (2004). Generalized quotient image, *IEEE Proceeding Conference on Computer Vision and Pattern Recognition*, Vol.2, pp. 498 - 505

Zhang, Y.; Tian, J.; He, X. & Yang, X. (2007). MQI Based Face Recognition Under Uneven Illumination, *Advances in Biometrics*, Vol. 4642, pp. 290-298

9

Liveness Detection for Face Recognition

Gang Pan, Zhaohui Wu and Lin Sun
Department of Computer Science, Zhejiang University
China

1. Introduction

Biometrics is an emerging technology that enables uniquely recognizing humans based upon one or more intrinsic physiological or behavioral characteristics, such as faces, fingerprints, irises, voices (Ross et al., 2006). However, spoofing attack (or copy attack) is still a fatal threat for biometric authentication systems (Schukers, 2002). Liveness detection, which aims at recognition of human physiological activities as the liveness indicator to prevent spoofing attack, is becoming a very active topic in field of fingerprint recognition and iris recognition (Schuckers, 2002; Bigun et al., 2004; Parthasaradhi et al., 2005; Antonelli et al., 2006).

In face recognition community, although numerous recognition approaches have been presented, the effort on anti-spoofing is still very limited (Zhao et al., 2003). The most common faking way is to use a facial photograph of a valid user to spoof face recognition systems. Nowadays, video of a valid user can also be easily captured by needle camera for spoofing. Therefore anti-spoof problem should be well solved before face recognition could be widely applied in our life.

Most of the current face recognition works with excellent performance, are based on intensity images and equipped with a generic camera. Thus, an anti-spoofing method without additional device will be preferable, since it could be easily integrated into the existing face recognition systems.

In Section 2, we give a brief review of spoofing ways in face recognition and some related work. The potential clues will be also presented and commented. In Section 3, a real-time liveness detection approach is presented against photograph spoofing in a non-intrusive manner for face recognition, which does not require any additional hardware except for a generic webcamera. In Section 4, databases are introduced for eyeblink-based anti-spoofing. Section 5 presents an extensive set of experiments to show effectiveness of our approach. Discussions are in Section 6.

2. Spoofing in face recognition

Generally speaking, there are three ways to spoof face recognition:

a. Photograph of a valid user
b. Video of a valid user
c. 3D model of a valid user

Photo attack is the cheapest and easiest spoofing approach, since one's facial image is usually very easily available for the public, for example, downloaded from the web, captured unknowingly by a camera. The imposter can rotate, shift and bend the photo before the camera like a live person to fool the authentication system. It is still a challenging task to detect whether an input face image is from a live person or from a photograph.

Video spoofing is another big threat to face recognition systems, because it is very similar to live face and can be shot in front of legal user's face by a needle camera. It has many physiological clues that photo does not have, such as head movement, facial expression, blinking et al.

3D model has 3D information of face, however, it is rigid and lack of physiological information. It is also not very easy to be realistic with live person who the 3D model imitates. So photo and video are most common spoofing ways to attack face recognition system.

In general, human is able to distinguish a live face and a photograph without any effort, since human can very easily recognize many physiological clues of liveness, for example, facial expression variation, mouth movement, head rotation, eye change. However, the tasks of computing these clues are often complicated for computer, even impossible for some clues under the unconstrained environment.

From the static view, an essential difference between a live face and a photograph is that a live face is a fully three dimensional object while a photograph could be considered as a two dimensional planar structure. With this natural trait, Choudhary et al employed the structure from motion yielding the depth information of the face to detect live person or still photo (Choudhary et al., 1999). The disadvantages of depth information are that, firstly it is hard to estimate depth information when head is still. Secondly, the estimate is very sensitive to noise and lighting condition, becoming unreliable.

Compared with photographs, another prominent characteristic of live faces is the occurrence of the non-rigid deformation and appearance change, such as mouth motion, expression variation. The accurate and reliable detection of these changes usually needs either the input data of high-quality or user collaboration. Kollreider et al applies the optical flow to the input video to obtain the information of face motion for liveness judgement (Kollreider et al., 2005), but it is vulnerable to photo motion in depth and photo bending. Some researchers use the multi-modal approaches of face-voice against spoofing (Frischholz, & Dieckmann, 2000; Chetty & Wagner, 2006), exploiting the lip movement during speaking. This kind of method needs voice recorder and user collaboration. An interactive approach is tried by Frischholz et al, requiring user to act an obvious response of head movement (Frischholz & Dieckmann, 2000).

Besides, Li et al presented Fourier spectra to classify live faces or faked images, based on the assumption that the high frequency components of the photo is less than those of live face images (Li et al., 2004). With thermal infrared imaging camera, face thermogram also could be applied in to liveness detection (Socolinsky et al., 2003).

Table 1. summaries these anti-spoofing clues, in terms of data quality, hardware and user collaboration, for comparison.

Clues	Data Quality	Additional Hardware	User Collaboration
Facial expression	High	No	Middle
Depth information	High	No	Low
Mouth movement	Middle	No	Middle
Head movement	High	No	Middle
Eye blinking	Low	No	Low
Degradation	High	No	Low
Multi-modal	-	Yes	Middle/High
Facial thermogram	-	Yes	Low
Facial vein map	-	Yes	Middle
Interactive response	-	No	High

Table 1. Comparison of anti-spoofing clues for face recognition

3. Blinking-based liveness detection

Most of the current face recognition systems are based on intensity images and equipped with a generic camera. An anti-spoofing method without additional device will be preferable, since it could be easily integrated into the existing face recognition approach and system.

In this section, a blinking-based liveness detection approach is introduced for prevention of photograph-spoofing. It requires no extra hardware except for a generic webcamera. Eyeblink sequences often have a complex underlying structure. We formulate blink detection as inference in an undirected conditional graphical framework, and are able to learn a compact and efficient observation and transition potentials from data. For purpose of quick and accurate recognition of the blink behavior, *eye closity*, an easily-computed discriminative measure derived from the adaptive boosting algorithm, is developed, and then smoothly embedded into the conditional model.

3.1 Why blinking used?

We hope to find some easily computational, also hardly disguising clue for the photo-spoofing protection. Eyeblink is a physiological activity of rapid closing and opening of eyelids, which is an essential function of eyes that helps spread tears across and remove irritants from the surface of the cornea and conjunctiva. Although blink speed can vary with elements such as fatigue, emotional stress, behavior category, amount of sleep, eye injury, medication, and disease, researchers report that (Karson,1983; Tsubota, 1998), the spontaneous resting blink rate of a human being is nearly from 15 to 30 eyeblinks per minute. That is, a person blinks approximately once every 2 to 4 seconds, and a blink lasts averagely 250 milliseconds. Currently a generic camera can easily capture a face video with not less than 15 fps (frames per second), i.e. the frame interval is not more than 70 milliseconds. Thus, it is easy for a generic camera to capture two or more frames for each blink when a face looks into the camera. It is feasible to adopt eyeblink as the clue for anti-spoofing.

The advantages of eyeblink based approach lie in:
1. It can complete in a non-intrusive manner, generally without user collaboration.
2. No extra hardware is required.
3. Eyeblink behaviour is the prominently distinguishing character of a live face from a facial photo, which would be much helpful for liveness detection only from the generic camera.

There is little work addressing vision-based detection of eyeblink in the literature. Most of the previous efforts need highly controlled conditions and high-quality input data, for instance, the automatic recognition system of human facial action units (Tian et al., 2001). Moriyama's blinking detection method (Moriyama et al., 2002) is based on variation of average intensity in the eye region, sensitive to lighting conditions and noise. Ji et al have attempted to use an active IR camera to detect eyeblinks for prediction of driver fatigue (Ji et al., 2004).

3.2 Overview of the approach

An eyeblink behaviour could be represented as a temporal image sequence after being digitally captured by the camera. One typical method to detect blink is to classify each image in the sequence independently as one state of either close eye or open eye, for example, using the Viola's cascaded Adaboost approach like face detection (Viola & Jones, 2001). The problem with this method is that it assumes all of the images in the temporal sequence are independent. Actually, the neighboring images of blinking are dependent, since the blink is a procedure of eye eventually from opening to closure, then to opening. The temporal information is ignored for this method, which may be very helpful for recognition.

This independence assumption can be relaxed by disposing the state variables in a linear chain. For instance, an HMM (the hidden Markov model) (Rabiner, 1989) models a sequence of observations by assuming that there is an underlying sequence of states drawn from a finite state set. The features of image could be regarded as the observations, and the eye state label is for the underlying states. A HMM makes two independence assumptions to model the joint probability tractably. It assumes that each state depends only on its immediate predecessor, and that each observation variable depends only on the current state, depicted in Fig. 1(a). However, on one hand, the generative-model-based approaches should compute a model of $p(x)$, which is not needed for classification anyway. On the other hand, for our task of eyeblink recognition, the two independence assumptions are too restrictive, since, in fact, there exist dependencies among observations and states, which will benefit blink detection, in particular when the current observation is disturbed by noise such as highlight in eye region, variation of glasses' reflection.

We model eyeblink behaviors in an undirected Conditional Random Field framework, incorporated with a discriminative measure of eye sates for simplifying the complex of inference and simultaneously improving the performance. One of advantage of the proposed method is that allows us to relax the assumption of conditional independence of the observed data.

3.3 Conditional modeling of blinking behaviours

An eyeblink activity can be represented by an image sequence **S** consisting of T images, where $S=\{I_i, i=1,\ldots,T\}$. The typical eye states in the images are opening and closing, in

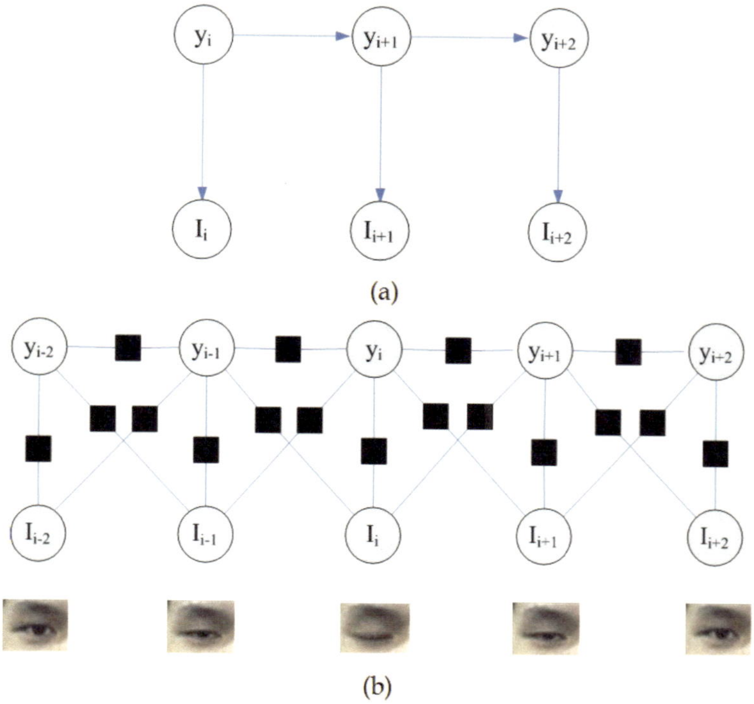

Fig. 1. Illustration of graphical structures. (a) Hidden Markov Model, (b) graphical model of a linear-chain CRF, where the circles are variable nodes and the black boxes are factor nodes, in this example the state depends on contexts of 3 neighbouring observations, that is, w=1.

addition, there is an ambiguous state when the eyeblinks from open state to close or from close state to open. We define a three-state set for eyes,

$$Q=\{\alpha : open,\ \gamma : close,\ \beta: ambiguous\}.$$

Thus, a typical blink activity can be described as a state change pattern of $\alpha \rightarrow \beta \rightarrow \gamma \rightarrow \beta \rightarrow \alpha$. Suppose that S is a random variable over observation sequences to be labeled, and *Y* is a random variable over the corresponding label sequences to be predicted, all of components y_i of *Y* are assumed to range over a finite label set Q. Let $G=(V, E)$ be a graph and *Y* is indexed by the vertices of *G*. Then (*Y*, S) is called a *conditional random field* (*CRF*) (Lafferty et al., 2001), when conditioned on S, the random variables *Y* and S obey the Markov property w.r.t. the graph:

$$p(y_v|S, y_u, u \neq v) = p(y_v|S, y_u, u \sim v) \tag{1}$$

Where $u \sim v$ means that *u* and *v* are neighbours in *G*.

We yield a linear chain structure, shown in Fig. 1(b). In this graphical model, a parameter of observation window size *W* is introduced to describe the conditional relationship between the current state and (2*W*+1) temporal observations around the current one, in the other word, it introduces the long-range dependencies in the model. Using the fundamental theorem by Hammersley & Clifford (Li, 2001), the joint distribution over the label sequence *Y* given the observation S can be written as the following form:

$$p_\theta(Y|S)=\frac{1}{Z_\theta(S)}exp(\sum_{t=1}^{T}\psi_\theta(y_t,y_{t-1},S)) \tag{2}$$

Where $Z_\theta(S)$ is a normalized factor summing over all state sequences, an exponentially large number of terms,

$$Z_\theta(S)=\sum_{Y}exp(\sum_{t=1}^{T}\psi_\theta(y_t,y_{t-1},S)). \tag{3}$$

The potential function $\psi_\theta(y_t,y_{t-1},S)$ is the sum of CRF features at time t:

$$\psi_\theta(y_t,y_{t-1},S)=\sum_{i}\lambda_i f_i(y_t,y_{t-1},S)+\sum_{j}\mu_j g_j(y_t,S) \tag{4}$$

With parameter $\theta=\{\lambda_1,...,\lambda_A;\mu_1,...,\mu_B\}$, to be estimated from training data.
The f_i and g_j are *within-label* and *between-observation-label* feature functions, respectively. λ_i and μ_j are the feature weights associated with f_i and g_j. Feature functions f_i and g_j are based on conjunctions of simple rules. The *within-label* feature functions f_i are:

$$f_i(y_t,y_{t-1},S)=1_{\{y_t=l\}}1_{\{y_{t-1}=l'\}} \tag{5}$$

Where $l,l'\in Q$, and $1_{x=x'}$ denotes an indictor function of x which takes the value 1 when $x=x'$ and 0 otherwise. Given a temporal window size W around the current observation, the *between-observation-label* feature functions g_j are defined as:

$$g_j(y_t,S)=1_{\{y_t=l\}}U(I_{t-w}) \tag{6}$$

Where $l\in Q$, $w\in[-W,W]$, $U(\cdot)$ is the eye closity, described in the next section. W is for a context window size around the current observation.
Parameter estimation of $\theta=\{\lambda_1,...,\lambda_A;\mu_1,...,\mu_B\}$ is typically performed by penalized maximum likelihood. Given a labeled training set $\{Y^{(i)}, S^{(i)}\}_{i=1,...,N}$, the conditional log likelihood is appropriate:

$$L_\theta=\sum_{i=1}^{N}log(p_\theta(Y^{(i)}|S^{(i)}))=\sum_{i=1}^{N}(\sum_{t=1}^{T}\psi_\theta(y_t^{(i)},y_{t-1}^{(i)},S^{(i)})-log(Z_\theta(S^{(i)}))) \tag{7}$$

In order to avoid over-fitting of a large number of parameters, the regularization technique is used, is a penalty on weight vectors whose norm is too large. For the function L_θ, every local optimum is also a global optimum because the function is convex. Regularization will ensure that L_θ is strictly convex. Finally, the optimization is solved by a limited-memory version of BFGS (Sha & Pereira, 2003), of quasi-Newton methods. The normalization factor $Z_\theta(S)$ can be computed by the idea forward-backward.
The inference tasks, for instance, to label an unknown instance $\boldsymbol{Y}^*=\mathrm{argmax}_Y\ p(Y|S)$, can performed efficiently and exactly by variants of the standard dynamic programming methods for HMM.

3.4 Eye closity: definition and computation

From the theoretical view, the original image data could be directly incorporated into the conditional model framework described above. However, obviously, it would dramatically increase the complexity and make the problem hard to solve. We hope to take advantage of the features extracted from the image for defining the intermediate observation. For example, silhouette features are commonly used in human motion recognition (Cristian et al., 2005; Gavrila, 1999}. Our goal is to develop a real-time approach, thus, we try to use as little feature as possible to reduce the computational cost, meanwhile the features should convey as much discriminative information for eye states as possible to improve the prediction accuracy.

Motivated by the idea of the adaptive boosting algorithm (Freund & Schapire, 1995), we define a real-value discriminative feature for the eye image, called *eye closity, U(I),* measuring the degree of eye's closeness, which is constructed by a linear ensemble of a series of weak binary classifiers and computed by an iterative procedure.

$$U_M(I) = \sum_{i=1}^{M} (log \frac{1}{\beta_i}) h_i(I) - \frac{1}{2} \sum_{i=1}^{M} log \frac{1}{\beta_i} \tag{8}$$

Where,

$$\beta_i = \varepsilon_i / (1 - \varepsilon_i) \tag{9}$$

and, $\{h_i(I): R^{Dim(I)} \rightarrow \{0,1\}, i=1,\ldots,M\}$ is a set of binary weak classifiers. Each classifier h_i is for classifying the input I as the open eye: {0}, or the close eye: {1}. Given a set of labelled training data, the efficient selection of h_i and the calculation of ε_i can be performed by an iterative procedure similar to adaptive boosting algorithm (Freund & Schapire, 1995).

The eye closity can be considered as a sense of the ensemble of effective features. From insight into the training procedure of Adaboost algorithm, we know that the positive value of *closity* indicates that the Adaboosted classifier will classify the input as the close eye, and the negative value as the open eye. Bigger the value of *closity is,* higher degree of eye closeness. A blinking activity sequence is shown in Fig.2, where the value is closity of the corresponding image, computed after training nearly by 1,000 samples of open eyes and 1,000 samples of close eyes. The closity value of zero is exactly the threshold for the Adaboosted classifier.

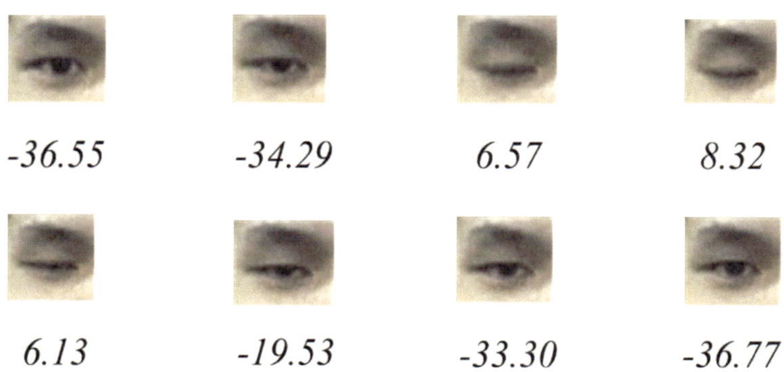

Fig. 2. Illustration of the closity for a blinking activity sequence. The closity value of each frame is below the corresponding frame. Bigger the value is, higher the degree of closeness. The closity value of zero is exactly the threshold of the Adaboost classifier.

4. Databases

To evaluate the proposed approach, we collected and built two databases: ZJU Eyeblink Database and ZJU Photo-Imposter Database.

4.1 ZJU eyeblink database

The ZJU Eyeblink Database is publicly available (http://www.cs.zju.edu.cn/~gpan or http://www.stat.ucla.edu/~gpan). It contains 80 video clips in AVI format of 20 individuals, collected by Logitech Pro 5000. There are 4 clips per subject: a clip for frontal view without glasses, a clip with frontal view and wearing thin rim glasses, a clip for frontal view and black frame glasses, and a clip with upward view without glasses. Each individual is required to perform blinking spontaneously in normal speed with the above four configurations. Each video clip is captured with 30 fps and size of 320x240 for each configuration, lasting about 5 seconds. The blink number in a video clip varies from 1 to 6 times. There are totally 255 blinks in the database. All the data are collected indoor without lighting control. Table 2 is demography of the blinking video database. Some samples are shown in Fig. 3.

Person#	Four clips for each person			Blinks#
	Clip#	View	Glasses	
20	1	frontal	none	255
	1	frontal	thin rim	
	1	frontal	black frame	
	1	upward	none	

Table 2. Demography of the blinking database. Totally 80 clips and approximately 1 to 6 blinks for each clip.

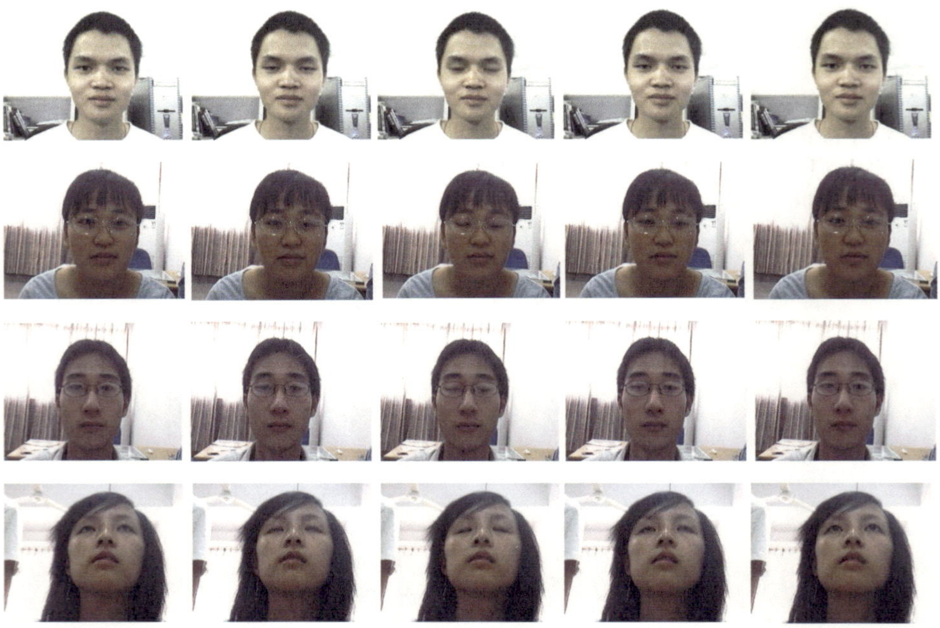

Fig. 3. Samples from the blinking database. The first row is for no glasses, the second row is with thin rim glasses, the third row for wearing black frame glasses, and the fourth row with upward view. The shown images are sampled every two frames.

4.2 ZJU photo-imposter database

To test the ability against photo imposters, we also collect a *photo-imposter database* with 20 persons. A high-quality photo of front view is taken for each person, then five categories of the photo-attacks are simulated before the camera:

1. Keep the photo still.
2. Move the photo horizontally, vertically, back and front.
3. Rotate the photo in depth along the vertical axis.
4. Rotate the photo in plane.
5. Bend the photo inward and outward along the central line.

For each attack, one video clip is captured with length of about 10 to 15 seconds and with size of 320 × 240. Five categories of the photo-attacks are shown in Fig. 4.

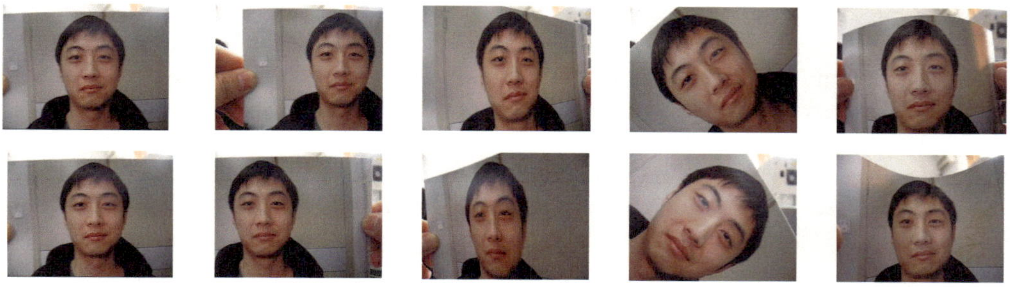

(1) (2) (3) (4) (5)

Fig. 4. Five categories of photo-attacks: (1) keep the photo still, (2) move the photo horizontally, vertically, back and front, (3) rotate the photo in depth along the vertical axis, (4) rotate the photo in plane, (5) bend the photo inward and outward along the central line.

5. Experiments

5.1 Setting

To compute *eye closity*, we need to train a series of efficient weak classifiers. A total of 1,016 labeled images of close eyes (positive samples) and 1,200 images of open eyes (negative samples) are used in the training stage. We do not differentiate between the left and right eyes. All the samples are scaled to a base resolution of 24×24 pixels. Some positive samples of closed eyes and negative samples of open eyes are shown in Fig. 5. Eventually 50 weak classifiers are selected for computing the *eye closity* (Equ.8).

In both the testing stage and the training stage of parameter estimation of blinking conditional model, the center of left and right eyes is automatically localized for each frame by a face key-point localization system developed by OMRON's face group. The eye images are extracted and normalized for training, whose size is determined by the distance between the two eyes. We adopt the *leave-one-out rule* to test the blinking video database. In other words, one clip is selected from 80 clips for test and the remainders act as the training data, then this test procedure is repeated 80 times over the 80 clips, finally get the detection rate. Each pattern of eye state variation $a \rightarrow \beta \rightarrow \gamma \rightarrow \beta \rightarrow a$ is accounted as one blink for this eye.

5.2 Performance measures

Three types of detection rates are for measuring the approach performance of liveness detection.

1. *One-eye detection rate*: it is the ratio of number of correctly detected blinks to the total blinks number in test data, where left and right eyes are calculated respectively.
2. *two-eye detection rate*: in fact, for each natural blink activity, both left and right eyes will blink. We can determine a live face if we correctly detect the blink of either left or right eye for each blink activity. Thus, *two-eye detection rate* is defined for this case as the ratio of number of correctly detected blink activities to the total blink activities in test data, where the simultaneous blinks of two eyes are accounted for one blink activity.
3. *clip detection rate*: the third measure is *clip detection rate*, in which case, the clip is considered as live face if any blink of single eye in the clip is detected.

5.3 Benefits of conditioned on observations

To investigate the benefits of the conditioned on the context of the current observation, an experiment with various windows size setting of $W = \{0, 1, 2, 3, 4\}$ (in Equ.6) is carried out. The results are shown in Fig. 6., from which we can find that the one-eye detection rate significantly increases when the windows size goes from zero to three, demonstrating there exists a strong dependency between the current state and the neighboring observations. Either one-eye detection rate or two-eye detection rate of performance is very close for $W = 3$ and $W = 4$, which shows the dependency becomes weak between the current state and the observations far from its corresponding observation. The window size of $W = 3$ means the

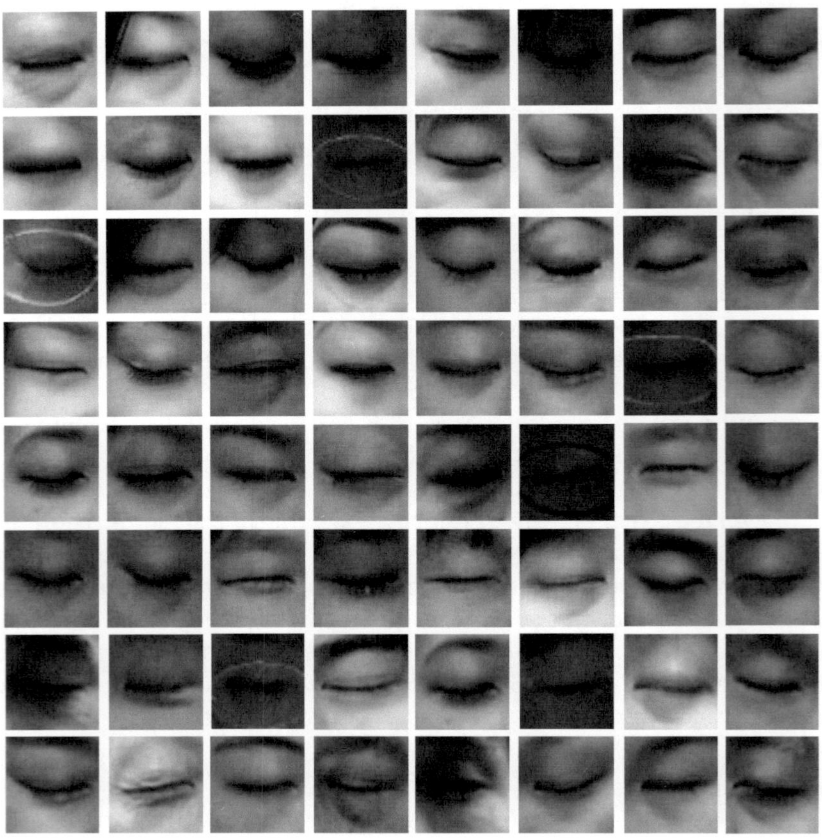

(a)

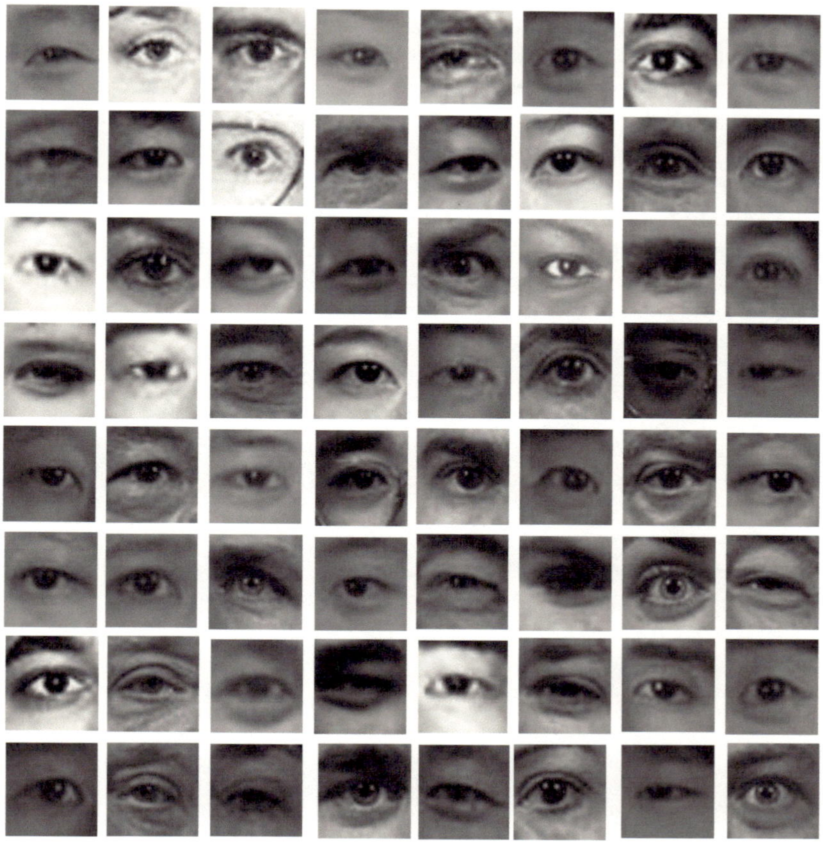

(b)

Fig. 5. Samples for computation of *eye closity*. (a) positive samples, (b) negative samples. Note that it includes glasses-wearing samples.

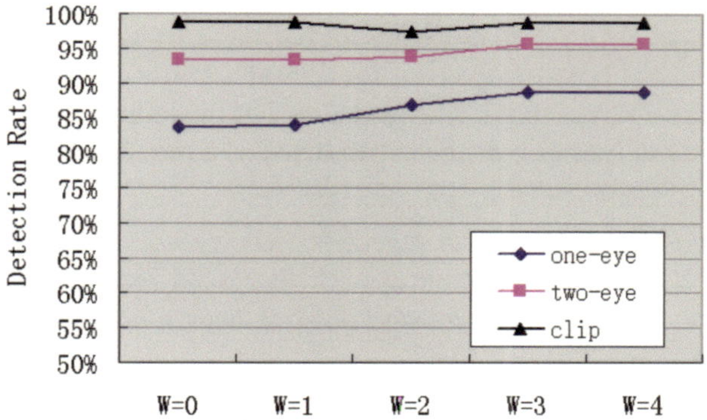

Fig. 6. Results of various window size: W = {0, 1, 2, 3, 4}.

contextual observations of 7 frames used for the conditional modeling. A blink activity average 7-8 frames (lasting nearly 250 ms), it can explain that the observations out range of a blink activity have little contribution to the blink detection.

Fig.7 shows three frames' results with W=3. In each frame, there are two bar graphs on the bottom depicting temporal variation of eye closity for both eyes respectively, where the closity of horizontal axis is equal to zero. The red bars indicate the temporal positions that have been labeled as blinking by our method. The temporal variation of closity in Fig. 7(a) is a typical blinking. The closity values of both eyes are greater than zero during blinking. The left eye in Fig. 7(a) and the right eye of Fig. 7(c) are two samples in which some closity values during blinking are below zero, where Adaboost will fail, while our approach still detects the blinking activities correctly. The right eye in Fig. 7(d) shows another example, where it will be classified as closed eye since the closity values of several neighboring frames are above zero, but our approach "knows" it is open.

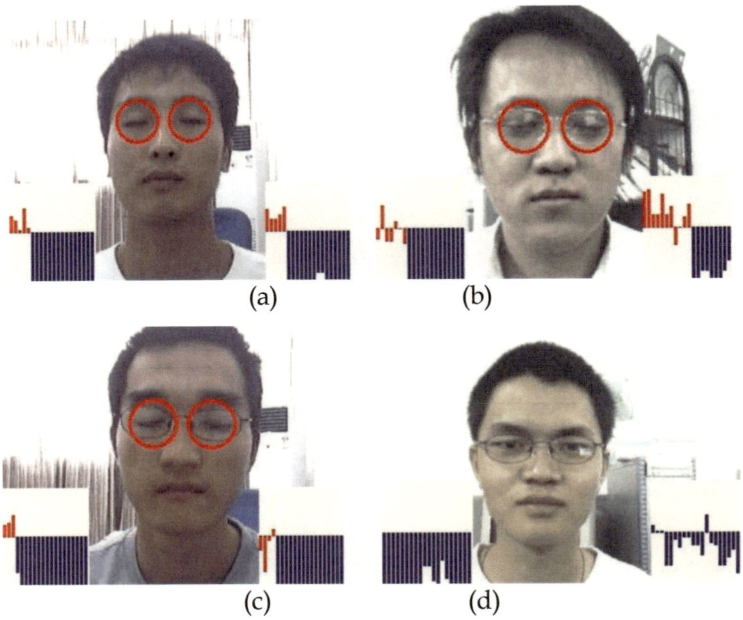

Fig. 7. Illustration of temporal variation of closity and blinking detection results. A bar graph shows the temporal variation of closity for each eye. In the bar graph, the vertical axis means eye closity, and the horizontal axis is for time steps. The closity of horizontal axis is equal to zero. The current time step is always located at the leftest of the bar graph. The time steps *in red* indicate these frames have been predicted as a part of a blink activity. The eye is circled in red if its blink is detected by our approach.

The computational cost of online test is very low, averagely 25 ms for one frame of 320-by-240 on P4 2.0GHz, 1GB RAM. Combining with the facial localization system, the whole system could achieve an online processing speed of nearly 20fps, which is reasonable for practical applications.

5.4 Comparison with cascaded Adaboost, HMM

The comparison experiments with cascaded Adaboost and HMM are also conducted. The labeled training samples for the cascaded Adaboost are similar to the training data for the *eye closity* computation, include 1,016 close eye samples with size of 24 × 24 and 1,200 background samples with the open eye (larger than 24 × 24). Finally, an optimal classifier consisting of eight stages and 73 features is obtained. For HMM, the eye closity of each frame is used as the observation data, same as our approach. The false alarm rates of all the three methods are controlled below 0.1% on the test data.

Fig. 8. shows the performance of cascaded Adaboost, HMM and our approach using three measures, one-eye detection rate, two-eye detection rate and clip detection rate. From the figure, it is obvious that our method (with *W*=3) always significantly outperforms cascaded Adaboost and HMM when different performance measures are used. Note that our approach exploits only 50 features while the cascaded Adaboost uses 73 features.

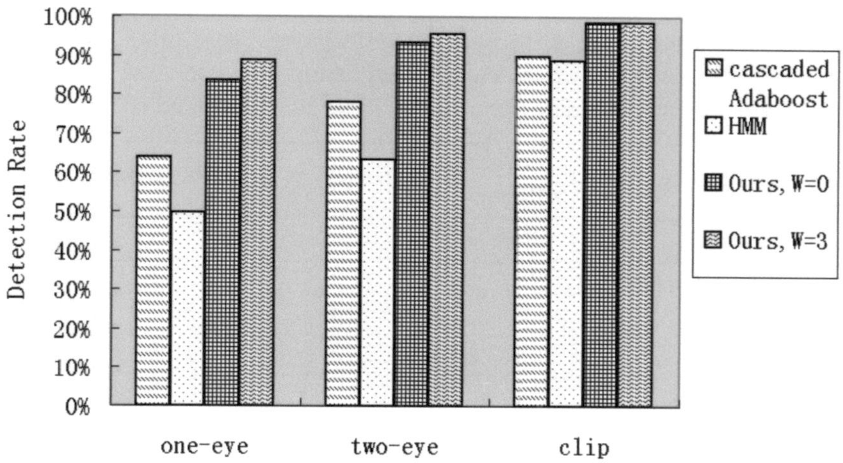

Fig. 8. Comparison with cascaded Adaboost and HMM using three performance measures.

Data	cas-Adaboost	HMM	W=0	W=1	W=2	W=3	W=4
One-eye detection rate							
Frontal w/o glasses	96.5%	69.6%	93.8%	93.8%	93.8%	93.8%	94.6%
Frontal w/ thin rim glasses	60.0%	43.9%	83.3%	84.1%	85.6%	85.6%	85.6%
Frontal w/ black frame glasses	46.9%	42.5%	80.6%	79.9%	82.1%	84.3%	84.3%
Upward w/o glasses	52.5%	45.5%	78.8%	79.6%	82.6%	84.9%	84.1%
Average	64.0%	49.6%	83.7%	84.1%	86.9%	**88.8%**	88.8%
Two-eye detection rate							
Frontal w/o glasses	98.2%	80.4%	98.2%	98.2%	98.2%	98.2%	98.2%
Frontal w/ thin rim glasses	80.0%	60.6%	93.9%	93.9%	93.9%	93.9%	93.9%
Frontal w/ black frame glasses	71.9%	55.2%	94.0%	92.5%	89.6%	91.0%	91.4%
Upward w/o glasses	62.3%	59.1%	87.9%	89.4%	92.4%	95.5%	95.5%
Average	8.1%	63.4%	93.3%	93.3%	93.7%	**95.7%**	95.7%

Table 3. Comparison with the cascaded Adaboost and HMM. (false alarm rate < 0.1%)

The detailed detection rates of the three methods are shown in Tab. 3, where the results of four conditions are listed respectively. Although the glasses-wearing and upward view have distinct effect on performance of all the three approaches, our approach still achieves good performance of the average one-eye rate of 88.8% and the average two-eye rate of 95.7% (W=3).

5.5 Photo imposter tests

The three methods trained above, cascaded Adaboost, HMM and our method, are also tested for their capability against photo spoofing using the photo-imposter video database. A total of five photo attacks are simulated in the database. Table 4 depicts the results. The number in the table shows how many clips failed during the attack test. It can be seen that the three methods have very similar performance, only 1-2 clips failed out of 100 clips.

Category of attacks	cas-Adaboost	HMM	W=0	W=1	W=2	W=3	W=4
Keep photo still	0	0	0	0	1	0	0
Move vert., hor., back and front	0	0	0	0	1	0	0
Rotate in depth	1	1	0	0	0	0	0
Rotate in plane	0	0	1	1	0	0	0
Bend inward and outward	0	1	0	0	0	1	0
Total	1	2	1	1	2	1	0

Table 4. Comparison of photo attack test using *photo-imposter database*, which includes 20 subjects, five categories of photo attacks for each, thus totally 100 video clips. The number shown in the table is the failed clip number.

6. Discussions

We investigate eyeblinks as a liveness detection clue against photo spoofing in face recognition. The advantages of eyeblink-based method are non-intrusion, no requirement of extra hardware. Undirected conditional graphical framework, which assumes dependencies among the observations and states, is employed to model eyeblink. A new-defined discriminative measure of eye states, called eye closity, can hasten inference as well as convey most effective discriminative information. Experiments demonstrate that the proposed approach achieves high performance by just using one generic webcamera under uncontrolled indoor lighting conditions, even glasses are worn. The comparison experiments show our approach outperforms cascaded Adaboost and HMM.

The proposed eyeblink detection approach, in nature, can be applied to a wide range of applications such as fatigue monitoring, psychological experiments, medical testing, and interactive gaming.

However, blinking-based liveness detection has some limitations. It would be affected by strong glasses reflection, which may cover eyes partially or totally. Blink clue also does not work for video spoofing. Anti-video spoofing is still a challenge to researchers.

7. Acknowledgements

This work was partly supported by NSFC grants (60503019, 60525202, 60533040), PCSIRT Program (IRT0652), 863 Program (2008AA01Z149), and a grant from OMRON corporation.

8. References

Antonelli, A.; Cappelli, R. & Maio, D. & Maltoni, D. (2006). Fake finger detection by skin distortion analysis. IEEE Trans. Information Forensics and Security, Vol.1, No.3, pp. 360-373, 2006

Bigun, J.; Fronthaler, H. & Kollreider, K. (2004). Assuring liveness in biometric identity authentication by real-time face tracking,IEEE Conference on Computational Intelligence for Homeland Security and Personal Safety (CIHSPS'04), pp.104-111, July 2004

Chetty, G. & Wagner, M. (2006). Multi-level Liveness Verification for Face-Voice Biometric Authentication, Biometric Symposium 2006, Baltimore, Maryland, Sep 2006

Choudhury, T.; Clarkson, B. & Jebara, T. & Pentland, A. (1999). Multimodal person recognition using unconstrained audio and video, International Conference on Audio- and Video-Based Biometric Person Authentication (AVBPA'99), pp.176-181, Washington DC, 1999

Cristian, S.; Kanaujia, A. & Li, Z. & Metaxas, D. (2005). Conditional Models for Contextual Human Motion Recognition, IEEE International Conference on Computer Vision (ICCV'05), pp.1808-1815, 2005

Freund, Y. & Schapire, R. (1995). A decision-theoretic generalization of on-line learning and an application to boosting, Second European Conference on Computational Learning Theory, pp.23-37, 1995

Frischholz, R.W. & Dieckmann, U. (2000). BioID: A Multimodal Biometric Identification System, IEEE Computer, Vol. 33, No. 2, pp.64-68, February 2000

Frischholz, R.W. & Werner, A. (2003). Avoiding Replay-Attacks in a Face Recognition System using Head-Pose Estimation, IEEE International Workshop on Analysis and Modeling of Faces and Gestures (AMFG'03), pp.234- 235, 2003

Gavrila,D. (1999). The Visual Analysis of Human Movement: A Survey, Computer Vision and Image Understanding, Vol.73, No.1, pp.82-98, 1999

Ji, Q.; Zhu, Z. & Lan, P. (2004). Real Time Nonintrusive Monitoring and Prediction of Driver Fatigue, IEEE Trans. Vehicular Technology, Vol.53, No.4, pp.1052-1068, 2004

Karson, C. (1983). Spontaneous eye-blink rates and dopaminergic systems. Brain, Vol.106, pp.643-653, 1983

Kollreider, K.; Fronthaler, H. & Bigun, J. (2005). Evaluating liveness by face images and the structure tensor, Fourth IEEE Workshop on Automatic Identification Advanced Technologies, pp.75-80, Oct. 2005

Lafferty, J.; McCallum, A. & Pereira, F. (2001) Conditional Random Fields: Probabilistic Models for Segmenting and Labeling Sequence Data. International Conference on Machine Learning (ICML'01), pp.282-289, 2001

Li, J.; Wang, Y. & Tan, T. & Jain, A. (2004). Live Face Detection Based on the Analysis of Fourier Spectra, Biometric Technology for Human Identification, Proceedings of SPIE, Vol. 5404, pp. 296-303, 2004

Li, S.Z. (2001) Markov Random Field Modeling in Image Analysis. Springer-Verlag, 2001

Moriyama, T.; Kanade, T. & Cohn,J.F. & Xiao, J. & Ambadar, Z. & Gao, J. & Imamura, H. (2002). Automatic Recognition of Eye Blinking in Spontaneously Occurring Behavior. IEEE International Conference on Pattern Recognition (ICPR'02), 2002

Parthasaradhi, S.; Derakhshani R. & Hornak, L. & Schuckers, S. (2005). Time-series detection of perspiration as a liveness test in fingerprint devices. IEEE Trans. Systems, Man and Cybernetics, Part C, Vol.35, No.3, pp. 335-343, Aug. 2005

Rabiner, L.R. (1989). A tutorial on hidden markov models and selected applications in speech recognition. Proceedings of the IEEE, Vol.77, No.2, pp.257-286, 1989

Ross, A.; Nandakumar, K. & Jain, A.K. (2006). Handbook of Multibiometrics, Springer Verlag.

Schuckers, S. (2002). Spoofing and Anti-Spoofing Measures. Information Security Technical Report, Vol.7, No.4, 56-62, Elsevier

Sha, F. & Pereira, F. (2003). Shallow Parsing with Conditional Random Fields. Proc. Human Language Technology, NAACL, pp. 213-220, 2003

Socolinsky, D.A.; Selinger, A. & Neuheisel, J. D. (2003). Face Recognition with Visible and Thermal Infrared Imagery, Computer Vision and Image Understanding, vol.91, no. 1-2, pp. 72-114, 2003

Tian, Y.; Kanade, K. & Cohn, J.F. (2001). Recognizing Action Units for Facial Expression Analysis. IEEE Trans. Pattern Analysis and Machine Intelligence, Vol.23, No.2, pp.97-115, 2001

Tsubota, K. (1998). Tear Dynamics and Dry Eye. Progress in Retinal and Eye Research, Vol.17, No.4, pp565-596, 1998

Viola, P. & Jones, M.J. (2001). Rapid Object Detection using a Boosted Cascade of Simple Features. IEEE Computer Society Conference on Computer Vision and Pattern Recognition (CVPR'01), pp.511-518, 2001.

Zhao, W.; Chellappa, R. & Phillips, J. & Rosenfeld, A. (2003). Face Recognition: A Literature Survey. ACM Computing Surveys, pp.399-458, 2003

10

2D-3D Mixed Face Recognition Schemes

Antonio Rama Calvo[1], Francesc Tarrés Ruiz[1],
Jürgen Rurainsky[2] and Peter Eisert[2]
[1]Department of Signal Theory and Communications
Universitat Politècnica de Catalunya (UPC)
[2]Image Processing Department
Fraunhofer Institute for Telecommunications Heinrich-Hertz-Institut (HHI)
[1]Spain
[2]Germany

1.Introduction

Automatic recognition of people is a challenging problem which has received much attention during the recent years [FRHomepage, AFGR, AVBPA] due to its potential applications in different fields such as law enforcement, security applications or video indexing. Face recognition is a very challenging problem and up to date, there is no technique that provides a robust solution to all situations and different applications that face recognition may encounter.

Most of the face recognition techniques have evolved in order to overcome two main challenges: illumination and pose variation [FRVT02, FRGC05, Zhao03, Zhao06]. Either of these problems can cause serious performance degradation in a face recognition system. Illumination can change the appearance of an object drastically, and in the most of the cases these differences induced by illumination are larger than differences between individuals, what makes difficult the recognition task. The same statement is valid for pose variation. Usually, the training data used by face recognition systems are frontal view face images of individuals [Brunelli93, Nefian96, Turk91, Pentland94, Lorente99, Belhumeur97, Bartlett02, Moghaddam02, Delac05, Kim02, Schölkopf98, Schölkopf99, Yang02, Yang04, , Wang06, Yu06, Heo06]. Frontal view images contain more specific information of a face than profile or other pose angle images. The problem appears when the system has to recognize a rotated face using this frontal view training data. Furthermore, the appearance of a face can also change drastically if the illumination conditions vary [Moses94]. Therefore, pose and illumination (among other challenges) are the main causes for the degradation of 2D face recognition algorithms.

Some of the new face recognition strategies tend to overcome both challenges from a 3D perspective. The 3D data points corresponding to the surface of the face may be acquired using different alternatives: a multi camera system (stereoscopy) [Onofrio04, Pedersini99, structured light [Scharstein02, 3DRMA], range cameras or 3D laser and scanner devices [Blanz03, Bowyer04, Bronstein05]. The main advantage of using 3D data is that depth information does not depend on pose and illumination and therefore the representation of the object do not change with these parameters, making the whole system more robust.

However, the main drawback of the majority of 3D face recognition approaches is that they need all the elements of the system to be well calibrated and synchronized to acquire accurate 3D data (texture and depth maps). Moreover, most of them also require the cooperation or collaboration of the subject making them not useful for uncontrolled or semi-controlled scenarios where the only input of the algorithms will be a 2D intensity image acquired from a single camera.
All these requirements can be available during the training stage of many applications. When enrolling a new person in the database, it could be performed off-line, with the help o human interaction and with the cooperation of the subject to be enrolled. On the contrary, the previous conditions are not always available during the test stage. The recognition will be in most of the cases in a semi-controlled or uncontrolled scenario, where the only input to the system will probably consist of a 2D intensity image acquired from a single camera. One possible example of these application scenarios are video surveillance or control access. This leads to a new paradigm using some mixed 2D-3D face recognition systems where 3D data is used in the training but either 2D or 3D information can be used in the recognition depending on the scenario. Following this concept, where only part of the information (partial concept) is used in the recognition, a novel method is presented in this work. This has been called Partial Principal Component Analysis (P^2CA) since it fuses the partial concept with the fundamentals of the well known PCA algorithms. Both strategies have been proven to be very robust in pose variation scenarios showing that the 3D training process retains all the spatial information of the face while the 2D picture effectively recovers the face information from the available data. Simulation results have shown recognition rates above 91% when using face images with a view range of 180° around the human face in the training stage and 2D face pictures taken from different angles (from -90° to +90°) in the recognition stage.

2.State-of-the art face recognition methods

2.1 2D face recognition

The problem of still face recognition can be simply stated as: given a set of face images labelled with the person identity (learning set) and an unlabeled set of face images from the same group of people (the test set), identify each person in the test images. This problem statement is also known as person identification.
Different schemes and strategies have been proposed for the problem of face recognition. The categorization of these approaches is not easy and different criteria are usually used in literature. One popular classification scheme is the attending of the holistic/non-holistic philosophy of the methods[Zhao03, Zhao06]. Holistic methods try to recognize the face in the image using overall information, that is, the face as a whole. These methods are commonly referred as appearance-based approaches. On the contrary, non-holistic approaches are based on identifying particular features of the face such as the nose, the mouth, the eyes, etc. and their relations to make the final decision. Some recent methods try to exploit the advantages of both approaches at the same time and therefore they are classified as hybrid. The number of 2D face recognition algorithms is immense and they enclose a huge variety approaches so it would be impossible to make an exhaustive enumeration of all publications related with 2D face recognition.
Kanade's face identification system [Kanade73] was the first automated system to use a top-down control strategy directed by a generic model of expected feature characteristics of the

face. Later Brunelli et al. and Nefian have used correlation-based approaches [Brunelli93, Nefian96]. In this kind of methods, the image is represented as a bidimensional array of intensity values (I_T) and is compared with a single template (T) that represents the whole face. Nevertheless, one important date for face recognition was beginning of the 90's when Turk and Pendland implemented the Eigenfaces approach [Turk91, Pentland94], which is surely the most popular face recognition method. This was the beginning of the appearance-based methods for face recognition. After Eigenfaces, different statistical approaches have appeared that improve the results of Eigenfaces under certain constraints. For example, the most representative ones are Fisherfaces which is more robust towards illumination conditions [Belhumeur97], Kernel PCA [Kim02] and Independent Component Analysis [Bartlett98] which exploit higher-order statistics, or a recent two dimensional extension of the PCA [Yang04].

Another strategy that has been used to solve face recognition is neural networks [Kohonen88, Fadzil94, Lawrence97, Lin97, Haddadnia02 Palanivel03]. Neural networks approaches promise good performance but these have to be further improved and investigated mainly because of the difficulty of the training the system. One method that intends to solve the conceptual problems of conventional artificial neural networks,, and should be also mentioned, is Elastic Graph Matching [Lades93, Wiskott99]. Face recognition using Elastic Graph Matching (EGM) [Lades93] is based on the neural information processing concept, the Dynamic Link Architecture (DLA). In EGM, a face is represented by a set of feature vectors (Gabor responses) positioned on nodes of a rectangular grid placed on the image. Comparing two faces corresponds to matching and adapting a grid taken from one image to the features of the other image. Rotation in depth is compensated for by elastic deformation of the graphs.

Although all methods report encouraging and excellent results, the real fact is that approaches based on statistical appearance-based methods like Principal Component Analysis (PCA) and Elastic Graph Matching [Lades93, Wiskott99] are the algorithms which present the best face recognition rates [Zhang97]. For a more detailed survey about all the different methods, the author is addressed to the work of Zhao et al. [Zhao03 Zhao06].

2.2 3D face recognition approaches

The 3D structure of the human face intuitively provides high discriminatory information and is less sensitive to variations in environmental conditions like illumination or view-point. For this reason, recent techniques have been proposed employing range images, i.e. 3D data in order to overcome the main challenges of 2D face recognition: Pose and illumination. Next section a review of the most relevant approaches in 3D face recognition will be presented. In fact, the section has been divided into three main groups: Curvature-based algorithms, multimodal approaches and finally model-based methods.

2.2.1 Early work in 3D face recognition: curvature-based approaches

3D Face Recognition is a relatively recent trend although early work was done over a decade ago [Cartoux89, Lee90, Gordon91]. The first contributions to the field [Cartoux89, Lee90, Gordon91] were mainly based on the extraction of a curvature representation of the face from ranging images. Then a set of features were obtained or created from these curvature face representations and used to match the different faces. For example, in [Cartoux89], a profile curve is computed from the intersection of the face range image and the profile plane. This profile plane is defined as the one that segments the face in two quasi-symmetric parts. In order to find it, Cartoux et al. propose an iterative method where the correspondence between points of the convex-concave representation of the face is analyzed. Very high recognition rates were reported (100%) for experiments carried out on a very small database of 18 face images which correspond to 5 persons. Another curvature-based method is the one presented in [Lee90]. An Extended Gaussian Image (EGI) is created from the parameterization to the Gaussian Sphere of the curvature maps (in fact, only the points which represent the convex regions of the face). To establish the correspondence between two different EGIs a region a graph-matching approach is applied. This graph-matching algorithm incorporates relational constraints that account for the relative spatial locations of the convex regions in the domain of the range image. Similar to the previous approach Gordon et al. [Gordon91] acquire range data from a laser scanner and parameterize it into a cylindrical coordinate representation. Afterwards, the *principal curvature* maps for this range data are computed and used for the segmentation of the face range image (four different regions: concave, convex and two types of saddle). Two different ways of matching the faces were proposed: The first one is a depth template-based approach, and the second one is a comparison between feature vectors composed of some fiducial points and their relationships. A recognition rate of 100% is reported for a database of 26 individuals and a probe set of 8 faces under 3 different views. Tanaka et al. [Tanaka98] extended the work of Lee [Lee90] and proposed a spherical correlation of the EGIs. Experiments are reported with a 100% recognition rate utilizing a set of 37 range images from the National Research Council of Canada database.

A more recent curvature-based approach [Feng06] extracts two sets of facial curves from a face range image. The authors present a novel facial feature representation, the affine integral invariant that mitigates the effect of pose on the facial curves. The authors claim that a human face can be characterized by 12 affine invariant curves, which are located near the face center profile, center and corner of eye regions. Each curve is projected onto a 8 dimensional space to construct a feature vector with a resulting performance by a 3-NN classifier of 92.57% recognition accuracy for a database of 175 face images.

The main drawback of these methods is that there are only few fiducial points (features) that can be reliably extracted from a 2D face image and would be insensitive to illumination, pose, and expression variations.

A recent and successful method which cannot be classified in this curvature-based category but that intends to perform recognition from geodesic distances between points of the face is the one presented by the Bronstein twins [Bronstein05]. The authors focused their research on a very robust system towards facial expression variations. Under the assumption that the facial skin does not stretch significantly, facial expressions can be modeled as *isometries*, i.e. a transformation that bends the surface such that the object (face) does not "feel" it. In other words, the main idea is to find a transformation which maps the geodesic distances between a certain numbers of sample points on the facial surface to Euclidean distances. This transformation is called the *canonical form*. The authors reported 100% recognition rate for a database of 30 subjects with big variations in facial expression even though two of the 30 subjects are the Bronstein twins.

A similar approach based also in geodesic distances detects surface creases, ravines and ridges [Antini06] which are less sensitive then the fiducial points needed for extracting the curves of previous approaches [Cartoux89, Lee90, Gordon91, Tanaka98, Feng06]. These surface variations provide important information about the shape of 3D objects. Intuitively, these salient traits can be defined as those curves on a surface where the surface bends sharply. Then, a theory for modeling spatial relationships between curves in the 3D domain has been developed. Finally, a graph matching solution is proposed for the comparison between the spatial relationships computed on curves extracted from a template model and those of reference models. The results presented are worse than the ones shown by the Bronstein twins [Bronstein05] but it should be also mentioned that the database used for the experiments is composed of the double of subjects (61 persons).

2.2.2 2D+3D multimodal approaches

A second type of 3D Face Recognition approaches could be the so called multimodal algorithms. Basically, the general idea is to apply conventional statistical *appearance-based* methods (like PCA, LDA, ICA...) not only to texture but also to depth images [Tsalakanidou04, Chang05, Samani06]. It could be foreseen as two different face recognition experts (one for each modality) whose opinions are combined in a final stage in order to claim the identity of the person. The advantage of this category of 3D FR methods is that it adds depth information to conventional approaches without increasing too much the computational cost. These multimodal methods report generally better recognition rates for texture than for depth information when performing the recognition separately. Nevertheless, in all the cases an improvement of the recognition is reported when using both modalities together.

Tsalakanidou et al. [Tsalakanidou04] report on multimodal face recognition using color and 3D images. The input data of the system is a color frontal view face image with its corresponding frontal depth map (range image). The recognition algorithm is based on the application of PCA to the different color planes and to the range image individually. Experiments are carried out on a subset of 40 persons from the XM2VTS database. Again the best reported results show a 99% of accuracy for the multimodal algorithm which clearly outperforms the recognition rates of each modality (range and color) alone.

A similar, but most extended, 2D+3D proposal is presented by Chang et al [Chang05]. The study involves 198 persons in the gallery and either 198 or 670 time-lapse probe images. PCA-based methods are used separately for each modality and match scores in the separate face spaces are combined for multimodal recognition. The authors conclude that 2D and 3D have similar recognition performance when considered individually and that a simple weighting scheme combination of both modalities outperforms either 2D or 3D alone. Chang et al compare also the multimodal scheme with a 2D multi-image proposal, showing that again is better to use both modalities together rather than using multiple images of the same modality.

A more recent approach [Samani06] fuses both modalities before applying the statistical method. A range and an intensity image are obtained using two digital cameras in a stereo setup and both images are rearranged in a higher dimensional vector representation called *composite image*. The authors reported better results when using this combined depth-texture representation and then applying PCA, rather than applying PCA to each modality alone.

2.2.3 3D model-based approaches

One main drawback of all the methods reviewed so far (curvature-based and multimodal approaches) is that the input of the recognition stage of these approaches should maintain the same data format as the training images, i.e. if *frontal views* have been used during the training stage then a depth and/or intensity *frontal image* is required in the recognition stage [Chang05]. Opposite to those two previous 3D face recognition categories, 3D model based approaches train the system with 3D data but then they perform the recognition using only one single intensity image. This last category can be enclosed in a 2D-3D mixed face recognition framework.

3D model-based approaches use complete morphable 3D models of a face to perform the recognition [Beymer95, Georghiades01, Ansari03, Blanz03, Lu05, Lu06]. These approaches build a 3D model (3D mesh) using some 3D scans by means of special 3D devices, structured light, or multiple camera in the training stage. Then the input data for the recognition stage is one simple 2D intensity image which can correspond to any pose of a face. The model-based approach try to fit this image to the 3D face model (a generic one of one for each person on the database) and then, it tries to recognize the person. In fact, fitting the 3D morphable model to test images can be used in two ways for recognition across different viewing conditions as stated in [Blanz03]:

Paradigm 1. After fitting the model, recognition can be based on model coefficients, which represent intrinsic shape and texture of faces, and are independent of imaging conditions. For identification, all gallery images are analyzed by the fitting algorithm, and the shape and texture coefficients are stored. Given a test image, the fitting algorithm computes the again the coefficients which are compared with all gallery data in order to find the nearest neighbor [Ansari03, Blanz03]

Paradigm 2. Three-dimension face reconstruction can be employed to generate synthetic views from gallery or probe images [Beymer95, Georghiades01, Lu05, Lu06]. The synthetic views are then transferred to a second viewpoint-dependent recognition algorithm, i.e. using some of the 2D Face Recognition methods presented in Section 2.1.

The most representative model-based approach using Paradigm 1 is the outstanding method presented by Blanz and Vetter [Blanz03]. The authors use an analysis-by-synthesis technique. First, a generic 3D morphable model is learned and created from a set of textured 3D scans (depth and texture maps) of heads. In fact, the morphable model is based on a vector space representation of faces. The authors, align 200 textured 3D scans of different persons using an optical-flow algorithm to a reference scan. Then using the 200 aligned textured 3D scans they apply PCA to shape and texture separately in order to construct the 3D morphable model. The fitting process of the model to an image optimizes shape coefficients, texture coefficients and 22 additional rendering parameters (camera parameters, illumination, viewpoint, etc), i.e. given an input image the fitting procedure minimizes a cost function that takes into account all these parameters. The goal of this fitting procedure can be defined as an analysis-by-synthesis loop, that tries to find the model and scene parameters such that the model, rendered by computer graphics algorithms, produces an image as similar as possible to the input image. The authors presented recognition rates on large databases (FERET and CMU-PIE) above the 95% and stated that their algorithm has been evaluated with 10 more face recognition systems in the Face Recognition Vendor Test 2002 [FRVT02] obtaining better results for non-frontal face images for 9 out of 10 systems.

On the other hand, one of the most recent examples of the second paradigm is the work presented by Lu et al. [Lu05, Lu06]. For each subject, a 3D face model is constructed by integrating several 2.5D face scans which are captured from different views. The authors considered a 2.5D surface as a simplified version of the 3D (x, y, z) surface representation that contains at most one depth value (z direction) for every point in the (x, y) plane. Each

3D model has also its associated texture map. The recognition stage consists of two components: Namely, surface matching and appearance-based matching. The surface matching component is based on a modified Iterative Closest Point (ICP) algorithm. This surface matching returns a small candidate list from the whole gallery that is used for appearance matching. This combination of surface and appearance matching reduces the complexity of the system. Three-dimensional models in the gallery are used to synthesize new appearance samples with pose and illumination variations and the synthesized face images are used in discriminant subspace analysis. Experimental results are given for matching a database of 200 3D face models with 598 2.5D independent test scans acquired under different pose and some lighting and expression changes.
The main drawback of 3D model-based approaches, independent of what paradigm do they use, is the high computational burden of the fitting procedure of the intensity image to the 3D generic model in an accurate manner that do not degrade recognition results. Thus, section 0 will introduce a novel 2D-3D face recognition framework which can be foreseen as a gap between pure 2D and pure 3D face recognition methods.
For a more detailed survey about all the different 3D Face Recognition methods, the author is addressed to the work. [Bowyer04, Chang05, Zhao03, Zhao06].

3. Partial principal component analysis: a 2D-3D mixed face recognition scheme

3.1.1 Fundamentals of the 2DPCA method

Like in the majority of face recognition methods, in 2DPCA [Yang04] the dimensionality of the face images is reduced through the projection into a set of M optimal vectors which composed the so called *feature space* or *face space*. The vectors representing the i^{h} individual are obtained as:

$$\mathbf{r}_k^{\,i} = (\mathbf{A}_i - \mu) \cdot \mathbf{v}_k \qquad k = 1,..,M \tag{1}$$

,where A_i is the mxn texture image representing individual i , μ is the *mean* image of the training set, and v_k are the M optimal projection vectors that maximize the energy of the projected vectors r_k averaged through the whole database. These vectors could be interpreted as unique signatures that identify each person. The projection described in Equation (1) is depicted in Fig. 1. Note that each vector r_k^i has m components where m is the dimension of the matrix A_i in the vertical direction (height of the face image).

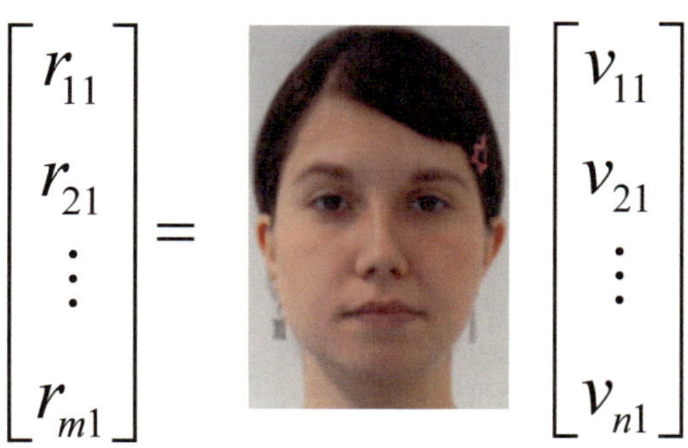

Fig. 1. Representation of a face in 2DPCA using only one vector (v_1)

The set of ortonormal vectors which maximize the projection of Equation (1) may be obtained as the solution to the following optimization problem: Find v_k for k=1,..,M such that $\xi = \sum_k \sum_l (r_k^l)^T \cdot r_k^l$ is maximum, where r_k^l is defined as the projection of image l through the vector v_k and l accounts for the number of images in the training set. The function to be maximized may be expressed as:

$$\xi = \sum_k \sum_l ((A_l - \mu) \cdot v_k)^T \cdot ((A_l - \mu) \cdot v_k) = \sum_k v_k^T \left(\sum_l (A_l - \mu)^T \cdot (A_l - \mu) \right) \cdot v_k \quad (2)$$

,which states that the optimum projection vectors may be obtained as the eigenvectors associated to the M largest eigenvalues of the nxn non-negative definite Covariance matrix C_s

$$C_s = \sum_l (A_l - \mu)^T \cdot (A_l - \mu) \quad (3)$$

Therefore, a total of M feature vectors are available, with n (width of the face image) components each as depicted in Fig. 1. The image has been compressed to a total of mxM scalars with M always being smaller than n.
After computing the *face space*, at least one signature ($\mathbf{r}_k^i$) will be extracted for each person of the database by projecting one (or more) representative image (usually one frontal face image with a neutral expression) in the face space. During the recognition stage, when a new image is input to the system, the mean image is subtracted ant the result is projected into the face space resulting in a new signature r_k with k=1,…,M. The best match is found for the identity i that minimizes the Euclidean distance:

$$\min_i \left\{ \xi_k = \sum_{k=1}^{M} \sum_{l=1}^{n} \left(r_k(l) - r_k^{\,i}(l) \right)^2 \right\} \qquad i = 1,..,L \quad (4)$$

where L represents the number of individuals in the database.
The procedure is quite different from conventional PCA, since in 2DPCA the whole image is represented as a 2D matrix instead of a 1D vector like in PCA. Certainly, in PCA a scalar number is obtained when the vector image is projected to one eigenvector, whereas in 2DPCA, an m-dimensional vector ($\mathbf{r}_k$) is obtained, when the image (in matrix form) is projected to an eigenvector. It can seem that the 2DPCA approach demands more computational cost because it uses vectors instead of numbers to represent the projections. However, the number of eigenvectors $\{\mathbf{v}_k\}$ needed in 2DPCA for an accurate representation is much lower than in PCA [Yang04].
The authors report extensive simulations of these algorithms in different data sets that include images of individuals under different expressions and taken in different dates (AR database) and compare the performance of the method with Fisherfaces, ICA, Eigenfaces and Kernel Eigenfaces. In most simulations 2DPCA has shown better or at least equal performance than the other alternatives. Probably, the main reason for the improvement is that the covariance matrix is of lower order and therefore can be better estimated using a reduced number of samples. Another inherent advantage of the procedure is the computational time for the feature extraction and the computation of eigenvectors is significantly below the PCA.

3.2 A novel mixed 2D-3D FR scheme: Partial Principal Component Analysis (P^2CA)

As already mentioned, the main objective is to implement a face recognition framework which takes advantage of 3D data in the training stage but then use either 2D or 3D in the recognition stage.

The most used definition of the term "3D face data" could be the data that represents the three-dimensional shape of a face from all the possible view angles with a texture map overlaid on this 3D depth map [Zhao06]. In this work, however, the main objective was to show the validity of the method; thus, we will refer to the multi-view texture maps (180° cylindrical texture representations) as the "3D data". Nevertheless, all the fundamentals and experiments explained below and in the following sections are also valid when using "complete 3D data" (depth and texture maps) as shown in [Onofrio06].

The 3D face information required in the training stage could be obtained by means of 3D laser scanners, by structured light reconstruction systems, by multicamera camera sets using stereoscopic techniques, or by simple morphing techniques. A simple approach based on semiautomatic morphing of 2D pictures taken from different view has been followed in this work for its simplicity since our main objective, as already stated, is a mixed 2D-3D face recognition framework and not an accurate 3D face reconstruction system.

Let us present the main idea of P^2CA which is based on the fundamentals of 2DPCA [Yang04] explained in the previous section. Now, let us take the mxn 180° texture map of the subject i and rotate it 90° as shown in Fig 2. Now we can reformulate Equation (1) by changing A_i with A_i^T so that the transposed texture image is represented by the M vectors r_k^i. Now, unlike in the previous section, each vector r_k^i has m components where m is the dimension of the matrix A_i in the horizontal direction (width of the original texture map).

$$\mathbf{r}_k^{\,i} = \mathbf{A}_i^T \cdot \mathbf{v}_k \quad k = 1,..,M \tag{5}$$

Note also, that the mean is not subtracted when computing the signature of individual i. This fact does not represent a problem and will lead only to the necessity of using one more eigenvector as can be mathematically demonstrated.

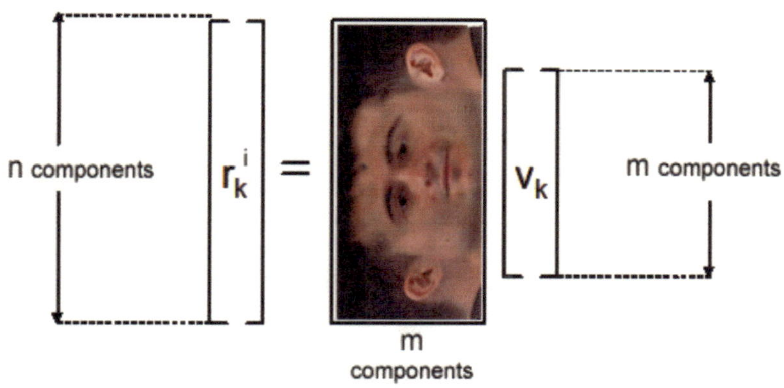

Fig. 2. Description of a cylindrical coordinate image by means of projection vectors (training stage)

During the recognition procedure if complete 3D data of the individual is available, the recognition stage is straightforward. In fact, it is only necessary to convert the 3D data to cylindrical coordinates (texture maps) and compute the resulting M vectors r_k. The best

match is found for the identity i that minimizes the Euclidean distance formulated in Equation (4).
The main advantage of this representation scheme is that it can also be used when only partial information of the individual is available. Consider, for instance, the situation depicted in Fig 3, where it is supposed that only one 2D picture of the individual is available. Each of the 2D pictures of the subject (frontal and lateral) show a high correlation with the corresponding area of the cylindrical representation of the 3D image. The procedure for extracting the information of a 2D picture is illustrated in Fig 4.

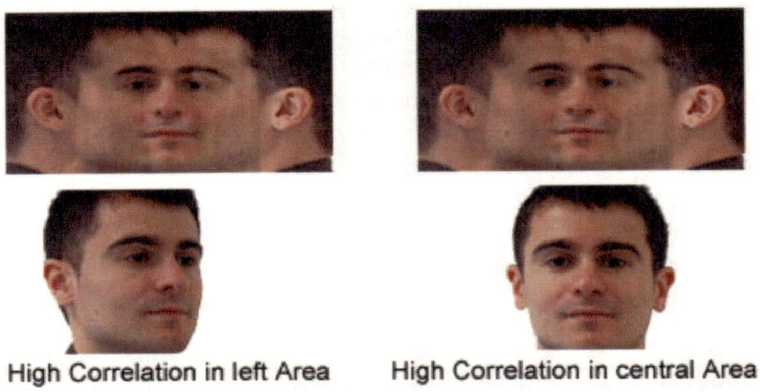

Fig. 3. Comparing 2D pictures with a cylindrical representation of the subject

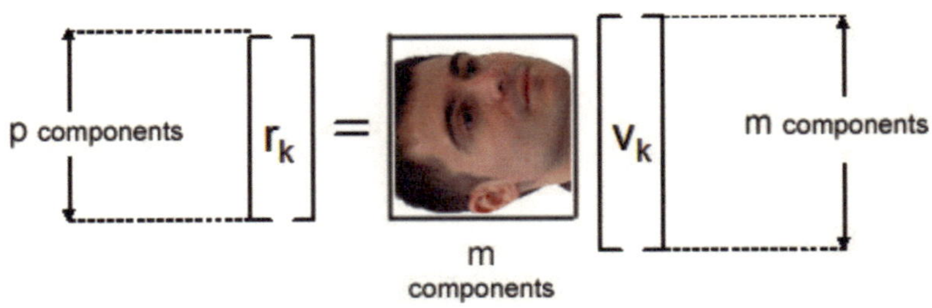

Fig. 4. Projection of a partial 2D picture through the vector set v_k (recognition stage)

In this case, mxp 2D picture will be represented by M vectors r_k with a reduced dimension p. However, it is expected that these p components will be highly correlated with a section of p components in the complete vectors r_k^i computed during the training stage. Therefore, the measure proposed below can be used to identify the partial available information (p components) through the vectors r_k^i:

$$\min_{(i,j)}\left\{\sum_{k=1}^{M}\sum_{l=1}^{p}\left(r_k(l)-r_k^{\,i}(l+j)\right)^2\right\} \qquad (6)$$
$$i=1,..,L; \quad j=0,..,n-p$$

The most outstanding point of P²CA is that the image projected in the n-dimensional space does not need to have dimension mxn (3D data) during the recognition stage so that only partial information (2D data) can be used as illustrated in Fig 4. It is possible to use a reduced *mxp* ($p<n$) image which is projected to a smaller subspace. Fig 5 depicts the general block diagram of the P²CA technique explained above and its flexibility. The whole system is trained with the 3D data (texture maps in the bottom part of Fig 5) and the feature vectors r_k^i are computed for each individual of the database (a total of L individuals). The recognition procedure is illustrated in the top part of Fig 5. If the scenario permits to acquire 3D face images, these are projected to the *face space* obtained *m*-dimensional signatures which can be directly compared with the ones stored in the database using Euclidean Distance. On the other hand, if only one normal 2D face image is available, then the resulting *p*-dimensional signatures are compared with the database ones applying some correlation methods like the criteria defined in Equation (6). For more details about Partial Principal Component Analysis the reader is addressed to the work of Rama et al. [Rama05a, Rama05b, Rama06].

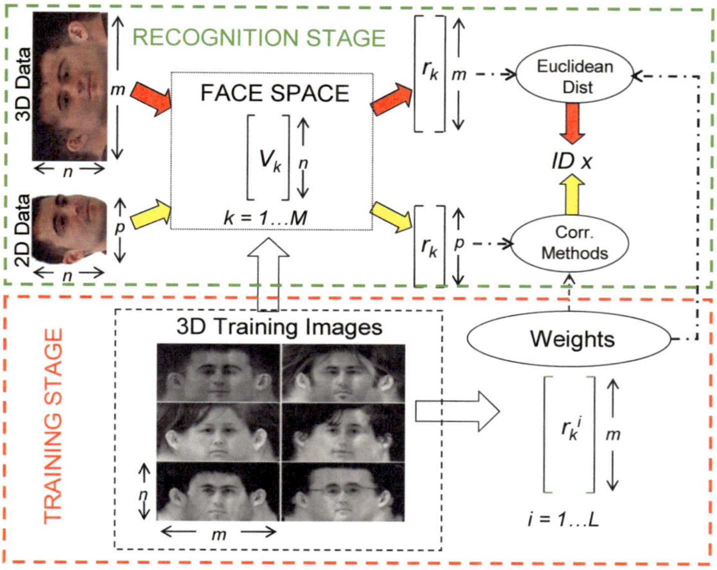

Fig. 5. General Block Diagram of P²CA Approach

4. Aligned texture map creation

4.1 Introduction

Multi view image analysis and synthesis is used for a variety of computer vision and graphics approaches. Combining or stitching of several captured views to one complete virtual representation can be achieved by interpolation between the real captured views. In the articles of Akimoto et al. and Soh et al. [Akimoto93, Soh95] the creation of virtual views for a face is described by using a cylindrical projection onto the real or almost real object surface. A multi resolution edge based approach to align real views are described in the article of Lee et al. [Lee00]. Cylindrical approximations of a human face is used for head motion tracking, like in the publication of Brown, Cascia et al. and in the article of Xiao et al. [Brown01, Cascia98, Xiao93]. Spherical approximation of the head, which is more reliable for head motions, like in the used video sequences is described in the conference publication of

Lui and Chen [Liu03]. A complete mosaicking scheme for the creation of a virtual face image used for face recognition purposes is described in the journal publication of Singh and Ross [Singh07]. A hierarchical registration model is used to align the single views before the stitching and blending via multiresolution splines tales place. Marker points placed on the human face are used for panoramic face mosaicking is described in the journal publication of Yang et al. [Yang]. The markers are removed from the finale virtual view representation.
We present an approach, which aims to use just a cylinder not only for the frontal part but for a complete ±90° projection of a face. There image analysis is compensated by the calibration data of the capture setup. The main advantage is the simple approximation of a human head in contrast to a detailed surface representation used for similar results.
For further processing of such face projections additional steps have to be applied, which depend on the purpose of usage. In the case of face recognition input images are aligned before analyzing them, e.g. the eye centers are very often used for this purpose and other face features are usually not received attention. In the conference publication of Kouzani and Sammut [Kouzani99] the advantage of a local face feature analysis is demonstrated. The importance of local aligned face features for recognition is described in the conference publication of Tsapatsoulis et al. [Tsapatsoulis98], where the local alignment is described as resizing. We present an approach for the local alignment of not only the eye center but for any face feature, e.g. eye corners, nose, mouth and chin. This method is based on a feature wire grid model rendered on the graphics card. The result is a face image with face features aligned to a reference, so that a component analysis does not reflects the differences of one face feature but the properties. The novelty of the face feature alignment is the handling of the face feature area by using affine transformation.

4.2 Aligned texture maps

The goal is it to create a cylindrical projection of a face, like the one shown in Fig 6 with a desired view angle range of ±90° using multi view images. Such image can be used as texture map for 3D models or pose invariant face recognition tasks. The creation of texture maps from one or multiple views are described in many publications. The common idea is to project the captured images onto a cylinder using a more or less detailed surface representation or to find registration data, which related one captured view to another. Blending rules at the overlapping areas define the quality of the synthetic image. Our approach is based on a simple approximation of a human head in contrast to a detailed surface representation used for similar results. Therefore a detailed reconstruction of the face is not required. Registration techniques require high frequency parts, which maybe not available for the complete face or hair. Marker points are not very likely, because of the more complicated capture and removal process. On the other hand, ghost edges are very likely, if the cylindrical approximation is not placed at the right position or the system calibration is not adequate.
In addition selected face features are aligned through several created texture maps. The importance of local aligned face features for recognition is described in the conference publication of Tsapatsoulis et al. [Tsapatsoulis98], where the local alignment is described as resizing. For the alignment of face features we propose a method consisting of a global alignment using 2D affine transformation and a local feature alignment based on textured wire grid deformation using graphics card rendering. The local alignment is also using an affine transformation, but this time of the area around the desired face feature. Feature

points are associated to one feature and connected to the used wire grid model, comparable to a 3D alignment. Using such transformed images for a PCA will reflect more the properties of face features and not the differences.

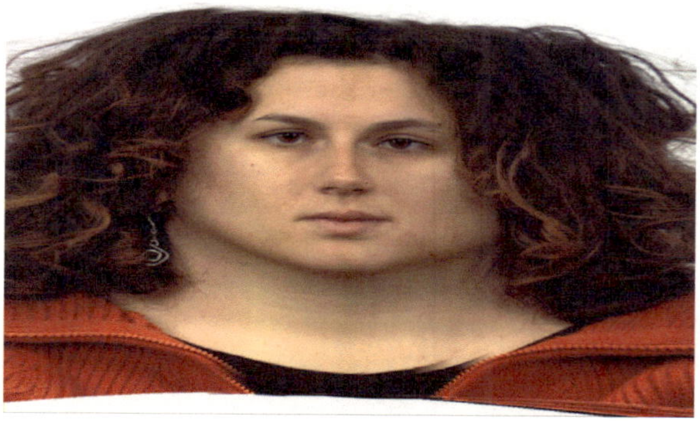

Fig. 6. Texture map created from an image set of nine images captured with

4.2.1 Stitching multiview images

The following paragraphs will explain the creation of cylindrical face projections from several different views. Our goal is to use a very simple approximation instead of a detailed object surface. We have used a cylinder as approximation of a human head. The combination of several views captured with a system as shown in Fig 7 to a synthetic image as shown in Fig 6 requires information about the surface of the captured object. Such

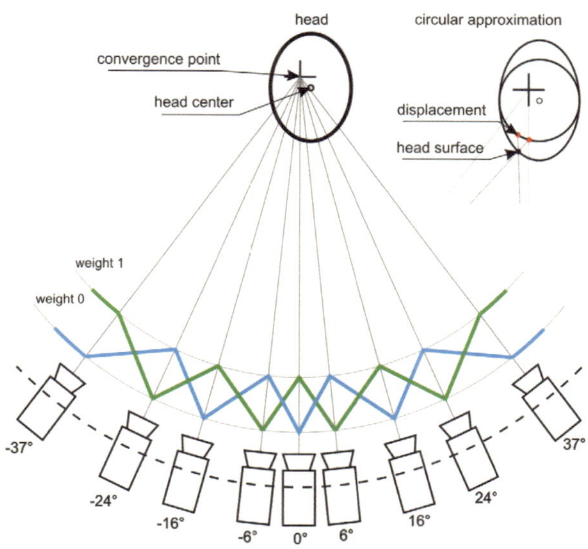

Fig. 7. Capture system for training data acquisition consists of nine cameras at different horizontal angles. (left) face surface point displacement due to the circular approximation. (middle) Blending rule for the combining of the input images

information can range from an exact 3D model over some points in 3D space to an approximation of the basic shape. If such surface information are not available, they can be extracted from the captured view images with a wide variety of methods. Triangulation only requires corresponding point pairs in two views. Surface point reconstruction for a couple of corresponding point pairs allows the definition of an approximation of the desired surface up to a detailed representation. If the captured images show a unique silhouette, a method known as shape from silhouette can be used to reconstruct a volume model. This method is limited to convex surfaces. Other methods use registration information, created from gradients or marker positions.
A cylindrical approximation is adapted to the captured head and positioned in the middle of the assumed head axis. Head dimensions are defined in the book of Farkas [Farkas95] with average values of 151mm for the width of a head and 197mm for the depth of a head. Similar numbers can also be found in the report of Young [Young93]. Considering a head with hair and two ears, a circular assumption is one possible approximation to the ellipse shaped head therefore suitable for the given problem. Besides the head size (radius for the cylinder), which can be taken from the mentioned statistical publications, there are other remaining unknown positions. Both offsets (x- and z-axis) have to be estimated.
Therefore the following equation describes the problem.

$$r^2 = (x - o_x)^2 + (z - o_z)^2$$

This non-linear equation can be solved by Levenberg-Marquadt approach as described in the book of Scales [Scales85]. We have used the 3D reconstructed locations of both eye pupil centers as well as left and right eye corner of both eyes as fitting locations. The radius was fixed to a slightly bigger value than given for the head depth by the statistical publications, because of the requirements for the resulting texture map (±90°). The determined cylinder offset parameter for the x- and z-axis are used to place the cylinder at the face surface with the highest impact for the alignment, like the eyes and mouth. Therefore, the edges of these features are aligned and the displacement error for other features are not visible, e.g. nose tip. The fitted cylinder and a face surface model are shown in Fig 8. Therefore, some face surface points are reconstructed using the calibration data and perspective projection. Due to the fact, that several views provide 2D locations of the same feature point, a multi view approach for the reconstruction is used for more reliable 3D feature point locations. The handling of outliers, which can be a result of the point correspondences or calibration data, is crucial at this step. The average of permuted reconstructed 3D point locations using two views as well as a closed-form solution for all views have the drawback of moving the solution to one or more outliers. We have used a combination of the permutation and closed-form solution, which takes advantage of the back projection error in all considered views and is therefore an iterative solution. The consideration of the minimum back projection error as measurement for the 3D point localization accuracy leads to reliable surface points and identifies possible problems with 2D point locations. The evaluation result can not only be used for more exact 3D point locations by excluding outliers, but also to define weights according to the quality of back projection and therefore to define the influence of each view to the to be created texture map.
The composition is mainly described by the projection of each view onto the object surface and in our case a cylindrical approximation. The perspective warping of images onto a cylindrical surface is described in the technical report of Szeliski [Szeliski04]. Afterwards a projection will

take place, in order to create the texture map. Sampling the cylinder surface with the desired resolution of the virtual view is used for this approach. This method allows a set of DOFs, like the horizontal and vertical resolution as well as defining a specific region of interest. A linear blending rule, like the one shown in Fig 7 is used to incorporate adjacent views. For each horizontal position along the circumference left and right views are selected according to the camera rotation around the y-axis. The angle differences between the view vector and the selected left and right views are converted to weights. This method is constrained on the assumption, that the views are now rotating around the head and cylinder center and not longer around the convergence point of all views. The 3D reconstructed face features show a very small offset along the x axis and a strong offset along the z axis, so that middle view still refers to the most frontal face view. Using a linear interpolation between adjacent views leads to a weight of 0.5 in the middle of these both views.

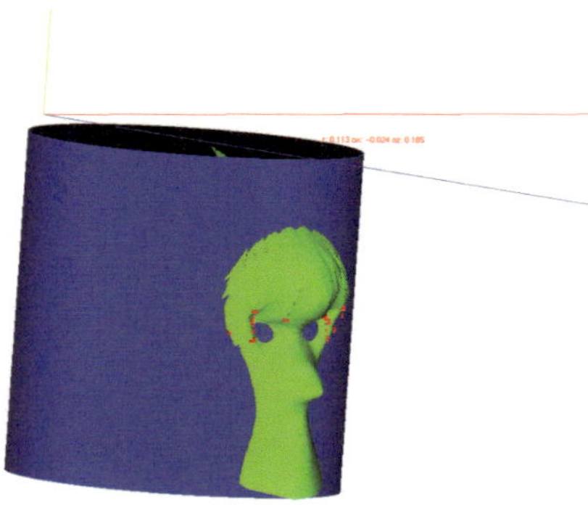

Fig. 8. Interpolated face surface model with a cylinder fitted at both eyes.

The result is a texture map shown in Fig 6, where nine views are incorporated to one cylindrical projected face image showing ±90°. At the top and the bottom of the created image some ghost parts are visible. These wrong stitched parts are caused by the cylindrical assumption and the difference to the real object surface. A more detailed 3D object would decrease such miss alignments of the regions below the chin.

4.3 Global and local alignment

In order to use the created texture maps for the mentioned pose invariant face recognition approach, an alignment has to take place. Common is to align the input images globally, by using the eye centers as reference points. With the publication of Tsapatsoulis et al. [Tsapatsoulis98] the positive influence of local aligned face features is described, if only a resizing takes place. We extend this idea to a complete affine transformation of the area around the desired face feature and applying the transformation under the support of graphics card rendering. Global alignment is based on 2D affine transformation and performed for each created texture map separably. The parameters for the transformation are determined by using selected face feature locations in all created virtual images. The average feature point location is used as reference and all transformations are calculated with respect to these data. The feature point locations used for the texture map creation are transformed, in order to use them for the alignment. The accuracy of these locations are good enough, compared a manual selections, considering the depth distance between approximation and real object surface.

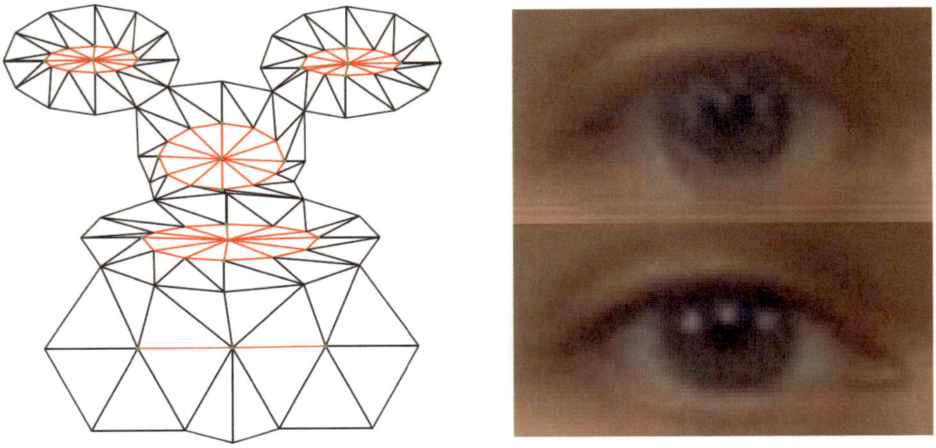

Fig. 9. (left) Adapted triangle mesh used for the local alignment of selected face features (both eyes, nose, mouth and chin). (right) Average images after (right top) global and (right bottom) local alignment of 30 images of right eyes from male persons.

The alignment result for 30 right eyes is shown in the upper part of Fig 9. In order to achieve a better alignment result, the regions around selected face features are aligned locally. The generic triangle mesh from Fig 9 is adapted and placed at the global transformed face feature locations and the associated texture information for each triangle is extracted. The face feature locations are transformed to the desired position and the associated textured triangles will perform the texture map interpolation. The feature region warping is supported by the graphics hardware by rendering the deformed triangle mesh.

Fig. 10. Average image of 25 texture maps of different persons (male and female mixture) after global and local alignment of selected face features (both eyes, nose, mouth and chin).

Using this approach leads to locally aligned virtual texture maps, as can be seen in Fig 10. The average image shows a very good definition in the locally aligned facial features. A closer look and direct comparison between just global and global plus local aligned right eyes is given in Fig 10, which shows again the alignment of 30 right eyes.

5. Experimental results

5.1 Dataset and experiment description

Two different databases have been created in order to show the performance of the Partial Principal Component Analysis (P^2CA) approach and the improvement in the recognition accuracy when using the automatic approach for the creation of the virtual alignment texture maps.

The first one: The UPC face database [UPC-FaceDatabase] contains a total of 756 images corresponding to 28 persons with 27 pictures per person acquired under different pose views (0°, $\pm 30^o$, $\pm 45^o$, $\pm 60^o$ and $\pm 90^o$) and three different illuminations (environment or natural light, strong light source from an angle of 45°, and finally an almost frontal mid-strong light source). The images have been normalized to an output resolution of 122x100 pixels. The 180° cylindrical training images have been created by manually morphing five images (0°, $\pm 45^o$and $\pm 90^o$) that have been acquired in a different session than the rest of the pictures under environmental light conditions. This database is used for testing the P^2CA approach towards pose and illumination variations and also for comparing this technique with the conventional Eigenfaces approach [Turk91].

The second dataset has been created using the method proposed above for the automatic creation of texture maps. Although this database contains only 20 different subjects it will be used to show the improvement of the local alignment method proposed. For each subject two different texture maps have been created: One using only global alignment, and another texture map using the global and local alignment process described in Section 4.3. So for this database, two different training sets have been created for the training stage of the face recognition system: Training set T1 using the global alignment maps; and training set T2 using the local alignment maps. These training sets will be also used as gallery sets. The test set is composed of a total of 9 different views for each subject (180 test images) acquired in a second session using the setup depicted in Fig 7.

A total of three different experiments have been performed: The first one tries to evaluate the P^2CA technique under different assumptions using the UPC Face Database. The second experiment is focused on a comparative between the Partial Principal Component Analysis technique and the conventional *Eigenfaces* approach. Finally, the third experiment is carried out on the second dataset and it shows the improvement in the recognition rate when introducing the proposed automatic creation and alignment of the texture maps.

5.2 Results

In the first experiment we will identify which view angles present lower recognition accuracy using P^2CA. For this reason, the test set of the UPC-FaceDatabase is divided in subsets depending on the angle view of the face image to obtain Table 1 and Table 2. The first Table represents the recognition results when using only the images under the neutral illumination for the evaluation, whereas the second Table considers the three different illuminations of the test set.

Angle	Recog.	Angle	Recog.	Angle	Recog.
-90°	82.14%	-30°	92.85%	+45°	96.43%
-60°	85.71%	0°	100%	+60°	82.14%
-45°	96.43%	+30°	82.14%	+90°	85.71%

Table 1. Recognition Accuracy of P²CA under natural light (neutral illumination)

Angle	Recog.	Angle	Recog.	Angle	Recog.
-90°	72.63%	-30°	73.80%	+45°	70.23%
-60°	71.42%	0°	75%	+60°	70.23%
-45°	73.80%	+30°	69.05%	+90°	70.23%

Table 2. Recognition under 3 different illumination conditions

Table 1 shows that the new technique is considerably robust towards changes in the pose of the face. On the other hand, when testing the images under the three different illuminations (especially the strong light source from an angle of 45°) the algorithm presents lower recognition accuracy as depicted in Table 2. Moreover, it can also be concluded that the positive pose variations present a lower recognition rate. The reason for this reduction of the recognition accuracy is that one of the three illuminations of the UPC-FaceDatabase corresponds to a very strong spotlight coming from the positive side

In the next experiment, we verify the robustness of P²CA in front of the conventional 2D strategies. Thus, Eigenfaces (PCA), and 2DPCA have been implemented. For the training of the conventional 2D strategies, 5 different face views for each subject have been used as training and gallery data.

Method \ Exp.	Neutral illumination	3 illuminations
PCA / Eigenfaces	72.22%	60.45%
2DPCA	75%	61.24%
P²CA	91.91%	72.9%

Table 3. Recognition Accuracy of the different algorithms

The results presented in Table 3 show that the novel 2D-3D mixed scheme (P²CA) outperforms its respective two dimensional approaches (PCA and 2DPCA) when varying pose.

Finally, in the third experiment we analyze the advantages of creating the virtual images with the global and the local alignment method. Table 4 summarizes the results for face recognition when using the datasets described above.

	Training Set T1 (global alignment)	Training Set T2 (global + local alignment)
Recognition Rate	93.33%	96.66%

Table 4. Improvement using the local alignment method

Although only 20 different persons are used in the experiments, results show that the local aligned virtual images present a slight improvement in the recognition rate. The improvement of this rate has been obtained for the 0° and $\pm 8^{\circ}$ views since these views enclose all the face features used for the alignment.

6. Conclusions and future work

Face processing is one of the most active research fields as demonstrated by more than 1000 publications that have appeared in different conferences and journals in the last two years. Additionally, it is also a mature topic with more than 30 years. Recently, a new trend of 3D face recognition approaches showed an increase in the recognition rate if 3D data is available. Nevertheless, cost of the set-up, acquisition time and cooperation of the subjects are still some of the requirements for obtaining accurate 3D data that may not be available during the recognition stage. Thus, we have presented here a possible alternative following a mixed 2D-3D face recognition philosophy, i.e. the system is trained with 3D data but it can use either 2D or 3D data in the test stage. We have presented the extension of the 2D statistical PCA method [Turk91, Yang04] to a 2D-3D face recognition scheme (Partial Principal Component Analysis). However, this philosophy may be extended also to other face recognition statistical approaches like LDA or ICA with have shown a higher robustness in the presence of illumination variations. Additionally, we have presented an automatic approach for the creation of aligned virtual view images using nine different views. These aligned virtual view images are used as training data for the P^2CA technique. The virtual view image is created by using a cylindrical approximation for the real object surface. The alignment is done by global and local transformations of the whole image and face features, respectively. Results show an improvement in the recognition rate when using the local alignment procedure proposed.

7. References

General

[3DRMA] 3D RMA Database http://www.sic.rma.ac.be/~beumier/DB/3d_rma.htm

[AFGR] *Proceedings of International Conference on Automatic Face and Gesture Recognition*

[AVBPA] *Proceedings of International Conference on Audio and Video-Based Person Authentication*

[FRGC05] P. J. Phillips, P. J. Flynn, T. Scruggs, K. W. Bowyer, J. Chang, K. Hoffman, J. Marques, J. Min, and W.Worek, "Overview of the Face Recognition Grand Challenge," *IEEE Conf. Computer Vision and Pattern Recognition(CVPR)*, 2005

[FRHomepage] Face Recognition Homepage, in http://www.face-rec.org/

[FRVT02] P. J. Phillips, P. Grother, R. Micheals, D. Blackburn, E. Tabassi, and J. Bone , "Face Recognition Vendor Test 2002: Evaluation Report". NISTIR 6965, National Institute of Standards and Technology, 2003. http://www.frvt.org

[Zhao03] W. Zhao, R. Chellappa, P. J. Phillips, and A. Rosenfeld, "Face Recognition: A Literature Survey" *ACM Computing Surveys*, Vol.35, N°4, December 2003

[Zhao06] W. Zhao, and R.Chellapa, "Face Processing: Advanced modeling and methods", Academic Press, 2006

2D face recognition

[Bartlett02] M. S. Barlett, J.R. Movellan, T.J.Sejnowski, "Face Recognition by Independent Component Analysis", on *IEEE Trans. On Neural Networks*, vol 13, no. 6, Nov 2002

[Bartlett98] M. S. Bartlett, H. M. Lades, and T. J. Sejnowski, "Independent component representations for face recognition," in *Proc. SPIE Symp. Electon. Imaging: Science Technology – Human Vision and Electronic Imaging III*, vol. 3299, T. Rogowitz and B. Pappas, Eds., San Jose, CA, 998, pp. 528–539.

[Belhumeur97] R.N. Belhumeur, J.P. Hespanha, D.J. Kriegman, "Eigenfaces vs Fisherfaces: Recognition Using Class Specific Linear Projection" *in IEEE Transacations Pattern Analysis and Machine Intelligence*, vol 19, N. 7, July 1997

[Brunelli93] R. Brunelli and T. Poggio, "Face Recognition: Features vs Templates" *IEEE Trans. Pattern Analysis and Machine Intelligence*, vol.15, no. 10, pp 1042-1053. Oct 1993

[Delac05] Delac, K., Grgic, M., Grgic, S., Independent Comparative Study of PCA, ICA, and LDA on the FERET Data Set, *International Journal of Imaging Systems and Technology*, Vol. 15, No. 5, 2005

[Fadzil94] Mohamad Hani Ahmad Fadzil, Abu Bakar H. "Human Face Recognition Using Neural Networks" *ICIP (3) 1994*: 936-939. 1994

[Haddadnia02] J. Haddadnia, K. Faez, M. Ahmadi, "N-Feature Neural Network Human Face Recognition," *Proc. of 15th International Conference on Vision Interface*, Calgary, May 2002, pp. 300-307

[Heo06] J. Heo, Ma. Savvides, R. Abiantun, Ch. Xie, and B.V.K. Vijayakumar "Face Recognition With Kernel Correlation Filters On A Large Scale Database", in *IEEE International Conference on Acoustics, Speech and Signal Processing*, Toulouse, May 14th- 19th, 2006

[Kanade73] T. Kanade, "Picture processing system by computer complex and recognition of human faces", Dept. of Information Science, Kyoto University, 1973

[Kim02] K. I. Kim, K. Jung, H.J. Kim, "Face Recognition Using Kernel Principal Component Analysis", *IEEE Signal Processing Letters*, Vol.9, No. 2, February 2002

[Kohonen88] T. Kohonen, "Self-Organization and Associative Memory". Berlin: Springer. 1988

[Lades93] M. Lades, J.C. Vorbruggen, J. Buhmann, J. Lange, C. von der Malsburg, R.P. Wurtz, W. Konen. "Distortion Invariant Object Recognition in the Dynamic Link Architecture" *IEEE Transactions on Computers* archive Volume 42 , Issue 3 Pages: 300 - 311. 1993

[Lawrence97] S. Lawrence, C. L. Giles, A. C. Tsoi and A.D. Back, "Face Recognition: A Convolutional Neural-Network Approach", *IEEE Transactions Neural Networks*, Vol. 8, No. 1, 1997, pp. 98-113. IDIAP--RR 03-20

[Lin97] S. H. Lin, S. Y. Kung, and L.J. Lin, "Face Recognition/Detection by Probabilistic Decision-Based Neural Network" *IEEE Transactions on Neural Networks*, 8(1):114-132.1997

[Lorente99] L. Lorente, L. Torres, "*Face recognition of video sequences in a MPEG-7 context using a global eigen approach*", *International Conference on Image Processing*, Kobe, Japan, October 25-29, 1999

[Moghaddam02] B. Moghaddam, Principal manifolds and probabilistic subspaces for visual recognition, *in IEEE Transactions Pattern Analysis and Machine Intelligence* 24 (2002), 780- 788.

[Moses94] Y. Moses, Y. Adani, and S. Ullman. "Face Recognition: The problem of compensating for changes in illumination direction", *in Proceedings European Conference on Computer Vision* pp. 286-2996, 1994

[Nefian96] A.V. Nefian. "Statistical Approaches To Face Recognition". Qualifying Examination Report. Georgia Institute of Technology. Dec 1996

[Palanivel03] S. Palanivel, B.S.Venkatesh and B.Yegnanarayana, "Real time face recognition system using Autoassociative Neural Network models," *in IEEE International Conference on Acoustics, Speech and Signal Processing*, Hong Kong, April 2003, pp. 833-836

[Pentland94] A. P. Pentland, B. Moghaddam, T. Starner and M. Turk, "*View-based and modular eigenspaces for face recognition*", *Proceedings of the IEEE Computer Society Conference on Computer Vision and Pattern Recognition*, pp. 84-91,1994.

[Schölkopf98] B.Schölkopf, A. Smola, K. Müller, „Non-linear Component Analysis as a Kernel Eigenvalue Problem", *Neural Computers*, vol. 10, pp. 1299-1319, 1998

[Schölkopf99] B.Schölkopf, A. Smola, K. Müller, "Kernel Principal Component Analysis" in *Advances in Kernel Methods-Support Vector Learning*, pp. 327-352, MIT Press, 1999

[Turk91] M. A. Turk, A. P. Pentland, "Face recognition using eigenfaces", *Proc. of the IEEE Comp. Soc. Conf. on CVPR*, pp. 586-591, Hawaii 1991

[Wang06] J. Wang, K. N. Plataniotis, A. N. Venetsanopoulos, "Selecting Kernel Eigenfaces For Face Recognition With One Training Sample Per Subject", ", in *IEEE International Conference & Multimedia Expo*, Toronto, Canada, July 9th-12th 2006

[Wiskott99] L. Wiskott, J.M. Fellous, N. Kruger, and C. von der Malsburg, "Face recognition by elastic bunch graph matching" *IEEE Trans. Pattern Analysis and Machine Intelligence*, vol. 19, no. 7, pp. 775—779. Revised version 1999

[Yang02] M.H. Yang, "Kernel Eigenfaces vs. Kernel Fisherfaces: Face Recognition Using Kernel Methods", in *Proceedings of IEEE International Conference on Automatic Face and Gesture Recognition (FG'02)*, pp. 215-220, May 2002.

[Yang04] J. Yang, D. Zhang, A.F. Frangi, and J.Yang, "Two-Dimensional PCA: A New Approach to Appearance-based Face Representation and Recognition", in *IEEE Trans. on Pattern Analysis and Machine Intelligence*, Jan. 2004

[Yu06] J. Yu, Q. Tian, "Constructing descriptive and discriminant features for face classification" in *IEEE International Conference on Acoustics, Speech and Signal Processing*, Toulouse, May 14th- 19th, 2006

[Zhang97] J. Zhang, Y. Yan, M. Lades, "*Face recognition: eigenface, elastic matching, and neural nets*", *Proceedings of the IEEE*, Vol. 85, No. 9, pp. 1423-1435, September 1997

3D-face recognition

[Antini06] G. Antini, S. Berretti, A. Del Bimbo, P. Pala, "3D Face Identification Based On Arrangement Of Salient Wrinkles", in *IEEE International Conference & Multimedia Expo*, Toronto, Canada, July 9th-12th 2006

[Beymer95] D. Beymer and T. Poggio , "Face Recognition from One model View", in *Proc. Fifth Int'l Conf. Computer Vision*, 1995

[Blanz03] V. Blanz, and T. Vetter, "Face Recognition based on fitting 3D morphable model", in *IEEE Trans. Pattern Analysis and Machine Intelligence*, 25(9):1063-1074, 2003

[Bowyer04] K. Bowyer, K. Chang, and P. Flynn, "A Survey of Approaches to 3D and Multi-Modal 3D+2D Face Recognition," *IEEE Intl.Conf. on Pattern Recognition*, 2004.

[Bronstein05] A. M. Bronstein, M. M. Bronstein, R. Kimmel, "Three-dimensional face recognition „ in *International Journal of Computer Vision* Vol.64/1, pp. 5-30, August 2005

[Cartoux89] J. Y. Cartoux, J. T. Lapreste, and M. Richetin. "Face authentification or recognition by profile extraction from range images." *In Workshop on Interpretation of 3D Scenes*, pages 194- 199, 1989

[Chang05] K. I. Chang, K. W. Bowyer, and P. J. Flynn, "An Evaluation of Multimodal 2D+3D Face Biometrics", in *IEEE Trans. on Pattern Analysis and Machine Intelligence*, Vol.27, pp 619-624, April 2005

[Feng06] S. Feng, H. Krim, I. Gu, M. Viberg, "3D Face Recognition Using Affine Integral Invariants" in *IEEE International Conference on Acoustics, Speech and Signal Processing*, Toulouse, May 14th- 19th, 2006

[Georghiades01] A. S. Georghiades, P. N. Belhumeur, and D. J. Kriegman, "From Few to Many: Illumination Cone Models for Face Recognition" in *IEEE Transactions on Pattern Analysis and Machine Intelligence*, 23(6):643-- 660, 2001

[Gordon91] Gaile G. Gordon. Face recognition based on depth maps and surface curvature. In *Geometric Methods in Computer Vision*, volume 1570 of *SPIE Proceedings*, pages 234- 247, 1991

[Lee90] John Chun Lee and E. Milios. Matching range images of human faces. *In Proc. IEEE International Conference on Computer Vision*, pages 722- 726, 1990

[Lu05] X. Lu, and A.K. Jain, "Integrating Range and Texture Information for 3D Face Recognition", in *Proc. IEEE WACV*, Breckenridge, Colorado 2005

[Lu06] X. Lu, and A.K. Jain, "Matching 2.5D face scans to 3D models", in *IEEE Transactions Pattern Analysis and Machine Intelligence*, Jan. 2006 Volume: 28, pp: 31- 43

[Onofrio06] D. Onofrio, A. Rama, F. Tarres, S. Tubaro, "P^2CA: How Much Information is needed", *IEEE International Conference on Image Processing*, Atlanta, USA, October 2006

[Rama05a] A.Rama, F.Tarrés, D.Onofrio, and S. Tubaro, "Using partial information for face recognition and pose estimation", in *IEEE International Conference & Multimedia Expo*, Amsterdam, July 6th-8th 2005

[Rama05b] A.Rama, and F.Tarrés, "P^2CA: A new face recognition scheme combining 2D and 3D information", in *IEEE International Conference on Image Processing*, Genoa, Italy, September 11th-14th 2005

[Rama06] A.Rama, F.Tarres, D.Onofrio, and S.Tubaro, "Mixed 2D-3D Information for pose estimation and face recognition" in *IEEE International Conference on Acoustics, Speech and Signal Processing*, Toulouse, May 14th- 19th, 2006

[Samani06] A. Samani, J. Winkler, M. Niranjan, „Automatic Face Recognition Using Stereo Images", in *IEEE International Conference on Acoustics, Speech and Signal Processing*, Toulouse, May 14th- 19th, 2006

[Tanaka98] Hiromi T. Tanaka, Masaki Ikeda, and Hisako Chiaki. Curvature-based face surface recognition using spherical correlation - principal direcions for curved object recognition. *In Proc. IEEE International Conference on Automatic Face and Gesture Recognition*, pages 372- 377, 1998

[Tsalakanidou04] F. Tsalakanidou, S. Malassiotis, and M. Strintzis, "Integration of 2D and 3D Images for enhanced face authentication". *Sixth International Conference on Automated Face and Gesture Recognition*, pages 266-271, May 2004

[UPC-FaceDatabase] "UPC Face Database" in http://gps-tsc.upc.es/GTAV

3D face modelling, reconstruction and texture map creation

[Akimoto93] Akimoto, T., Suenaga, Y.,Wallace, R.S.: Automatic Creation of 3D Facial Models. IEEE Computer Graphics and Applications 13 (1993) 16–22

[Ansari03] A. Ansari, M. Abdel-Mottaleb, "3D Face Modelling Using Two Ortogonal Views and a Generic Face Model", *in Proc. of Int. Conf. and Multimedia and Expo*, July 2003

[Brown01] Brown, L.M.: 3D Head Tracking Using Motion Adaptive Texture-Mapping. In: Proceedings of the IEEE Computer Society Conference on Computer Vision and Pattern Recognition, Hawaii, IEEE Computer Society (2001) 998–1003

[Cascia98] Cascia, M.L., Isidoro, J., Sclaroff, S.: Head Tracking via Robust Registration in Texture Map Images. In: Proceedings of the IEEE Computer Society Conference on Computer Vision and Pattern Recognition, Santa Barbara, CA, USA, IEEE Computer Society (1998) 508

[Farkas95] Farkas, L.G.: Anthropometry of the Head and Face. 2nd edn. Raven Press (1995)

[Forster01] Forster, F., Lang, M., Radig, B., 2001. Real-time 3D and colour camera. In: Proc. Internat. Conf. on Augmented, Virtual Environments and 3D Imaging, Mykonos, 2001. pp. 45–48.

[Kouzani99] Kouzani, A., Sammut, K.: Quadtree principal component analysis and its application to facial expression classification. In: Proceedings of the IEEE International Conference on Systems, Man, and Cybernetics, Hawaii (1999) 835–839

[Lee00] Lee, W.S., Magnenat-Thalmann, N.: Fast head modeling for animation. Image and Vision Computing 18 (2000) 355–364(10)

[Liu03] Liu, X. and Chen, T., Geometry-assisted statistical modeling for face mosaicing, IEEE Transactions on Systems, in Proc. IEEE Int. Conf. Image Process, 2003, Volume 2, page 883-886

[Onofrio04] D. Onofrio, A. Sarti, and S. Tubaro, "Area Matching Based on Belief Propagation with Applications to Face Modeling", in *IEEE International Conference on Image Processing*, Singapore 2004

[Onofrio05] D. Onofrio, S. Tubaro, A. Rama, F. Tarres, "3D Face Reconstruction with a four camera acquisition system". *Proc. International Workshop on Very Low Bitrate Video Coding (VLBV05)*, Costa Rei, Sardinia, 15-16 September 2005

[Pedersini99] F. Pedersini, A. Sarti, S. Tubaro, "Multicamera Systems: Calibration and Applications," *IEEE Signal Processing Magazine, Special Issue on Stereo and 3D Imaging*, vol. 16, N. 3, pp. 55-65, May 1999

[Scales85] Scales, L.E.: Introduction to non-linear optimization. Springer-Verlag New York, Inc., New York, NY, USA (1985)

[Scharstein02] D. Scharstein, R. Szeliski, "A Taxonomy and Evaluation of Dense Two-Frame Stereo Correspondence Algorithms," *Int'l J. Computer Vision*, vol. 47, N. 1, pp 7-42, 2002.

[Singh07] Singh, R. and Ross, A., A Mosaicing Scheme for Pose-Invariant Face Recoginition, IEEE Transactions on Systems, Man, and Cybernetics - Part B: Cybernetics, Volume 37(5), 2007

[Soh95] Soh, A.W.K., Yu, Z., Prakash, E.C., Chan, T.K.Y., Sung, E.: Texture Mapping of 3D Human Face for Virtual Reality Environments. International Journal of Information Technology 8 (2002) 54–65

[Szeliski04] Szeliski, R.: Image Alignment and Stitching: A Tutorial. Technical Report MSR-TR-2004-92, Microsoft Research (2004)

[Tsapatsoulis98] Tsapatsoulis, N., Doulamis, N., Doulamis, A., Kollias, S.: Face extraction from non-uniform background and recognition in compressed domain. In:

Proceedings of the IEEE International Conference on Acoustics, Speech and Signal Processing. Volume 5, Seattle, WA, USA (1998) 2701–2704

[Xiao93] Xiao, J., Kanade, T., Cohn, J.F.: Robust Full-Motion Recovery of Head by Dynamic Templates and Re-registration Techniques. International Journal of Imaging Systems and Technology 13 (2003) 85–94

[Young93] Young, J.W.: Head and Face Anthropometry of Adult U.S. Civilians. Technical Report ADA268661, Civil Aeromedical Institute, Federal Aviation Administration (1993)

11

Recognizing Face Images with Disguise Variations

Richa Singh, Mayank Vatsa and Afzel Noore
Lane Department of Computer Science & Electrical Engineering, West Virginia University
USA

1. Introduction

Automatic face recognition, required in law enforcement applications such as surveillance, border security and forensic investigation, is a process in which an individual is identified or verified based on facial characteristics. Researchers have proposed several algorithms that can effectively recognize individuals in controlled environment with minor variations in pose, expression, and illumination (Zhao et al., 2003), (Li & Jain, 2005), (Wechsler, 2006), (Delac & Grgic, 2007). In recent face recognition test reports such as FRVT 2002, FRGC 2004, and FRGC 2006 (Philips et al., 2006 & Philips et al., 2007), the results show that under normal changes in constrained environment, the performance of existing face recognition systems is greatly enhanced. However, in most real world applications, images may not be of good quality or user may not be cooperative or there may be temporal variations and dissimilarities in facial characteristics that are artificially created using disguise accessories.

Challenges in automatic face recognition can be classified into six categories: illumination, image quality, expression, pose, aging, and disguise. Among these challenges, recognition of faces with disguise is a major challenge and has only been recently addressed by few researchers (Alexander & Smith, 2003), (Ramanathan et al, 2004), (Silva & Rosa, 2003), (Singh et al., 2008). As shown in Fig. 1, the inter-personal and intra-personal characteristics can be modeled using disguise accessories to alter the appearance of an individual, to impersonate another person, or to hide one's identity. For example, a criminal can alter facial features and appearance using makeup tools and accessories to remain elusive from law enforcement. The challenges due to disguise cause change in visual perception, alter actual data, make pertinent facial information disappear, mask features to varying degrees, or introduce extraneous artifacts in the face image. Existing face recognition algorithms may not be able to provide the desired level of security for such cases.

In literature, Ramanathan et al. (Ramanathan et al., 2004) studied facial similarity for several variations including disguise by forming two eigenspaces from two halves of the face, one using the left half and other using the right half. From the test image, optimally illuminated half face is chosen and is projected into the eigenspace. This algorithm has been tested on the AR face database (Martinez & Benavente, 1998) and the National Geographic database (Ramanathan et al., 2004) which consists of variations in smile, glasses, and illumination. An accuracy of around 39% for best two matches is reported on the AR database. Silva and Rosa

(Silva & Rosa, 2003) proposed using Eigen-eyes to handle several challenges of face recognition including disguise. Using the Yale database (Yale face database), the algorithm was able to achieve an accuracy of around 87.5%. The advantage of the algorithm is that alterations in the facial features excluding the eye region do not affect the accuracy. Pamudurthy et al. (Pamudurthy et al., 2005) proposed a face recognition algorithm which uses dynamic features obtained from skin correlation and the features are matched using nearest neighbor classifier. On a database of 10 individuals, authors reported that this approach gives accurate results. Alexander and Smith (Alexander & Smith, 2005) used PCA based algorithm with Mahalanobis angle as the distance metric. The results show an accuracy of 45.8% on the AR database (Martinez & Benavente, 1998). The limitation of these algorithms is that the performance degrades when important regions such as the eye and mouth are covered. Moreover, the AR and Yale databases do not contain many images with disguise and therefore are not ideal for validating algorithms under comprehensive disguise scenarios.

Fig. 1. Face disguise: use of makeup tools and accessories to alter facial features and appearance of the same individual.

In this chapter, we focus on the problem of recognizing faces that are altered due to variations in disguise, i.e. the ability to recognize individuals when their appearances are intentionally altered to defraud law enforcement and the public using disguises. Specifically, in this research we identify different types of disguise accessories that can be used to alter facial information and analyze their effect on face recognition algorithms. Eight face recognition algorithms, including state-of-the-art algorithms and algorithms that are tailored for disguise, are evaluated using a heterogeneous face database and the face disguise database. Experimental results suggest that the performance of appearance and feature based algorithms is affected when features are altered or hidden whereas texture based algorithms fail to perform with multiple disguises. Further, results indicate that face recognition with variations in disguise is a major challenge and the performance of existing algorithms are not adequate. The next section identifies the types of disguise that can alter facial appearance and features pertinent for face recognition.

2. Types of disguises

The performance of face recognition algorithms can be affected by alteration in appearance, feature and combination of multiple variations. The possible variations of disguise can be classified into the following eight categories depending on their effect on facial appearance and features.

1. **Minimal variations**: Two face images captured at different time instances can have minimal variations in appearance and features. In such cases, face recognition algorithms usually yield correct results.
2. **Variations in hair style**: Hair style can be changed to alter the appearance of a face image or hide facial features. Fig. 2 shows an example of facial variations of an individual due to changes in hair style.

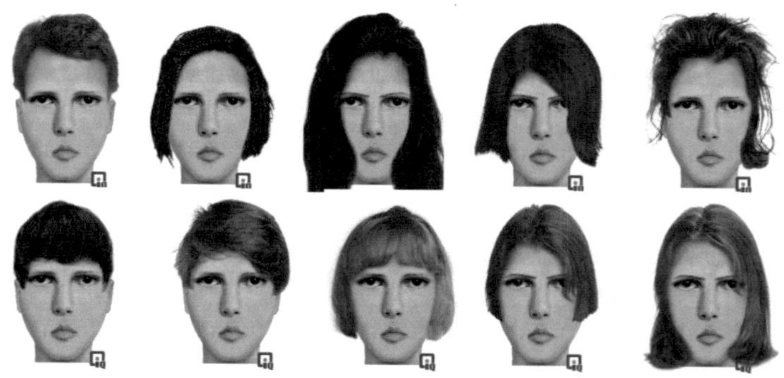

Fig. 2. Face images with variation in hair style

3. **Variations due to beard and moustache**: Facial hair such as beard and moustache can alter facial appearance and features in the lower half of the face, specifically near mouth and chin regions. Fig. 3 shows an example where face images with and without beard and moustache show different appearance.

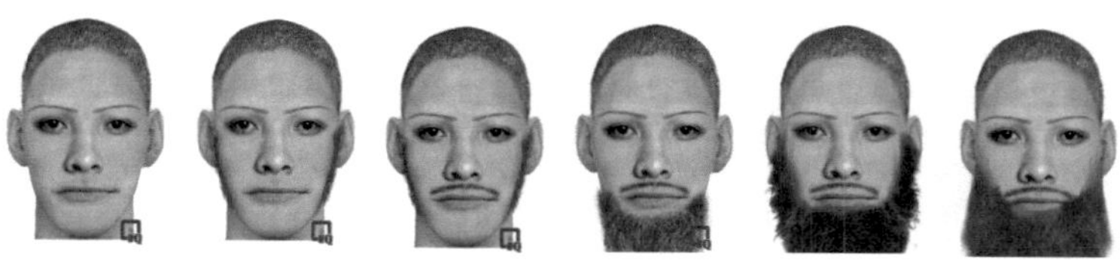

Fig. 3. Face images with variation in beard and moustache

4. **Variations due to glasses**: Glasses, especially sun-glasses are one of the easiest ways to alter facial appearance. In general, glasses affect upper facial region by hiding the facial features (e.g. eyes and eyebrows). As shown in Fig. 4, structural differences in glasses and opacity of lens can also change the appearance of an individual.

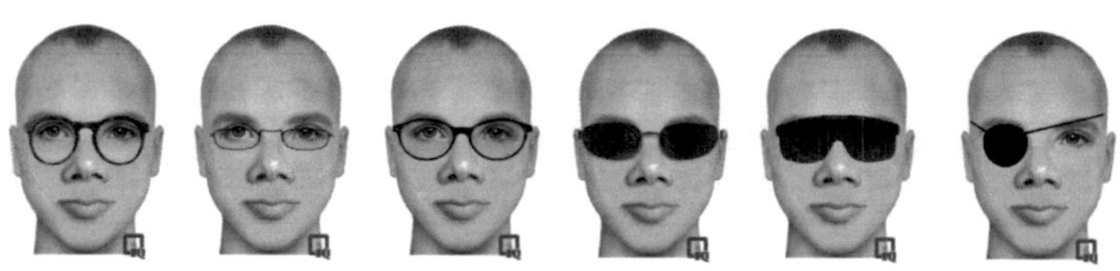

Fig. 4. Face images with variation in eye glasses

5. **Variations due to cap and hat**: In general, use of cap and hat hides hairs and some part of the forehead which are not used by the recognition algorithms. However, as shown in Fig. 5, some specific types of cap and hat (e.g., monkey cap) can hide pertinent facial features, thereby affecting the performance of face recognition algorithms.

Fig. 5. Face images with variation in cap and hat

6. **Variations due to lips, eyebrows and nose**: Makeup tools can be used to alter the shape and size of lips, eyebrows and nose (Fig. 6). These key local features, if altered, can affect the performance of feature based face recognition algorithms.

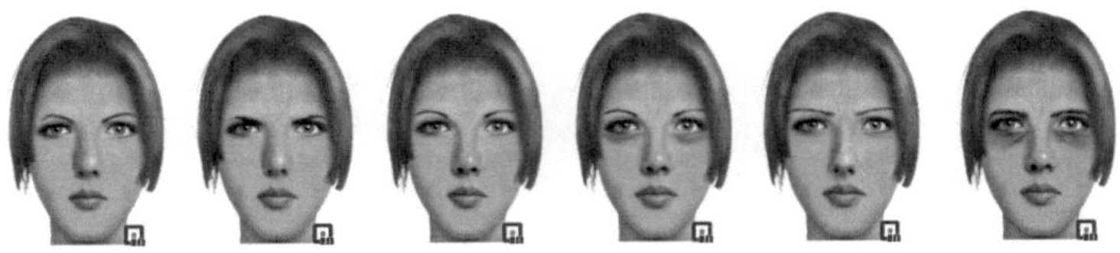

Fig. 6. Face images with variation in lips, eyebrow and nose characteristics

7. **Variations due to aging and wrinkles**: Aging can be natural (due to age progression) and artificial (using makeup tools). In both the cases, aging and wrinkles can severely affect the performance of face recognition algorithms. An example of facial variations due to aging and wrinkles is shown in Fig. 7.

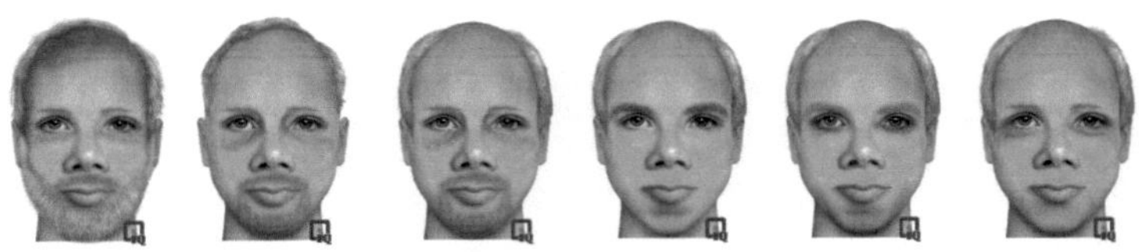

Fig. 7. Face images with aging and wrinkle variations

8. **Multiple variations**: A combination of the above mentioned variations can be used to disguise and defraud law enforcement. Fig. 8 shows an example in which multiple variations are used to alter the appearance and features of an individual.

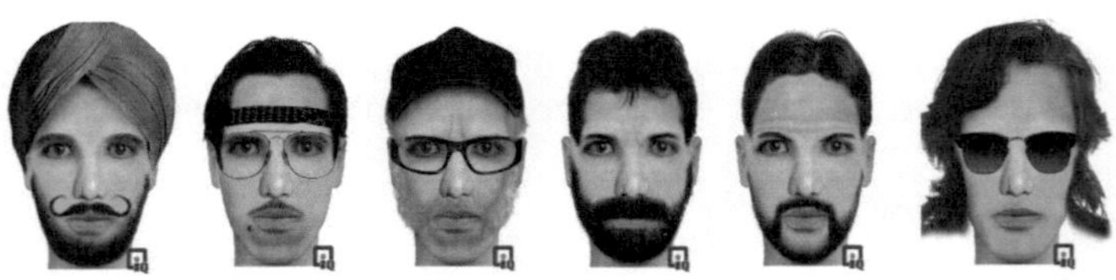

Fig. 8. Face images of an individual with multiple disguise variations

3. Characteristics of face recognition algorithms used for evaluation

In general, face recognition algorithms can be broadly classified into three classes (1) appearance based algorithms, (2) feature based algorithms, and (3) texture based algorithms. To compare the performance of these algorithms; eight algorithms are selected and are briefly explained below.

1. **Appearance based algorithms**: Three appearance based algorithms are used in experiments that are specifically tailored for recognizing individuals with altered

appearances. These algorithms are: (1) PCA algorithm with Mahalanobis distance (Alexander & Smith, 2005), (2) Half-face based algorithm (Ramanathan et al., 2004), and (3) Eigen-eyes based algorithm (Silva & Rosa, 2003). Additional details of these algorithms are explained in the Introduction section.

2. **Feature based algorithms**: Two feature based algorithms are selected namely, Geometrical Feature (GF) (Cox et al., 1996) and Local Feature Analysis (LFA) (Penev & Atick, 1996).
   Geometrical feature based recognition algorithm (Cox et al., 1996) uses mixture distances of the facial features for matching. This algorithm works on the distance between geometrical features. Facial features such as nose, mouth, eyes, and ears are extracted and their shape information is computed. For matching two images, this shape information is matched using Euclidean distance measure. Hence, the algorithm depends on the correspondence between the facial features and works only in cases when this information is preserved. If the facial features are occluded using accessories such as glasses, beard, moustache, and scarf, then the performance decreases.
   Local feature analysis (Penev & Atick, 1996) is one of the most widely used face recognition algorithms which can accommodate some changes in facial expression. LFA refers to a class of algorithms that extract a set of geometrical metrics and distances from facial images and use these features as the basis for representation and comparison. The recognition performance is dependent on a relatively constant environment and quality of the image.
3. **Texture based algorithms**: In the third class of face recognition algorithms, i.e., texture based, three algorithms are selected namely Independent Gabor Features (IGF) (Liu & Wechsler, 2003), Local Binary Pattern (LBP) (Ahonen et al., 2006), and 2D-log polar Gabor transform and Neural Network (2DLPGNN) (Singh et al., 2008).
   Independent Gabor features (Liu & Wechsler, 2003) extract Gabor features from the face image and then reduces the dimensionality using PCA. The independent Gabor features are obtained from the reduced dimensionality feature vector by applying Independent Component Analysis. These independent Gabor features are classified using Bayes classifier and then matched using the Manhattan distance measure.
   Local binary pattern based face recognition algorithm (Ahonen et al., 2006) extracts textural feature from the face images. In this algorithm, a face image is divided into several regions and weighted LBP features are extracted to generate a feature vector. Matching of two LBP feature vectors is performed using weighted Chi square distance measure based algorithm.
   2D-log polar Gabor and neural network based face recognition algorithm (Singh et al., 2008) extracts phase features from the face images. It uses dynamic neural network architecture to extract the phase features using 2D log polar Gabor transform. The phase features are divided into frames which are matched using hamming distance.

4. Characteristics of face databases and experimental protocol

The experiments are divided into two parts. In the first part, the performance of face recognition algorithms is evaluated on a heterogeneous face database that contains variations due to pose, expression and illumination. This experiment is performed as the baseline experiment. The second experiment is performed to evaluate the effect of disguises on face recognition algorithms. For these experiments, we have created two face databases, (1) heterogeneous face database and (2) face disguise database.

1. **Heterogeneous face database**: For evaluating the performance on a large database with challenging intra-class variations, we combined images from multiple face databases and created a heterogeneous database of 882 subjects. Table 1 lists the databases used and the number of subjects selected from the individual databases. The CMU-AMP database (CMU-AMP face database) contains images with large expression variations while the CMU-PIE dataset (Sim et al., 2003) contains images with variation in pose, illumination and facial expressions. The Equinox database (Equinox face database) has images captured under different illumination conditions with accessories and expressions. The AR face database (Martinez & Benavente, 1998) contains face images with varying illumination and accessories, and the FERET database (Philips et al., 2000) has face images with different variations over a time interval of 3-4 years. The Faces in the Wild database (Huang et al., 2007) contains real world images of celebrities and popular individuals. This database contains images of more than 1600 subjects from which we selected 294 subjects that have at least 6 images. To the best of our knowledge, there is no single database available in the public domain which encompasses all these types of intra-class variations.

Face database	Number of subjects
CMU-AMP	13
CMU-PIE	65
Equinox	90
AR	120
FERET	300
Faces in the Wild	294
Total	882

Table 1. Composition of the heterogeneous face database

2. **Face disguise database**: This database is prepared by the authors. It contains real and synthetic face images from 125 subjects. For every subject, disguise variations are collected based on the eight classes of disguise variations described in Section 2. The database contains real face images of 25 individuals with 15-25 different disguise variations of each individual. Since our goal is to evaluate the performance of the face recognition algorithms on disguise, the database contains frontal face images with less emphasis on variations due to illumination, expression and pose. Fig. 9 shows an example of this database. Further, we used FACES software (Faces software) to generate 4000 frontal face images of 100 subjects with a comprehensive set of variations for disguise. An example of the synthetic face database is shown in Fig. 10. The complete face disguise database is used to broadly evaluate the performance of the proposed algorithm for disguised images.
3. **Experimental protocol**: For both the experiments, the images are partitioned into two sets: (1) the training dataset is used to train the individual face recognition algorithms and (2) the gallery-probe dataset (the test set) is used to evaluate the performance of the recognition algorithms. The training set comprises of randomly selected three images of each subject and the remaining images are used as the test data to evaluate the

algorithms. This train-test partitioning is repeated 20 times (cross validation) and the Receiver Operating Characteristics (ROC) curves are generated by computing the genuine accept rates (GAR) over these trials at different false accept rates (FAR). Furthermore, verification accuracies are reported at 0.01% FAR.

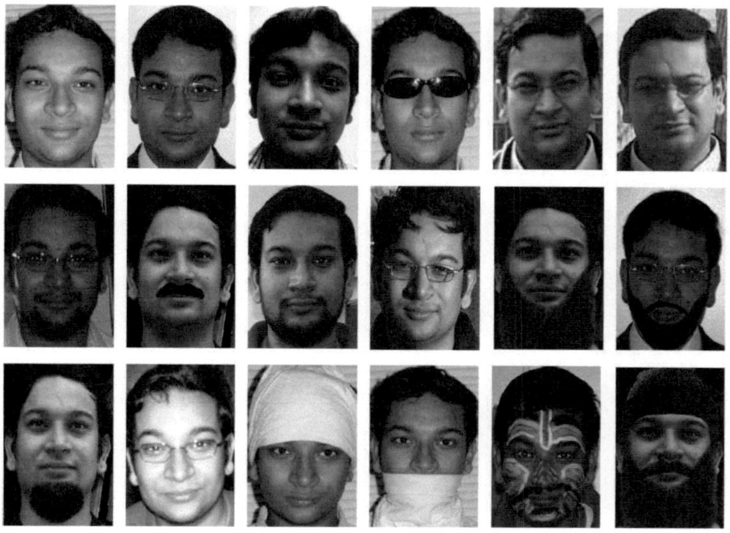

Fig. 9. Sample images from the real face database of the same individual.

5. Performance evaluation

The experiments are divided into two parts: (1) evaluation using the heterogeneous face database, and (2) evaluation using the disguise database. Experimental protocol described in Section 4 is used for training and testing. Training images are used to train the face recognition algorithms and testing images are used for gallery probe matching and evaluation.

5.1 Evaluation using heterogeneous face database

This experiment is conducted to evaluate the effect of three covariates namely pose, expression, and illumination on the performance of face recognition. Fig. 11 shows the ROC plot and Table 2 illustrates the verification accuracies at 0.01% FAR. The key results and their analysis are summarized below:

1. From Table 2, covariate analysis suggests that among the three covariates, variations in pose cause a large reduction in verification accuracy compared to expression and illumination.
2. Results also suggest that the texture based algorithms yield better accuracy compared to appearance and feature based algorithms. This is because pose, expression and illumination variations can cause substantial changes in appearance and spurious/missing features, thereby reducing the verification performance.
3. Among all the algorithms, 2DLPGNN yields the best verification accuracy of 84.2%, which is at least 12% better than other algorithms. The 2DLPGNN algorithm effectively encodes textural features that can handle minor to moderate variations in pose, expression and illumination.

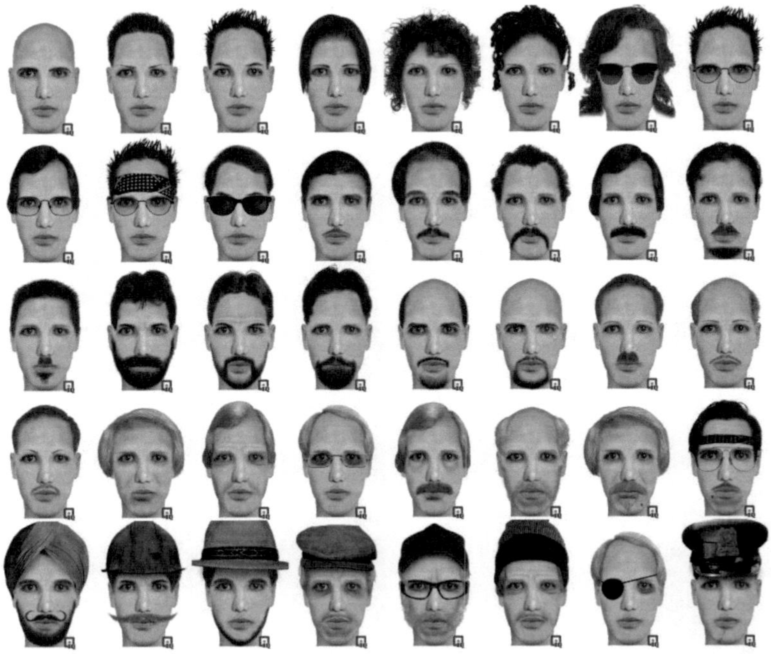

Fig. 10. Sample disguise variations of the same image from the synthetic face database

Effect of disguises on accuracy

In this section, we analyze the performance of face recognition algorithms for each disguise category using the disguise database. The ROC plot in Fig. 12 and Table 3 summarizes the performance of face recognition algorithms. The key results of the experiments are explained below.

1. For most of the disguise variations, appearance based algorithms yield lower verification accuracy because these algorithms use facial appearance to determine the identity, and the makeup tools and accessories significantly alter the facial information. Similarly, feature based algorithms suffer due to feature alterations that are caused by disguise accessories.
2. Texture based algorithms provide significantly better verification accuracy compared to appearance based algorithms. Conversely, these algorithms do not yield good verification accuracy with moderate to large disguise variations.
3. 2DLPGNN algorithm (Singh et al., 2008) yields the best verification performance. However, for the challenging scenarios of multiple disguise variations, the accuracy is only 65.6% but still outperforms other algorithms. This shows that existing algorithms are not efficient enough to handle large degree of disguise variations.
4. Another important comparison is among pose, expression, illumination and multiple disguise variations. From Table 2 and 3, it is quite clear that multiple disguise variations is the most difficult challenge to handle (e.g. 2DLPGNN yields accuracies in the range of 75-86% for pose, expression and illumination whereas for multiple disguise variations, it is only 65%).

These comprehensive experimental results indicate that further research is needed to address high degree of disguise variations.

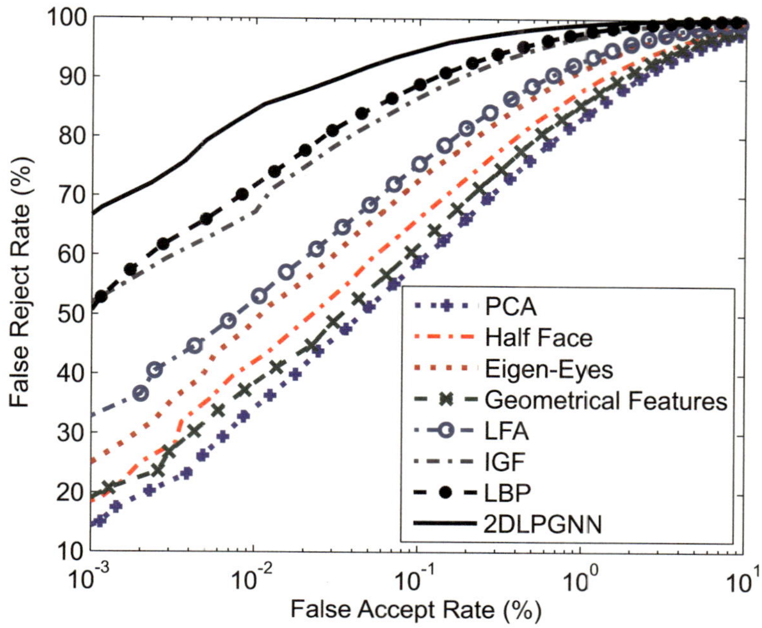

Fig. 11. ROC to evaluate the performance of face recognition algorithms on the heterogeneous face database

Verification accuracy at 0.01% FAR								
Covariates	Appearance based algorithms			Feature based algorithms		Texture based algorithms		
	PCA	Half-face	Eigen-eyes	GF	LFA	IGF	LBP	2D-LPGNN
Pose	31.9	36.6	29.7	35.4	50.1	60.7	73.2	75.3
Expression	35.5	42.1	78.6	38.2	52.3	69.8	71.4	87.6
Illumination	35.3	45.2	45.8	41.7	53.5	68.6	70.9	86.5
Overall	34.4	41.8	49.3	38.9	52.7	67.3	72.1	84.2

Table 2. Verification performance of appearance, feature and texture based face recognition algorithms for different covariates.

6. Conclusion

Currently, many security applications use human observers to recognize the face of an individual. In some applications, face recognition systems are used in conjunction with limited human intervention. For autonomous operation, it is highly desirable that the face recognition systems be able to provide high reliability and accuracy under multifarious conditions, including disguise. However, most of the algorithms are not robust to high

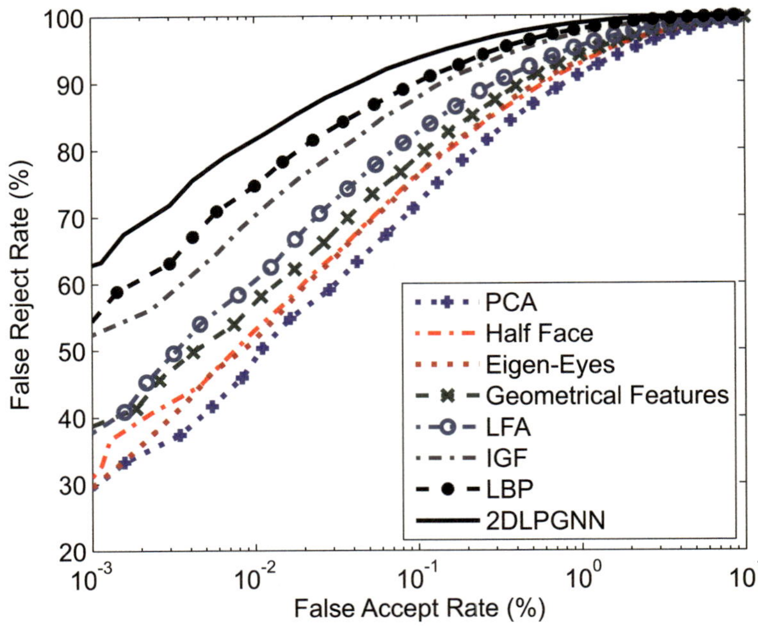

Fig. 12. ROC to evaluate the performance of face recognition algorithms on the face disguise database

Verification accuracy at 0.01% FAR								
Variations	Appearance based algorithms			Feature based algorithms		Texture based algorithms		
	PCA	Half-face	Eigen-eyes	GF	LFA	IGF	LBP	2DLPGNN
Minimal variations	60.3	59.5	63.1	61.3	63.7	74.2	85.5	96.9
Hair	56.8	61.4	57.2	61.9	63.1	73.8	85.1	96.4
Beard and moustache	32.2	34.1	60.5	53.2	54.5	58.7	61.0	77.3
Glasses	41.4	44.6	6.9	52.4	53.8	57.6	62.5	81.9
Cap and hat	55.7	56.8	50.4	58.9	61.4	71.0	80.4	86.3
Lips, nose, and eyebrow	56.3	59.2	47.7	49.1	56.3	70.9	78.6	89.2
Aging and wrinkles	49.6	53.9	41.6	51.8	54.9	55.1	70.3	80.8
Multiple variations	14.7	16.4	30.3	31.6	32.0	32.8	50.3	65.6
Overall	48.2	52.9	51.1	58.0	60.4	70.1	74.7	82.0

Table 3. Verification performance of the appearance, feature and texture based face recognition algorithms for different disguise variations

security applications such as border crossing and terrorist watch list, when an individual attempts to defraud law enforcement by altering his or her physical appearance with disguises. This chapter emphasizes this important aspect of face recognition. It describes different types of disguise variations and experimentally analyzes their effect on face recognition algorithms. The performance of appearance based algorithms, feature based algorithms, and texture based algorithms are compared using the heterogeneous face database and the disguise face database. Experimental results suggest that high degree of disguise variations is more challenging to address compared to variations in pose, expression and illumination. Furthermore, it also suggests that a careful and thorough investigation is required to develop a robust face recognition algorithm that can fulfil the operational needs of real world applications.

7. Acknowledgement

The authors would like to thank NIST, Robotics Institute CMU, CMU AMP Research Lab, Dr. A.R. Martinez, Dr. E.G.L. Miller and Equinox Corporation for granting us access to the face databases used in this research.

8. References

Ahonen, T.; Hadid, A. & Pietikäinen, M. (2006). Face description with local binary patterns: application to face recognition. *IEEE Transactions on Pattern Analysis and Machine Intelligence*, Vol. 28, No. 12, pp. 2037-2041

Alexander, J. & Smith, J. (2003). Engineering privacy in public: Confounding face recognition, privacy enhancing technologies. *Proceedings of International Workshop on Privacy Enhancing Technologies*, pp. 88–106

CMU AMP face database: http://amp.ece.cmu.edu/projects/FaceAuthentication/download.htm

Cox, I.J.; Ghosn, J. & Yianilos, P.N. (1996). Feature-based face recognition using mixture-distance. *Proceedings of International Conference on Computer Vision and Pattern Recognition*, pp. 209-216

Delac, K. & Grgic, M. (2007) Face recognition, I-TECH Education and Publishing

Equinox face database: http://www.equinoxsensors.com/products/HID.html

Faces software: http://www.iqbiometrix.com/products_faces_40.html

Huang, G.B.; Ramesh, M.; Berg, T. & Learned-Miller E. (2007). Labeled faces in the wild: A database for studying face recognition in unconstrained environments. University of Massachusetts, Amherst, Technical Report

Liu, C. & Wechsler, H. (2003). Independent component analysis of Gabor features for face recognition. *IEEE Transactions on Neural Networks*, Vol. 14, No. 4, pp. 919-928

Li, S. & Jain, A. (2005) Handbook of face recognition. New York: Springer

Martinez, A. & Benavente, R. (1998). The AR face database. Computer Vision Center, Technical Report.

Pamudurthy, S.; Guan, E.; Mueller, K. & Rafailovich M. (2005). Dynamic approach for face recognition using digital image skin correlation. *Proceedings of Audio- and Video-based Biometric Person Authentication*, pp. 1010–1018

Penev, P. & Atick, J. (1996). Local feature analysis: a general statistical theory for object representation. *Network: Computation in Neural Systems*, Vol. 7, pp. 477-500

Phillips, P.J.; Moon, H.; Rizvi, S. & Rauss, P.J. (2000). The FERET evaluation methodology for face recognition algorithms. *IEEE Transactions on Pattern Analysis and Machine Intelligence*, Vol. 22, No. 10, pp. 1090–1104

Phillips, P.; Flynn, P.; Scruggs, T.; Bowyer, K. & Worek, W. (2006). Preliminary face recognition grand challenge results, *Proceedings of International Conference on Automatic Face and Gesture Recognition*, pp. 15–24

Phillips, P.; Scruggs, W.; O' Toole, A.; Flynn, P.; Bowyer, K.; Schott, C. & Sharpe, M. (2007). FRVT 2006 and ICE 2006 large-scale results, NIST Technical Report NISTIR 7408

Ramanathan, N.; Chowdhury, A. & Chellappa, R. (2004). Facial similarity across age, disguise, illumination and pose, *Proceedings of International Conference on Image Processing*, Vol. 3, pp. 1999–2002

Silva P. & Rosa, A.S. (2003). Face recognition based on eigeneyes. *Pattern Recognition and Image Analysis*, Vol. 13, No. 2, pp. 335–338

Sim, T.; Baker, S. & Bsat, M. (2003). The CMU pose, illumination, and expression database. *IEEE Transactions on Pattern Analysis and Machine Intelligence*, Vol. 25, No. 12, pp. 1615-1618

Singh, R.; Vatsa, M. & Noore A., (2008). Face recognition with disguise and single gallery images. *Image and Vision Computing*, doi:10.1016/j.imavis.2007.06.010

Wechsler, H. (2006). Reliable Face Recognition Methods: System Design, Implementation and Evaluation. Springer

Yale face database: http://cvc.yale.edu/projects/yalefaces/yalefaces.html

Zhao, W.-Y.; Chellappa, R.; Phillips, P. J. & Rosenfeld A. (2003). Face recognition: A literature survey. *ACM Computing Survey*, Vol. 35, No. 4, pp. 399–458

Discriminant Subspace Analysis for Uncertain Situation in Facial Recognition

Pohsiang Tsai, Tich Phuoc Tran, Tom Hintz and Tony Jan
School of Computing and Communications – University of Technology, Sydney Australia

1. Introduction

Facial analysis and recognition have received substential attention from researchers in biometrics, pattern recognition, and computer vision communities. They have a large number of applications, such as security, communication, and entertainment. Although a great deal of efforts has been devoted to automated face recognition systems, it still remains a challenging uncertainty problem. This is because human facial appearance has potentially of very large intra-subject variations of head pose, illumination, facial expression, occlusion due to other objects or accessories, facial hair and aging. These misleading variations may cause classifiers to degrade generalization performance.

It is important for face recognition systems to employ an effective feature extraction scheme to enhance separability between pattern classes which should maintain and enhance features of the input data that make distinct pattern classes separable (Jan, 2004). In general, there exist a number of different feature extraction methods. The most common feature extraction methods are subspace analysis methods such as principle component analysis (PCA) (Kirby & Sirovich, 1990) (Jolliffe, 1986) (Turk & Pentland, 1991b), kernel principle component analysis (KPCA) (Schölkopf et al., 1998) (Kim et al., 2002) (all of which extract the most informative features and reduce the feature dimensionality), Fisher's linear discriminant analysis (FLD) (Duda et al., 2000) (Belhumeur et al., 1997), and kernel Fisher's discriminant analysis (KFLD) (Mika et al., 1999) (Scholkopf & Smola, 2002) (which discriminate different patterns; that is, they minimize the intra-class pattern compactness while enhancing the extra-class separability). The discriminant analysis is necessary because the patterns may overlap in decision space.

Recently, Lu et al. (Lu et al., 2003) stated that PCA and LDA are the most widely used conventional tools for dimensionality reduction and feature extraction in the appearance-based face recognition. However, because facial features are naturally non-linear and the inherent linear nature of PCA and LDA, there are some limitations when applying these methods to the facial data distribution (Bichsel & Pentland, 1994) (Lu et al., 2003). To overcome such problems, nonlinear methods can be applied to better construct the most discriminative subspace.

In real world applications, overlapping classes and various environmental variations can significantly impact face recognition accuracy and robustness. Such misleading information make Machine Learning difficult in modelling facial data. According to Adini et al. (Adini et al., 1997), it is desirable to have a recognition system which is able to recognize a face insensitive to these within-personal variations.

However, in (Adini et al., 1997), the authors mainly focused their empirical experiments on variations due to changes in illumination. They stated that within-personal variation is larger than between-personal separation. These variations between images of the same individual faces make difficult machine learning. Therefore, in a facial recognition system if the extracted input data contains misleading information (ambiguous regions), classifiers may produce a degraded classification performance (Jan, 2004). Specifically, in this chapter, we will mainly focus our empirical experiments on variations due to changes in facial expression that are less emphasized in (Adini et al., 1997) and deal with the impact of facial expression changes as individuals deform/express their faces either naturally or deliberately in a real-time face recognition system. As Adini et al. (Adini et al., 1997) stated that a facial recognition system should recognize a face insensitive to these within-personal variations. Limited success is reported for face recognition systems that are invariant of facial expression changes (Liu et al., 2002b) (Liu et al., 2003) (Martinez, 2000) (Martinez, 2002) (Seow et al., 2003) (Chen & Lovell, 2004). Our earlier research on a facial expression invariant system demonstrated its challenging nature (Tsai et al., 2005) (Tsai & Jan, 2005). If the number of individuals is increased (along with their varying facial expressions), the facial data will largely overlap. Thus, the variations of individual facial expressions will increase the range of uncertainty. This makes classification difficult.

The aim of this chapter was first to address the issue of within-personal variations due to facial expression changes. We then used a kernel-based discriminant analysis technique to reduce the uncertainty (overlapping) in the feature subspace applied before learning so as to improve classification rates. This chapter also examined other linear and nonlinear techniques (PCA, FLD, and KPCA) for comparison. Their transformation effects on a subsequent classification performances were then tested in combination with learning algorithms (multi-layered perceptron neural networks (MLPNNs), radial basis function neural networks (RBFNNs), and support vector machines (SVMs)). The algorithms were then applied to face database with facial expression changes. We found that the transformation of kernel-based discriminant analysis had a beneficial effect to the classification performance. The experimental results indicates that non-linear discrimininant analysis method may robustly deal with the uncertainty problem. It appears that a facial recognition system may be robust to facial expressio changes, and thus be applicable.

The structure of this chapter is as follows: First, we provide a concise overview of the facial expression analysis. Second, we discuss the expression variant problem in facial recognition. Third, we introduce a concise overview of the subspace feature extraction methods. Then, in the final part of this chapter, we analyse different subspace transformation methods and their transformation capabilities. We finally present the results of the experiments and discuss them from several aspects, focusing on the advantages and disadvantages of each subspace feature extraction method.

2. Facial expression analysis

Human faces contain abundant information of human facial behaviors (Cohn et al., 1999). According to Johansson's point-light display experiment (Johansson, 1973) (Johansson, 1976), facial expressions can be described by the movements of points that belong to the facial features such as eye brows, eyes, nose, mouth and chin and analyzed by the relationships between those features in movements (Pantic & Rothkrantz, 2000b). Hence, point-based visual properties of facial expressions can then be used for facial gesture analysis. We present a literature review regarding facial expression analysis in the following subsections.

2.1 Facial muscle analysis

Facial features such as eyes, eyebrows, mouth, facial lines and bulges will change human facial appearances when their facial muscles are contracted. The contracted muscles will deform those features temporarily and the change of the muscular movements can only last for a few seconds (Fasel & Luettin, 2003) (Pantic & Rothkrantz, 2004). Those facial muscles include frontalis, corrugator, procerus, depressor supercilli, orbicularis oculi, levator labii superioris, nasalis, zygomatic minor, zygomatic major, caninus, depressor labii, buccinator, orbicularis oris, masseter, depressor labii, mentalis, triangularis, platysman, and risorius. Readers who are interested in the anatomy of facial muscles can refer to dataface website[1] for rigorous exposition.

2.2 Action Units (AUs)

The FACS is called Facial Action Coding system, which is used to describe facial movements/motions/actions of facial muscles in behavior science (Ekman & Friesen, 1975) (Donato et al., 1999) (Essa & Pentland, 1997). This system is based on action units (Aus). Each AU represents some facial movement. For example, AU1 stands for upward pull of the inner portion of the eyebrows. There are 44 AUs in total. Different sets of combinations of AUs accur in different facial expression categories; for example, the combination of 'surprise' consists of AUs1+2. In Figure 1, it shows the upper facial muscles that correspond to action units 1,2,4,6 and 7.

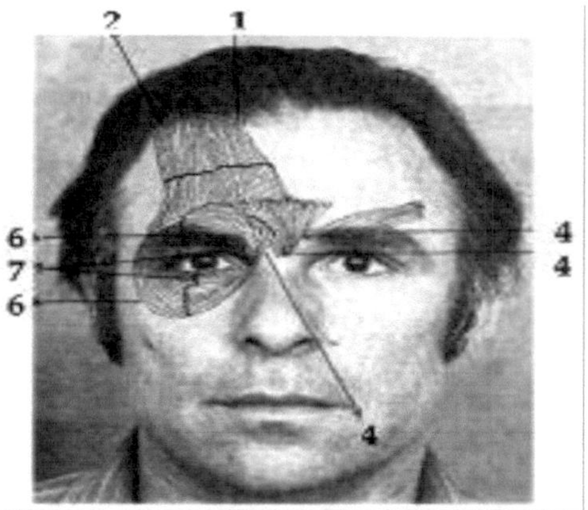

Fig. 1. The corresponding action units to the upper facial muscle (Donato et al., 1999).

Moreover, those action units can also be used to detect subtle changes of facial expression (Pantic & Rothkrantz, 2004, Tian et al., 2001). The Automatic Facial Analysis (AFA) system

[1] http://face-and-emotion.com/dataface/general/homepage.jsp

(Tian et al., 2001) and FACS+ (Essa & Pentland, 1997) were developed to improve FACS system (Ekman & Friesen, 1975).

2.3 Facial expression data extraction

Detection of feature points of a still image is very important in facial expression analysis because by knowing which expression the current image is and which facial muscle actions produce such an expression (Pantic & Rothkrantz, 2004, Vukadinovic & Pantic, 2005). There are three types of face representation for analyzing facial expressions (Donato et al., 1999). They are template-based (holistic), feature-based (analytic), and hybrid (analytic to holistic) methods (Pantic & Rothkrantz, 2000a). See Figure 7.2 and literature (Pantic & Rothkrantz, 2004) (Cootes et al., 1998) (Huang & Huang, 1997) (Kobayashi & Hara, 1992) (Valstar & Pantic, 2006) (Cohn et al., 1998) (Lyons et al., 1998) (Zhang et al., 1998). Interested readers can refer to those references for rigorous explanations.

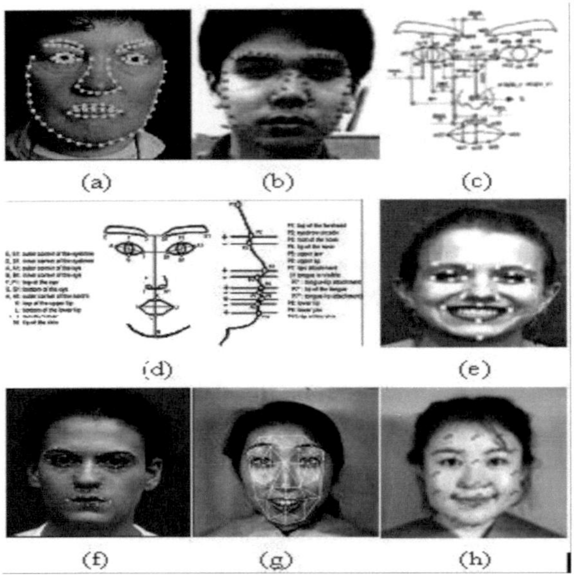

Fig. 2. Different ways of detecting facial fiducial points (Cootes et al., 1998) (Huang & Huang, 1997) (Kobayashi & Hara, 1992) (Pantic & Rothkrantz, 2004) (Valstar & Pantic, 2006) (Cohn et al., 1998) (Lyons et al., 1998) (Zhang et al., 1998) .

2.4 Facial model

About 55% of human communication relies on facial expressions. Facial expressions; however, are the normative units of the non-verbal communication (Pantic & Rothkrantz, 2000b). There are prototypic (Six basic emotional expressions: sadness, happiness, anger, disgust, fear and surprise) and non-prototypic (blended emotional expression) expressions (Ekman & Friesen, 1975, Pantic & Rothkrantz, 2000b). In addition, *facial fiducial points* are the special facial points such as the corners of the eyes, corners of the eyebrows, and the tip of the chin etc. (Vukadinovic & Pantic, 2005). Examples using facial feature points are (Pantic & Rothkrantz, 2004) which used 19 fiducial facial feature points and (Vukadinovic & Pantic, 2005) (Valstar & Pantic, 2006) which used 20 fiducial facial feature points as in Figure 3.

The frontal-view face model is composed of 30 features (F1-F30, please see (Pantic & Rothkrantz, 2000b)) , which are defined by a set of 20 facial fiducial points. For example, F3 is the distance between point A and E and F18 is the distance between point C and point M etc. (See Table 1 (Right) for some examples). These points are illustrated in Figure 3 and described in Table 1 (Right).

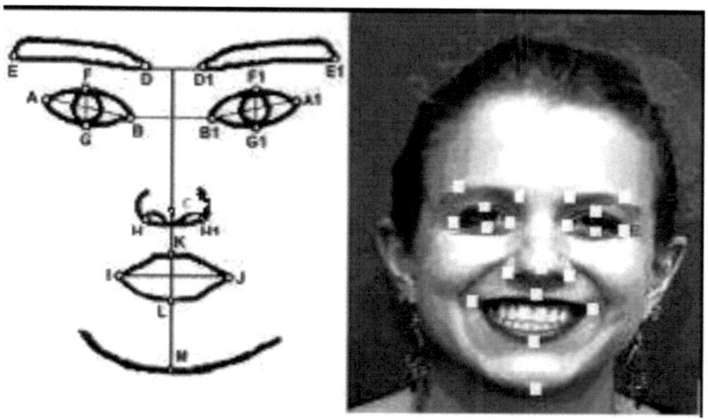

Fig. 3. Twenty Facial fiducial points (Pantic & Rothkrantz, 2004).

Point	Point Description
A	Left eye outer corner, stable point
A1	Right eye outer corner, stable point
B	Left eye inner corner, stable point
B1	Right eye inner corner, stable point
C	The medial point between left and right nostril centers
D	Left eyebrow inner corner, non-stable
D1	Right eyebrow inner corner, non-stable
E	Left eyebrow outer corner, non-stable
E1	Right eyebrow outer corner, non-stable
F	Top of the left eye, non-stable
F1	Top of the right eye, non-stable
G	Bottom of the left eye, non-stable
G1	Bottom of the right eye, non-stable
K	Top of the upper lip, non-stable
L	Bottom of the lower lip, non-stable
I	Left corner of the mouth, non-stable
J	Right corner of the mouth, non-stable
M	Tip of the chin, non-stable

Feature	Feature description
F1	Angle BAD
F2	Angle B1A1D1
F3	Distance AE
F4	Distance A1E1
F5	Distance cF, c is the centre of AB
F6	Distance c1F1, c1 is the centre of A1B1
F7	Distance cG
F8	Distance c1G1
F9	Distance FG
F10	Distance F1G1
F11	Distance CK, C is 0.5HH1 (f0)
F12	Distance IB
F13	Distance JB1
F14	Distance CI
F15	Distance CJ
F16	Distance IJ
F17	Distance KL
F18	Distance CM

Table 1. (Left) Facial fiducial point description of the frontal-view model; (Right) Some examples of the features of the frontal-view model (Pantic & Rothkrantz, 2000b).

3. Related work in expression invariant facial recognition

The facial expression variation problem not only exist in facial recognition but also in any multimedia databases that require image retrieval. The recognition performance of facial recognition system that trained with only neural faces will drop if there are facial expression variations in the appearance of facial images. Image retrieval from multimedia databases requires semantic queries to help a user to obtain or to manipulate data without knowing its detailed syntactic structure. An emerging technology in this area is the image-based query from a user's input. In particular, in the context of facial images, it is of interest to retrieve information based on faces. There are many research have been conducted to tackle pose or illumination problems. However, little work has been conducted to tackle expressions. When images of the databases appear at different facial expressions, most currently available face recognition approaches encounter the expression-invariant problem in which neutral faces are difficult to recognize.

For example, (Liu et al., 2002b) (Liu et al., 2003), a quantified statistical facial asymmetry method under 2D facial expression changes (called AsymFaces) was used for person identification. PCA was then applied to AsymFaces for dimension reduction. AsymFaces were claimed to be invariant to facial expression changes. In (Martinez, 2000) (Martinez, 2002), a local and probabilistic weighting method that weights the local areas of facial features independently, which are less sensitive to expression changes. In (Seow et al., 2003), a learning algorithm based on L2-norm approximation was proposed and applied to face expression variant database so as to evaluate the problem of facial expression changes for face recognition. In (Chen & Lovell, 2004), an adaptive principle component analysis (APCA) method was used to deal with one sample problem under both illumination and facial expression changes simultaneously. APCA method was applied to 2D face images after applying standard PCA method in order to construct a subspace for image representation and to improve class separability. A Bayes classifier was then used for classification.

However, their apperance-based approaches still suffer from high dimensionality problem; that is to say, this problem will require expensive computation and increase the sparse data distribution. Our earlier research (Tsai et al., 2005) (Tsai & Jan, 2005) used seventeen Euclidean distance-based facial features of multiple training images in each class and applied subspace model analysis to develop a facial recognition system that was tolerant to facial expression changes. The dimensionality of the Euclidean distance-based facial features was reduced greatly compared to the appearance-based approaches. Our previous work also demonstrated its challenging nature. If the number of individuals is increased (along with their varying facial expressions), the facial data will largely overlap. That is, the variations of individual facial expressions will increase the range of uncertainty. This makes classification difficult. Therefore, the extensive work of our previous research in this chapter aimed to reduce the uncertainty (overlapping) in the feature subspace applied before learning so as to improve the classification rates.

4. An overview of subspace analysis in feature extraction

Feature extraction in subspace analysis aims to transform a multidimensional feature space of initial objects to be classified (data points) into a reduced low dimensional feature space before executing a learning algorithm so as to improve classification performance and to reduce the dimensionality of the data. That is, the initial data feature set is transformed into another transformed feature set so as to yield a more efficient and faster classification. The approach of subspace analysis methods can be either linear or nonlinear. We then discuss these methods in the following sections. Our aim is to help the reader gain a unified view of these feature extraction methods and get some ideas about their usage.

4.1 Linear-based suspace analysis

Subspace analysis methods are the processes of projecting high dimensional data to a lower dimensional subspace which are used for visualization or dimensionality reduction in pattern recognition applications. Subspace Analysis methods such as Principle Component Analysis (PCA) and Fisher's Linear Discriminant (FLD) analysis are used for the extraction of low-dimensional forms consisted of statistically uncorrelated or independent variables which is crucial in machine learning that tends to simplify tasks such as regression, classification, and density estimation .

4.1.1 Principle Component Analysis (PCA)

PCA is a classical feature extraction and data representation technique also known as Karhunen-Loeve Expansion. It is a linear method that projects the high-dimensional data onto a lower dimensional space. It seeks a weight projection that best represents the data, which is called principle components. It has been used in the areas of pattern recognition and computer vision. Sirovich and Kirby (1987 and 1990) first used PCA to efficiently represent pictures of human faces. Turk and Pentland presented the well-known Eigenfaces methods for face recognition in 1991 (Turk & Pentland, 1991a) (Turk, 2001). However, its main limitation is that it does not consider class separability.

Let a face image X_i be a two-dimensional $m \times m$ array of intensity values, an image may also be considered as a vector of dimension x^2. Denote the training set of n face images by $X = (X_1, X_2, \ldots, X_n) \subset R^{m^2 \times n}$, and we assume that each image belongs to one of c classes. Define the covariance matrix as follows (Bishop, 1995) (Duda et al., 2000):

$$\Sigma = \frac{1}{n}\sum_{i=1}^{n}(X_i - \overline{X})(X_i - \overline{X})^T = \Phi\Phi^T \tag{1}$$

where $\Phi = (\Phi_1, \Phi_2, \ldots, \Phi_n) \subset \Re^{m^2 \times n}$ and $\overline{X} = (1/n)\Sigma_{i=1}^{n} X_i$. Then, the eigenvalues and eigenvectors of the covariance Σ are calculated. Let $U=(U_1,U_2,\ldots,U_r) \subset \Re^{m^2 \times n} (r<n)$ be the r eigenvectors corresponding to the r largest eigenvalues. Thus, for a set of original face images $X \subset \Re^{m^2 \times n}$, their corresponding eigenface-based feature $Y \subset \Re^{r \times n}$ can be obtained by projecting X onto the eigen-based feature space as follows:

$$Y = U^T X \tag{2}$$

4.1.2 Linear Discriminant Analysis (LDA)

While PCA is unsupervised method that constructs the face space without using the face class (category) information, the LDA aims to find an "optimal" way to represent the face vector space to maximize the discrimination between different face classes. Exploiting the class infomration can be helpful to the identification tasks.

FLD is also a linear projection of discriminant analysis. It is not just the choice of discriminant itself but the choice of dimensionality reduction. Therefore, it is a specific choice of direction for projection of the data right down to one dimension. Its objective is to preserve the class discriminatory information as much as possible while reducing the dimensionality from original n dimension space into $(c-1)$ dimension space in order to classify c classes of objects. Therefore, if the data is linearly separable, the results of FLD will be globally optimal because of its linear transformation which maximizes the ratio of the determinant of the between-class scatter matrix of the projected samples to the determinant of the with-class scatter matrix of the projected samples (Bishop, 1995) (Duda et al., 2000).

However, its limitations include "the separability criterion is not directly related to the classification accuracy in the output space" and "if the distributions are significantly non-Gaussian, the LDA projections will not be able to preserve any complex structure of the data, which may be needed for classification" (Lotlikar & Kothari, 2000).

Let a face image X_i be a two-dimensional $m \times m$ array of intensity values, an image may also be considered as a vector of dimension x^2. Denote the training set of n face images by $X = (X_1, X_2, ..., X_n) \subset R^{m^2 \times n}$, and we assume that each image belongs to one of c classes. Define the between-class scatter and the within-class scatter matrices as follows:

$$S_B = \sum_{i=1}^{c} n^i (\overline{X}^i - \overline{X})(\overline{X}^i - \overline{X})^i \tag{3}$$

$$S_W = \sum_{i=1}^{c} \sum_{X_k \in X_i} (X_k - \overline{X}^i)(X_k - \overline{X}^i)^T \tag{4}$$

where $\overline{X} = (1/n)\sum_{j=1}^{n} X_j$ is the mean image of input vectors, and $\overline{X}^i = (1/n^i)\sum_{j=1}^{n^i} X_j^i$ is the mean image of the ith class, n^i is the number of samples in the ith class and c is the number of classes. Therefore, If S_W is nonsingular, the optimal projection W_{opt} is chosen as the matrix with orthonormal columns which maximizes the ratio of the determinant of the between-class scatter matrix of the projected input samples to the determinant of the with-class scatter matrix of the projected input samples. The optimal projection W_{opt} is defined as follows:

$$W_{opt} = \arg\max_{W} \frac{\left|W^T S_B W\right|}{\left|W^T S_W W\right|} = \left[W_1, W_2, ..., W_m\right] \tag{5}$$

where $\left\{W_i \mid i = 1, 2, ..., c-1\right\}$ is the set of generalized eigenvectors of S_B and S_W corresponding to the $c-1$ largest generalized eigenvalues $\left\{\lambda_i \mid i = 1, 2, ..., c-1\right\}$,i.e.,

$$S_W^{-1} S_B W = \lambda_i W \tag{6}$$

Thereby, the feature vectors Z for any probe face images X in the most discriminant subspace can be calculated as follows:

$$Z = W_{opt}^{T} \cdot X \tag{7}$$

4.2 Non-linear subspace analysis

The combination of subspace analysis methods with NN-based classifiers is to reduce the dimensionality of input data so as to reducing the NN structure and computational complexity; hence increasing the classification accuracy. KPCA and KFLD are kernel-based PCA and FLD subspace analysis methods. These two kernel-based methods are ideal to use in nonlinearly complex real-world problems. They firstly nonlinearly map the input data into some high dimensional feature space F by using kernel functions, and secondly apply the PCA and FLD methods in the mapped feature space (Schölkopf et al., 1998) (Mika et al., 1999). Some further details of KPCA and KFDA in face recognition are provided in (Yang et al., 2000) (Liu et al., 2002a) (Kim et al., 2002) (Yang, 2002).

4.2.1 Kernel principle component analysis

Given a set of centered input data $X = \{x_k\}\Big|_{k=1,...,n,k\in R^{d\times n}}$, where n the number of input data is, d is the number of dimensions, the input data is projected onto a high dimensional feature space F by nonlinear kernel mapping $\Phi{:}X\in R^{d\times n} \rightarrow f\in F$, in which the mapped data $\Phi(x_k)$ is centered as $\sum_{k=1}^{N}\Phi(x_k) = 0$. In the feature space F, the estimate of the covariance matrix of the mapped data $\Phi(x_k)$ is defined as:

$$C^{\Phi} = \frac{1}{n}\sum_{k=1}^{n} \Phi(x_k)\Phi(x_k)^{T} \tag{8}$$

and the eigenvalues and eigenvectors of the covariance matrix C^{Φ} is calculated as

$$\lambda w^{\Phi} = C^{\Phi} w^{\Phi} \tag{9}$$

where eigen-values $\lambda \geq 0$ and eigenvectors $w^{\Phi} \in F \setminus \{0\}$. As $C^{\Phi} w^{\Phi} = \frac{1}{n}\sum_{k=1}^{n}(\Phi(x_k)\cdot w^{\Phi})\Phi(x_k)$, all solutions w^{Φ} with $\lambda \neq 0$ must lie in the span of $\Phi(x_1),...,\Phi(x_N)$; hence, equation **Error! Reference source not found.** is equivalent to

$$\lambda(\Phi(x_k)\cdot w^{\Phi}) = (\Phi(x_k)\cdot C^{\Phi} w^{\Phi}) \ \forall k = 1,...,n \tag{10}$$

The expansion of w^{Φ} is formed as

$$w^{\Phi} = \sum_{i=1}^{n} \alpha_i \Phi(x_i) \tag{11}$$

where any solution $\{\alpha_i | i=1...n\}$ must lie in the span of all samples in F.

Combining (10) and (11), and also defining an $n\times n$ matrix K by $k_{ij} = (\Phi(x_i)\Phi(x_j))$, which produces an eigenvalue problem, is defined as

$$M\lambda k\alpha = k^2\alpha \equiv M\lambda\alpha = k\alpha \tag{12}$$

Now, we can solve the eigenvalue problem (12) in F by finding the r largest leading eigenvectors $\{\alpha_i | i = 1,2,..,r\}$ of $M\lambda$ corresponding to r largest eigenvalues $\{\lambda_i | i = 1,2,..,r\}$. Finally, we can project $\Phi(x)$ to a lower dimensional subspace spanned by eigenvectors w^{Φ}, i.e.

$$w^{\Phi}\Phi(x) = \sum_{i=1}^{n} \alpha_i k(x_i, x) \tag{13}$$

, which is the nonlinear principle component corresponding to Φ.

4.2.2 Kernel fisher's linear discriminant analysis

Let the centered input data $X = \bigcup_{i=1}^{c} x_{n_i}^{i}$ be samples from c classes with total samples $n = \sum_{i=1}^{c} n_i$, where each class has n_i samples. The input data is projected into an implicit feature space F by nonlinear kernel mapping $\Phi : x \in R^{d \times n} \rightarrow f \in F$. The kernel functions such as Gaussian RBF or polynomial is used to compute the dot products of the training patterns in some feature space F, instead of computing Φ explicitly. We then compute Fisher's linear discriminant in F. Let Φ be a non-linear mapping to F, we need to find the vector $w^{\Phi} \in F$ which maximizes

$$J(w^{\Phi}) = \frac{(w^{\Phi})^T S_B^{\Phi} w^{\Phi}}{(w^{\Phi})^T S_W^{\Phi} w^{\Phi}} \tag{14}$$

so as to find the linear discriminant in F. We define between-class scatter matrix S_B^{Φ} and within-class scatter matrix S_W^{Φ} in the feature space F as

$$S_B^{\Phi} = \frac{1}{c(c-1)} \sum_{i=1}^{c} \sum_{j=1}^{c} (u_i^{\Phi} - u_j^{\Phi})(u_i^{\Phi} - u_j^{\Phi})^T \tag{15}$$

$$S_W^{\Phi} = \frac{1}{c} \sum_{i=1}^{c} \frac{1}{ni} \sum_{j=1}^{ni} (\Phi(x_j^i) - u_i^{\Phi})(\Phi(x_j^i) - u_i^{\Phi})^T \tag{16}$$

where $u_i^{\Phi} = \frac{1}{ni} \sum_{j=1}^{ni} \Phi(x_j^i)$ denotes the sample mean of class i in F. Therefore, any solution $\{\alpha_i | i=1...n\}$ must lie in the span of all samples in F. The expansion of w^{Φ} is formed as

$$w^{\Phi} = \sum_{i=1}^{n} \alpha_i \Phi(x_i) \tag{17}$$

by (17) and u_i^{Φ}, we write the projection of u_i^{Φ} onto w^{Φ} as

$$((w^{\Phi})^T \cdot u_i^{\Phi}) = \frac{1}{n_i} \sum_{j=1}^{n} \sum_{k=1}^{n_i} \alpha_j k(x_j, x_k^i) = \alpha^T U_i \tag{18}$$

where $(U_i)_j = \frac{1}{n_i} \sum_{k=1}^{n_i} k(x_j, x_k^i)$, and the dot products is replaced by the kernel function. Therefore, it follows that

$$(w^{\Phi})^T S_B^{\Phi} w^{\Phi} = \alpha^T MB\alpha \tag{19}$$

$$(w^{\Phi})^T S_W^{\Phi} w^{\Phi} = \alpha^T NW\alpha \tag{20}$$

where $M_B = \frac{1}{c(c-1)} \sum_{i=1}^{c} \sum_{j=1}^{c} (m_i - m_j)(m_i - m_j)^T$ and $N_W = \frac{1}{c} \sum_{i=1}^{c} \frac{1}{n_i} \sum_{j=1}^{n_i} (\xi_j - m_i)(\xi_j - m_i)^T$ with $\xi_j = \sum_{j=1}^{n_i} k(x_n, x_j)^T$.

We then replace N_W with $N_W + \mu I$ for numerical issues and regularization(Mika et al., 1999). Thus, combining (19) and (20), we can choose the $(c-1)$ optimal projection α_{opt}, which maximize the Fisher's linear discriminant in F by

$$J(\alpha) = \frac{\alpha^T M_B \alpha}{\alpha^T N_W \alpha} \tag{21}$$

The optimal projection α_{opt} is defined as finding the $(c-1)$ leading eigenvectors $\{\alpha_i | i = 1, 2, .., c-1\}$ of $N_W^{-1} M_B$ corresponding to the $(c-1)$ largest eigenvalues $\{\lambda_i | i = 1, 2, .., c-1\}$, i.e

$$N_W^{-1} M_B \alpha_i = \lambda_i \alpha_i \tag{22}$$

Finally, we can project $\Phi(x)$ to a lower dimensional subspace spanned by eigenvectors w^{Φ}, i.e.

$$((w^{\Phi})^T \cdot \Phi(x)) = \sum_{i=1}^{n} \alpha_i k(x_i, x) \tag{23}$$

5. Experiments

Experiments will consist of comparing the face recognition rates under varying expressions for different types of classifiers. In the following sections, we discuss the analyses of different feature extractors.

5.1 Facial expression database and performance evaluation

One of the databases of facial expression images used in this chapter is the Japanese Female Facial Expression (JAFFE) database[2]. This database is used for facial expression analysis and

---

[2] http://www.kasrl.org/jaffe.html

recognition (Lyons et al., 1998) (Zhang et al., 1998) (Lyons et al., 1999). It contains 213 gray-scale images of 6 facial expressions (happiness, sadness, surprise, anger, disgust, fear) plus one neutral face posed by 10 Japanese women. Each woman posed for two, three or four examples of each of the six basic facial expressions and a neutral face. Each individual pose is for various extents of facial expression changes. Some individuals pose similar facial expression changes, while others pose different ones. Also, some individuals have slight pose variations when they pose facial expressions. The size of each image is 256x256, resulting in an input dimensionality of $d = 65536$. Figure 4 displays the sample images in the database.

Moreover, we will conduct the hold-out procedure for our performance evaluation; that is, a certain amount of data is used for training and the remaining is used for testing. That is, one-third of the data for testing and two-thirds for training.

Fig. 4. Facial Expression Images from JAFFE database.

5.2 Geometric feature-based analysis

Features in facial images include eyes, nose, mouth, and chin. In facial recognition, geometric properties and relations such as areas, distances and angles between the features are selected as the descriptors of faces for recognition . Therefore, the geometric attributes provide benefits in data reduction and less sensitivity to variations in illumination, viewpoint, and expressions. Ivancevic et al. (Ivancevic et al., 2003) stated that, there are

about 80 landmark points on a human face Figure 5, and the number of points chosen is application-dependant. However, some authors used more than 80 facai points.
For example, Cootes et al.(Cootes et al., 1998) used 122 landmark points, Huang and Huang (Huang & Huang, 1997) used 90 facial feature points, Kobayashi and Hara (Kobayashi & Hara, 1992) used 30 facial characteristic points, Pantic and Rothkrantz (Pantic & Rothkrantz, 2004) used 19 facial fiducial points, Valstar and Pantic (Valstar & Pantic, 2006) used 20 facial fiducial points, Cohn et al. (Cohn et al., 1998) used 46 fiducial points, and Zhang et al.(Zhang et al., 1998) used 34 fidicial points.
Therefore, based on works in feature point tracking(Cohn et al., 1999, Cohn et al., 1998), action units recognition for facial expression analysis (Tian et al., 2001) (Valstar & Pantic, 2006) (Donato et al., 1999) (Essa & Pentland, 1997) (Pantic & Rothkrantz, 2004) (Tian et al., 2001), review papers in facial expression analysis (Fasel & Luettin, 2003) (Pantic & Rothkrantz, 2000b) (Pantic & Rothkrantz, 2000a), and the aforementioned works, we manually selected 18 fiducial characteristic points on each of the images for representing the original 17 Euclidean distance-based facial features superimposed on the subject's face image in Figure 6 Fig. 6. The 18 fiducial points on the subject's face image in the database. Note that we chose 'a' as the base point because that point does not move when changing expressions. These features are marked as F1, F2 ... F17 (See Table 2). Hence, these facial features provided certain discriminative information when individuals change expressions.

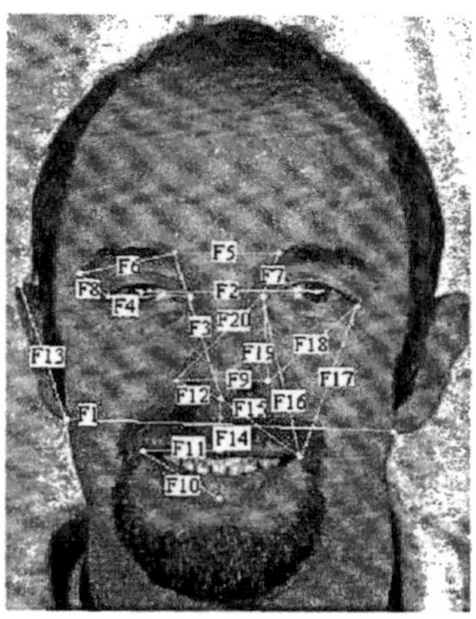

Fig. 5. Pre-selected facial features in the sample of 80 facial images from the test database

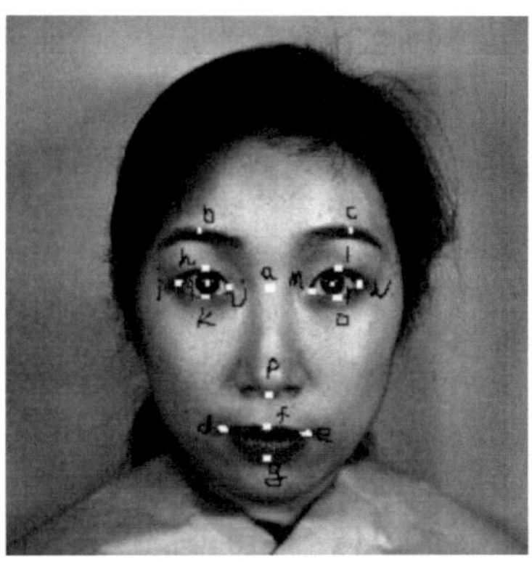

Fig. 6. The 18 fiducial points on the subject's face image in the database.

Features	F1	F2	F3	F4	F5	F6	F7	F8	F9
Distances	a_b	a_c	A_d	a_e	a_f	a_g	a_h	a_i	a_j
Features	F10	F11	F12	F13	F14	F15	F16	F17	
Distances	a_k	a_l	A_m	a_n	a_o	a_p	a_q	a_r	

Table 2. The original 17 pre-selected facial feature distances

5.3 Subspace tranformation analysis

The input facial features were normalized to have zero mean and unit variance so as to improve the performance of proposed methods. Figure 7 displays the first two components of the original 17 facial features (dimensions) of three and ten individuals respectively. Each shape symbol stands for each individual's name (e.g. KA, MK or NM etc.). The figure shows the nonlinear nature of image distribution and the increased overlapping problem of intra-personal variations under facial expression changes.

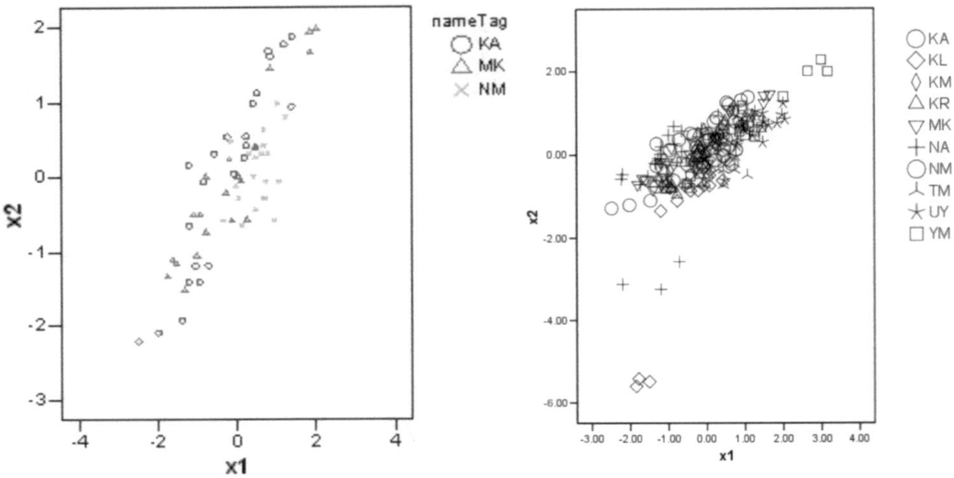

Fig. 7. (Left) First two components of 17 facial features of 3. (Right) 10 individuals after normalization.

Hence, these normalized input data were used for KPCA and KFLD subspace analysis methods. The Gaussian kernel $k(x,y)=\exp(-\|x-y\|^2/2\sigma^2)$ was used for the following analyses, where σ is Gaussian width. We will examine the impacts of KPCA and KFLD in the following subsections.

5.3.1 Linear-based subspace analysis results

In PCA-based Subspace Analysis, the original normalized 17 facial features of 3 and 10 individuals were reduced to 2 and 9 features after using PCA as shown in Figure 9 (Left) and Figure 9 (Right), respectively.

Figure 9 (Left) demonstrates that the original 17 facial features of three individuals were complex and non-separable after PCA. The result of this extraction thereby provided some insight to the original structure of feature distribution. However, Figure 9 (Right)

demonstrates that the original facial features of ten individuals became more complex and non-separable after PCA due to the increased number of subjects as shown in Figure 8.
Therefore, in some cases, PCA looses discriminant information. FLD promised to retain discriminant information.
In FLDA-based Subspace Analysis, the original normalized 17 facial features of three and ten individuals were reduced to two and nine features after using FLD as shown in Figure 9 (Left) Figure 9 (Left) and Figure 9 (Right), respectively. Figure 9 (Left) shows that the original 17 facial features of three individuals were well clustered after FLD; it was better than PCA for for clustering and classification. Figure 9 (Right) shows that the original features were overlapped due to the more dispersed data distribution as shown in Figure 7 (Right); however, the data distribution is still better than that of the PCA-based subspace of the 10 subjects. Hence, the results are very application-specific. Further classifiers are sometimes necessary to discriminate between these clusters using - MLP and/or RBFNN.

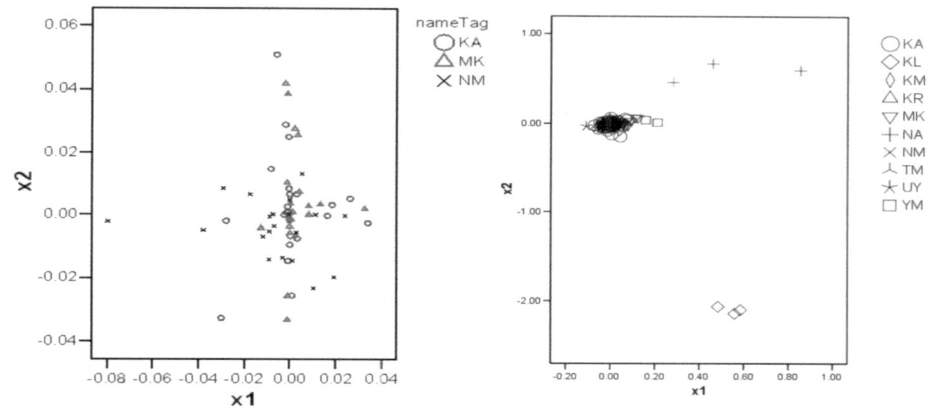

Fig. 8. (Left) Normalized 17 facial features of 3 individuals reduced to 2 features (prince-ple components) after PCA (left). (Right) First two components of PCA-transformed matrix ($d = 9$).

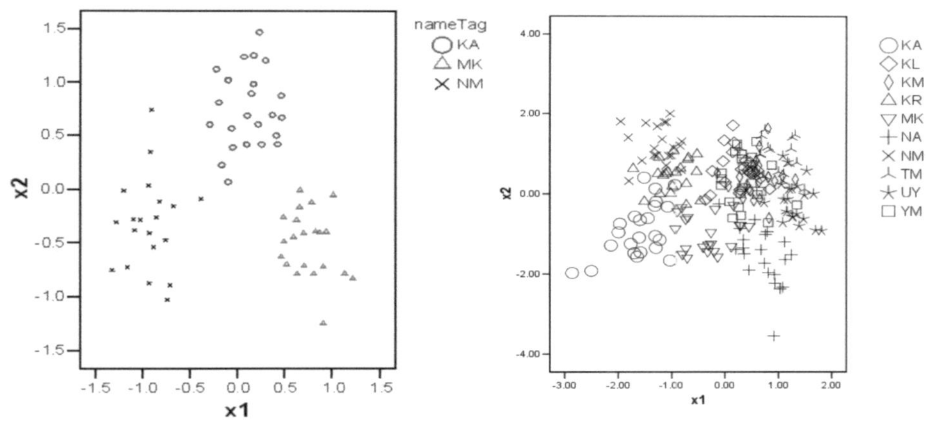

Fig. 9. (Left) Normalized 17 facial features of 3 individuals reduced to 2 features (c -1) after FLD. (Right) First two components of FLDA-transformed matrix ($d = 9$)

5.3.2 KPCA-based subspace analysis results

In KPCA-based Subspace Analysis, the normalized input data were reduced to 9 dimensions ($c - 1$) after using KPCA (same as in PCA). The first two components of the transformed matrix of 10 individuals are shown in Figure 10 (Left). This figure demonstrates that the resultant data distribution was less complex and overlapping than that of PCA (Figure 8(Right)). Clearly, the finding indicates that KPCA still tends to lose discriminant information. KFLD promises to retain discriminant information. In the following subsection, we will examine the results of KFLDA.

In KFLDA-based Subspace Analysis, the normalized input data were reduced to 9 dimensions ($c - 1$) after using KFLDA (same as in FLDA). The first two components of the transformed matrix of 10 individuals are shown in Figure 10 (Right). This figure shows that the resultant data distribution was well compacted and separated compared to that of FLDA (Figure 9 (Right)). The findings indicate that KFLDA was better than PCA, FLDA and KPCA for classification purpose. Thus, KFLDA can deal with uncertainty problem.

As the transformation results obtained from the above subspace analysis methods, we will use different classifiers to evaluate their transformation capabilities in the following section.

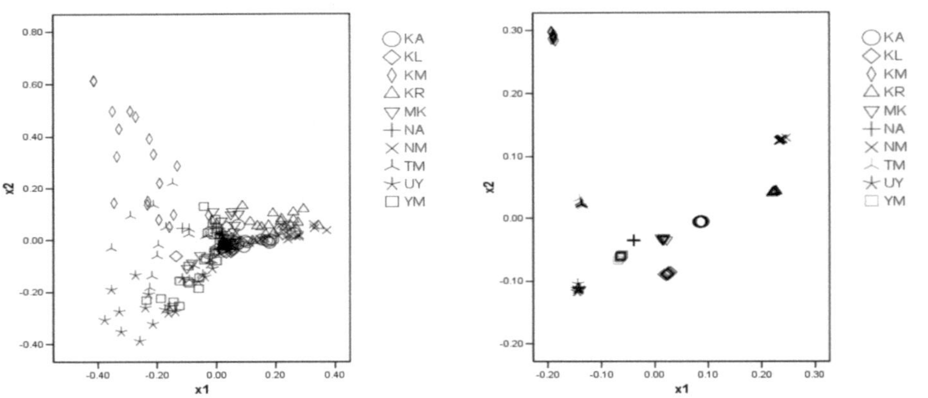

Fig. 10. (Left) First two components of KPCA-transformed matrix ($\sigma = 1$; $d = 9$). (Right) first two components of KFLD-transformed matrix ($\sigma = 1$; $d = 9$)

6. Results and discussion

Experiments will consist of comparing the face recognition rates under varying expressions for different types of classifiers. The original normalized facial features were fed to ANN-based classifiers and its results are compared to the results when the outputs of subspace analysis were fed to MLP, RBF or SVM classifiers.

The experimental results are shown in Table 3. Note that we focused on the transformation capability of each extractor instead of each classifier.

It shows that the classification performances of MLP and RBF neural networks were 90.9% and 45.5%, respectively. The classification performances of the PCA-based subspace analysis in sequence with ANNs for 3 individuals were 31.8% for both MLP and RBF models. The results from PCA subspace analysis showed to achieve poor classification performances. It is because the data distribution for PCA-based subspace provides less discriminative features. The classification performances of the FLD-based subspace analysis in sequence with ANNs for 3 individuals were 100% for both MLP and RBF models. The results used the FLD subspace analysis method were shown to achieve better classification performances. This is due to the data distribution for FLD-based subspace being perfectly separated and each class well-clustered. However, if the number of sample subjects is increased to 10, there is an obvious decrease of performance rates (Please see the averaged classification performances as shown in Table 3) due to the increased complexity of data distribution, which makes the PCA and/or FLD-based subspace analysis method more difficult to extract the informative and/or discriminant information for further classification. Hence, it appears that subspace analysis is crucial in pattern classification because of the importance of selecting optimal feature dimensionality. In summary, the experimental results of linear mapping subspace analyses showed that the existence of large within-class variation under facial expression changes will degrade the classification performance. This degradation is aggravated especially when the number of subjects is increased; and this happens frequently in the real world. Because of the limitation on linear mapping methods, more advanced methods will be employed to deal with the inherent nature of nonlinear data distribution of facial images by using the kernel-based discriminant analysis method.

Extractors	MLP	RBF	SVM	Average
		3 subjects		
None(all)	90.9	45.5	95.5	77.3
PCA (2)	31.8	31.8	36.4	33.3
FLD(2)	100	100	100	100
		10 subjects		
None(all)	84.9	42.5	83.6	70.3
PCA (9)	6.8	21.9	45.6	24.8
FLD (9)	45.2	63.0	87.7	65.3
KPCA(9)	75.3	39.7	72.6	62.5
KFLD(9)	100	100	100	100

Table 3. Classification performance of different classifiers (%)

PCA achieved the poorest classification performance. It is due to the data distribution for the PCA-based subspace being in ill-clustered features.

Note too that using the original features also directly returns fairly good classification performances due to the original feature subspace being tighter compact than that of PCA and all the three complex classifiers are powerful for dealing with nonlinear data distribution. PCA is of a linear nature; hence sometimes it is inadequate for non-linear problems. FLDA achieved better classification performance than PCA. It is because the image data distribution for the FLDA-based subspace is much better separated and clustered than that of the PCA-based subspace. However, these two linear mapping methods are incapable of dealing with the nonlinear image data problem adequately. They are poor in dealing with the uncertainty (overlapping) problem. The uncertainty problem can cause poor generalization in classification. Therefore, we used the two kernel-based nonlinear methods (KPCA and KFLDA) for coping with the aforementioned problem. KPCA achieved much better performance than that of the PCA method, but slightly poorer performance than that of FLDA. It is likely due to the fact that KPCA obtained better salient information than PCA, but less discriminative separability than FLDA. KFLDA achieved the highest performance among all methods considerd here because it obtained the most compact and discriminant subspace. Therefore, the average classification performances of MLP, RBF and SVM classifiers for each feature set have obviously shown that the proposed KFLDA method is the most powerful extractor among all the others.

In concusion, the findings indicate that the use of geometric features of facial behavior might provide individual unique cues to some extent and the proposed method might achieve superior classification performance with reduced feature dimensions. The nonlinear supervised transformation has the tendency to perform better than the linear and nonlinear unsupervised methods. Hence, it appears that face recognition should be robust to facial expression changes and have potential applicability if an automatic measurement of facial features can be employed. However, the main drawback of kernel-based methods is that computing the kernel matrix is very expensive, and the transformation of kernel methods attempts to find the minimum compact within-class variations and the maximum discrimination of between-class separations; whereas it is indirectly avoided the varying changes of data points (Indirect Invariance).

7. Conclusion and future work

The purpose of this research is three fold: (1) to demonstrate that the within-class variation under facial expression changes will increase the uncertain regions for classification; hence, degrades the classification performance, (2) the low-dimensional subspace with enhanced discriminatory power could provide better feature space for classification, and (3) facial behaviors could also be used as another behavioural biometric for human identification and verification.

This experiment attempted to analyze the uncertainty (overlapping) problem in facial recognition under expression changes by using kernel-based subspace analysis methods and ANN-based classifiers so as to provide an insight of possible solutions for the expression variations problem in face recognition. Moreover, we also emphasized the empirical experiments on variations due to changes in facial expression that are less emphasized in (Adini et al., 1997).

Only 17 facial features of 18 fiducial points were selected. The selected features were shown to provide expressive information and demonstrated that facial expression could be used as another behavior biometric. They also showed that the feature dimensionality was reduced greatly compared to appearance-based or image-based feature extraction.

Our proposed non-linear discriminant analysis method dealt very well with the uncertainty (overlapping) due to expression changes. We found that the transformation of kernel-based discriminant analysis has a beneficial effect on the classification performance. The experimental results showed that a face recognition system with optimal design may eventually be developed, which is robust to the problem of facial expression changes.

8. References

ADINI, Y., MOSES, Y. & ULLMAN, S. (1997) Face recognition: the problem of compensating for changes in illumination direction. *IEEE Transactions on Pattern Analysis and Machine Intelligence,* 19, 721-732.

BELHUMEUR, P. N., HESPANHA, J. P. & KRIEGMAN, D. J. (1997) Eigenfaces versus Fisherfaces: Recognition using class specific linear projection. *IEEE Transactions on Pattern Analysis and Machine Intelligence,* 19, 711-729.

BICHSEL, M. & PENTLAND, A. (1994) Human face recognition and the face image set's topology. *CVGIP: Image Understand.,* 59, 254-261.

BISHOP, C. M. (1995) *Neural Networks for Pattern Recognition,* Oxford, Oxford University Press.

CHEN, S. & LOVELL, B. C. (2004) Illumination and expression invariant face recognition with one sample image. *Proceedings of the 17th International Conference on Pattern Recognition.*

COHN, J., ZLOCHOWER, A., LIEN, J. J. & KANADE, T. (1999) Automated face analysis by feature point tracking has high concurrent validity with manual FACS coding. *Psychophysiology,* 36, 35-43.

COHN, J. F., ZLOCHOWER, A. J., LIEN, J. J. & KANADE, T. (1998) Feature-point tracking by optical flow discriminates subtle differences in facial expression. *IEEE International Conference on Automatic Face and Gesture Recognition.* Nara.

COOTES, T. F., EDWARDS, G. J. & TAYLOR, C. J. (1998) Active Appearance Models. *Computer Vision – ECCV'98.* Springer Berlin / Heidelberg.

DONATO, G., BARTLETT, M. S., HAGER, J. C., EKMAN, P. & SEJNOWSKI, T. J. (1999) Classifying facial actions. *IEEE Transactions on Pattern Analysis and Machine Intelligence,* 21, 974-989.

DUDA, R. O., HART, P. E. & STORK, D. G. (2000) *Pattern Classification,* New York, Wiley

EKMAN, P. & FRIESEN, W. V. (1975) *Unmasking the Face,* New Jersy, Prentice Hall.

ESSA, I. A. & PENTLAND, A. P. (1997) Coding, analysis, interpretation, and recognition of facial expressions. *IEEE Transactions on Pattern Analysis and Machine Intelligence,* 19, 757-763.

FASEL, B. & LUETTIN, J. (2003) Automatic facial expression analysis: a survey. *Pattern Recognition,* 36, 259-275.

HUANG, C.-L. & HUANG, Y.-M. (1997) Facial Expression Recognition Using Model-Based Feature Extraction and Action Parameters Classification. *Journal of Visual Communication And Image Representation,* 8, 278-290.

IVANCEVIC, V., KAINE, A. K., MCLINDIN, B. A. & SUNDE, J. (2003) Factor analysis of essential facial features. *International conference on information technology interfaces.*

JAN, T. (2004) Learning and Generalization using Kernel Based Subspace Model Approaches. *Department of Computer Systems.* Sydney, University of Technology, Sydney.

JOHANSSON, G. (1973) Visual perception of biological motion and a model for its analysis. *Perception & Psychophysics,* 14, 201-211.

JOHANSSON, G. (1976) Spatio-temporal differentiation and integration in visual motion perception. *Psychological Research,* 38, 379-393.

JOLLIFFE, I. T. (1986) *Principle Component Analysis,* New York, Springer-Verlag.

KIM, K. I., JUNG, K. & KIM, H. J. (2002) Face recognition using kernel principal component analysis. *IEEE Signal Processing Letters,* 9, 40-42.

KIRBY, M. & SIROVICH, L. (1990) Application of the Karhunen-Loeve procedure for the characterization of human faces. *IEEE Transactions on Pattern Analysis and Machine Intelligence,* 12, 103-108.

KOBAYASHI, H. & HARA, F. (1992) Recognition of Six basic facial expression and their strength by neural network. *IEEE International Workshop on Robot and Human Communication.* Tokyo.

KROEKER, K. L. (2002) Graphics and security: exploring visual biometrics. *IEEE Computer Graphics and Applications,* 22, 16-21.

LI, S. Z. & LU, J. (1999) Face Recognition Using the Nearest Feature Line Method. *IEEE trans. Neural Networks,* 10, 439-443.

LIU, Q., RUI, H., LU, H. & MA, S. (2002a) Face recognition using kernel based fisher discriminant analysis. *IEEE International Conference on Automatic Face and Gesture Recognition.*

LIU, Y., SCHMIDT, K. L., COHN, J. F. & MITRA, S. (2003) Facial asymmetry quantification for expression invariant human identification. *Computer Vision and Image Understanding: CVIU,* 91, 138-159.

LIU, Y., SCHMIDT, K. L., COHN, J. F. & WEAVER, R. L. (2002b) Facial asymmetry quantification for expression invariant human. *Proceedings of Fifth IEEE International Conference on Automatic Face and Gesture Recognition.*

LOTLIKAR, R. & KOTHARI, R. (2000) Fractional-step dimensionality reduction. *IEEE Transactions on Pattern Analysis and Machine Intelligence,* 22, 623-627.

LU, J., PLATANIOTIS, K. N. & VENETSANOPOULOS, A. N. (2003) Face recognition using kernel direct discriminant analysis algorithms. *IEEE Transactions on Neural Networks,* 14, 117-126.

LYONS, M., AKAMATSU, S., KAMACHI, M. & GYOBA, J. (1998) Coding facial expressions with Gabor wavelets. *IEEE International Conference on Automatic Face and Gesture Recognition.* Nara

LYONS, M. J., BUDYNEK, J. & AKAMATSU, S. (1999) Automatic classification of single facial images. *IEEE Transactions on Pattern Analysis and Machine Intelligence,* 21, 1357-1362.

MARTINEZ, A. M. (2000) Semantic access of frontal face images: the expression-invariant problem. *Proceedings of IEEE Workshop on Content-based Access of Image and Video Libraries.*

MARTINEZ, A. M. (2002) Recognizing imprecisely localized, partially occluded, and expression variant faces from a single sample per class. *IEEE Transactions on Pattern Analysis and Machine Intelligence,* 24, 748-763.

MIKA, S., RATSCH, G., WESTON, J., SCHOLKOPF, B. & MULLERS, K. R. (1999) Fisher discriminant analysis with kernels. *Proceedings of the 1999 IEEE Signal Processing Society Workshop Neural Networks for Signal Processing IX.*

NABNEY, T. (2002) *NETLAB: Algorithms for Pattern Recognition,* London, Springer.

PANTIC, M. & ROTHKRANTZ, L. J. M. (2000a) Automatic analysis of facial expressions: the state of the art. *IEEE Transactions on Pattern Analysis and Machine Intelligence,* 22, 1424-1445.

PANTIC, M. & ROTHKRANTZ, L. J. M. (2000b) Expert system for automatic analysis of facial expressions. *Image and Vision Computing,* 18, 881-905.

PANTIC, M. & ROTHKRANTZ, L. J. M. (2004) Facial action recognition for facial expression analysis from static face images. *IEEE Transactions on Systems, Man and Cybernetics, Part B.,* 34, 1449-1461.

SCHÖLKOPF, B., SMOLA, A. & MÜLLER, K. R. (1998) Nonlinear component analysis as a kernel eigenvalue problem. *Neural Comput.,* 10, 1299–1319.

SCHOLKOPF, B. & SMOLA, A. J. (2002) *Learning with Kernels: Support Vector Machines, Regularization, Optimization, and Beyond,* Cambridge, MIT.

SEOW, M.-J., VALAPARLA, D. & ASARI, V. K. (2003) L2-norm approximation based learning in recurrent neural networks for expression invariant face recognition. *IEEE International Conference on Systems, Man and Cybernetics.*

TIAN, Y. I., KANADE, T. & COHN, J. F. (2001) Recognizing action units for facial expression analysis. *IEEE Transactions on Pattern Analysis and Machine Intelligence,* 23, 97-115.

TSAI, P. & JAN, T. (2005) Expression-Invariant Face Recognition System Using Subspace Model Analysis. *Proceedings of IEEE International Conference on Systems, Man and Cybernetics* ,Hawaii, USA.

TSAI, P., JAN, T. & HINTZ, T. (2005) Expression-Invariant Face Recognition for Small Class Problem. *Proceedings of IEEE International Conference on Computational Intelligence for Measurement Systems and Applications.* Sicily, Italy.

TURK, M. A. (2001) A random walk through eigenspace. *IEICE Trans. Inf. Systems,* E84-D, 1586-1695.

TURK, M. A. & PENTLAND, A. P. (1991a) Eigenfaces for recognition. *Journal of Cognitive Neuroscience,* 3, 71-86.

TURK, M. A. & PENTLAND, A. P. (1991b) Face recognition using eigenfaces. *Proceedings of IEEE Computer Society Conference on Computer Vision and Pattern Recognition.*

VALSTAR, M. & PANTIC, M. (2006) Fully Automatic Facial Action Unit Detection and Temporal Analysis. *2006 Conference on Computer Vision and Pattern Recognition Workshop.*

VUKADINOVIC, D. & PANTIC, M. (2005) Fully Automatic Facial Feature Point Detection Using Gabor Geature Based Boosted Classifiers. *IEEE International Conference on Systems, Man and Cybernetics.* Waikoloa, Hawaii.

YANG, M.-H. (2002) Kernel Eigenfaces vs. Kernel Fisherfaces: Face Recognition Using Kernel Methods. *Proceedings of the Fifth IEEE International Conference on Automatic Face and Gesture Recognition.*

YANG, M. H., AHUJA, N. & KRIEGMAN, D. (2000) Face recognition using kernel eigenfaces. *International Conference on Image Processing.*

ZHANG, Z., LYONS, M., SCHUSTER, M. & AKAMATSU, S. (1998) Comparison between geometry-based and Gabor-wavelets-based facial expression recognition using multi-layer perceptron. *IEEE International Conference on Automatic Face and Gesture Recognition*. Nara.

13

Blood Perfusion Models for Infrared Face Recognition

Shiqian Wu, Zhi-Jun Fang, Zhi-Hua Xie and Wei Liang
School of information technology, Jiangxi University of Finance and Economics, China

1. Introduction

Infrared (IR) technology has traditionally been applied to military use and remote sensing. During the last two decades, the cost of IR cameras (especially uncooled imagers) has been significantly reduced with the development of CCD technology, and therefore civil applications have increased constantly due to its unique features. One of such applications is IR face recognition (Prokoski et al., 1992, Prokoski, 2000, Kong et al., 2005). The fundamentals behind it are, as indicated by Kong et al (Kong et al., 2005) that IR images are independent of external illumination. While visible images represent the reflectance information of the face surface, IR face images contain more fundamental information about faces themselves, such as anatomical information (Prokoski, et al., 1992, Prokoski, 2000); the thermal characteristics of faces with variations in facial expression and make-up remain nearly invariant (Socolinsky & Selinger, 2002) and the tasks of face detection, localization, and segmentation are relatively easier and more reliable than those in visible images (Kong et al., 2005). It has been pointed by Prokoski et al. (Prokoski et al., 1992) that humans are homoiotherm and hence capable of maintaining constant temperature under different surroundings. The thermal images collected over 20 years have demonstrated that the thermal measurements of individuals are highly repeatable under the same conditions. Furthermore, as discussed by Prokoski (Prokoski, 2000), a facial thermal pattern is determined by the vascular structure of each face, which is irreproducible and unique.
Based on the assumption that facial thermal patterns are determined by blood vessels transporting warm blood, Prokoski tried to extract the blood vessel minutiae (Prokoski, 2001) or vascular network (Buddharaju et al., 2004, Buddharaju et al., 2005) as the facial features for recognition. The basic idea is to extract such features using image segmentation. It has been indicated by Guyton & Hall (Guyton & Hall, 1996) that the average diameter of blood vessels is around 10~15μm, which is too small to be detected by current IR cameras (limited by the spatial resolution); the skin directly above a blood vessel is on average 0.1°C warmer than the adjacent skin, which is beyond the thermal accuracy of current IR cameras. The methods using image segmentation in (Prokoski, 2001, Buddharaju et al., 2004, Buddharaju et al., 2005) are heuristic, and it still remains a big challenge to capture the pattern of blood vessels on each face.
On the other hand, the phenomenon of "homoiotherm" due to human temperature regulation has led to the direct use of thermograms for recognition (Wilder et al., 1996,

Socolinsky & Selinger, 2002, Wu et al., 2003, Chen et al., 2005). Wilder et al. (Wilder et al., 1996) used three different feature-extraction and decision-making algorithms for test. The recognition results revealed that both visible and IR imageries perform similarly across algorithms. The real-time IR face recognition system developed by Wu et al. (Wu et al., 2003) achieves good performance. Especially, Socolinsky & Selinger (Socolinsky & Selinger, 2002) simultaneously registered the IR and visible images of each candidate under controlled conditions. It has been concluded from their experimental results that (1) variations of IR images are less than those of visible images; (2) IR images are less sensitive to facial expression changes. The experiments conducted with the common methods like principle component analysis (PCA), linear discriminant analysis (LDA), local feature analysis (LFA) and independent component analysis (ICA) demonstrated that using thermal infrared imagery yields higher performance than using visible images under many circumstances (Socolinsky & Selinger, 2002).

It is noted that the aforementioned database mainly involved same-session data (i.e., nearly-simultaneous acquisition of training and testing data). Besides the same-session test, Chen et al. (Chen et al., 2005) paid more attention to test of time-lapse data (i.e., training data and testing data being collected in different time sessions). The intervals among training data and testing data are several weeks, several months or even one year respectively. The large-scale studies involving both same-session and time-lapse data indicated that in a same-session scenario, neither modality is significantly better than the other using the PCA-based recognition; however, using visible imagery outperforms that using IR imagery for time-lapse data.

When we mention that humans are homoiothermal, it should be highlighted that the so called "homoiotherm" only refers to the approximately constant temperature in deep body (i.e., the core temperature), whereas the skin temperature distribution fluctuates with the ambient temperature, changes from person to person, and from time to time, as shown in (Houdas & Ring, 1982, Guyton & Hall, 1996, Jones & Plassmann, 2000). It should also be noted that an IR camera can only capture the apparent temperature instead of deep temperature. As indicated by Housdas & Ring (Houdas & Ring, 1982), the variations in facial thermograms result from not only external conditions, such as environmental temperature, imaging conditions, but also various internal conditions, such as physiological or psychological conditions. Socolinsky & Selinger (Socolinsky & Selinger, 2004A, Socolinsky & Selinger, 2004B) also explored such variations.

To improve the performance of IR face recognition for time-lapse session, more efforts have been put on classifier design (Socolinsky & Selinger, 2004A, Socolinsky & Selinger, 2004B, Srivastava & Liu, 2003). Meanwhile, some researchers focus on feature extraction. Yoshitomi et al. (Yoshitomi et al., 1997) used both thermal information and geometrical features for recognition. Wu et al. (Wu et al., 2005A) proposed a model to convert the thermograms to blood perfusion data and the performance on time-lapse data is significantly improved. The modified blood perfusion model by Wu et al. (Wu et al., 2007) further improves the time-lapse performance.

In this chapter, we will provide a comprehensive study on the proposed blood perfusion models. It is revealed that the transforms by the blood perfusion models reduce the within-class scatter of thermograms and obtains more consistent features to represent human faces. In the following Section, the thermal pattern variations are analyzed. The blood perfusion models are presented and analyzed in Section 3. A variety of experiments on blood perfusion and thermal data are performed in Section 4, and the conclusions are drawn in Section 5.

2. Thermal pattern variations and analysis

Although IR images are independent of illumination, fluctuations in thermal appearance occur in relation to ambient conditions, subject's metabolism and so on. It is necessary to learn how the thermal patterns vary in different situations before presenting the proposed methods. Some of the factors affecting thermal distribution are presented in the following subsections.

2.1 Deep body temperature vs skin temperature

In 1958, Aschoff and Wever introduced the terms "thermal core", the temperatures of which remain almost exactly constant, within +/- 0.6°C, day in and day out except when a person develops a febrile illness (Guyton & Hall, 1996). Blatteis (Blatteis, 1998) indicates that even if ambient temperature varies widely, core temperature does not change as a function of ambient temperature. This is due to the presence of a closed control loop with negative feedback in the body system which prevents mean body temperature from deviating extensively from this value taken under thermoneutral conditions (Blatteis, 1998). In fact, a rise in core temperature of only 0.5 °C causes extreme peripheral vasodilation (flushing of the skin in humans). This stability implies that the heat produced in the body and that lost from it stay in relative balance, despite the large variations in ambient temperature (Blatteis, 1998).
The skin temperature, in contrast to the core temperature, fluctuates with the temperature of the surroundings (Guyton & Hall, 1996, Blatteis, 1998). One may infer, therefore, that in order to maintain core temperature stable, the rate of heat flow from core to skin is djusted according to the body's thermal needs and that, as a result, skin temperature varies more widely than core temperature in relation to ambient temperature (Blatteis, 1998). Under steady-state conditions in a thermoneutral environment, (i.e., one in which neither the mechanism for heat production nor for heat loss is activated and the perceived thermal comfort is optimal), core temperature thus is higher than skin temperature (Blatteis, 1998). For resting, naked adults, this zone of ambient temperature lies between 28 and 30 °C (Blatteis, 1998).
There is no single temperature level that can be considered to be normal because measurements on many normal people have shown a *range* of normal temperature measured orally, from less than 36.1°C to 37.5°C (Guyton & Hall, 1996). When excessive heat is produced in the body by strenuous exercise, temperature can rise temporarily to as high as 38.33-40.0°C. On the other hand, when the body is exposed to cold, the temperature can often fall to values below 96°F (35.56°C) (Guyton & Hall, 1996).

2.2 Variation with ambient conditions

The works by Chen et al. Chen et al., 2005), Socolinsky & Selinger (Socolinsky & Selinger, 2004A, Socolinsky & Selinger, 2004B), Wu et al. (Wu et al., 2005A, Wu et al., 2007) have illustrated that variations in ambient temperature significantly change the thermal characteristics of faces, and accordingly affect the performances of recognition. Fig. 1 shows the thermal distribution of the same face in different ambient temperatures. All of the images are observed (the red part) from the pixel values ranging from 238 to 255. It is observed from Fig.1 that the skin temperature of the cheeks, tip of nose and hair increases as the ambient temperature increases. The intensities of the forehead region start off as bright when the ambient temperature is low. As the ambient temperature increases (above 27.9 °C ~ 28.1 °C), the intensities of the forehead region drops drastically due to the effect of sweating. It was indicated by Blatteis (Blatteis, 1998) that the human body has about three million sweat glands, the greatest density being found on the palms, soles and forehead. Thermoregulatory sweating increases with elevation in core temperature (Blatteis, 1998), and therefore the forehead region emits sweat easily when the ambient temperature increases. Evaporation takes place once the sweat reaches the surface, hence causing the skin temperature to lower down.

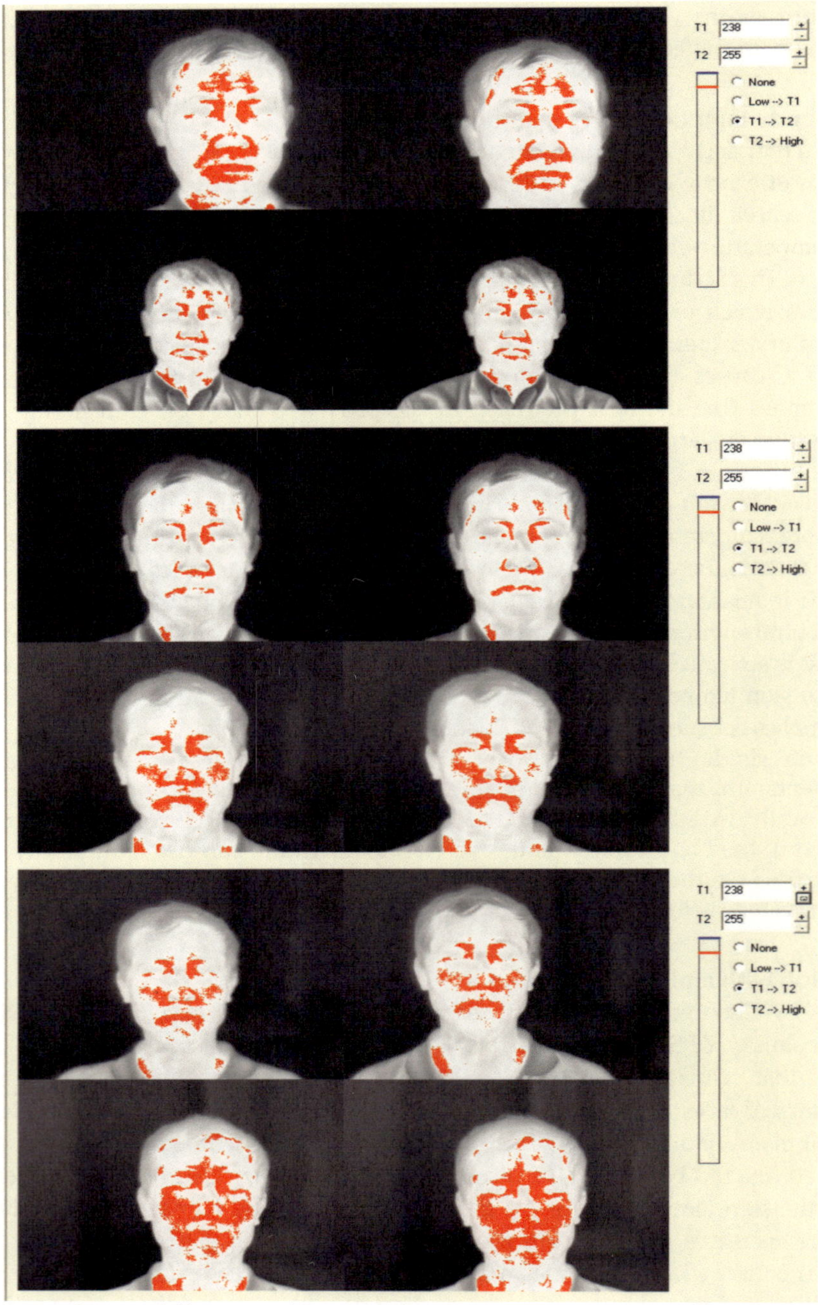

Fig. 1. Images taken at different ambient conditions (1st row: 24.8 °C ~ 25.0 °C, 2nd row: 25.7 °C ~ 26.1 °C, 3th row: 27.1 °C ~ 27.4 °C, 4th row: 27.9 °C ~ 28.1 °C, 5th row: 28.4 °C ~ 28.7 °C, 6th row: 28.9 °C ~ 29.3 °C)

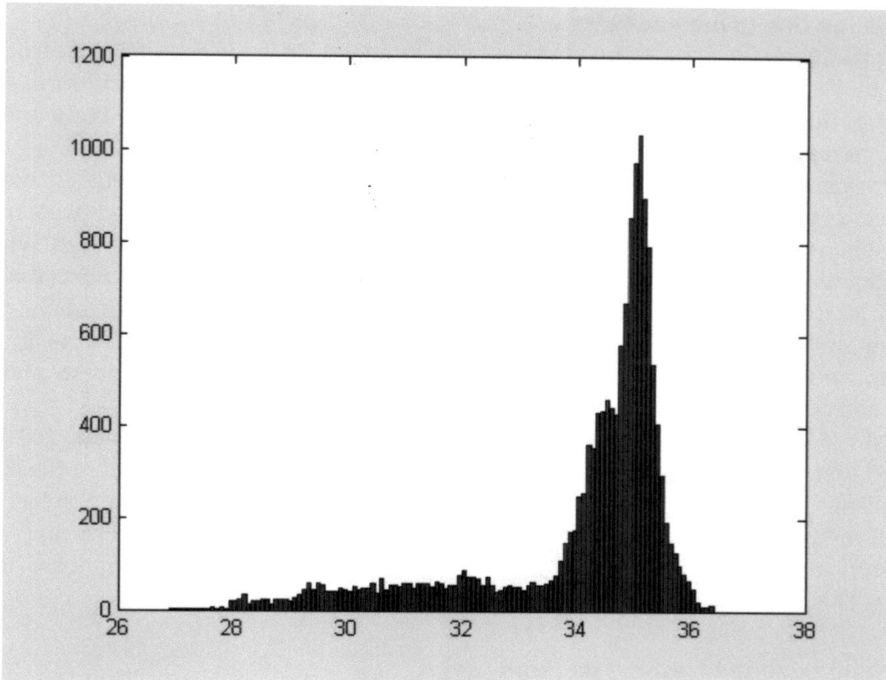

(a) Histogram in ambient temperature 24.8 °C ~ 25.0 °C

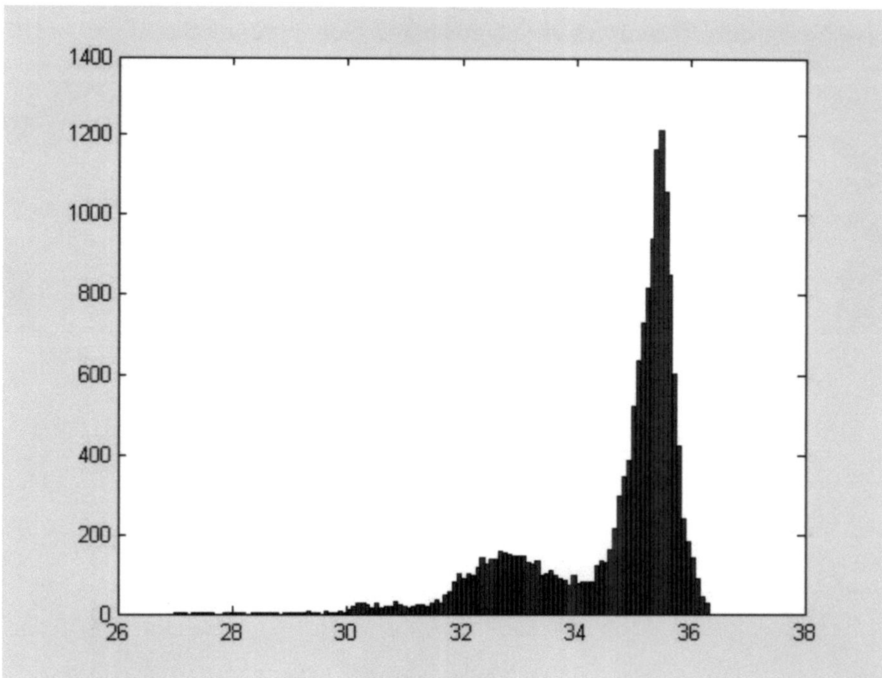

(b) Histogram in ambient temperature 28.9 °C ~ 29.3 °C

Fig. 2. Histograms in different ambient temperatures of the same face

2.3 Variation due to metabolism

Ganong (Ganong, 2001) indicates that the body temperature is lowest during sleep, slightly higher in the awake but relaxed state, and rises with activity. For activities such as exercising, the heat produced by muscular contraction accumulates in the body and cause the body temperature to rise (Ganong, 2001).

Body temperature also rises slightly during emotional excitement, probably owing to unconscious tensing of the muscles (Ganong, 2001). It is chronically elevated by as much as 0.5 °C when the metabolic rate is high, as in hyperthyroidism, and lowered when the metabolic rate is low, as in hypothyroidism (Ganong, 2001). There is an additional monthly cycle of temperature variation characterized by a rise in basal temperature at the time of ovulation for women (Ganong, 2001). Temperature regulation is less precise in young children, and they may normally have a temperature that is 0.5 °C or so above the established norm for adults (Ganong, 2001).

Socolinsky & Selinger (Socolinsky & Selinger, 2004A, Socolinsky & Selinger, 2004B) also analysed that additional fluctuations in thermal appearance could be related to the subject's metabolism. During their data collection, an uncontrolled portion of the subjects was engaged in strong physical activity at different periods prior to imaging. The time elapsed from physical exertion to imaging was uncontrolled and known to be different for different sessions. This further contributes to the change in thermal appearance.

2.4 Variation due to breathing patterns

Fig.3 shows the images when the person is breathing in (the first one), breathing out (the middle one) and no breathing (last one), and the curve below represents the reversed cumulative histograms. The curves in red, green and blue represent the subject breathing in,

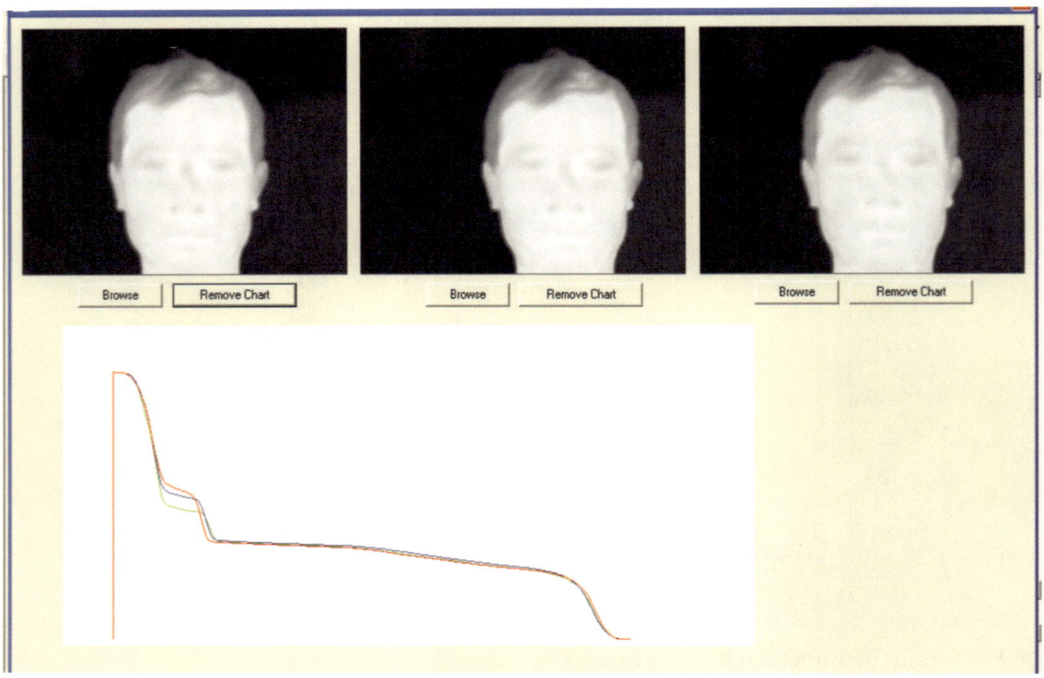

Fig. 3. Reversed cumulative histogram for inhalation & exhalation

breathing out and no breathing respectively. It can be seen that a relatively larger area of the face is subjected to low temperature (left part in the curve) when the subject breathes in and high temperature when breathes out. The area of the face with higher temperature part (right part in the curve) stays almost constant regardless of whether the subject is breathing in or out. Such change is obvious: when the subject exhales, the region directly below nose (i.e., region around nose and mouth) becomes warmer since exhaled air is at core body temperature, which is several degrees warmer than skin temperature.

2.5 Variation due to alcohol consumption

The variation in thermal distribution when the subject is under alcohol consumption is shown in Fig.4. It is generally known that alcohol increases body temperature because it dilates blood vessels in the skin. The flushed complexion associated with drinking is due to central vasomotor depression. In Fig.4, the top left image is taken immediately after consumption of alcohol, the top right image is taken 15 min later after consumption, bottom left image is taken after 35 min delay and finally the bottom right image is taken 100 min later. It can be observed that there are changes in the appearance of the thermal images at different timings after a single session of drinking alcohol. More regions of the face, especially the cheeks and forehead became warm as time passes after consumption. This is due to the fact that alcohol concentration in the blood flowing in the human face peaked only some time after consumption.

Alcohol consumption can normally affect thermal distribution for each individual differently. It depends on the amount of dosage and how fast the rate of absorption of alcohol takes place in the body. The rate of absorption can in turn be determined by whether there was any food consumption beforehand or whether the subject had his / her pyloric valves removed surgically (Goodwin, 2000).

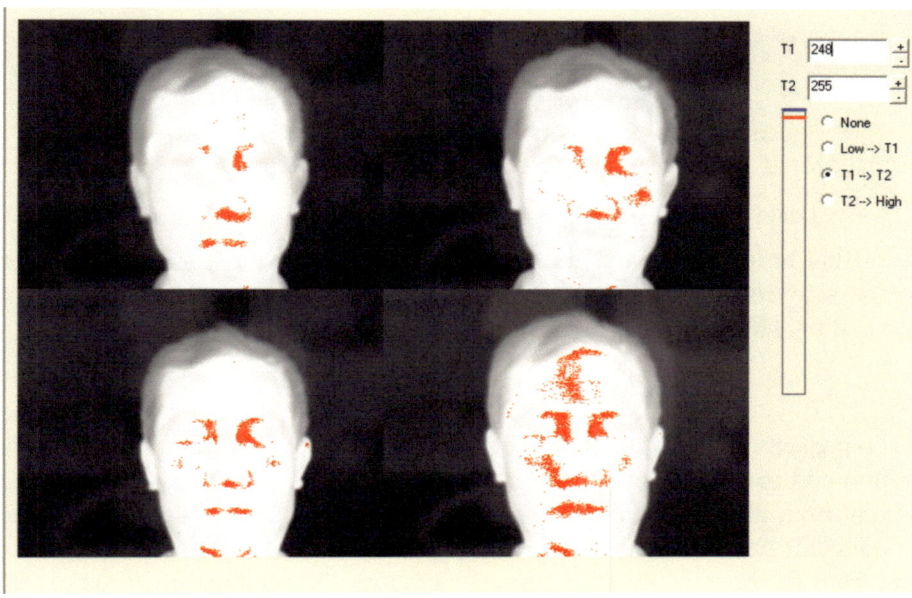

Fig. 4. Images taken at different timings after alcohol consumption

Actually, many other factors affect the thermograms. These include imaging condition (e.g., thermal drift, distance, glasses etc), psychological condition (e.g., angry, blushing, stress etc) and physiological condition (toothache, headache etc). As indicated by Jones & Plassmann (Jones & Plassmann, 2000), "the skin temperature distribution changes from person to person, and from time to time". It is difficult to extract the unique features of a face.

3. Blood perfusion models

It is assumed that the ambient condition is stable without wind and sun effect, and the subjects are in the steady state without temperature regulation, i.e., the following assumptions are made:

Assumption 1: The deep body temperature is constant, and no thermal regulation (e.g., sweating) is considered;

Assumption 2: The ambient temperature is lower than body temperature (e.g., indoor condition is considered);

Assumption 3: Pathological conditions (e.g., fever, headache, inflammation, etc) and psychological conditions (e.g., anger, blush, etc) are not considered.

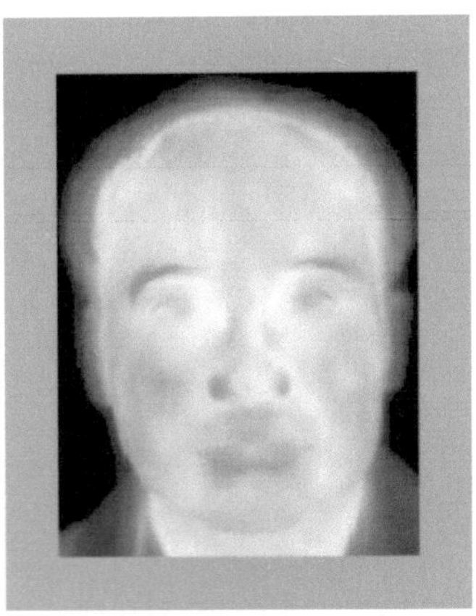

(a) Thermal data ($T_e = 26.2\,^{o}\mathrm{C}$);

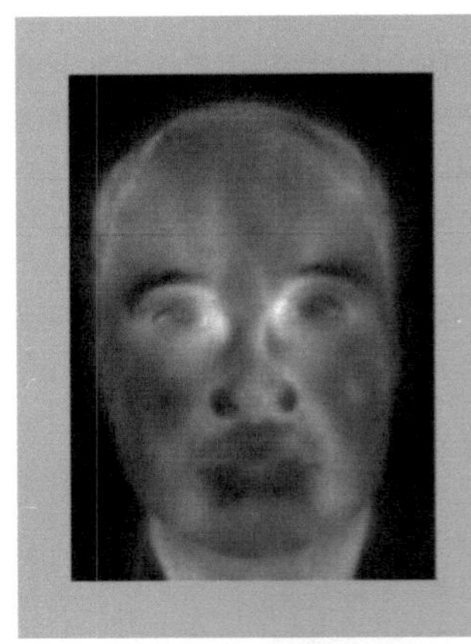

(b) Corresponding blood perfusion data

Fig. 5. Thermal data vs blood perfusion data

In view of the heat transfer and thermal physiology under these assumptions, the heat transfer on skin surface can be described by the following heat equilibrium equations (Houdas & Ring, 1982):

$$H_r + H_e + H_f = H_c + H_m + H_b \tag{1}$$

where H represents the heat flux per unit area. The subscripts r, e and f stand for radiation, evaporation and convection respectively. These three terms on left hand are the outflows which point from the skin surface to the environment. The subscripts c, m and b stand for body conduction, metabolism and blood flow convection. These are the influx terms in the direction from the body to the skin surface. Based on the analysis in (Wu et al., 2005A), blood perfusion is expressed as follows:

$$\omega = \frac{\varepsilon\sigma(T_s^4 - T_e^4) + A\mu\, d^{3M-1}(\mathrm{P}\, g\beta/\nu^2)^M (T_s - T_e)^{M+1} - k(T_c - T_s)/D - H_m}{\alpha c_b (T_a - T_s)} \tag{2}$$

where the specific parameters are tabulated in Table 1. Equation (2) defines the thermogram to blood perfusion transform, with which a thermal datum $T(x, y)$ at location (x, y) can be therefore converted into the corresponding blood perfusion $\omega(x,y)$. An example of the conversion is shown in Fig. 5.

symbol	description	Value
ω	Blood perfusion	
σ	Stefan-Boltzmann constant	$5.67*10^{-8}$ W $m^{-2}K^{-4}$
ε	Tissue/skin thermal emissivity	0.98
T_s	Skin temperature	
T_e	Ambient temperature	
T_a	Artery temperature	312.15K
T_c	Core temperature	312.15K
k	tissue/skin thermal conductivity	$0.2Wm^{-1}K^{-1}$
μ	Air thermal conductivity	0.024 W $m^{-1}K^{-1}$
c_b	blood specific heat	$3.78*10^3$ J kg^{-1} K^{-1}
H_m	metabolic heat flux per unit area	4.186W m^{-2}
α	tissue/skin countercurrent exchange ratio	0.8
P	Prandtl constant	0.72
ν	kinematic viscosity of air	$1.56*10^{-5}$ m^2/s
β	air thermal expansion coefficient	$3.354*10^{-3}K^{-1}$
g	local gravitational acceleration	$9.8m^2/s$
A	constant	0.27
M	constant	0.25
d	Characteristic length of a face	0.095
D	Distance from body core to skin surface	0.095

Table 1. Nomenclature

The proposed blood perfusion model by equation (2) defines a transform from the thermal space to the blood perfusion space. It is a point-wise transform and has the following characteristics: the location of the facial features is preserved; the shape of the subject is identical to the thermograms. It is noted that the concept of blood perfusion is meaningful only for skin part; for the non-skin part (e.g., hair and background), it could be viewed as an equivalent "blood perfusion".

It is easy to derive the differential of blood perfusion to temperature T as follows:

$$\frac{d\omega}{dT} = \frac{[4\varepsilon\sigma T^3 + A\mu\, d^{3M-1}(P\, g\beta/\nu^2)^M (T - T_e)^M + kT/D](T_c - T) + S}{\alpha c_b (T_a - T)^2} \tag{3}$$

where

$$S = \varepsilon\sigma(T^4 - T_e^4) + A\mu d^{3M-1}(Pg\beta/v^2)^M (T - T_e)^{M+1} - k(T_c - T)/D - H_m \tag{4}$$

As $T > T_e$ according to Assumption 2, $T_a > T$, and S is always positive since the blood perfusion is positive, $\frac{d\omega}{dT}$ is definitely positive. This implies that the relationship between the skin temperature T and the blood perfusion ω is monotonous. The skin area with relatively high temperature results in high blood perfusion as demonstrated in Fig.5.

From the perspective of image processing, the proposed transform is a nonlinear one, as can be seen from Fig. 6. In essence, it increases the dynamic range of IR images and enhances the overall image contrast as visually demonstrated in Fig. 5. More specific and also importantly, it expands the contrast on high-temperature part (i.e., skin) and suppresses the contrast on low-temperature part (i.e., hair, background, etc.). As mentioned in Section 2, the thermal variations are usually big in low-temperature part due to environmental changes, but very small in high-temperature part because of the temperature regulation. Since the high-temperature part is the most meaningful portion of the signal for the decision making, the proposed blood-perfusion-based transform is appropriate since it overcomes the inherent variations in thermogram data.

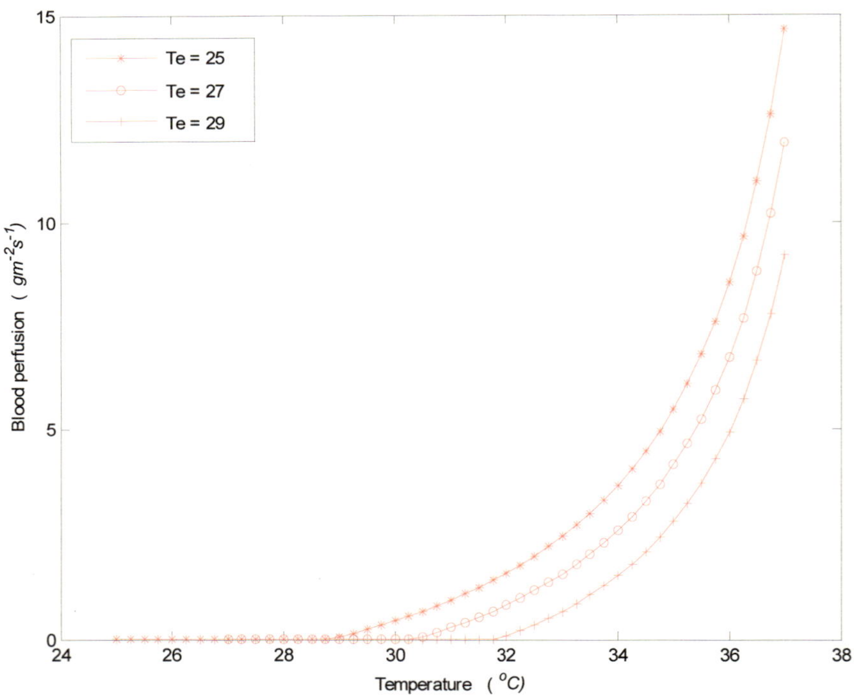

Fig. 6. The relationship between temperature data and blood perfusion data

Using the parameters shown in Table 1, it is found that H_f has much less effect (second-order effect) on blood perfusion than H_r. If T_e has a change ΔT_e, and we neglect the small variation of H_f, we have:

$$\Delta\omega \approx \frac{\varepsilon\sigma T^4}{\alpha c_b (T_a - T)}\{[1-(\frac{T_e}{T})^4]-[1-(\frac{T_e+\Delta T_e}{T})^4]\} \tag{5}$$

i.e.,

$$\Delta\omega \approx \zeta[(\frac{T_e+\Delta T_e}{T})^4 - (\frac{T_e}{T})^4] \tag{6}$$

where

$$\zeta = \varepsilon\sigma T^4 / \alpha c_b (T_a - T) \tag{7}$$

Expanding equation (6):

$$\Delta\omega \approx \zeta[4\frac{T_e^3}{T^3}\frac{\Delta T_e}{T} + 6\frac{T_e^2}{T^2}(\frac{\Delta T_e}{T})^2 + 4\frac{T_e}{T}(\frac{\Delta T_e}{T})^3 + (\frac{\Delta T_e}{T})^4)] \tag{8}$$

If $\Delta T_e / T$ is small (note: the unit of T is Kelvin temperature), and ignore the high-order terms, we obtain:

$$\Delta\omega \approx 4\zeta\frac{T_e^3}{T^4}\Delta T_e \tag{9}$$

It reveals from equation (9) that if T_e has a small variation, the change of blood perfusion is almost linear, which is illustrated in Fig. 7. However, the gradient for each point is the function of its temperature.

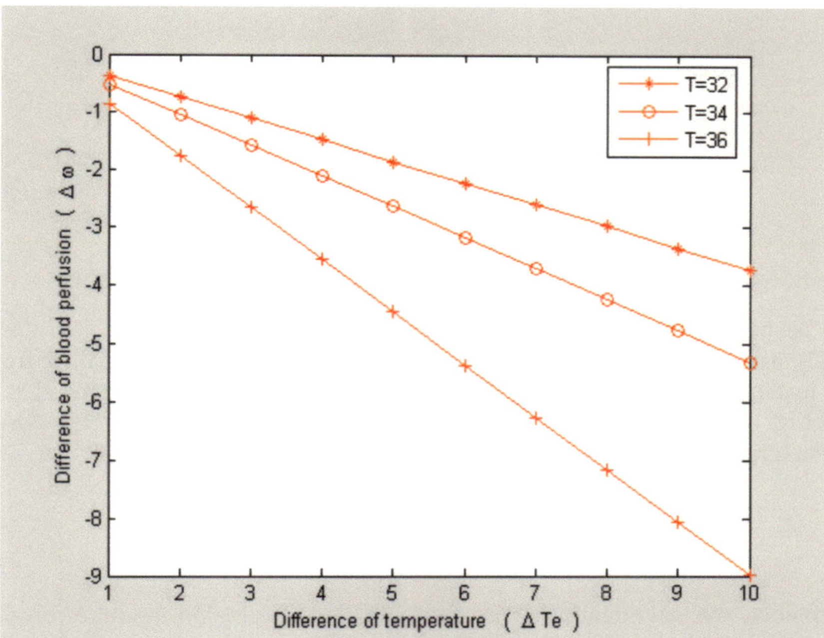

Fig. 7. The difference of blood perfusions vs different ambient temperatures ($T_e = 23^0 C$)

Let $\eta = 4\zeta T_e^3 / T^4$, which determines the transform from the ΔT_e to $\Delta\omega$, and use equation (7), we have:

$$\eta = 4\frac{\varepsilon\sigma T_e^3}{\alpha c_b(T_a - T)} \tag{10}$$

Using the parameters specified in Table 1, and setting $T_e = 15 \sim 30^0 C$, and $T = 32 \sim 36^0 C$, the variations of parameter η are demonstrated in Fig. 8. It is observed that the smaller T and T_e are, the smaller η is. Even when $T_e = 30^0 C$ and $T = 36^0 C$, η is less than 0.7. This implies that if the ambient temperature has variation ΔT_e, the resultant variation of blood perfusion $\Delta\omega$ is always less than ΔT_e. Hence, from the perspective of pattern recognition, the transform in equation (2) reduces the within-class scatter resulting from ambience, and obtains more consistent data to represent the human face.

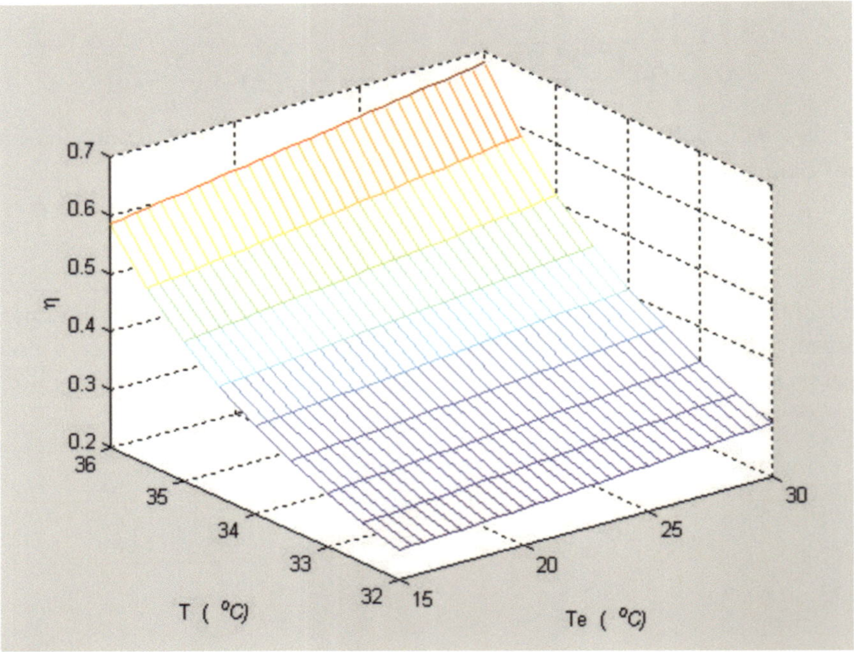

Fig. 8. The transform coefficient η from ΔT_e to $\Delta\omega$ in different temperatures

It should be highlighted that some parameters, for example *M*, *D*, *d* etc., described in equation (2) are obtained from experiments. These values should vary or differ from person to person instead of constants as shown in Table 1. Furthermore, it is found that terms H_f, H_c, H_m and H_e are less significant compared to other terms. Therefore, it is reasonable to ignore these terms to obtain a simplified blood perfusion model as follows:

$$\omega = \frac{\varepsilon\sigma(T^4 - T_e^4)}{\alpha c_b(T_a - T)} \tag{11}$$

For convenience, we call equation (2) as complex blood perfusion model or original blood perfusion (OBP) model and equation (11) as modified blood perfusion (MBP) model. The relationship between the two models is depicted in Fig. 9. It is observed that both models have similar properties, for example, nonlinear and monotonous increase, but with different gradients.

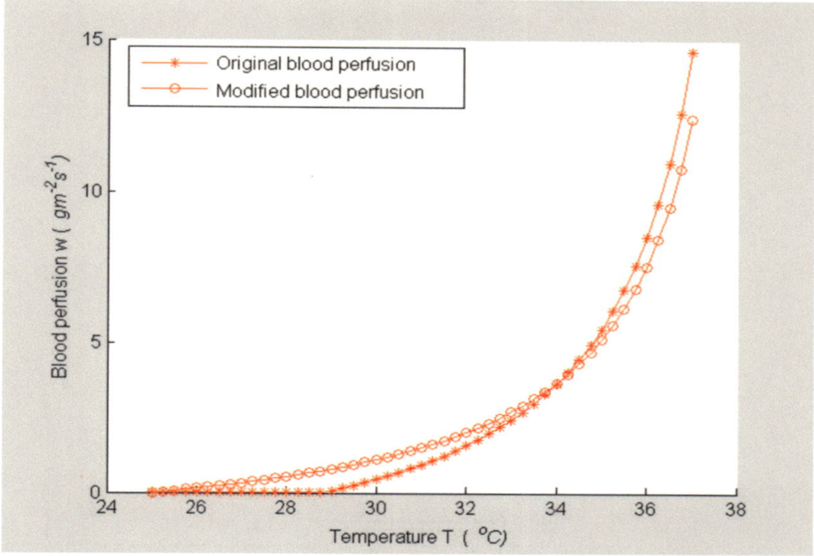

Fig. 9. Original blood perfusion model vs modified blood perfusion model

4. Experimental results

4.1 IR face recognition system

The experiments were performed using the real-time IR face recognition system as described in (Wu et al., 2003). The schematic diagram of the system is shown in Fig.10. After an image is captured, its quality is evaluated by an objective measurement (Wu et al., 2005B). Only the image with good quality is inputted to the following detection and then recognition modules. Before normalize the face in a specific size, the face orientation is detected by single linkage clustering (Wu et al. 2006). Then, the facial features are extracted by the principle component analysis and Fisher's linear discriminant method, and the classifier employs the RBF neural network as shown in (Wu et al. 2003) for details. The performance is evaluated in terms of maximum recognition score.

4.2 Database collection

The IR images were captured by the ThermoVision A40 made by FLIR Systems Inc. This camera, which uses an uncooled microbolometer sensor with resolution of 320×240 pixels and the spectral response is 7.5 ~ 13 microns, is specially designed for accurate temperature measurement. The sensitivity is as high as 0.08 °C. One of its prominent features is the function of automatic self-calibration to cope with the temperature drift. Furthermore, we have a blackbody MIKRON M340 to check and compensate the accuracy of measurement.

The database used in experiments comprises 850 data of 85 individuals which were carefully collected at the same condition: i.e., same environment under air-conditioned control with temperature around 24.3 ~ 25.3°C, and each person stood at a distance of about 1 meter in front of the camera. Each person has 10 templates: 2 in frontal-view, 2 in up-view, 2 in down-view, 2 in left-view, and 2 in right-view. All the 10 images of each subject were acquired within 1 minute. As glass is opaque to IR, people are required to remove their eyeglasses.

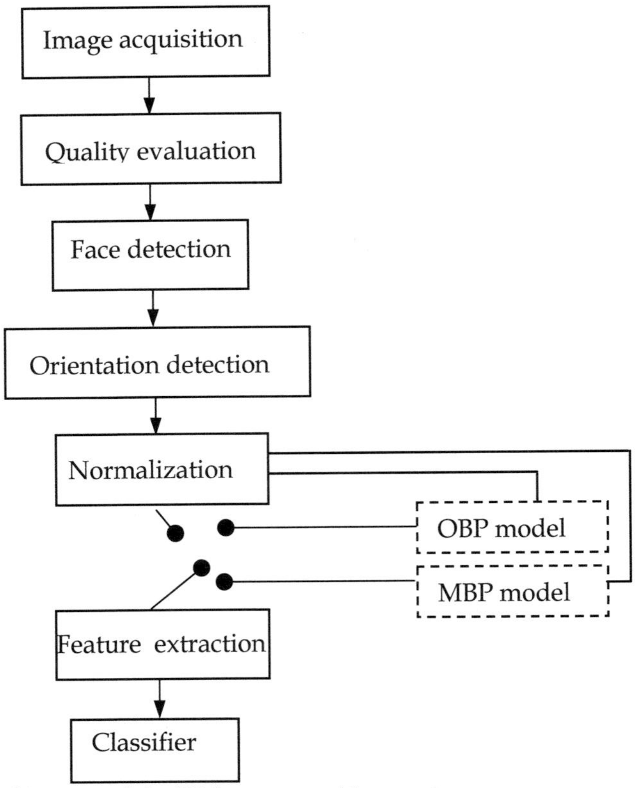

Fig. 10. Schematic diagram of the IR face recognition system

4.3 Recognition results for same-session data

The test situation is similar to the watchlist scenario described in FRVT 2002 (Bone & Blackburn, 2002). The subject is allowed to walk slowly back and forth in front of the camera at a distance between 0.7m and 1.4m. He/she may have different poses and facial expressions. For different purposes, the subjects were asked to wear/remove eyeglasses.

A. Effect of eyeglasses

During the first part of this experiment, the subjects were required to remove their eyeglasses. These testing images were captured right after collecting the training data. Here, the numbers of subjects and probe images are 10 and 114 respectively.

Immediately after the first part of the experiment, the same group of testing persons was instructed to put on their eyeglasses for the next round of image capturing. The number of probe images is 108. The recognition results performed on thermal data, original blood perfusion (OBP) model and modified blood perfusion (MBP) model are tabulated in Table 2 and Table 3. The recognition scores are demonstrated in Fig.11 and Fig. 12 respectively.

Ambient Condition 24.3 °C - 25.3 °C	Thermal data	OBP model	MBP model
Recognition Rate	96.4%	100%	100%
Mean Score	0.825	0.913	0.874
Variance	0.299	0.289	0.280

Table 2. Recognition rate for same-session data without eyeglasses

Ambient Condition 24.3 °C - 25.3 °C	Thermal data	OBP model	MBP Model
Recognition Rate	80.9%	91.7%	91.7%
Mean Score	0.705	0.803	0.764
Variance	0.448	0.418	0.437

Table 3. Recognition rate for same-session data with eyeglasses

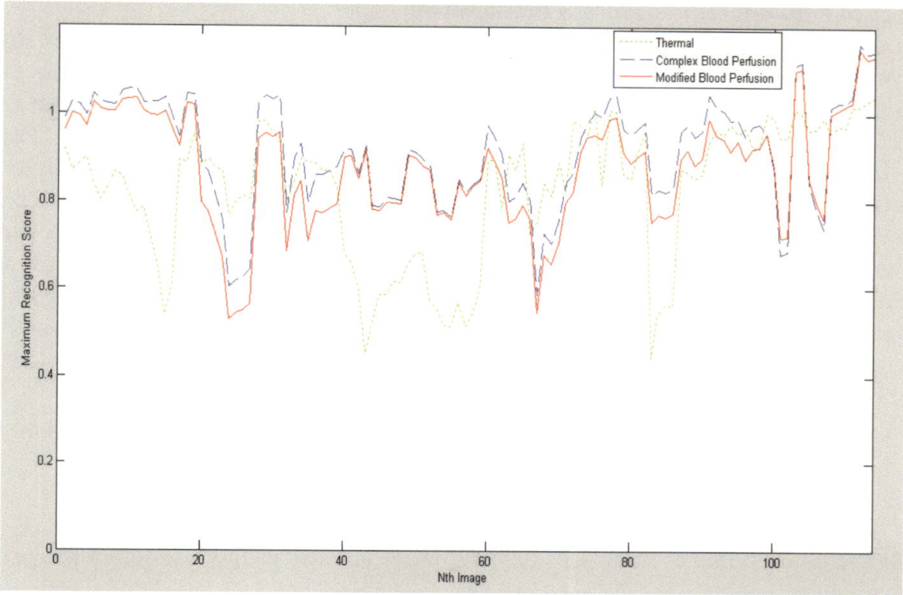

Fig. 11. Maximum recognition score for same-session data without eyeglasses

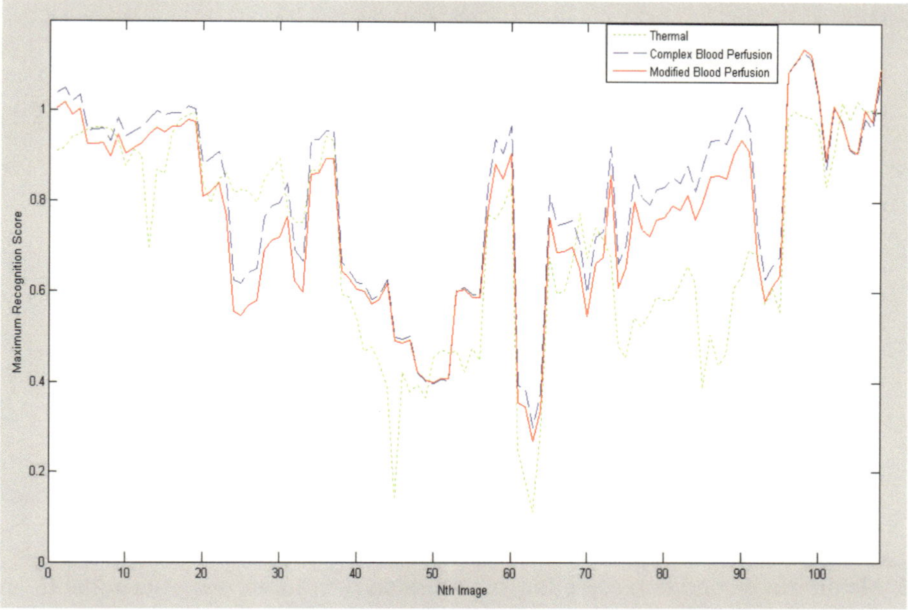

Fig. 12. Maximum recognition score for same-session data with eyeglasses

From Table 2, it can be seen that the recognition rates for both blood perfusion models are excellent (achieved 100% recognition rate). The maximum recognition scores obtained are generally high for all the three models. The small variances indicate that the performances are robust.
It is observed from Table 3 that wearing eyeglasses leads to decrease of recognition rate, especially for thermal images. The effects on OBP model and MBP model are similar and both the blood perfusion models greatly outperform the thermal model in terms of recognition rates and scores.

B. Effect of ambient temperature & metabolism

In this experiment, 15 subjects were engaged in some physical activity prior to imaging. They came to register their images in the afternoon between 1 p.m. to 4 p.m. The outdoor condition on that day was a warm and sunny weather, with ambient temperature ranging around 28.3 °C- 29.5 °C, while the indoor temperature is around 25.1 °C- 25.3 °C. There are totally 150 probe images collected. In this case, body temperature has significantly changes due to different activities and ambient temperatures. Accordingly, the performance in this situation decreases in terms of the recognition rates, recognition scores and score variances as shown in Table 4 and Fig.13, although the interval between training and testing is around 2 minutes. As discussed in Section 2, the thermal characteristics indeed change under

Ambient Condition 28.3°C - 29.5 °C to 25.1 °C- 25.3 °C	Thermal data	OBP model	MBP Model
Recognition Rate	64.7%	81.7%	80.3%
Mean Score	0.461	0.474	0.470
Variance	0.488	0.428	0.430

Table 4. Recognition rate of same-session data under variations due to ambient temperature and metabolism

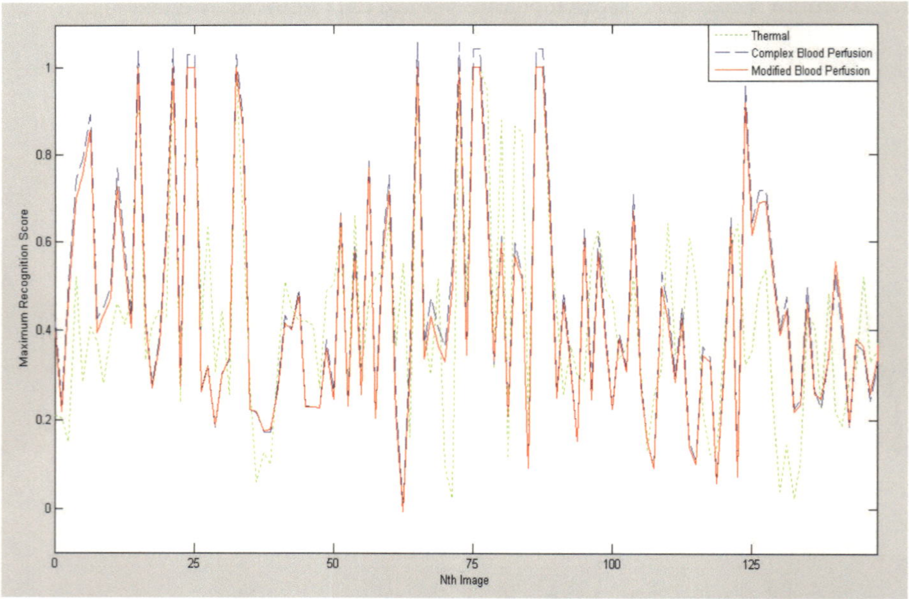

Fig. 13. Maximum recognition score for same-session data under variations due to ambient temperature and metabolism

variations due to ambient temperature and metabolism. In light of this, limitations are posed for recognition using thermal imaging. It is also observed that blood perfusion models try to alleviate these variations and yield reasonably performances. However, the recognition scores are relatively low and the variances are relatively high.

C. Effect of breathing patterns

In Sect 2.4, we analyzed the effects on thermal variation associated with breathing. Here, experiments are conducted to obtain the recognition results when the subject is inhaling, exhaling, followed by breathing normally. First, we performed the experiments when the subjects are inhaling. The number of probe images collected is 140. Table 5 illustrates the recognition rates obtained by the three different models and Fig. 14 shows the maximum recognition scores.

Ambient Condition	Data Type	Recognition Rate
24.3˚C - 25.3 ˚C	Thermal	69.8%
	Complex Blood Perfusion	90.1%
	Modified Blood Perfusion	87.1%

Table 5. Recognition rate for same-session data when inhalation

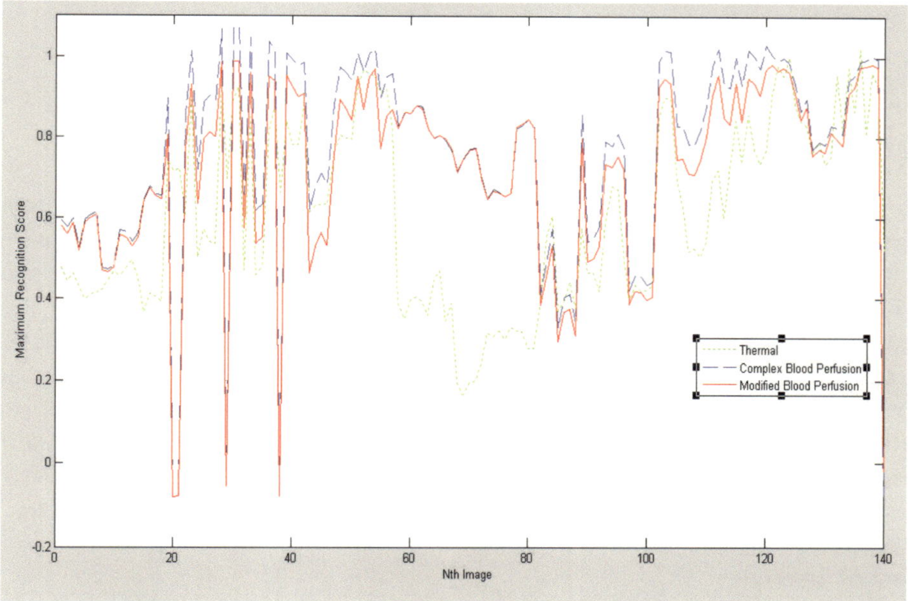

Fig. 14. Maximum recognition scores for same-session data when inhalation

In the next experiment, with the same group of people for test, they are instructed to only exhale during recognition. The total number of probe images in this case is 140. Table 6 shows the recognition rates and the recognition scores are depicted in Fig.15.

Ambient Condition	Data Type	Recognition Rate
24.3˚C - 25.3 ˚C	Thermal	84.1%
	Complex Blood Perfusion	89.8%
	Modified Blood Perfusion	89.8%

Table 6. Recognition rate for same-session data when exhalation

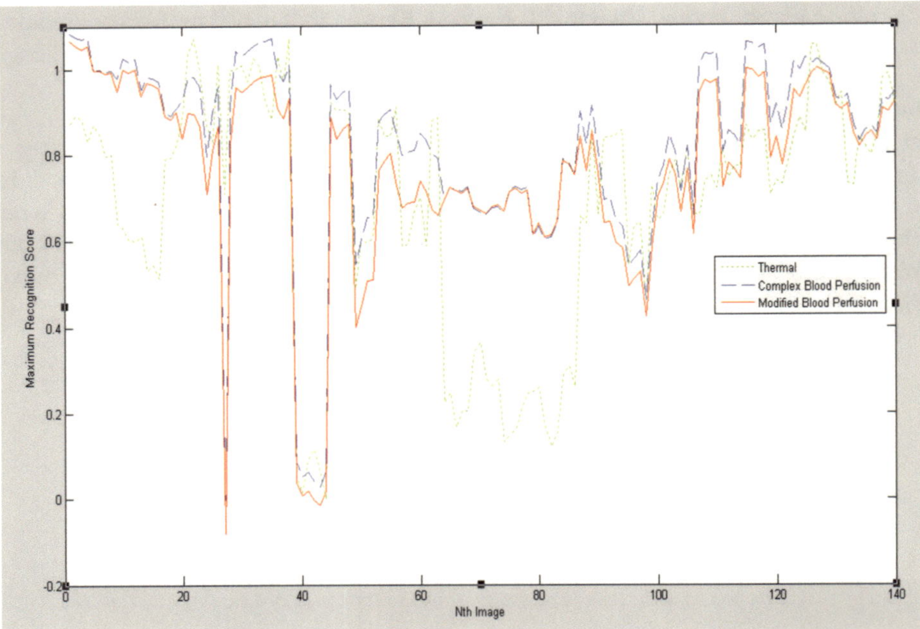

Fig. 15. Maximum recognition scores for same-session data when exhalation

The same group of people involved in the previous two breathing experiments is then instructed to breathe without any restraints in the next series of experiments. The number of probe images of subjects breathing normally is totally 135. The performances are shown in Table 7 and Fig. 16.

It is interesting to note how the recognition rates obtained from the thermal model vary under the three scenarios. It can be seen that the thermal model results in big change of performances (14.3%), and yields the best recognition rate result (84.1%) during the exhalation experiments. For both the blood perfusion models, the recognition rate results obtained from the three different scenarios are comparable, and yields the best recognition rate result (94.1%) during the normal breathing. This is further verified that the blood perfusion models are efficient.

D. Effect of hairstyle

It is also interesting to find the effect of hair on recognition performance as the hair/hairstyle keeps change frequently. Table 8 and Fig. 17 illustrate the recognition results for a person with no hair, while Fig. 18 shows the recognition results for a female with long hair.

Ambient Condition	Data Type	Recognition Rate
24.3°C - 25.3 °C	Thermal	77.8%
	Complex Blood Perfusion	94.1%
	Modified Blood Perfusion	94.1%

Table 7. Recognition rate for same-session data when normal breathing

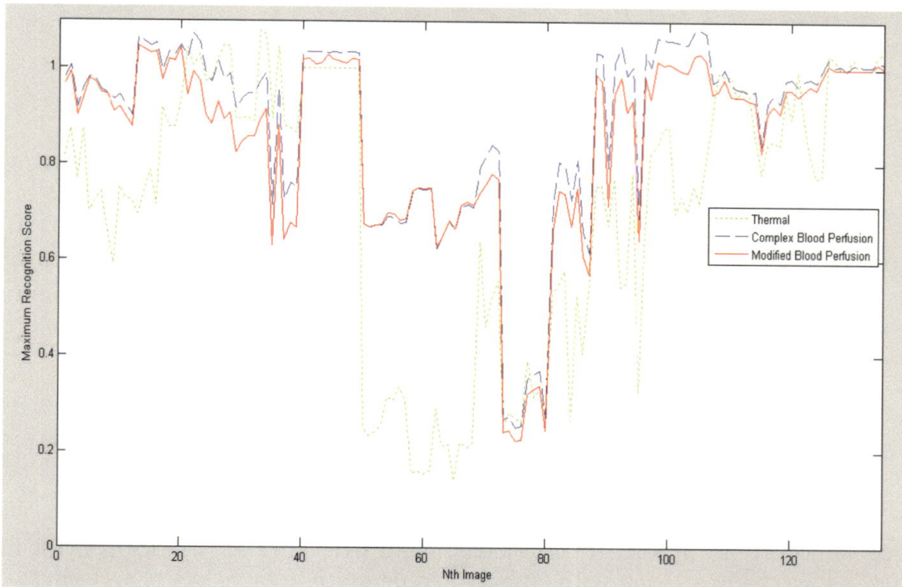

Fig. 16. Maximum recognition scores for same-session data when normal breathing

Ambient Condition 24.3 °C - 25.3 °C	Thermal data	OBP model	MBP Model
Recognition Rate	80%	100%	100%
Mean Score	0.5132	0.6892	0.6632
Variance	0.3189	0.1853	0.1850

Table 8. Mean and variance of recognition scores for a bald subject

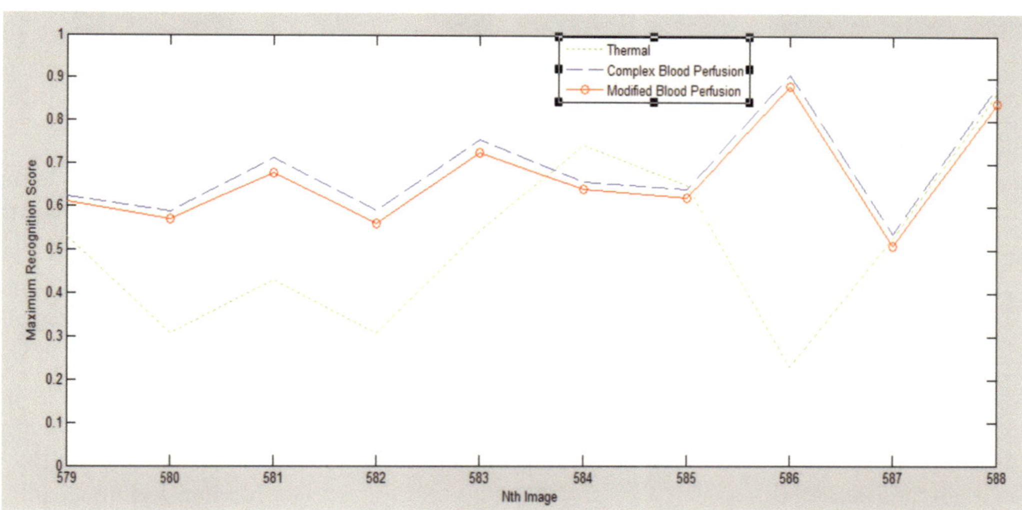

Fig. 17. Maximum recognition score for a bald subject

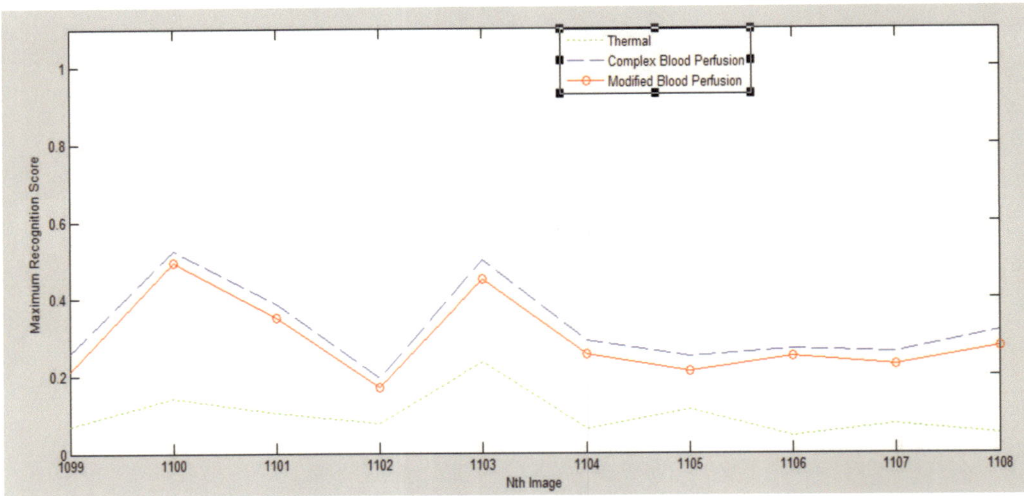

Fig. 18. Maximum recognition score for a female with long hair

Hair is an annoying factor for both segmetation and normalization of faces. As the thermal pattern of a face changes along with ambient temperature, psychological and physiological conditions, and the geometrical features of a face in an IR image is not clear, it is difficult to locate the facial features in IR images for face segmentation and normalization. In our recognition system (Wu et al., 2003), a face is segmented by temperature disparity between ambience and a face. Such method accordingly yields segmentation error by hair. Such situation is more serious for a female with long hair: for the same person, the segmentation results are significantly different caused by hair in different poses as shown in Figs. 19 and 20 respectively. On the other hand, hair is not a feature for recognition and accordingly affects performances. Therefore, the performance in terms of recognition rate and scores on subjects with bald head outperforms that on subjects with long hair.

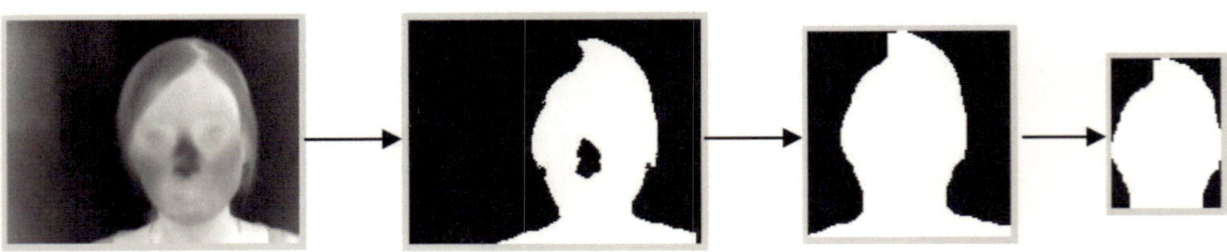

Testing image acquired

Normalized image after face detection program

Fig. 19. Testing person with long hair: image 1 obtained after face detection program

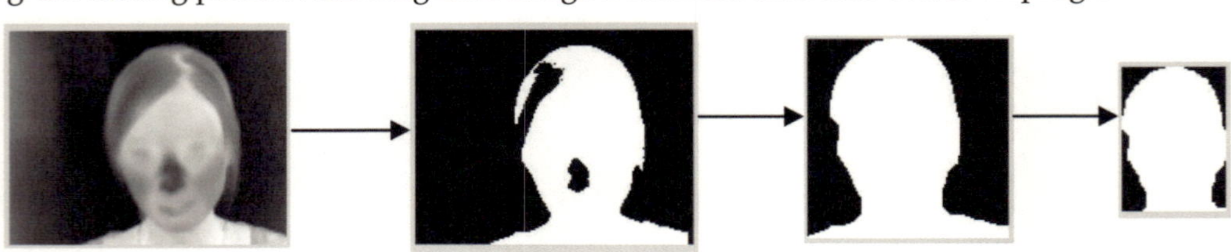

Testing image acquired

Normalized image after face detection Program

Fig. 20. Testing person with hair: image 2 obtained after face detection program

It is interesting to find from Table 8 that 2 images are not recognized correctly for the bald subject when the thermal images are used , although the segmentation is excellent for such subjects as demonstrated in Fig.21. This is mainly caused by big pose variations. However, the 2 images can be recognized correctly by employing the proposed blood perfusion models.

Testing image acquired

Normalized Image after Face Detection Program

Fig. 21. Testing person with bald head: image obtained after face detection program

E. Overall results for same-session data

Considering all the aforementioned effects that can affect recognition performance, an overall recognition performance results based on same-session testing is generated. The number of subjects participating in this experiment is 85 and the number of probe images used here is 1780. Table 9 illustrates the overall results obtained.

These results illustrate that both the blood perfusion models are less sensitive to variations to the factors as aforementioned, than the thermal data. It can also be observed that the recognition rate obtained from the OBP model is only slightly better than that of the MBP model. This suggests that the MBP model not only aids in reducing complexity and the computational time, it can also perform as well as the OBP model for same-session data.

Ambient Condition	Model	Recognition Rate
24.3 °C - 25.3 °C	Thermal data	66.9%
	OBP model	86.6%
	MBP model	86.4%

Table 9. Recognition rate for same-session data

4.4 Recognition results for time-lapse data

Time-lapse recognition was conducted based on the data collected one month later. The testing situation and environmental condition are similar to that when collecting the training data, under the temperature ranging from 24.3 °C - 25.3 °C. The number of probe images is 180. The results obtained are indicated in Table 10 and Fig.22.

As the testing data were captured in air-conditioned room, it is considered that the testing individuals are in steady state without body temperature regulation. However, these time-lapse data comprise a variety of variations: ambient temperature (although it is small), face shape resulted from hair styles, and physiology etc. The effect of hair styles leads to inconsistence in face normalization, and accordingly results in decrease of recognition rate. However, we found that one crucial factor came from physiology, for example, relaxed in morning, and tired in afternoon and at night. It was shown that even the ambient temperature was almost the same, the face images collected when the person was overtired cannot be recognized at all, and the effect of physiology on recognition rate varies from person to person. It is the key reason to affect the performance identified on time-lapse data.

The experimental results shown in Table 10 and Fig.22 reveal that it is difficult to use the thermograms to identify the person accurately under time-lapse scenarios. The recognition rate, using temperature data, decreases significantly from 66.9% (for same- session data) to 23.8%. The performance using OBP model also yields big change ranged from 86.6% for same-session data to 76.6% for time-lapse data. However, it should be highlighted from Table 10 that the MBP model achieves better performance than the OBP model under time-lapse testing. The recognition rate (83.7%) on time-lapse data is comparable to that of same-session data. It is also observed from Fig. 22 that the scores performed on the MBP model is the highest amongst the three models at most times. Therefore, it is concluded that the MBP model is more suitable for real IR face recognition system.

Ambient Condition	Model	Recognition Rate
24.3 °C - 25.3 °C	Thermal data	23.8%
	OBP model	76.6%
	MBP model	83.7%

Table 10. Recognition rate for time-lapse data

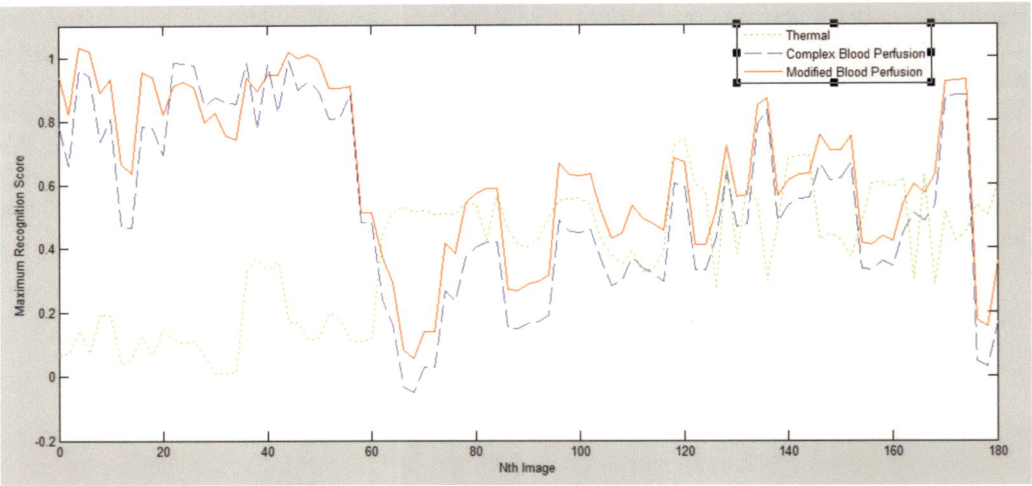

Fig. 22. Maximum recognition score for time-lapse data

5. Conclusion

Infrared imagery has been proposed for face recognition because it is independent on external illumination and shading problem. However, the thermal pattern of a face is also severely affected by a variety of factors ranging from eyeglasses, hairstyle, environmental temperature to changes in metabolism, breathing patterns and so on. To alleviate these variations, blood perfusion models are proposed to convert thermal information into physiological data. The transforms are nonlinearly monotonous, and are able to reduce the within-class scatter resulting from ambience, metabolism and so on, and more consistent features which represent the human faces are obtained. The extensive experiments demonstrated that the recognition performances with blood perfusion models are substantially better than that with thermal data in different situations, especially for time-lapse data.

It should be highlighted that physiological (e.g., fever) and psychological (e.g., happy, angry and sad etc) conditions also affect the thermal patterns of faces. Further analysis and experiments on these variations will be our future work.

6. References

Blatteis, C. M. (1998). *Physiology and Pathophysiology of Temperature Regulation*, World Scientific Publishing Co

Bone, M. & Blackburn, D. (2002). Face Recognition at a Chokepoint - Scenario Evaluation Results, http://www.dodcounterdrug.com/facialrecognition/DLs/ChokePoint_Results.pdf, November 14, 2002

Buddharaju, P.; Pavlidis I. & Kakadiaris I. A. (2004). Face recognition in the thermal infrared spectrum, *Proceedings of IEEE International Conference on Computer Vision and Pattern Recognition Workshop*, pp. 133-133, Washington DC, USA, 2004

Buddharaju, P.; Pavlidis I. & Tsiamyrtzis, P. (2005). Physiology-based face recognition using the vascular network extracted from thermal facial images: a novel approach, *Proceedings of IEEE Advanced Video and Signal Based Surveillance*, pp. 354-359, Lake Como, Italy, 2005

Chen, X.; Flynn, P. J. & Bowyer, K. W. (2005). IR and visible light face recognition, *Computer Vision and Image Understanding*, Vol. 99, No. 3, pp. 332-358, 2005

Ganong, W. F. (2001). *Review of Medical Physiology*, 20th ed., McGraw-Hill Medical Publishing Division

Goodwin, D. W. (2000). *Alcoholism: the facts*, 3rd ed., Oxford University Press, USA

Guyton, A. C. & Hall, J. E. (1996). *Textbook of Medical Physiology*, 9th ed., Philadelphia: W.B. Saunders Company, 1996

Houdas, Y. & Ring, E. F. J. (1982). *Human Body Temperature: Its Measurement and Regulation*. New York: Plenum Press, 1982

Jones, B. F. & Plassmann, P. (2002). Digital infrared thermal imaging of human skin, *IEEE Engineering in Medicine & Biology Magazine*, Vol. 21, No. 6, pp.41-48, 2002

Kong, S. G.; Heo. J.; Abidi, B. R. Paik, J. & Abidi, M. A. (2005). Recent advances in visual and infrared race recognition - a review, *Computer Vision and Image Understanding*, Vol. 97, No. 1, pp. 103-135, 2005

Prokoski, F. J.; Riedel, B. & Coffin, J. S. (1992). Identification of individuals by means of facial thermography, *Proceedings of IEEE Int. Conf. Security Technology, Crime Countermeasures*, pp. 120-125, Atlanta, USA, Oct. 1992

Prokoski, F. J. (2000). History, current status, and future of infrared identification, *Proceedings of IEEE Workshop on Computer Vision beyond Visible Spectrum: Methods and Applications*, pp. 5-14, Hilton Head, SC, USA, 2000

Prokoski, F. J. (2001). Method and apparatus for recognizing and classifying individuals based on minutiae, US Patent: 6173068B1, January 9, 2001.

Socolinsky, D. A. & Selinger, A. (2002). A comparative analysis of face recognition performance with visible and thermal infrared imagery, *Proceedings of Int. Conf. Pattern Recognition*, pp. 217-222, Quebec, Canada, 2002

Socolinsky, D. A. & Selinger, A. (2004A). Thermal face recognition in an operational scenario, *Proceedings of IEEE Conference on Computer Vision and Pattern Recognition*, pp. 1012-1019, Washington DC, USA, 2004

Socolinsky, D. A. & Selinger. A. (2004B). Thermal face recognition over time, *Proceedings of Int. Conf. Pattern Recognition*, pp. 187-190, Cambridge, UK, 2004

Srivastava, A. & Liu, X. (2003). Statistical hypothesis pruning for identifying faces from infrared images, Image and Vision Computing, Vol. 21, No. 7, pp. 651-661, 2003

Wilder, J. Phillips, P. J.; Jiang, C. & Wiener, S. (1996). Comparison of visible and infrared imagery for face recognition, *Proceedings of the 2nd Int. Conf. Automatic Face and Gesture Recognition*, pp. 182-187, Killington, Vermont, USA, 1996

Wu, S. Q., Jiang, L. J.; Cheng, L. et al. (2003). RIFARS: a real-time infrared face recognition system, *Proceedings of Asian Biometrics Workshop*, pp. 1-6, Singapore, 2003

Wu, S. Q.; Song, W.; Jiang, L. J. et al. (2005A). Infrared face recognition by using blood perfusion data, *Proceedings of Audio- and Video-based Biometric Person Authentication*, pp. 320-328, Rye Brook, NY, USA, 2005

Wu, S. Q.; Lin, W. S.; Jiang, L. J. et al. (2005B). An objective out-of-focus blur measurement, *Proceedings 5th Int. Conf. Inform., Comm. & Sign. Proc.*, pp. 334-338, Bangkok, Thailand, 2005

Wu, S. Q.; Jiang, L. J.; Xie, S. L. & Yeo, C. B. (2006) A robust method for detecting facial orientation in infrared images, Patt. Recog., Vol. 39, No. 2, pp. 303-309, 2006

Wu, S. Q; Gu, Z. H; Chia, K. A. & Ong, S. H. (2007). Infrared facial recognition using modified blood perfusion, *Proceedings 6th Int. Conf. Inform., Comm. & Sign. Proc.*, pp. 1-5, Singapore, Dec, 2007

Yoshitomi, Y.; Miyaura, T.; Tomita, S. & Kimura, S. (1997). Face identification using thermal image processing, *Proceedings of IEEE Int. Workshop of Robot and Human Communication*, pp. 374-379, Sendai, Japan, 1997

14

Discriminating Color Faces for Recognition

Jian Yang[1], Chengjun Liu[2] and Jingyu Yang[1]
[1]*School of Computer Science and Technology, Nanjing University of Science and Technology, Nanjing 210094,*
[2]*Department of Computer Science, New Jersey Institute of Technology, Newark, NJ 07102,*
[1]*P. R. China*
[2]*USA*

1. Introduction

Color provides useful and important information for object detection, tracking and recognition, image (or video) segmentation, indexing and retrieval, etc. [1-15]. Color constancy algorithms [13, 14] and color histogram techniques [5, 10-12], for example, provide efficient tools for indexing in a large image database or for object recognition under varying lighting conditions. Different color spaces (or color models) possess different characteristics and have been applied for different visual tasks. For instance, the *HSV* color space and the YC_bC_r color space were demonstrated effective for face detection [2, 3], and the modified $L^*u^*v^*$ color space was chosen for image segmentation [7]. Recently, a selection and fusion scheme of multiple color models was investigated and applied for feature detection in images [15].

Although color has been demonstrated helpful for face detection and tracking, some past research suggests that color appears to confer no significant face recognition advantage beyond the luminance information [16]. Recent research efforts, however, reveal that color may provide useful information for face recognition. The experimental results in [17] show that the principle component analysis (PCA) method [35] using color information can improve the recognition rate compared to the same method using only luminance information. The results in [18] further reveal that color cues do play a role in face recognition and their contribution becomes evident when shape cues are degraded. Other research findings also demonstrate the effectiveness of color for face recognition [19-22, 38].

If color does help face recognition, then a question arises: how should we represent color images for the recognition purpose? One common practice is to convert color images in the RGB color space into a grayscale image by averaging the three color component images before applying a face recognition algorithm for recognition. However, there are neither theoretical nor experimental justifications for supporting that such a grayscale image is a good representation of the color image for the recognition purpose. Other research effort is to choose an existing color space or a color component configuration for achieving good recognition performance with respect to a specific recognition method. For instance, Rajapakse et al. [19] used the RGB color space and nonnegative matrix factorization (NMF) method for face recognition. Torres et al. [17] suggested using the YUV color space or the configuration of S and V components from the HSV color space together with PCA for feature extraction. Shih and Liu [21] showed that the color configuration YQC_r, where Y and Q color components are from the YIQ color space and C_r is from the YC_bC_r color space, was effective for face recognition using the enhanced Fisher linear discriminant (FLD) model [23]. In summary, current research efforts apply a separate strategy by first choosing a color image representation scheme and then evaluating its effectiveness using a recognition method. This separate strategy cannot theoretically guarantee that the chosen color image representation scheme is best for the subsequent recognition method and therefore cannot guarantee that the resulting face recognition system is optimal in performance.

The motivation of this chapter is to seek a meaningful representation and an effective recognition method of color images in a unified framework. We integrate color image representation and recognition into one discriminant analysis model: color image discriminant (CID) model. In contrast to the classical FLD method [24], which involves only one set of variables (one or multiple discriminant projection basis vectors), the proposed CID model involves two sets of variables: a set of color component combination coefficients for color image representation and one or multiple discriminant projection basis vectors for image discrimination. The two sets of variables can be determined optimally and simultaneously by the developed, iterative CID algorithm. The CID algorithm is further extended to generate three color components (like the three color components of the RGB color images) for further improving face recognition performance.

We use the Face Recognition Grand Challenge (FRGC) database and the Biometric Experimentation Environment (BEE) system to assess the proposed CID models and algorithms. FRGC is the most comprehensive face recognition efforts organized so far by the US government, and it consists of a large amount of face data and a standard evaluation system, known as the Biometric Experimentation Environment (BEE) system [25, 26]. The BEE baseline algorithm reveals that the FRGC version 2 Experiment 4 is the most challenging experiment, because it assesses face verification performance of controlled face images versus uncontrolled face images. We therefore choose FRGC version 2 Experiment 4 to evaluate our algorithms, and the experimental results demonstrate the effectiveness of the proposed models and algorithms.

2. CID model and algorithm

In this section, we first present our motivation to build the color image discriminant model and then give the mathematical description of the model and finally design an iterative algorithm for achieving its optimal solution.

2.1 Motivation

We develop our general discriminant model based on the RGB color space since it is a fundamental and commonly-used color space. Let **A** be a color image with a resolution of $m \times n$, and let its three color components be **R**, **G**, and **B**. Without loss of generality, we assume that **R**, **G**, and **B** are column vectors: $\mathbf{R}, \mathbf{G}, \mathbf{B} \in R^N$, where $N = m \times n$. The color image **A** is then expressed as an $N \times 3$ matrix: $\mathbf{A} = [\mathbf{R}, \mathbf{G}, \mathbf{B}] \in R^{N \times 3}$.

How should we represent the color image **A** for the recognition purpose? Common practice is to linearly combine its three color components into one grayscale image:

$$\mathbf{E} = \tfrac{1}{3}\mathbf{R} + \tfrac{1}{3}\mathbf{G} + \tfrac{1}{3}\mathbf{B} \qquad (1)$$

The grayscale image **E** is then used to represent **A** for recognition. However, theoretical explanation is lacking in supporting that such a grayscale image is a good representation of image **A** for image recognition.

The motivation of this chapter is to seek a more effective representation of the color image **A** for image recognition. Our goal is to find a set of optimal coefficients to combine the **R**, **G**, and **B** color components within a discriminant analysis framework. Specifically, let **D** be the combined image given below:

$$\mathbf{D} = x_1\mathbf{R} + x_2\mathbf{G} + x_3\mathbf{B}, \tag{2}$$

where x_1, x_2 and x_3 are the color component combination coefficients. Now, our task is to find a set of optimal coefficients so that **D** is the best representation of the color image **A** for image recognition.

Given a set of training color images with class labels, we can generate a combined image **D** for each image $\mathbf{A} = [\mathbf{R}, \mathbf{G}, \mathbf{B}]$. Let us discuss the problem in the *D*-space, i.e., the pattern vector space formed by all the combined images defined by Eq. (2). In order to achieve the best recognition performance, we borrow the idea of Fisher linear discriminant analysis (FLD) [24] to build a color image discriminant (CID) model. Note that the CID model is quite different from the classical FLD model since it involves an additional set of variables: the color component combination coefficients x_1, x_2 and x_3. In the following, we will show the details of a CID model and its associated CID algorithm for deriving the optimal solution of the model.

2.2 CID model

Let c be the number of pattern classes, A_{ij} be the *j*-th color image in class *i*, where $i = 1, 2, \cdots, c$, $j = 1, 2, \cdots, M_i$, and M_i denotes the number of training samples in class *i*. The mean image of the training samples in class *i* is

$$\bar{\mathrm{A}}_i = \frac{1}{M_i}\sum_{j=1}^{M_i}\mathrm{A}_{ij} = [\bar{\mathrm{R}}_i, \bar{\mathrm{G}}_i, \bar{\mathrm{B}}_i]. \tag{3}$$

The mean image of all training samples is

$$\bar{\mathrm{A}} = \frac{1}{M}\sum_{i=1}^{c}\sum_{j=1}^{M_i}\mathrm{A}_{ij} = [\bar{\mathrm{R}}, \bar{\mathrm{G}}, \bar{\mathrm{B}}], \tag{4}$$

where *M* is the total number of training samples, i.e., $M = \sum_{i=1}^{c} M_i$.

The combined image of three color components of the color image $\mathrm{A}_{ij} = [\mathrm{R}_{ij}, \mathrm{G}_{ij}, \mathrm{B}_{ij}]$ is given by

$$\mathrm{D}_{ij} = x_1\mathrm{R}_{ij} + x_2\mathrm{G}_{ij} + x_3\mathrm{B}_{ij} = [\mathrm{R}_{ij}, \mathrm{G}_{ij}, \mathrm{B}_{ij}]\mathrm{X} \tag{5}$$

Let $\bar{\mathrm{D}}_i$ be the mean vector of the combined images in class *i* and $\bar{\mathrm{D}}$ the grand mean vector:

$$\bar{\mathrm{D}}_i = \bar{\mathrm{A}}_i \mathrm{X} \tag{6}$$

$$\bar{\mathrm{D}} = \bar{\mathrm{A}} \mathrm{X} \tag{7}$$

The between-class scatter matrix $\mathrm{S}_b(\mathrm{X})$ and the within-class scatter matrix $\mathrm{S}_w(\mathrm{X})$ in the *D*-space are defined as follows:

$$\begin{aligned} \mathrm{S}_b(\mathrm{X}) &= \mathrm{s} \\ &= \sum_{i=1}^{c} P_i[(\bar{\mathrm{A}}_i - \bar{\mathrm{A}})\mathrm{X}][(\bar{\mathrm{A}}_i - \bar{\mathrm{A}})\mathrm{X}]^T \\ &= \sum_{i=1}^{c} P_i[(\bar{\mathrm{A}}_i - \bar{\mathrm{A}})\mathrm{X}\mathrm{X}^T(\bar{\mathrm{A}}_i - \bar{\mathrm{A}})^T] \end{aligned} \tag{8}$$

$$\begin{aligned} \mathrm{S}_w(\mathrm{X}) &= \sum_{i=1}^{c} P_i\left(\frac{1}{M_i - 1}\sum_{j=1}^{M_i}(\mathrm{D}_{ij} - \bar{\mathrm{D}}_i)(\mathrm{D}_{ij} - \bar{\mathrm{D}}_i)^T\right) \\ &= \sum_{i=1}^{c} P_i \frac{1}{M_i - 1}\sum_{j=1}^{M_i}[(\mathrm{A}_{ij} - \bar{\mathrm{A}}_i)\mathrm{X}][(\mathrm{A}_{ij} - \bar{\mathrm{A}}_i)\mathrm{X}]^T \\ &= \sum_{i=1}^{c} P_i \frac{1}{M_i - 1}\sum_{j=1}^{M_i}[(\mathrm{A}_{ij} - \bar{\mathrm{A}}_i)\mathrm{X}\mathrm{X}^T(\mathrm{A}_{ij} - \bar{\mathrm{A}}_i)^T] \end{aligned} \tag{9}$$

where P_i is the prior probability for Class *i* and commonly evaluated as $P_i = M_i / M$. Since the combination coefficient vector **X** is an unknown variable, the elements in $\mathrm{S}_b(\mathrm{X})$ and $\mathrm{S}_w(\mathrm{X})$ can be viewed as linear functionals of **X**.
The general Fisher criterion in the *D*-space can be defined as follows:

$$J(\boldsymbol{\varphi}, \mathbf{X}) = \frac{\boldsymbol{\varphi}^T \mathbf{S}_b(\mathbf{X})\boldsymbol{\varphi}}{\boldsymbol{\varphi}^T \mathbf{S}_w(\mathbf{X})\boldsymbol{\varphi}}, \tag{10}$$

where $\boldsymbol{\varphi}$ is a discriminant projection basis vector and **X** a color component combination coefficient vector.
Maximizing this criterion is equivalent to solving the following optimization model:

$$\begin{cases} \max\limits_{\boldsymbol{\varphi}, \mathbf{X}} \mathrm{tr}\{\boldsymbol{\varphi}^T \mathbf{S}_b(\mathbf{X})\boldsymbol{\varphi}\} \\ \text{subject to } \boldsymbol{\varphi}^T \mathbf{S}_w(\mathbf{X})\boldsymbol{\varphi} = 1 \end{cases}, \tag{11}$$

where $\mathrm{tr}(\cdot)$ is the trace operator. We will design an iterative algorithm to simultaneously determine the optimal discriminant projection basis vector $\boldsymbol{\varphi}^*$ and the optimal combination coefficient vector **X*** in the following subsection.

2.3 CID algorithm

First of all, let us define the color-space between-class scatter matrix $\mathbf{L}_b(\boldsymbol{\varphi})$ and the color-space within-class scatter matrix $\mathbf{L}_w(\boldsymbol{\varphi})$ as follows

$$\mathbf{L}_b(\boldsymbol{\varphi}) = \sum_{i=1}^{c} P_i[(\overline{\mathbf{A}}_i - \overline{\mathbf{A}})^T \boldsymbol{\varphi}\boldsymbol{\varphi}^T (\overline{\mathbf{A}}_i - \overline{\mathbf{A}}), \tag{12}$$

$$\mathbf{L}_w(\boldsymbol{\varphi}) = \sum_{i=1}^{c} P_i \frac{1}{M_i - 1} \sum_{j=1}^{M_i} [(\mathbf{A}_{ij} - \overline{\mathbf{A}}_i)^T \boldsymbol{\varphi}\boldsymbol{\varphi}^T (\mathbf{A}_{ij} - \overline{\mathbf{A}}_i)]. \tag{13}$$

$\mathbf{L}_b(\boldsymbol{\varphi})$ and $\mathbf{L}_w(\boldsymbol{\varphi})$ are therefore 3×3 non-negative definite matrices. Actually, $\mathbf{L}_b(\boldsymbol{\varphi})$ and $\mathbf{L}_w(\boldsymbol{\varphi})$ can be viewed as dual matrices of $\mathbf{S}_b(\mathbf{X})$ and $\mathbf{S}_w(\mathbf{X})$.
Based on the definition of $\mathbf{L}_b(\boldsymbol{\varphi})$ and $\mathbf{L}_w(\boldsymbol{\varphi})$, we give the following proposition:

Proposition 1: $\boldsymbol{\varphi}^T\mathbf{S}_b(\mathbf{X})\boldsymbol{\varphi} = \mathbf{X}^T\mathbf{L}_b(\boldsymbol{\varphi})\mathbf{X}$, and $\boldsymbol{\varphi}^T\mathbf{S}_w(\mathbf{X})\boldsymbol{\varphi} = \mathbf{X}^T\mathbf{L}_w(\boldsymbol{\varphi})\mathbf{X}$.

Proof:
$$\boldsymbol{\varphi}^T\mathbf{S}_b(\mathbf{X})\boldsymbol{\varphi} = \sum_{i=1}^{c} P_i[\boldsymbol{\varphi}^T(\overline{\mathbf{A}}_i - \overline{\mathbf{A}})\mathbf{X}][\mathbf{X}^T(\overline{\mathbf{A}}_i - \overline{\mathbf{A}})^T\boldsymbol{\varphi}]$$

$$= \sum_{i=1}^{c} P_i[\mathbf{X}^T(\overline{\mathbf{A}}_i - \overline{\mathbf{A}})^T\boldsymbol{\varphi}][\boldsymbol{\varphi}^T(\overline{\mathbf{A}}_i - \overline{\mathbf{A}})\mathbf{X}]$$

$$= \mathbf{X}^T\{\sum_{i=1}^{c} P_i[(\overline{\mathbf{A}}_i - \overline{\mathbf{A}})^T\boldsymbol{\varphi}\boldsymbol{\varphi}^T(\overline{\mathbf{A}}_i - \overline{\mathbf{A}})\}\mathbf{X}$$

$$= \mathbf{X}^T\mathbf{L}_b(\boldsymbol{\varphi})\mathbf{X}.$$

Similarly, we can derive that $\boldsymbol{\varphi}^T\mathbf{S}_w(\mathbf{X})\boldsymbol{\varphi} = \mathbf{X}^T\mathbf{L}_w(\boldsymbol{\varphi})\mathbf{X}$. □

The model in Eq. (11) is a constrained optimization problem, which can be solved using the Lagrange multiplier method. Let the Lagrange functional be as follows:

$$L(\boldsymbol{\varphi}, \mathbf{X}, \lambda) = \boldsymbol{\varphi}^T\mathbf{S}_b(\mathbf{X})\boldsymbol{\varphi} - \lambda(\boldsymbol{\varphi}^T\mathbf{S}_w(\mathbf{X})\boldsymbol{\varphi} - 1), \tag{14}$$

where λ is the Lagrange multiplier. From Proposition 1, we have

$$L(\boldsymbol{\varphi}, \mathbf{X}, \lambda) = \mathbf{X}^T\mathbf{L}_b(\boldsymbol{\varphi})\mathbf{X} - \lambda(\mathbf{X}^T\mathbf{L}_w(\boldsymbol{\varphi})\mathbf{X} - 1), \tag{15}$$

First, take the derivative of $L(\boldsymbol{\varphi}, \mathbf{X}, \lambda)$ in Eq. (14) with respect to $\boldsymbol{\varphi}$:

$$\frac{\partial L(\boldsymbol{\varphi}, \mathbf{X}, \lambda)}{\partial \boldsymbol{\varphi}} = 2\mathbf{S}_b(\mathbf{X})\boldsymbol{\varphi} - 2\lambda\mathbf{S}_w(\mathbf{X})\boldsymbol{\varphi} \tag{16}$$

Equate the derivative to zero, $\frac{\partial L(\boldsymbol{\varphi}, \mathbf{X}, \lambda)}{\partial \boldsymbol{\varphi}} = 0$, then we have the following equation:

$$\mathbf{S}_b(\mathbf{X})\boldsymbol{\varphi} = \lambda \mathbf{S}_w(\mathbf{X})\boldsymbol{\varphi} \tag{17}$$

Second, take the derivative of $L(\boldsymbol{\varphi}, \mathbf{X}, \lambda)$ in Eq. (15) with respect to **X**:

$$\frac{\partial L(\boldsymbol{\varphi}, \mathbf{X}, \lambda)}{\partial \mathbf{X}} = 2\mathbf{S}_b(\boldsymbol{\varphi})\mathbf{X} - 2\lambda \mathbf{S}_w(\boldsymbol{\varphi})\mathbf{X} \tag{18}$$

Equate the derivative to zero, $\frac{\partial L(\boldsymbol{\varphi}, \mathbf{X}, \lambda)}{\partial \mathbf{X}} = 0$, then we have the following equation:

$$\mathbf{L}_b(\boldsymbol{\varphi})\mathbf{X} = \lambda \mathbf{L}_w(\boldsymbol{\varphi})\mathbf{X} \tag{19}$$

And finally, take the derivative of $L(\boldsymbol{\varphi}, \mathbf{X}, \lambda)$ in Eq. (14) with respect to λ and equate it to zero, and we have the following equation:

$$\boldsymbol{\varphi}^T \mathbf{S}_w(\mathbf{X})\boldsymbol{\varphi} = 1, \tag{20}$$

which is equivalent to

$$\mathbf{X}^T \mathbf{L}_w(\boldsymbol{\varphi})\mathbf{X} = 1. \tag{21}$$

Therefore, finding the optimal solutions $\boldsymbol{\varphi}^*$ and **X*** of the optimization problem in Eq. (11) is equivalent to solving the following two sets of equations:

$$\textit{Equation Set I}: \quad \begin{cases} \mathbf{S}_b(\mathbf{X})\boldsymbol{\varphi} = \lambda \mathbf{S}_w(\mathbf{X})\boldsymbol{\varphi} \\ \boldsymbol{\varphi}^T \mathbf{S}_w(\mathbf{X})\boldsymbol{\varphi} = 1 \end{cases} \tag{22}$$

$$\textit{Equation Set II}: \quad \begin{cases} \mathbf{L}_b(\boldsymbol{\varphi})\mathbf{X} = \lambda \mathbf{L}_w(\boldsymbol{\varphi})\mathbf{X} \\ \mathbf{X}^T \mathbf{L}_w(\boldsymbol{\varphi})\mathbf{X} = 1 \end{cases} \tag{23}$$

Theorem 1 [27] Suppose that **A** and **B** are two $n \times n$ nonnegative definite matrices and **B** is nonsingular. There exist *n* eigenvectors $\xi_1, \cdots, \xi_n$ corresponding to eigenvalues $\lambda_1, \cdots, \lambda_n$ of the generalized eigen-equation $\mathrm{A}\xi = \lambda \mathrm{B}\xi$, such that

$$\boldsymbol{\xi}_i^T \mathbf{A} \boldsymbol{\xi}_j = \begin{cases} \lambda_i & i = j \\ 0 & i \neq j \end{cases} \quad i, j = 1, \cdots, n \tag{24}$$

and

$$\boldsymbol{\xi}_i^T \mathbf{B} \boldsymbol{\xi}_j = \begin{cases} 1 & i = j \\ 0 & i \neq j \end{cases} \quad i, j = 1, \cdots, n. \tag{25}$$

From Theorem 1, we know the solution of *Equation Set I*, i.e., the extremum point $\boldsymbol{\varphi}^*$ of $J_F(\boldsymbol{\varphi}, \mathbf{X})$, can be chosen as the eigenvector of the generalized equation $\mathbf{S}_b(\mathbf{X})\boldsymbol{\varphi} = \lambda \mathbf{S}_w(\mathbf{X})\boldsymbol{\varphi}$ corresponding to the largest eigenvalue, and the solution of *Equation*

Set II, i.e., the extremum point **X*** of $J_F(\varphi,\mathbf{X})$, can be chosen as the eigenvector of the generalized equation $\mathbf{L}_b(\varphi)\mathbf{X}=\lambda\,\mathbf{L}_w(\varphi)\mathbf{X}$ corresponding to the largest eigenvalue. Based on this conclusion, we can design an iterative algorithm to calculate the extremum points φ^* and **X***.

Let $\mathbf{X}=\mathbf{X}^{[k]}$ be the initial value of the combination coefficient vector in the *k*-th iteration. In the first step, we construct $\mathbf{S}_b(\mathbf{X})$ and $\mathbf{S}_w(\mathbf{X})$ based on $\mathbf{X}=\mathbf{X}^{[k]}$ and calculate their generalized eigenvector $\varphi=\varphi^{[k+1]}$ corresponding to the largest eigenvalue. In the second step, we construct $\mathbf{L}_b(\varphi)$ and $\mathbf{L}_w(\varphi)$ based on $\varphi=\varphi^{[k+1]}$ and calculate their generalized eigenvector $\mathbf{X}^{[k+1]}$ corresponding to the largest eigenvalue. $\mathbf{X}=\mathbf{X}^{[k+1]}$ is used as initial value in the next iteration.

The CID algorithm performs the preceding two steps successively until it converges. Convergence may be determined by observing when the value of the criterion function $J(\varphi,\mathbf{X})$ stops changing. Specifically, after k+1 times of iterations, if $|J(\varphi^{[k+1]},\mathbf{X}^{[k+1]})-J(\varphi^{[k]},\mathbf{X}^{[k]})|<\varepsilon$, we think the algorithm converges. Then, we choose $\varphi^*=\varphi^{[k+1]}$ and $\mathbf{X}^*=\mathbf{X}^{[k+1]}$. The CID algorithm is illustrated in Figure 1.

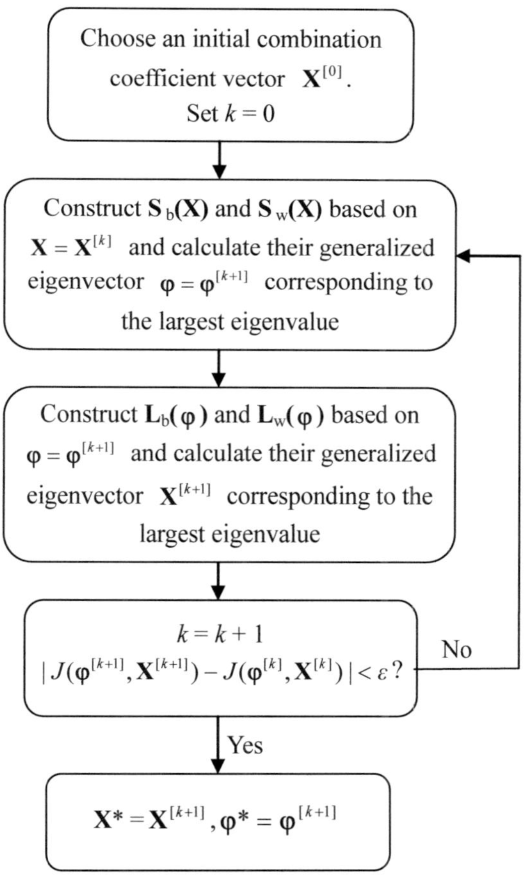

Fig. 1. An overview of the CID Algorithm

2.4 Extended CID algorithm for multiple discriminating color components

Using the CID algorithm, we obtain an optimal color component combination coefficient vector $\mathbf{X}^*=[x_{11},x_{21},x_{31}]^T$, which determines one discriminating color component $\mathrm{D}^1 = x_{11}\mathrm{R}+x_{21}\mathrm{G}+x_{31}\mathrm{B}$. In general, one discriminating color component is not enough for the discrimination of color images. Actually, analogous to the three color components in the RGB color space, we can derive three discriminating color components for image recognition. Let us denote the three discriminating color components of the color image $\mathrm{A}=[\mathrm{R},\mathrm{G},\mathrm{B}]$ as follows:

$$\mathbf{D}^i = x_{1i}\mathbf{R}+x_{2i}\mathbf{G}+x_{3i}\mathbf{B} = [\mathbf{R},\mathbf{G},\mathbf{B}]\,\mathbf{X}_i,\ i=1,2,3 \tag{26}$$

where $\mathbf{X}_i$ ($i=1,2,3$) are the corresponding combination coefficient vectors. These coefficient vectors are required to be $\mathbf{L}_w(\varphi)$-orthogonal[1], that is

$$\mathbf{X}_i^T\mathbf{L}_w(\varphi)\mathbf{X}_j = 0, \quad \forall i \neq j, \quad i,j=1,2,3. \tag{27}$$

Let the first combination coefficient vector be $\mathbf{X}_1 = \mathbf{X}^*$ and $\varphi=\varphi^*$, which have been determined in the foregoing subsection. Since the second combination coefficient vector is assumed to be $\mathbf{L}_w(\varphi)$-orthogonal to the first one, we can choose it from the $\mathbf{L}_w(\varphi)$-orthogonal complementary space of $\mathbf{X}_1$. We know $\mathbf{X}_1$ is chosen as the generalized eigenvector $\mathbf{u}_1$ of $\mathbf{L}_b(\varphi)$ and $\mathbf{L}_w(\varphi)$ corresponding to the largest eigenvalue after the CID algorithm converges. Let us derive $\mathbf{L}_b(\varphi)$ and $\mathbf{L}_w(\varphi)$'s remaining two generalized eigenvectors $\mathbf{u}_2$ and $\mathbf{u}_3$, which are $\mathbf{L}_w(\varphi)$-orthogonal to the first one. We choose the second combination coefficient vector $\mathbf{X}_2=\mathbf{u}_2$ and the third combination coefficient vector $\mathbf{X}_3=\mathbf{u}_3$.

After calculating three color component combination coefficient vectors $\mathbf{X}_1$, $\mathbf{X}_2$ and $\mathbf{X}_3$, we can obtain the three discriminating color components of the color image **A** using Eq. (26). In order to further improve the performance of the three discriminating color components, we generally center $\mathbf{X}_2$ and $\mathbf{X}_3$ in advance so that each of them has zero mean.

3. Experiments

This section assesses the performance of the proposed models and algorithms using a large scale color image database: the Face Recognition Grand Challenge (FRGC) version 2 database [25, 26]. This database contains 12,776 training images, 16,028 controlled target images, and 8,014 uncontrolled query images for the FRGC Experiment 4. The controlled images have good image quality, while the uncontrolled images display poor image quality, such as large illumination variations, low resolution of the face region, and possible blurring. It is these uncontrolled factors that pose the grand challenge to face recognition performance. The Biometric Experimentation Environment (BEE) system [25] provides a computational experimental environment to support a challenge problem in face

[1] This conjugate orthogonality requirement is to eliminate the correlations between combination coefficient vectors. The justification for this is given in Ref. [36].

recognition, and it allows the description and distribution of experiments in a common format. The BEE system uses the PCA method that has been optimized for large scale problems as a baseline algorithm, and it applies the whitened cosine similarity measure. The BEE baseline algorithm shows that FRGC Experiment 4, which is designed for indoor controlled single still image versus uncontrolled single still image, is the most challenging FRGC experiment. We therefore choose the FRGC Experiment 4 to evaluate our method. In our experiments, the face region of each image is first cropped from the original high-resolution still images and resized to a spatial resolution of 32×32. Figure 2 shows some example FRGC images used in our experiments.

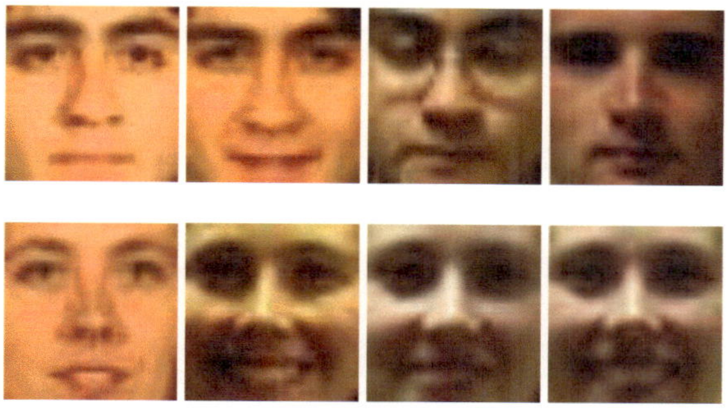

Fig. 2. Example FRGC images that have been cropped to 32x32.

According to the FRGC protocol, the face recognition performance is reported using the Receiver Operating Characteristic (ROC) curves, which plot the Face Verification Rate (FVR) versus the False Accept Rate (FAR). The ROC curves are automatically generated by the BEE system when a similarity matrix is input to the system. In particular, the BEE system generates three ROC curves, ROC I, ROC II, and ROC III, corresponding to images collected within semesters, within a year, and between semesters, respectively. The similarity matrix stores the similarity score of every query image versus target image pair. As a result, the size of the similarity matrix is $T \times Q$, where T is the number of target images (16,028 for FRGC version 2 Experiment 4) and Q is the number of query images (8,014 for FRGC version 2 Experiment 4).

3.1 Face recognition based on one color component image

Following the FRGC protocol, we use the standard training set of the FRGC version 2 Experiment 4 for training. The initial value of the CID algorithm is set as $\mathbf{X}^{[0]} = [1/3, 1/3, 1/3]$, and the convergence threshold of the algorithm is set to be $\varepsilon = 0.1$. After training, the CID algorithm generates one optimal color component combination coefficient vector $\mathbf{X}_1 = [x_{11}, x_{21}, x_{31}]^T$ and a set of 220 optimal discriminant basis vectors since there are 222 pattern classes. The combination coefficient vector $\mathbf{X}_1$ determines one discriminating color component $\mathbf{D}^1 = x_{11}\mathbf{R} + x_{21}\mathbf{G} + x_{31}\mathbf{B}$ for color image representation and the set of discriminant basis vectors determines the projection matrix for feature extraction. In comparison, we also implement the FLD algorithm on grayscale images and choose 220 discriminant features.

For each method mentioned, the cosine measure [33] is used to generate the similarity matrix. After score normalization using Z-score [34], the similarity matrix is analyzed by the

BEE system. The three ROC curves generated by BEE are shown in Figure 3 and the resulting face verification rates at the false accept rate of 0.1% are listed in Table 1. The performance of the BEE baseline algorithm is also shown in Figure 3 and Table 1 for comparison. Figure 3 and Table 1 show that the proposed CID algorithm achieves better performance than the classical FLD method using grayscale images. In particular, the CID algorithm achieves a verification rate of 61.01% for ROC III, which is a nearly 10% increase compared with the FLD method using the grayscale images.

Method	ROC I	ROC II	ROC III
BEE Baseline	13.36	12.67	11.86
FLD on grayscale images	52.96	52.34	51.57
CID	**60.49**	**60.75**	**61.01**

Table 1. Verification rate (%) comparison when the false accept rate is 0.1%

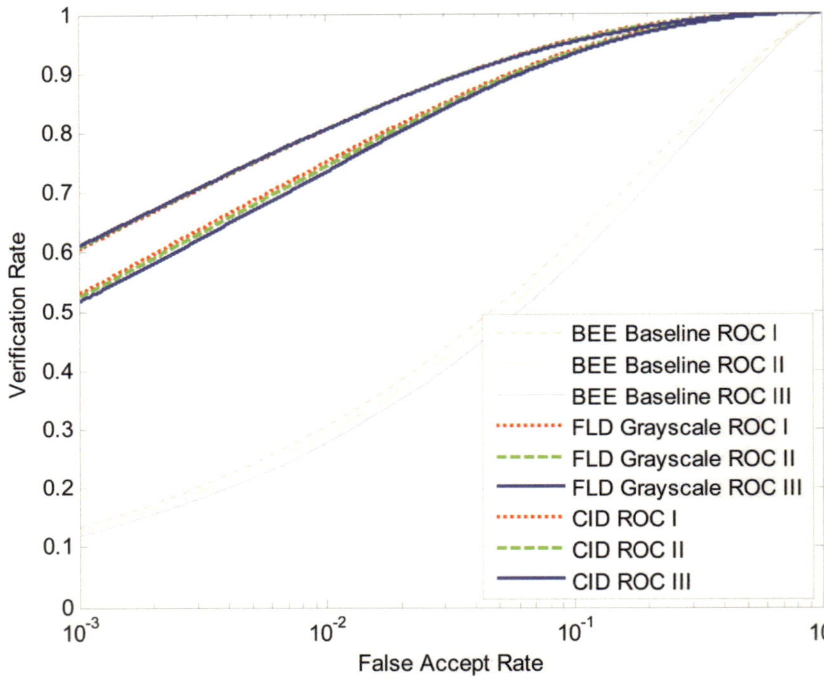

Fig. 3. ROC curves corresponding to the BEE Baseline algorithm, FLD on grayscale images and the CID Algorithm

It should be pointed out that the convergence of the CID algorithm does not depend on the choice of the initial value of $\mathbf{X}^{[0]}$. We randomly generate four set of initial values (four three-dimensional vectors). The convergence of the CID algorithm corresponding to these four set of initial values and the originally chosen initial values $\mathbf{X}^{[0]} = [1/3, 1/3, 1/3]$ is illustrated in Figure 4. Figure 4 shows that the convergence of the CID algorithm is independent of the choice of initial value of $\mathbf{X}^{[0]}$. The algorithm consistently converges to a very similar value of the criterion function $J(\varphi, \mathbf{X})$, and its convergence speed is fast: it always converges within 10 iterations if we choose $\varepsilon = 0.1$.

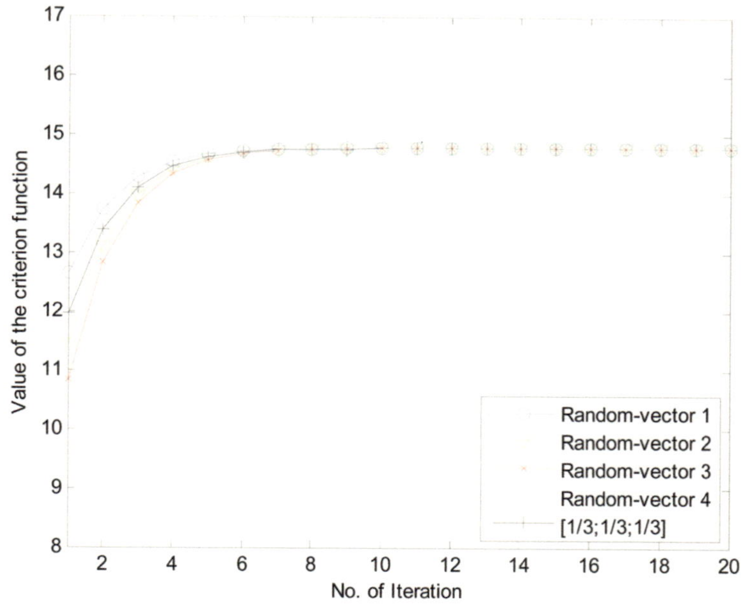

Fig. 4. Illustration of the convergence of the CID algorithm

3.2 Face recognition based on three color component images

In this experiment, we train the extended CID algorithm using the standard training set of the FRGC version 2 Experiment 4 to generate three color component combination coefficient vectors $\mathbf{X}_1$, $\mathbf{X}_2$ and $\mathbf{X}_3$, and based on these coefficient vectors we obtain three discriminating color components $\mathbf{D}^1$, $\mathbf{D}^2$ and $\mathbf{D}^3$ for each color image. The three discriminating color component images corresponding to one orginal image are shown in Figure 5.

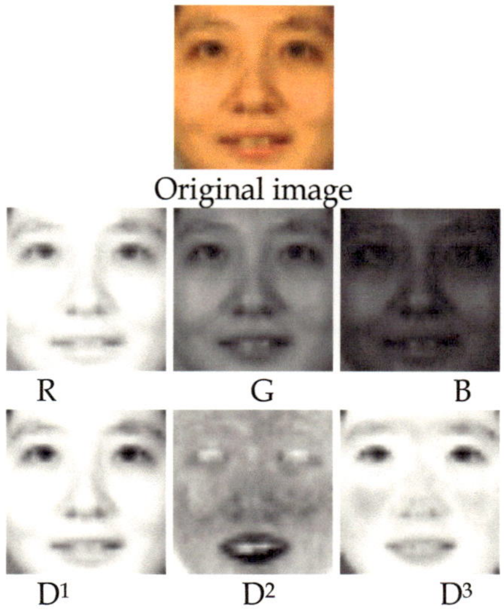

Fig. 5. Illustration of R, G, B color component images and the three color component images generated by the proposed method

We employ two fusion strategies, i.e., decision-level fusion and image-level fusion, to combine the information within the three discriminating color component images for recognition purpose. The decision-level fusion strategy first extracts discriminant features from each of the three color component images, then calculates the similarity scores and normalizes them using Z-score, and finally fuses the normalized similarity scores using a sum rule. The image-level fusion strategy first concatenates the three color components $\mathbf{D}^1$, $\mathbf{D}^2$ and $\mathbf{D}^3$ into one pattern vector and then performs PCA+FLD [23] on the concatenated pattern vector. To avoid the negative effect of magnitude dominance of one component image over the others, we apply a basic image normalization method by removing the mean and normalizing the standard deviation of each component image before the concatenation. To avoid overfitting, we choose 900 principal components (PCs) in the PCA step of the decision-level fusion strategy and 1000 PCs in the PCA step of the image-level fusion strategy. The frameworks of the two fusion strategies are shown in Figure 6.

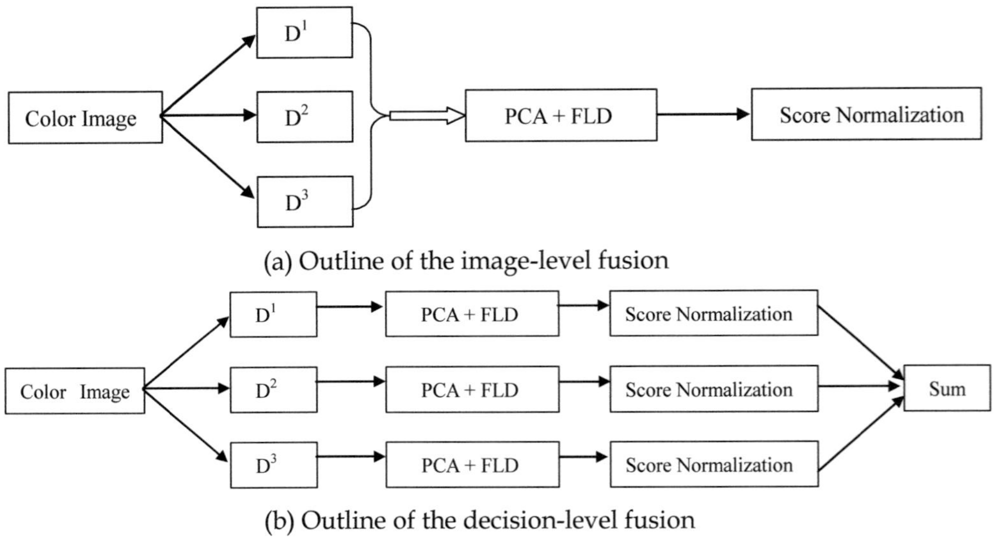

Fig. 6. Illustration of the decision-level and image-level fusion strategy frameworks

For comparison, we apply the same two fusion strategies to the R, G and B color component images and obtain the corresponding similarity scores. The final similarity matrix is input to the BEE system and three ROC curves are generated. Figure 7 shows the three ROC curves corresponding to each of three methods: the BEE Baseline algorithm, FLD using RGB images, and the extended CID algorithm using the decision-level fusion strategy. Figure 8 shows the ROC curves of the three methods using the image-level fusion strategy. Table 2 lists the face verification rates at the false accept rate of 0.1%. These results indicate that the fusion of the three discriminant color components generated by the extended CID algorithm is more effective for improving the FRGC performance than the fusion of the original R, G and B color components, no matter what fusion strategy is used.

In addition, by comparing the results of the two fusion strategies shown in Table 2, one can see that the three color components generated by the extended CID algorithm demonstrates quite stable face recognition performance while the R, G and B color components do not. For the three color components generated by the extended CID algorithm, the performance

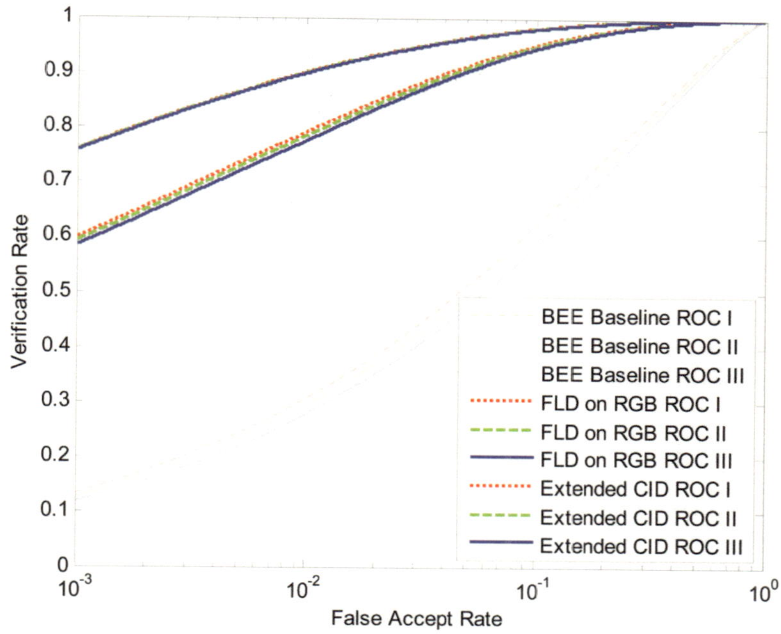

Fig. 7. ROC curves corresponding to the BEE baseline algorithm, FLD using the RGB images, and the extended CID algorithm (for three color components) using the decision-level fusion strategy

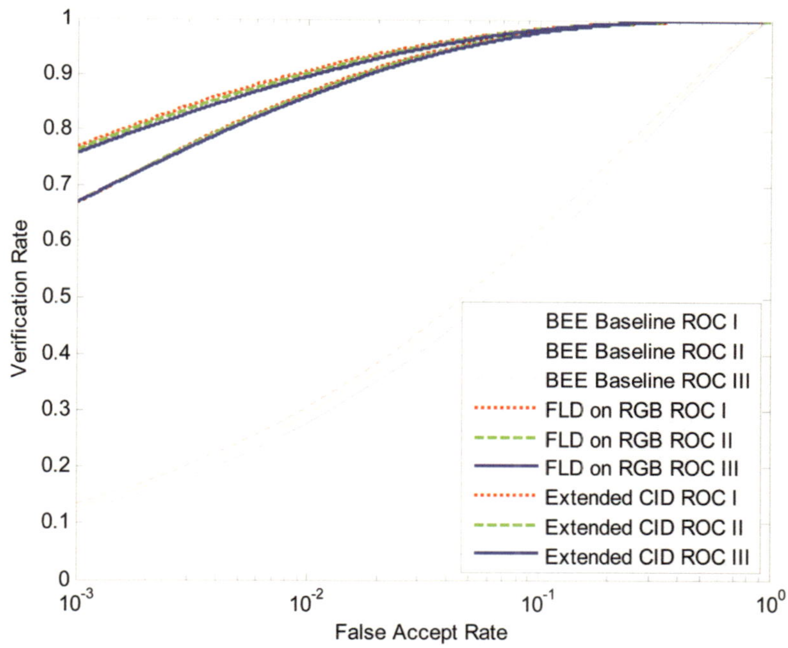

Fig. 8. ROC curves corresponding to the BEE baseline algorithm, FLD using the RGB images, and the extended CID algorithm (for three color components) using the image-level fusion strategy

difference between the two fusion strategies is at most 1.01%, whereas for the R, G and B color components, the performance difference between the two fusion strategies is as large as 8.55%. The RGB color space performs much worse when the decision-level fusion strategy is used.

Fusion strategy	Method	ROC I	ROC II	ROC III
Decision-level fusion	FLD on RGB images	59.75	59.14	58.34
	Extended CID	**75.73**	**75.74**	**75.66**
Image-level fusion	FLD on RGB images	66.68	66.85	66.89
	Extended CID	**76.72**	**76.25**	**75.64**

Table 2. Verification rate (%) comparison when the false accept rate is 0.1% using all of the three color components images

4. Conclusions

This chapter seeks to find a meaningful representation and an effective recognition method of color images in a unified framework. We integrate color image representation and recognition tasks into one discriminant model: color image discriminant (CID) model. The model therefore involve two sets of variables: a set of color component combination coefficients for color image representation and a set of projection basis vectors for color image discrimination. An iterative CID algorithm is developed to find the optimal solution of the proposed model. The CID algorithm is further extended to generate three color components (like the three color components of RGB color images) for further improving the recognition performance. Three experiments using the Face Recognition Grand Challenge (FRGC) database and the Biometric Experimentation Environment (BEE) system demonstrate the performance advantages of the proposed method over the Fisher linear discriminant analysis method on grayscale and RGB color images.

5. Acknowledgments

This work was partially supported by the National Science Foundation of China under Grants No. 60503026, No. 60632050, and the 863 Hi-Tech Program of China under Grant No. 2006AA01Z119. Dr. Chengjun Liu was partially supported by Award No. 2006-IJ-CX-K033 awarded by the National Institute of Justice, Office of Justice Programs, US Department of Justice.

6. References

[1] J. Luo, D. Crandall, "Color object detection using spatial-color joint probability functions" *IEEE Transactions on Image Processing*, June 2006, 15(6), pp. 1443 - 1453

[2] R. L. Hsu, M. Abdel-Mottaleb, and A.K. Jain, "Face detection in color images," *IEEE Trans. Pattern Anal. Machine Intell.*, vol. 24, no. 5, pp. 696–706, 2002.

[3] O. Ikeda, "Segmentation of faces in video footage using HSV color for face detection and image retrieval", *International Conference on Image Processing* (ICIP 2003), 2003.

[4] Y. Wu; T.S. Huang, "Nonstationary color tracking for vision-based human-computer interaction", *IEEE Transactions on Neural Networks*, July 2002, 13(4), pp. 948 - 960.

[5] T. Gevers, H. Stokman, "Robust histogram construction from color invariants for object recognition", *IEEE Transactions on Pattern Analysis and Machine Intelligence,* Jan. 2004, 26(1), pp. 113 - 118

[6] A. Diplaros, T. Gevers, and I. Patras, "Combining color and shape information for illumination-viewpoint invariant object recognition", *IEEE Transactions on Image Processing,* Jan. 2006, 15(1), pp. 1 - 11

[7] G. Dong, M. Xie, "Color clustering and learning for image segmentation based on neural networks", *IEEE Transactions on Neural Networks,* July 2005, 16(4), pp. 925 - 936

[8] H. Y. Lee; H. K. Lee; Y. H. Ha, "Spatial color descriptor for image retrieval and video segmentation", *IEEE Transactions on Multimedia,* Sept. 2003, 5(3), pp. 358 - 367

[9] A. W. M. Smeulders, M. Worring, S Santini, A. Gupta, and R. Jain, "Content-based image retrieval at the end of the early years," *IEEE Trans. Pattern Anal. Machine Intell.,* 2000, 22(12), pp. 1349–1380.

[10] M. J. Swain and D.H. Ballard, "Color indexing," *International Journal of Computer Vision,* vol. 7, no. 1, pp. 11–32, 1991.

[11] B. V. Funt, G.D. Finlayson, "Color constant color indexing", *IEEE Transactions on Pattern Analysis and Machine Intelligence,* May 1995, 17(5), Page(s):522 - 529

[12] D. A. Adjeroh, M. C. Lee, "On ratio-based color indexing", *IEEE Transactions on Image Processing,* Jan. 2001, 10(1), Page(s): 36 – 48.

[13] G. Healey and D. A. Slater, "Global color constancy: Recognition of objects by use of illumination invariant properties of color distributions," *Journal of the Optical Society of America A,* vol. 11, no. 11, pp. 3003–3010, 1994.

[14] G. D. Finlayson, S. D. Hordley, and P.M. Hubel, "Color by correlation: A simple, unifying framework for color constancy," *IEEE Trans. Pattern Anal. Machine Intell.,* vol. 23, no. 11, pp. 1209–1221, 2001.

[15] H. Stokman; T. Gevers, "Selection and Fusion of Color Models for Image Feature Detection", *IEEE Transactions on Pattern Analysis and Machine Intelligence,* March 2007, 29(3), Page(s): 371 - 381

[16] R. Kemp, G. Pike, P. White, and A. Musselman, "Perception and recognition of normal and negative faces: the role of shape from shading and pigmentation cues". *Perception,* 25, 37-52. 1996.

[17] L. Torres, J.Y. Reutter, L. Lorente, "The importance of the color information in face recognition", *International Conference on Image Processing* (ICIP 99), Oct. 1999, Volume 3, Page(s): 627 - 631

[18] A. Yip and P. Sinha, "Role of color in face recognition," *MIT tech report* (ai.mit.com) AIM-2001-035 CBCL-212, 2001.

[19] M. Rajapakse, J. Tan, J. Rajapakse, "Color channel encoding with NMF for face recognition", *International Conference on Image Processing* (ICIP '04), Oct. 2004, Volume 3, Page(s):2007- 2010.

[20] C. Xie, B. V. K. Kumar, "Quaternion correlation filters for color face recognition", *Proceedings of the SPIE,* Volume 5681, pp. 486-494 (2005).

[21] P. Shih and C. Liu, "Improving the Face Recognition Grand Challenge Baseline Performance Using Color Configurations Across Color Spaces", *IEEE International Conference on Image Processing, ICIP 2006,* 2006, October 8-11, Atlanta, GA.

[22] C. Jones III, A. L. Abbott, "Color face recognition by hypercomplex gabor analysis", *7th International Conference on Automatic Face and Gesture Recognition* (FGR 2006), April, 2006.

[23] C. Liu and H. Wechsler, "Gabor Feature Based Classification Using the Enhanced Fisher Linear Discriminant Model for Face Recognition", *IEEE Trans. Image Processing*, vol. 11, no. 4, pp. 467-476, 2002.

[24] K. Fukunaga, *Introduction to Statistical Pattern Recognition*, Academic Press, second edition, 1990.

[25] P.J. Phillips, P.J. Flynn, T. Scruggs, K.W. Bowyer, J. Chang, K. Hoffman, J. Marques, J. Min, and W. Worek, "Overview of the Face Recognition Grand Challenge," *Proc. IEEE Conf. Computer Vision and Pattern Recognition*, 2005.

[26] P. J. Phillips., P. J. Flynn, T.Scruggs, K.W. Bowyer, W. Worek, "Preliminary Face Recognition Grand Challenge Results", *Proceedings of the 7th International Conference on Automatic Face and Gesture Recognition* (FGR'06).

[27] P. Lancaster and M. Tismenetsky, The Theory of Matrices (Second Edition), Academic Press, INC. Orlando, Florida, 1985.

[28] D. L. Swets and J. Weng. "Using discriminant eigenfeatures for image retrieval", *IEEE Trans. Pattern Anal. Machine Intell.*, 1996,18(8), pp. 831-836.

[29] P. N. Belhumeur, J. P. Hespanha, and D. J. Kriengman, "Eigenfaces vs. Fisherfaces: recognition using class specific linear projection", *IEEE Trans. Pattern Anal. Machine Intell.* 1997, 19 (7), pp. 711-720.

[30] W. Zhao, A. Krishnaswamy, R. Chellappa, D. Swets, and J. Weng, "Discriminant analysis of principal components for face recognition", in *Face Recognition: From Theory to Applications*, Eds. H. Wechsler, P.J. Phillips, V. Bruce, F.F. Soulie and T.S. Huang, Springer-Verlag, pp. 73-85, 1998.

[31] J. Yang, J.Y. Yang, "Why can LDA be performed in PCA transformed space?" *Pattern Recognition*, 2003, 36(2), pp. 563-566.

[32] J. Yang, A. F. Frangi, J.-Y. Yang, D. Zhang, Z. Jin, "*KPCA Plus LDA: A Complete Kernel Fisher Discriminant Framework for Feature Extraction and Recognition", IEEE Trans. Pattern Anal. Machine Intell.*, 2005, 27(2), pp. 230-244.

[33] C. Liu, "Capitalize on Dimensionality Increasing Techniques for Improving Face Recognition Grand Challenge Performance", *IEEE Trans. Pattern Anal. Machine Intell.*, vol. 28, no. 5, pp. 725-737, 2006.

[34] A. Jain, K. Nandakumar, and A. Ross, "Score normalization in multimodel biometric systems", *Pattern Recognition*, 38 (2005), 2270-2285.

[35] M. Turk and A. Pentland, "Eigenfaces for recognition", J. Cognitive Neuroscience, 1991, 3(1), pp. 71-86.

[36] Z. Jin, J.Y. Yang, Z.S. Hu, Z. Lou, "Face Recognition based on uncorrelated discriminant transformation", *Pattern Recognition*, 2001,33(7), 1405-1416.

[37] J. Ye, R. Janardan, and Q. Li. "Two-Dimensional Linear Discriminant Analysis", *Neural Information Processing Systems (NIPS 2004).*

[38] J. Yang, C. Liu, "A General Discriminant Model for Color Face Recognition", *Eleventh IEEE International Conference on Computer Vision (ICCV 2007*), Rio de Janeiro, Brazil, October 14-20, 2007.

15

A Novel Approach to Using Color Information in Improving Face Recognition Systems Based on Multi-Layer Neural Networks

Khalid Youssef and Peng-Yung Woo
Northern Illinois University
USA

1. Introduction

Nowadays, machine-vision applications are acquiring more attention than ever due to the popularity of artificial intelligence in general which is growing bigger every day. But, although machines today are more intelligent than ever, artificial intelligence is still in its infancy. Advances in artificial intelligence promise to benefit vast numbers of applications. Some even go way beyond that to say that when artificial intelligence reaches a certain level of progress, it will be the key to the next economical revolution after the agricultural and industrial revolutions (Casti, 2008). In any case, machine-vision applications involving the human face are of major importance, since the face is the natural and most important interface used by humans. Many reasons lie behind the importance of the face as an interface. For starters, the face contains a set of features that uniquely identify each person more than any other part in the body. The face also contains main means of communications, some of which are obvious such as the eyes as image receptors and the lips as voice emitters, and some of which are less obvious such as the eye movement, the lip movement the color change in the skin, and face gestures. Basic applications involve face detection, face recognition and mood detection, and more advanced applications involve lip reading, basic temperature diagnoses, lye detection, etc. As the demand on more advanced and more robust applications increase, the conventional use of gray-scaled images in machine-vision applications in general, and specifically applications that involve the face is no longer sufficient. Color information is becoming a must.

It is surprising that until recent study demonstrated that color information makes contribution and enhances robustness in face recognition. The common belief was the contrary (Yip & Sinha, 2001). Thus, gray-scaled images were used to reduce processing cost (Inooka, et al., 1999; Nefian, 2002; Ma & Khorasani, 2004; Zheng, et al., 2006; Zuo, et al., 2006; Liu & Chen, 2007). Simply speaking, we know from nature that animals relying more on their vision as a means of survival tend to see in colors. For example, some birds are able to see a wider color spectrum than humans due to their need to locate and identify objects from very high distances. The truth is that due to its nature, color can be thought of as a natural efficiency trick that gives high definition accuracy with relatively little processing cost as will be shown later in this article. Up to a certain point in the past, a simple yes or no to a still image of a face with tolerable size and rotation restrictions was good enough for face recognition applications. For such a requirement, gray-scaled images did the job pretty well. Some even claim to have achieved recognition rates of upto 99.3% under these circumstances (Ahmadi, 2003). On the other hand, the demand on achieving human like level of recognition is ever-increasing, which makes the requirements even tougher. To be able to achieve these requirements, it is only intuitive to investigate how humans are able to do this. The human decision process in face recognition does not rely on mere fixed features extracted from shape information such as the shape of the nose, eyes, and lips. Humans use a combination of these and more sophisticated features that are ignored by the conventional face recognition techniques that rely on gray-scaled images, features like movement patterns, gestures, eyes color, and skin color.

Since color information plays a major role in achieving more advanced vision applications, and since the main reason behind using gray-scaled images is to reduce the processing cost, our goal in this article is to introduce the use of color information in these applications with minimal processing cost. This will be achieved by demonstrating new techniques that utilize color information to enhance the performance of face recognition applications based on artificial Neural Networks (NN) with minimal processing cost through a new network architecture inspired by the biological human vision system. It will be shown that conventional training algorithms based on Back Propagation (BP) can be used to train the network, and the use of the Gradient Descent (GD) algorithm will be explained in details. Further more, the use of Genetic Algorithm (GA) to train the network, which is not based on back propagation will also be explained. Although the application discussed in this article is face recognition, the presented framework is applicable to other applications.

The rest of this article is organized as follows. Section 2 gives a glimpse on previous work related to this subject. The proposed approach and the data processing behind it are given in section 3. Two basic trainig methods are explained in section 4. Experimental results and some observations are demonstrated in section 5, and the article is concluded in section 6.

2. Related work

Until recently, very little work where color information is used in face recognition applications could be found in the literature. Fortunately, this subject is attracting the attention of more researchers and the number of publications on this subject increased significantly in the last few years. However, most of the work that has been done so far basically belongs to at least one of two groups. The first group does not fully utilize color information, while the second group make better use of color information but at the cost of processing efficiency. The following is an example of each case respectively.

One approach suggests using gray-scaled images with an addition of the skin color as a new feature (Marcal & Bengio, 2002). This approach enhances the accuracy of face recognition with little extra processing cost. A 30x40 gray-scale image is used, which gives an input vector of dimension 1200. The additional vector that represents the skin color feature is of dimension 96. Thus, the input vector is of a total dimension 1296. This approach is good from the processing cost point of view and gives a better performance over similar approaches that only use gray-scale images, but it does not make a full use of the color information of the images. Marcal & Bengio also mentioned in their paper that their method has a weak point due to the color similarity of hair and skin pixels, which brings up an uncertainty to the extracted feature vector.

Another approach suggests to use color channel encoding with non-negative matrix normalization (NMF) (Rajapakse, et al., 2004) where the red, green, and blue (RGB) color channels act as separate indexed data vectors representing each image. NMF is then used for color encoding. Although this method makes better utilization of color information, there is a big inherent processing cost due to the encoding and the excessive iterative matrix operations that includes matrix inversion. Thus, in this case the performance enhancement is at the cost of processing efficiency.

NNs have proved to be among the best tools in face recognition applications and are widely used in approaches based on gray-scaled images. The approach followed in this article is originally proposed by us in a paper published in the proceedings of ICNN'07 (Youssef & Woo, 2007). This approach permits the use of NNs with colored images in a way that makes optimal use of color information without extra processing cost when compared to similar approaches that use gray-scaled images. In this article the original approach is elaborated with more illustration and demonstration of new methods to train the NN.

3. Proposed approach

3.1 Data processing preliminaries

Before the proposed approach is discussed, an introduction to the data processing behind it should be given.

All visible colors are a combination of three main color components, i.e., the red, green, and blue. In the human biological vision system, images are preprocessed before they are sent to the cortex which is responsible for the perception of the image. The image processing starts at the retina of the eye, which is not merely a transducer that translates light into nerve signals. The retina also extracts useful data and ignores redundant data before propagating it to the next stages. The retina of each eye contains 125 million receptors, called rods and cones. Cones are responsible for color vision, and rods are responsible for dim light vision. Naturally, rods cannot attain detailed vision, and they can merely identify shapes. Cones, on the other hand, use color information and are responsible for detailed vision. There are three basic types of cones: red, green, and blue.

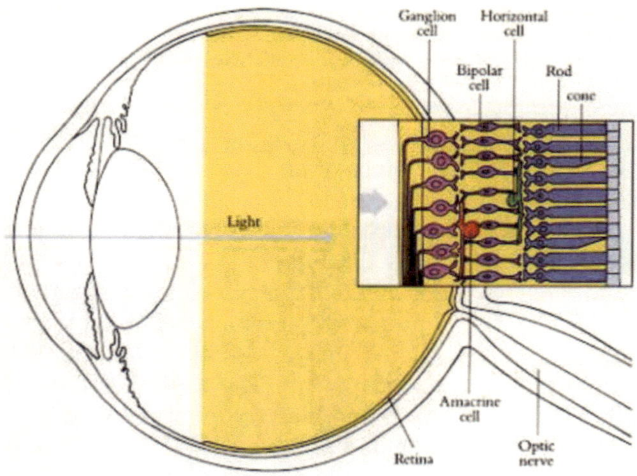

Fig. 1. Human Retina (Hubel, 1988)

In the RGB color system which is mostly used in computers, each of the color components is represented by a number ranging from 0 to 255 with 0 and 255 describing the absence and the full saturation of the color component, respectively. The combination of the different values of these components gives 256^3 = 16777216 different possible colors. A comparison between a face picture and its three RGB color components is shown in Fig. 2, where the top left picture is the original, the red component is on the top right, the green component on the bottom left and the blue component on the bottom right.

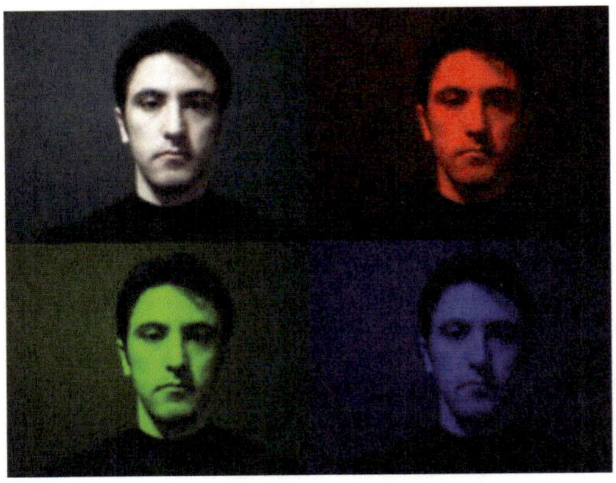

Fig. 2. RGB color components

Digital images are composed of pixels. The data contained in a pixel may vary depending on the pixel format. In general, this data carries information about the color, brightness, hue, and saturation of the pixel. Gray-scale images represent the luminance of the picture, and are usually achieved by extracting the luminance component from color spaces as YUV (Y is the luminance channel, and U and V are the color components), or by using a conversion method to convert pictures in RGB format into gray-scale images. One way to do this is to calculate the average of the red, green, and blue color components. In the method proposed in this article, the 24bit RGB format is used. The input data is divided into 4 channels, i.e., the red, green, and blue color channels, and the luminance channel which is attained by using the following formula:

$$Luminance = 0.299xR + 0.587xG + 0.114xB \quad (1)$$

Each color commponent in Fig. 2 is composed of the shades of one color channel that vary between 0 and 255 and can be considered a gray-scaled image, since in RGB, the shades of gray can be obtained by setting the values of all the components to the same number, i.e. (0,0,0), (1,1,1,) and (255,255,255) correspond to different shades of gray.The shades of gray gets darker as the number increases such that (0,0,0) represents white (complete absence), and (255,255,255) represents black (full saturation).

Note the similarity among the three filtered images of the same picture in Fig. 2. This similarity is inspected further by plotting a graph for a series of consecutive pixels that have the same location in each of the filtered images as shown in Fig. 3. Each line in Fig. 3 corresponds to the graph of a color component. The dashed line, the solid line, and the dotted line correspond to the red, green and blue components respictively. In this case, the pixels are presented in a 1-D vector that is a mapping of the 2-D positions of the pixels such that the vertical axis represents the value of the component, and the horizontal axis represents the pixel's position in the image.

Fig. 3 shows that in real face images, although the individual values of color components for a certain pixel are different in general, the relations among the values of different color components share a certain degree of similarity. Also, it is seen that the average magnitude of the blue color component is less than those of the red and green, because the best overall image quality is given, for the range of wavelengths, between 500 and 700 nanometers on the visible-light spectrum, which corresponds to colors between red and green wavelengths, while far-red and far-blue wavelengths provide little resolution (Elliot, 1999).

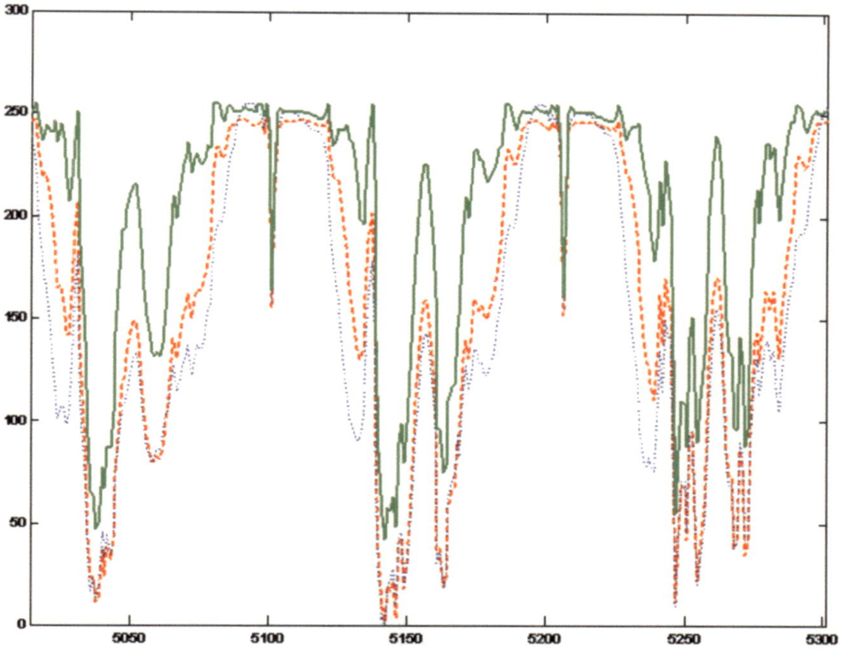

Fig. 3. 1-D pixel representation of color components

However, despite the similarity of the relation between pixel values of the color components, they are definitely not completely the same. In fact, the difference between the color components is where the extra information that is lost in gray-scaled images is embedded. Fig. 4 gives an idea of the difference between the color components. It shows the gray version of each indivdual component separately. The top left picture in Fig. 4 is a combination of all the components, the gray version of the red component is on the top right, the gray version of the green component on the bottom left and the gray version of the blue component on the bottom right.

In a complete face recognition application, face recognition is preceded by a face detection step that locates the face in the picture. Accurate face detection methods are studied by (Anifantis, et al., 1999; Curran, et al., 2005). However, in this article faces are manually cropped and resized to a face image of 19200 (160x120) pixels. The red, green, and blue color channels are extracted from the mage and the luminance channel is obtained by using Eq.(1), yielding four images that are different versions of the original picture. Each version of the image then goes through a process of smoothing and edge enhancement using convolution masks before it is mapped to a feature vector of length 19200. The images are also scaled such that all input values lie between zero and one.

Fig. 4. Gray version of the RGB color components

Convolution masks are used in image processing to detect the edges of objects in an image. Center-surround convolution masks are important in theories of biological vision. They implement an approximation to the Laplacian mathematical operator which is closely related to taking the second-order derivative of a function, and can be applied to digital images by calaculaing the difference between each pixel and the average of the pixels that surround it. Practical computer vision systems use masks that are related to the vertical and horizontal difference operations. Fig. 5 shows an example of a convoluted image and the detected edges of the image. On the left is the original picture, the convoluted image is shown in the middle and the edges after applying a threshold to the convoluted image is shown on the right. The edges are then enhanced.

Fig. 5. Edge detection

3.2 Network architecture

Motivated by the biological vision system where the color information input is derived from the three cone types that represent the red, green, and blue colors, and due to the similar nature of the relation among the color components of the pixels in real pictures, we propose an overall structure of a multi layer neural network (MLNN) where the neurons in the input layer are divided into three groups, each of which is connected to a separate input vector that represents one of the three color channels. This modification allows us to make full use of color information without extra processing costs. The overall structure of the MLNN is shown in Fig. 6 where a conventional MLNN is shown on the left and the proposed MLNN is shown on the right. It can be seen that the inputs of the proposed MLNN in Fig. 6 are not connected to each neuron in the first hidden-layer. Thus, although the number of inputs used here is three times larger than the number of inputs used in the conventional methods where only the gray-scale image is processed, the number of connections is still the same and therefore the processing cost remains the same. As we mentioned before, each training picture in the experiments conducted in this article consists of 19200 pixels. In a standard MLNN that uses the gray-scale images, all the N neurons in the first hidden-layer are connected to the input vector representing the luminance channel and therefore there are $19200N$ connections. On the other hand, in the proposed method, the neurons in the first hidden-layer are divided into three groups with each consisting of $N/3$ neurons that are connected to one of the three RGB color channels. Thus, there are $[19200*(N/3)]*3=19200N$ connections. It is seen that no extra processing cost is involved. The shades of gray using 32 and 256 levels are shown in the right and left sides of Fig. 7 respectively. In the proposed approach three color channels are used each of which has 256 levels giving a total number of 16777216 combinations.

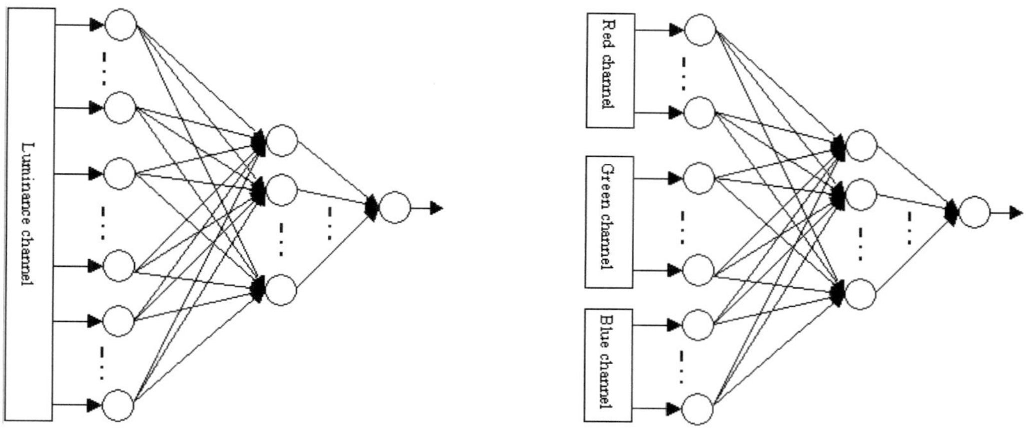

Fig. 6. Conventional v.s. proposed MLNN structures

Fig. 7. Shades of gray

4. Training methods

4.1 Back propagation

In a standard multi-layer neural network, each neuron in any layer is connected to ***all*** the neurons in the previous layer. It can be represented as follows:

$$a_i^0 = P_i, i = 1,2,\dots,N^0 \tag{2}$$

$$n_i^{m+1} = \sum_{j=1}^{N^m} w_{i,j}^{m+1} a_j^m + b_i^{m+1} \quad, m = 0,1,\dots,M-1, i = 1,2,\dots,N^{m+1} \tag{3}$$

$$a_i^{m+1} = f_i^{m+1}(n_i^{m+1}) \tag{4}$$

where p is the input of the MLNN, n and a are the input and output of a certain neuron, respectively, w is the weight, b is the bias and f is the activation function. The superscript m and the subscripts i and j are the indexes for the layers and neurons, respectively.
The MLNNs are usually trained by using a supervised training algorithm based on the EBP a.k.a. back propagation algorithm (BP) that was developed by P.J. Werbos whose Ph.D. thesis "Beyond Regression" is recognized as the original source of back propagation (Werbos, 1994). The EBP algorithm was rederived independently by D.B. Parker. Parker also derived a second-order back propagation algorithm for adaptive networks that approximates the Newton's minimization technique (Parker, 1987). After a careful review of the derivations in Werbos' thesis (Werbos, 1974) and Parker's paper (Parker, 1987), we conclude that the algorithms they derived can also be applied to an "incomplete" MLNN where not each neuron in a layer is connected to all the neurons in the previous layer.
The following steps summarize the back propagation algorithm:

- Propagate the input forward through the network to the output.
- Propagate the partial derivatives of the error function backward through the network.
- Update the weights and biases of the network.
- Repeat until stop condition is reached.

In the case of our proposed architecture, the inputs are not fully connected as usually assumed by the algorithms. The weights corresponding to missing connections can be simply ignored in the updating step, and when included in the calculation of the error they can be considered of zero value.

4.2 Genetic algorithm

Genetic algorithms (GA) are derivative-free stochastic optimization methods based on the features of natural selection and biological evolution (Siddique & Tokhi, 2001). The use of GAs to train MLNNs was introduced for the first time by D. Whiteley (Whiteley, 1989). Whiteley proved later, in other publication, that GA can outperform BP (Whiteley, et al., 1990). A good comparison between the use of BP and GA for training MLNN is conducted by Siddique & Tokhi. Many studies on improving the performance and efficiency of GA in training MLNNs followed, and the use of GA was extended further to tune the structure of NNs (Leung, et al., 2003).
The GA is a perfect fit for training our system. The structure of the MLNN does not matter for the GA as long as the MLNN's parameters are mapped correctly to the genes of the chromosome the GA is optimizing. For large-scale MLNNs as in our case, the preferred type of encoding is value encoding. Basically, each gene represents the value of a certain weight or bias in the MLNN, and the chromosome is a vector that contains these values such that each weight or bias corresponds to a fixed position in the vector as shown in Fig. 8.
The fitness function can be assigned from the recognition error of the MLNN for the set of pictures used for training. The GA searches for parameter values that minimize the fitness function, thus the recognition error of the MLNN is reduced and the recognition rate is maximized. The GA in general takes more time to train the MLNN than BP, thus the processing cost is increased. However, the processing cost of the training phase of the MLNN does not have a big weight, since the training is performed only once. Once the network is trained, it goes to what is known as the feedforward mode which is independent of the training algorithm. The feedforward mode is what counts the most when it comes to processing cost, since that is what is used in practice. When a search engine is searching for

a face in a database that contains millions of faces, the processing cost of the feedforward mode should be minimized as much as possible.

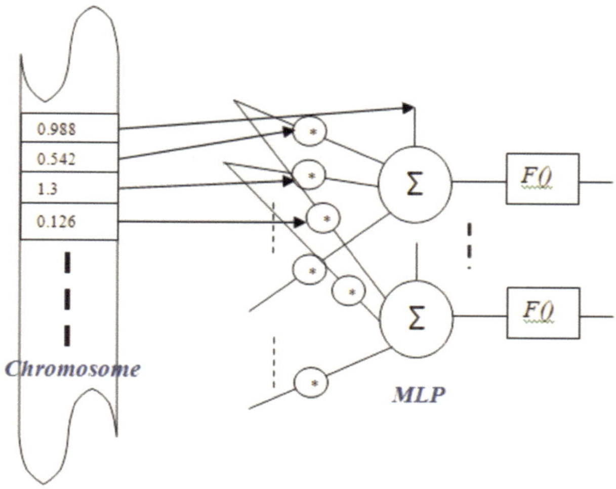

Fig. 8. Weight/bias mapping

5. Experimental results and observations

The modified MLNN used in the experiments consists of an input layer, two hidden-layers and an output layer. In our case each network is specialized in recognizing the face of one person, so there is only one neuron in the output layer. The network's output is a decimal number between 0 and 1. A threshold is then applied to the output to tune the network performance. A very high threshold enhances the false recognition rate (FRR), but at the same time decreases the true recognition rate (TRR). On the other hand, a very low threshold increases the TRR, but at the same time yields a higher FRR. The optimal threshold depends on the application requirement. In our experiments, the threshold is chosen in the middle point in order for the comparison between the performances of different systems to be fair.

The modified MLNN is trained to recognize the face of one person by using a number of pictures of the same person's face with different expressions, shooting angles, backgrounds and lighting conditions as well as a number of pictures of other people. Each MLNN is then tested by using pictures that have not been used in training. After the appropriate weights and biases that enable the system to recognize a certain person are found, they are saved in a file. This process is repeated for the faces of other people as well. The system can then be used to identify people that it has been previously introduced to. The system loads the files that it has in its memory, one file at a time, and performs the tests by using the data extracted from the picture to be identified and the weights and biases loaded from a certain file, keeping in mind that each file contains the weights and biases that correspond to a certain person. Note that the system now operates as a feedforward neural network, which simply calculates the output value. Dedicating a MLNN for each person makes it easier to expand to systems that search large numbers of faces, and it also simplifies adding new faces to the system.

The system is tested for a database of colored images of 50 people with 15 pictures for each including different expressions, shooting angles and lighting conditions. The pictures are obtained from the Georgia Tech face database. They are divided into two groups. The first group consists of 30 people, where nine pictures of each person are used for training the system, two pictures for validation and the remaining four pictures for testing. The second group consists of 20 people that are not used for training, but only for validation and testing. The same training and testing processes are also done for the standard MLNN by using gray-scale versions of the pictures. The success rates of the recognition tests without noise and with different noise levels for the standard and proposed MLNNs are recorded. Table 1 presents results of MLNNs trained using BP, and Table 2 presents results of MLNNs trained using GA.

It is clear from the results that the success rates of the recognition tests are higher for the proposed system. Furthermore, the difference gets more significant as the noise level increases. This demonstrates that our method is more robust to noise. It is not the objective of this article to find the optimal algorithm to train the MLNNs. Our objective is to demonstrate the superiority of the proposed system that operates with color pictures. Thus, a basic GA and the gradient descent algorithm are chosen for training, and a simple feature extraction technique is used in preprocessing. By using other GA and EBP algorithms and more advanced feature extraction techniques, the performance could be further enhanced.

Noise Mean Value	Color	Gray-scale
Without Noise	91.8%	89.1%
0.05	91.8%	89.1%
0.1	90.2%	88.4%
0.2	86.6%	81.3%

Table 1. Color v.s. gray-scale for BP

Noise Mean Value	Color	Gray-scale
Without Noise	94.3%	90.4%
0.05	94.1%	89.8%
0.1	91.6%	87.8%
0.2	84.7%	78.6%

Table 2. Color v.s. gray-scale for GA

Gray-scale methods basically use combinations of constant ratios of the RGB color channels to obtain the luminance channel. However, the ratios used do not necessarily correspond to the best distribution of the color channels. Furthermore, using constant ratios for color distribution does not dynamically adapt to the specific pictures in concern. On the other hand, in the system proposed in this article, the color distribution is determined by iteratively updating the weights that correspond to each color channel for the specific pictures in concern.

The inputs to the network are related directly to the pixels of the picture and therefore can be viewed as a 2-D grid of inputs, with each input giving a value of a certain color component for a certain pixel. Since each input has a weight related, the weights can also be viewed as a 2-D grid that corresponds to the 2-D grid of inputs. The obtained weights for one neuron in each of the three channels after training, between the input vector and the first hidden-layer, are put into three 2-D arrays. The obtained 2-D arrays are then plotted by using the (surf) function in Matlab that produces a 3-D plot where the x-axis and the y-axis correspond to the position of the element in the 2-D array, and the z-axis corresponds to the value of that element. When the (surf) function is used with the default color-map, higher values are assigned shades of red colors, middle values are assigned shades of yellow colors, and lower values are assigned shades of blue colors. Fig. 9 demonstrate the x-y view of the progress of wiegts' values in training for three neurons corresponding to the green, red, and blue input vectors, respictively. The first row in Fig. 9 corrsponds to the value of the weights before the network is trained, where they are set to random values. The second row shows the weights' values after four epochs of training using the GD algorithm. The third row shows the weights' values after eight epochs, and the last row shows the weights' values after the desired small error is reached. The first column in Fig. 9 (left) corresponds to the weights of a neuron connected to an input vector in the green color channel, the middle column corresponds to the weights of a neuron connected to an input vector in the red color channel, and the last column (right) corresponds to the weights of a neuron connected to an input vector in the blue color channel.

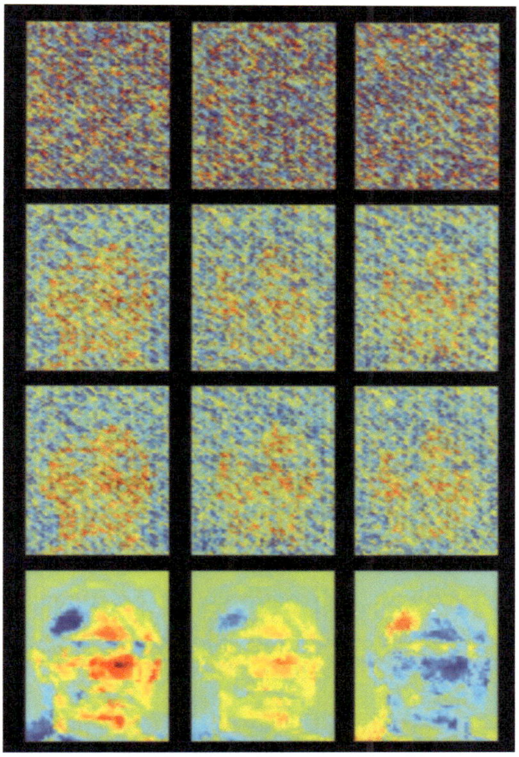

Fig. 9. Weights plot of neurons from the three color groups

The color distribution in the plots in Fig. 9 shows that neurons using the green channel input vector have the highest weight values at face features like the nose, the chin, and the forehead. Neurons using the red channel input vector have medium values, and neurons using the blue channel input vectors have the lowest values. This result agrees with what is depicted in Fig. 3.

6. Conclusion

Multi layer neural networks (MLNNs) have proved to be among the best existing techniques used in automatic face recognition due to their inherent robustness and generalizing ability. There are many papers in the literature that suggest different approaches in using neural networks to achieve better performance. The focus so far has been on studying different training algorithms and different feature extraction techniques. Yet, the majority of the work done in all face recognition methods in general and in methods that use neural networks specifically is based on grayscale face images. Until recent studies demonstrated that color information makes contribution and enhances robustness in face recognition. The common belief was the contrary. Grayscale images are used to save storage and processing costs. Colored images are usually composed of three components (Red, Green, Blue) while grayscale images are composed of one component only which is some form of averaging of the three color components, thus it basically requires one third of the cost. However, grayscale images only tell part of the story, and even though the enhancement that color adds might not seem very important to systems that use face recognition for basic identification applications, colors will be crucial for more advanced future applications where higher levels of abstraction is needed. There are many growing areas of computer vision in applications such as robotics, intelligent user interfaces, authentication in security systems and face search in video databases that are demanding color information important for future progress.

This article illustrates the importance of using color information in face recognition and introduces a new method for using color information in techniques based on MLNNs without adding mentionable processing cost. This method involves the new network architecture, and it can be used to enhance the performance of systems based on MLNNs regardless of the training algorithm or feature extraction technique. Motivated by how each pixel in a picture is comprised of its own unique color and the relation among those color components, we have proposed a new architecture. The new proposed network architecture involves the neurons in the input layer to be divided into three groups, each of which is connected to a separate input vector that represents one of the three color channels (Red, Green, Blue). This way, the modification allows us to make a full use of color information without extra processing costs. In addition, even though the input of the three color channels is larger than the standard input for the grayscale image, there is still the same number of connections, resulting in no further processing cost than the standard MLP. Experimental results that compare the performance of different approaches with and without using the proposed approach are demonstrated. Based on the aforementioned theoretical analysis and experimental results, the superiority of the proposed approach in face recognition is claimed, where the color distribution is determined by iteratively updating the weights that correspond to each color channel for the specific pictures in concern.

7. References

Ahmadi, M.; Faez, K. & Haddadnia, J. (2003). An Efficient Human Face Recognition System Using Pseudo-Zernike Moment Invariant and Radial Basis Function Neural

Network, *International Journal of Pattern Recognition and Artificial Intelligence*, Vol. 17, No. 1, Feb 2003, pp. 41-62, 0218-0014

Anifantis, D.; Dermatas, E. & Kokkinakis, G. (1999). A Neural Network Method For Accurate Face Detection on Arbitrary Images, *Proceedings of the International Conference on Electronics, Circuits, and Systems*, pp. 109-112, IEEE

Casti, J. (2008). Economics of the Singularity, *IEEE Spectrum*, Vol. 45, No.6, June 2008, pp. 45-50

Curran, K.; Li, X. & Caughley, N. (2005). The Use of Neural Networks In Real-time Face Detection, *Journal of Computer Sciences*, Jan 2005, pp 47-62, Science Publications

Elliott, C. (1999). Reducing Pixel Count Without Reducing Image Quality, *Information Display*, Vol. 15, December 1999, pp22-25

Hubel, D. (1988). *Eye, Brain, and Vision*, W H Freeman & Co, 978-0716750208, USA

Inooka, Y.; Fukumi, M. & Akamatsu, N. (1999). Learning and Analysis of Facial Expression Images Using A Five-Layered Hourglass-Type Neural Network, *Proceedings of the International Conference on Systems, Man, and Cybernetics*, pp 373-376, October 1999, IEEE

Leung, F.; Lam H.; Ling S. & Tam P. (2003). Tuning of the Structure and Parameters of a Neural Network Using an Improved Genetic Algorithm, *IEEE Transactions on Neural* Networks, Vol. 14, No. 1, Jan 2003, pp. 79-88

Liu, Y. & Chen, Y. (2007). Face Recognition Using Total Margin-Based Adaptive Fuzzy Support Vector Machines. *IEEE Transactions on Neural Networks*, Vol. 18, Jan 2007, pp. 178-192

Ma, L. & Khorasani, K. (2004). Facial Expression Recognition Using Constructive Feedforward Neural Networks, *IEEE Transactions on Systems, Man, and Cybernetics, Part B: Cybernetics*, Vol. 34, No. 3, June 2004, pp. 1588-1595

Marcel, S. & Bengio, S. (2002). Improving Face Verification Using Skin Color Information, *Proceedings of the International Conference on Pattern Recognition*, pp 378-381, August 2002

Nefian, A. (2002). Embedded Bayesian Networks for Face Recognition, *Proceedings of the International Conference on Multimedia and Expo*, pp. 133-136, 0780373049

Parker, D. (1987). Optimal Algorithms for Adaptive Networks: Second Order Back Propagation, Second Order Direct Propagation, and Second Order Hebbian Learning, *Proceedings of the International Conference on Neural Networks*, pp. 593-600, IEEE

Rajapakse, M.; Tan, J. & Rajapakse, J. (2004). Color Channel Encoding with NMF for Face Recognition, *Proceedings of the International Conference on Image Processing*, pp 2007-2010, October 2004

Siddique, M. & Tokhi, M. (2001). Training Neural Networks: Back Propagation vs. Genetic Algorithms, *Proceedings of International Joint Conference on Neural Networks*, pp. 2673-2678, 9780780370449,USA, July 2001, IEEE, Washington D.C.

Werbos, P. (1974). *Beyond Regression: New Tools for Prediction and Analysis Behavioral*, PhD Thesis, Harvard Univirsity

Werbos, P. (1994). *The Roots of Back Propagation: From Ordered Derivatives to Neural Networks and Political Forecasting*, Wiley-IEEE, 0471598976

Whiteley, D. (1989). Applying Genetic Algorithms to Neural Networks Learning, *Proceedings of Conference of the Society of Artificial Intelligence and Simulation of Behavior*, pp. 137-144, England, Pitman Publishing, Sussex

Whiteley, D.; Starkweather, T. & Bogart, C. (1990). Genetic Algorithms and Neural Networks: Optimizing Connection and Connectivity, *Parallel Computing*, Vol. 14, pp. 347-361

Yip, A. & Sinha, P. (2001). Role of Color in Face Recognition, *MIT AI Memos*, AIM-2001-035, (Dec 2001)

Youssef, K. & Woo, P.-Y. (2007). A New Method for Face Recognition Based on Color Information and a Neural Network, *Proceedings of the International Conference on Natural Computation*, pp. 585-589, 9780769528755, China, Aug 2007, IEEE, Haikou

Zheng, W.; Zho, X.; Zou, C. & Zhao, L. (2006). Facial Expression Recognition Using Kernel Canonical Correlation Analysis (KCCA), *IEEE Transactions On Neural Networks*, Vol. 17, No. 1, January 2006, pp 233-238

Zuo, W.; Zhang, D.; Yang, J. & Wang, K. (2006). BDPCA Plus LDA: A Novel Fast Feature Extraction Technique For Face Recognition, *IEEE Transactions on Systems, Man, and Cybernetics, Part B: Cybernetics*, Vol. 36, No. 4, August 2006, pp. 946-953